A SCOTS GREY
AT WATERLOO

A SCOTS GREY
AT WATERLOO

THE INCREDIBLE STORY OF TROOP
SERGEANT MAJOR WILLIAM CLARKE

Edited By
Gareth Glover

FRONTLINE
BOOKS

A SCOTS GREY AT WATERLOO
The Incredible Story of Troop Sergeant Major William Clarke

This edition published in 2017 by Frontline Books,
an imprint of Pen & Sword Books Ltd,
47 Church Street, Barnsley, S. Yorkshire, S70 2AS

ISBN: 978-1-47389-401-3

For more information on our books, please visit
www.frontline-books.com,
email info@frontline-books.com
or write to us at the above address.

Printed and bound by TJ International Ltd, Padstow, Cornwall
Typeset in 10.5/13 point Palatino

Contents

List of Plates

Foreword

Once in a while a real gem of a personal narrative written by a soldier in the ranks who fought at the Battle of Waterloo is still discovered and this narrative by Troop Sergeant Major William Clarke of the 2nd Royal North British Dragoons (Scots Greys) is certainly one of the best I have ever read. It has to be wondered where these treasures appear from after 200 years, but in this case we do have some reasons which may explain why it has lain hidden for such a long time. This huge single volume of over 600 handwritten pages was recently purchased by the John Rylands Library in Manchester[1] as an anonymous unpublished Victorian novel, giving the story of two soldiers discussing their lives over a few beers in a public house. It is probably because of this, that this failed 'novel' had simply sat within the collection of a Manchester bookseller for many years, largely ignored until his widow offered it to the library a couple of years ago. Luckily John Hodgson, Joint Head of Special Collections at the John Rylands, and I have had some previous contact over the huge archive of General Henry Clinton's papers also held at the library. John had rightly identified that although written as a novel, that there appeared to be the account of a genuine soldier who had fought at Waterloo in the Scots Greys running through the account, as it betrayed a very high level of knowledge of the life of a soldier. Although the book is anonymous, it at one point identifies the main character as simply as W.C., which John had surmised might well refer to Troop Sergeant Major William Clarke of the Scots Greys. At this point John kindly contacted me and I eagerly arranged to travel to the library to view and photograph every page to investigate it further and to transcribe it ready for publication.

William Clarke has left us two other short accounts of Waterloo which can definitely be attributed to him with certainty, a letter which he wrote to his parents dated from Nanterre near Paris on 8 July 1815[2] and a set of 'Extracts from the Journal of Sergeant William Clarke Scots Greys'[3] which is held by the National Library of Scotland. Having

---

1. John Rylands Special Collection Reference ENG MS 1439.
2. Published by the editor in his *Waterloo Archives* Volume 1.
3. NLS MS 15379.

studied these two versions, and then comparing them carefully with the soldier's tale as depicted within the novel, it is perfectly clear that it is simply a much fuller description of his experiences at the Battle of Waterloo; indeed before his description of Waterloo begins in the 'novel', he has abandoned such pretentions and simply narrates his experiences. The 'novel' in fact describes all of the military career of William Clarke from his enlistment in 1803 until he was discharged from the army in 1825, including his years on 'Home Service' across Britain including Ireland, often carrying out operations on the 'Prevention Service' with the local Customs Officers or 'policing' the cities at times of unrest. He paints an intriguing and fascinating picture of military life in the army of George III, but more particularly, he describes Waterloo, particularly the day after the battle, when he was part of the 'Burial Party,' in finer detail than anyone else I have ever read. His story culminates with an exceptionally detailed account of King George IV's state visit to Scotland in 1822, William's last great event before he retired. Everything that is described coincides perfectly with the known service history of William Clarke, including his marriage in Ireland in 1809, this is without doubt the life of Troop Sergeant Major William Clarke.

William Clarke was born at Prestonpans, Haddington, Scotland in 1785[4] and having tried work as a farm labourer and a gardener, he eventually enlisted for life[5] at the age of 18 into the Scots Greys at Glasgow on 19 July 1803 and began to learn the role of a cavalryman. William was a particularly fine specimen of a man for this period, being recorded at 6ft tall (1.83m), with dark brown hair, grey eyes,[6] and a brown (swarthy) complexion. He officially served as a private for 4 years and 306 days, becoming a corporal in 1808; in which capacity he then served for 5 years and 13 days before he became a sergeant in 1813; finally becoming a troop sergeant major after a further six years to the day on 1 August 1819. He finally served a further 6 years and 212 days before he was discharged from the army at Norwich on 21 December

---

4. This is taken from his Army Records, but no birth or baptism record has been discovered.
5. Being recruited for 'life' rather than a fixed term would earn him a much higher bounty payment for joining.
6. It is strange but true that a great number of recruits to the army were recorded as having grey eyes: this is markedly at odds with the percentage of grey eyes in the British population.

1825.[7] His length of service was officially listed as 22 years and 166 days, plus two additional years for serving at Waterloo. William retired to become a gardener, although he is recorded in his discharge papers as being 'worn out from length of service'. As to his conduct in the army, his official record would appear to be unblemished, his promotion being steady and he never suffered demotion for any misdemeanours; but his discharge papers record intriguingly that his conduct had been 'good, with the exception of having involved himself in pecuniary difficulty'. This may indicate that he may have got into trouble with the troop finances, but no official sanctions ensued, beyond perhaps a gentle 'persuasion' to retire. William Clarke was, however, 40 years of age and it was normal to retire at such an age, so perhaps it was not serious enough to cause his dismissal, we will probably never know.

William does occasionally mention having a brother named Mark in the army, who also served at Waterloo, both luckily surviving without a major injury, Mark only receiving a slight wound in the right leg. The only Mark Clarke[8] that can be discovered in the records who came from Scotland and served at Waterloo was a private in the 79th (Cameron Highlanders) Regiment of Foot. If indeed as seems likely, this is William's brother, then their parents were John Clark and Betty (née Bene). He was apparently two years younger than William being born on 6 November 1787 at Kilmadock near Perth, but he was also recruited when aged 18 at Glasgow for 'unlimited service' on 28 June 1805, his previous career also listed as a gardener. On his army records, Mark is shown as having been a little shorter than William at 5ft 9in (1.75m) but with a similar colouring, having dark brown hair, grey eyes and a dark (swarthy) complexion. Mark saw a great deal of service with the Cameronians, serving at Copenhagen in 1807, Portugal and Spain in 1808, the Walcheren campaign, Portugal, Spain and Southern France from 1810–14 including serving at the siege of Cadiz, the battles of Bussaco, Fuentes de Oñoro, Salamanca, the siege of Burgos, Nivelle, Nive, Toulouse and of course Waterloo, where he served in Captain Maclean's grenadier company. The regiment also served at Corunna and Vitoria, but presumably Mark was absent sick or on detached duty on these occasions. Intriguingly, Mark was discharged from the army

---

7. If anyone checks the number of days against his 'official' service record they will realise that there is a minor mistake made in the calculations and that he actually served 24 years and 179 days.

8. The army records show his surname without the final 'e.'

as 'unfit for service' within six weeks of his brother on 6 February 1826 at the age of 38 having served 22 years and 219 days (including his two years for Waterloo). His general conduct was listed as 'indifferent, but now improved', perhaps hinting at why he never rose in rank.

William also mentions marrying whilst in Ireland and the records do show one marriage at Dublin in 1809 between a William Clarke and Isabella Manders but no other details can be discovered and there is another reason to doubt this is the correct wedding. He rarely mentions his wife and never by name, but his letter home from Waterloo to his parents in Scotland would seem to indicate that his wife might still be residing in Ireland at this time. In this 1815 letter, however, he also mentions that he has two daughters, one of which has recently been born. There are few baptisms recorded at Dublin for a father named William Clarke, but one stands out – that of Mary, baptised 22 June 1815 at St Michael & John's in Dublin to a William and Mary Clarke (née Macavity) which fits perfectly with a girl born whilst he was serving in Belgium. There is also a record of an Elizabeth being baptised on 5 January 1812 at St Mary's in Dublin City to a William Clarke and an unnamed wife (left blank). These could be William's two girls, but unfortunately the records are poor and William never mentions them again. I do however suspect that our William married Mary Macavity in 1809.

Unfortunately, nothing certain has been discovered regarding the deaths of William, Mary or his brother Mark either, the name Clark or Clarke being too common to identify a death with any certainty.

I have reproduced the entire text as written, only adding chapters to aid the reader and footnotes to help identify individuals and places. Particularly in the early chapters, William does occasionally provide conversation in his text in Old Scottish; which to many will prove unintelligible, where this occurs I have added an English translation in [brackets], I can assure the reader that in many instances this is very necessary! In the early chapters, where William's story is in the format of a novel, it can be a little challenging, but I can assure the reader that if you persevere, you will discover a fascinating account of the military career of a young Scot's Grey, you will learn much and revel in a description of Waterloo and its aftermath which is second to none. This is William's story . . .

Memoirs of A Winter's Evening

Chapter 1

The Road to Enlisting

When dark December's gloomy mantle was spread over the face of nature and the chilling blast made fields and forests bare, I wandered forth one evening to a neighbouring village for the purpose of beguiling a dull hour among the farmers who usually met in the little ale-house in the evenings at that solitary season of each revolving year.

I had weathered my way thither through the rough storm and pondered for a time at the threshold of the lowly thatched hostelry, beating the snow from my shoes and lending an ear to robin red breast, as it perched on a withered stump opposite the door, with his feathers raised over his back, and chirping its pitiable plight in plaintive notes, through the sharpness of the frost-fraught gale which blew with unrelenting fury from the angry north.

A small stream which usually murmured down the glen at the back of the house, had now assumed the character of the mountain torrent. A temporary thaw had dissolved the snow on the neighbouring hills which now rushed down the hollow sounding glen with impetuous force. The thunder cloud burst at intervals overhead and rolled with dreadful sublimity along the face of the murky heavens which mingled with the roaring of the waters and howling storm fell in dread confusion on the ear, and all the sounds which attend the storm seemed here combined, as I hurried into the snug retreat, praising the all bountiful guide for that shelter and enjoyment which is secured to ungrateful man, so far beyond the reach of other creatures.

The villagers were gathered round a deep turf fire and on the table stood a smoking jug of old English beverage, with the landlady in the

1

middle of the group praising its goodness and assuring her friends that she never brought the same old brown stout above board except to her best customers.

I had scarcely seated myself amongst the happy squad, when two strangers entered and desired they might be allowed to stay till the following morning and after shaking the snow from their red mantles, they were desired to place themselves at the fire and were immediately enrolled in that body which the landlady termed her best customers.

The rustic song and unvarnished tale went gaily round and gladdened the blooming countenances which formed the happy circle, the widows smile accompanied the often-filled brown jug, as she placed it with its cheery contents on the table. The strangers were old soldiers and had spent their youth in the army; were now discharged and journeying once more towards their native country; they had after a long time of service bid adieu to the tented field, to war and all its boisterous accompaniments, intending to end their days where they began them in the land of their childhood and their hearts beat high as their minds were filled with the delightful hope of once more treading the mountain side on which they used with light hearts, to beguile the long gone by hours of their boyhood. They conversed together for some time; they were listened to with attention and at last requested by the company to entertain them with a short account of their wanderings. They were prepared to partake of such fare as the widow's provision afforded and after taking a draught from the foaming tankard, one of the veterans addressed himself to his comrade as follows.

'Comrade' said he, 'many years have rolled over our heads since we joined our good old regiment, many happy days have we enjoyed in it, occasionally mixed with little crosses to keep us in mind of ourselves; we have braved many a bitter blast and stood too in the range of fortune's sunshine.

'I dare say you have not forgot the night that made us first acquainted, our posts were separated only by the soulless and mouldering city walls when the hour of midnight was proclaimed by the bell of the venerable Cathedral of Canterbury and the dying notes born on the fresh imperceptible breeze o'er the post in which we stood.'[1]

---

1. The regiment was based at Canterbury in 1803–5, which is the time meant. The regiment did return there in 1814 and again in 1816–17.

His comrade sent a nod; which at once said, or meant 'All you have said is perfectly correct.' He requested his brother soldier to listen, and sank into a silent and attentive posture while his comrade proceeded as follows.

My father was a native of auld Scotland, poor indeed in purse, but at all times, carried with him, the dignity and deportment of an honest man; he struggled, in concert with her who was dear to him to his last moments, to teach & bring up a numerous family in the same path over which he had himself cautiously walked, and by his unwearied example shewed them the way, by which they might reach the high name which he himself had attained. A kind husband; a tender-hearted father, and universally esteemed friend. With him I spent my juvenile days among the romantic mountains of Perthshire, from which place they removed to Alva House[2] delightfully situated at the foot of the Oachle hills[3] about seven miles east from Stirling.

I had only attained my thirteenth or fourteenth year, when I began to form a notion of leaving home in search of; I knew not what! My father observed that I had a desire to stray from his happy hearth; and after many suitable advices, agreed that I should go for a short term to live with a farmer who had often before solicited his consent to the arrangement now concluded. He soon had an opportunity of seeing John Brown; for such was the farmer's name above alluded to and as he came every week to sell his butter in the little town of Alva; they struck the bargain at their first meeting & I was to prepare for my new situation on the following day.

John Brown was a plain, unassuming, worthy man; and if he be yet living, I hope he enjoys all the comforts this world can afford; and if not his memory will remain with those who knew him as a kind, honest and faithful friend as ever was clad in a broad blue bonnet and home spun coat.

I was highly delighted with the prospect of going from home on the morrow and with the rising sun I took the road, with a little bundle under my arm containing all my worldly gear, goods and chattels! Which consisted of a shirt or two & pairs of stockings, a Bible; some needles and thread and I think all is nearly told.

---

2. In the early 1800s Alva House was owned by the Johnstone family, and had previously been owned by Sir Charles Erskine. Alva House was used for military target practice in the Second World War and was completely destroyed. Alva had grown with the mining of silver in 1700 and the opening of a coal mine. In 1798 a modern woollen mill was established here.

3. Actually the Ochil Hills.

I had scarcely ever been out of sight of my father's snug little abode before and as I lost sight of [the] venerated clumps of trees which surrounded it, I found myself wiping away a tear which had stole into my eye and for which I could not account. However, I rallied again and trudged along; and after travelling nearly all day; sitting down occasionally by the wayside, refreshing myself with a crust of oatcake and cheese with which my mother had filled my pockets in the morning and a drink of the pure mountain stream which often crossed my path; I at last came in sight of my new abode. It was situated near Dunfermline; the farm was situated in the middle of a black and dreary moss and the solitary farmstead of Howfauld's[4] seen in the distance surrounded by a far expanse of barren and heath covered moorland where the scream of the lapwing and other feathered inhabitants of the dreary waste saluted the ear in sublime confusion. I saw no other of God's creatures as I entered within the boundary of the gloomy bog, except one solitary heron stalking in quest of its prey among the black pits from which John Brown and his fathers had dug their peats for many past ages. This sorry scenery fell far short of the beautiful valley I had left in the morning, and which folded in its bosom the happy cottage of my father. My mind was at once hurried back to the sweet spot! My wandering imagination beheld the village of Alva overlooked by the Oachle Hills, which were still in view, shooting their stupendous heads into the rolling clouds on the western horizon. The rugged & hanging rocks over which the tumbling cataract incessantly hurry on its roaring way down the Shelog Glen. The beauty of the scenery on either sides of the burn's romantic tract; the adjoining woods with their stately inhabitants under whose proud foliage I had often found a place of refuge from the blaze of the sultry summer sun, admiring the flowers in endless variety of colours, shooting their heads above the earth and cheering the senses with their exhaling odours; the varying songs of the linnet, the blackbird and the thrush mingling in sweet harmony with the more plaintive notes of robin red breast and the distant murmurs of the cooing Kushet.[5]

I also thought of the beautiful walks whose winding ways had so often led me through the charming recesses of the olive and myrtle

---

4.   This refers to the tiny village of Hawkiesfauld which stands two miles north of Dunfermline, the village has since been renamed Wellwood.

5.   Scottish – ring dove or wood pigeon.

groves until I had issued on the open boundary of the park, clothed in all the gay livery which adorn the field and forest.

Thus I mused as I slowly passed over the lonely heath, casting my eyes around in search of the dwellings of those who might inhabit the barren land, but no human abode; nor scarcely a hedge or tree were to be seen, except the farm house of Howfaulds and a small cottage situated close by; with a few scattered bourtree bushes[6] about the solitary stack yard[7] and the bare trunk, or remains of an old fir tree on which one green tuft still nodded to the passing breeze in the middle of the gloomy moss.

The miserable prospect filled my mind with anything the reader may think proper to imagine, comfort excepted. I stood still and glour'd frae me [stared] for a time; fleeting suggestions seemed to whisper 'turn back', but night had begun to lower the black mantle on the face of nature, such as it was; and at the same instant that these misgivings were working within, a swarm of moor fowl[8] that had intended to bivouac for the night, rose on wing from among the heather. The voice of their wings was like that of distant thunder which startled me from my reverie and I found myself unconsciously marching on and approaching my new abode.

I had arrived with all my riches under my arm, within a few yards of the mud wall which enclosed the stack yard and beheld something like a human figure, but it partook so much of the clay colour of all other objects around, that I was undecided as to whether it might be an animated sojourner in this queer world or not! However, it at last moved rather hastily to a gap in the feal dyke[9] & I instantly recognised the brown face of my old friend John Brown, who had posted himself there for the purpose of contemplating the industry of the inhabitants of his bee skeps[10] as well as to look out for my coming.

My heart became somewhat lighter on beholding, in this land of solitude, a face which I had seen before and John's voice was instantly

---

6. Scottish – for elder bushes.
7. Scottish – a yard stacked with peat cuts.
8. Old Scottish for red grouse.
9. Actually a fail dyke – Old Scots for a turf wall.
10. Bee skeps are now only occasionally used as they are awkward to remove the honey from in comparison with modern trays. It is formed as a large hollow dome which sits on the ground; made of wicker with a small post box entrance hole for the bees.

heard exclaiming 'Come awa ma' man! I thought ye was lint among the moss hags! Monie a glow'r 've gien ouer the heather for ye.' ['Come on lad, I thought that you were resting among the moss where the peat has been cut. I have given many a look over the heather for you.'] Then directing me how to enter the house, he retired and was ready to receive me at the front door.

I surveyed the ancient cut of his curious blue coat; the ample circumference of his bonnet set rather tastily ajee;[11] his long flapped waistcoat meeting about mid-thigh with the tops of his indefatigable gray mashes,[12] whose texture reflected no small degree of credit on the industry of his sister Jenny; who having by this time, been informed of my arrival, had left her milking pail & issued from the byre to welcome me home.

New wonders every moment unfolded themselves, Jenny's appearance was equally worthy of notice. Her garments were altogether of a clay colour and so numerous the patches and bracings, that secured one part to another that it was literally impossible to distinguish any part of the original among these and the endless variety of fringes which hung around the masculine bare legs and feet of the Howfauld's Venus, as she strode the dirty and broken pavement towards the door muttering 'Come in ouer my bairn, I'se warrant ye're beath hungry and dry' ['Come in my boy, I'll warrant you are both hungry and thirsty'].

My new mistress proceeded into the house and I followed with something whispering into my inexperienced lug 'There goes a kind heart taped up in dirt and rags.' I followed my leader into the dark kitchen, sending as I entered, a scrutinising glance around me, but all was darkness until Jenny had roused the parting life of a peat or two, which smothered among a heap of ashes in the middle of the floor; I then got a feint view of the smoky habitation.

Under foot was a damp earthen floor, on which stood in scattered irregularity, two or three old wooden seats of home manufacture, some wooden platters and rams-horn spoons lay on a tottering table in front of an old oaken box bed, which, with the walls and all their appendages, were of one dark and unvarying tinge, derived from the peat reek [smoke] which formed a dense cloud under the rafters which supported the roof and were adorned with a profusion of soot drops hanging like

---

11. Scottish – to the side or on a slant.
12. Stockings.

icicles & threatening their black fa' [fall] into any eye that dared to raise itself to their murky territory. A momentary chill crept over soul and body of me, as I contemplated my sorry situation. However, Jenny had observed my bewildered look & assuming a still more kindly tone, said 'Come, ma braw lad, poo in ouer a creepie an' warm ye' ['Come my brave lad, pull up a three-legged stool and warm yourself']. At the same time placing on a buffet stool before me, a wooden beaker full of good new milk and some well baked oatcakes, fare which has been palatable to me up to this hour.

These wholesome viands I was sparingly partaking of, when an old woman who inhabited the neighbouring cottage, came in, the vivid gleam of her small grey een,[13] from under the flannel tog[14] which she wore and which seemed by its appearance, to have secured her head from heats and cold, for many by-gone years; betokened ungovernable curiosity to see Jonnie Brown's new callant,[15] and accosted Jenny wi' a 'Whar's the Laddie?!'

'Here Effee, here' replied Jenny. 'He's a bra callant, but anco gentle poor man; I doot he disna like our mainland fare.' ['He's a fine young lad, but an awfully weak lad, I don't think he likes our mainland food'].

Effie on hearing this drew near, partly whistling with her shrill voice, 'Ye manna be blate birky, fill ye ye'r waine and ne'er fash your thum! I'se wid'a plack ye'r teeth's longer then y'er beard yet. Tak ye'r meat an ye'll do ye'r daurk I warrant ye my man' ['You mustn't be bashful and hungry, fill yourself boy and never worry about for them! I'll bet with coin that your teeth are longer than your beard for some time yet. Eat your meat and you'll do your day's work I'll warrant you boy']. And with such teasings old Effie pestered me till I had finished my repast, when she hobbled towards her cottage, leaving me alone to muse on the strange appearances around me; while Jenny finished her milking, and John performed such duties as were due to his route every evening.

These unvarying tasks being performed, John and his sister returned to the house where my new master held forth to me in a very kindly address, the comforts which awaited me under his homely roof; and after many assurances of his unchangeable friendship; he doffed

---

13. Scottish – for eye.
14. Scottish – for clothes.
15. Scottish – for a lad or young boy.

his blue bonnet and with a reverential aspect, commanded Jenny to pass him the muckle[16] Bible frae the boll[17] at the back o' the cum [cupboard] and prepared to perform family worship; the last duty of the evening. He turned over the leaves of the sacred volume and at last found a portion to his mind, while Jenny to throw a light upon the good work placed herself by him with a handful of chips of the wood which had been dug out of the moss and which to all probability had been deposited there from the time that Noah and his zoological friends had rocked on the general deluge. She lighted one after another and John began to read the 9th Chapter of Joshua, but the ancient record, which had long inhabited the same smoky quarters had now become dirty and difficult to read. However, he persevered, half reading, half spelling and sometimes over-leafing a king or two, whose names were rather hard to pronounce; until he arrived at the 17th verse; where under the walls of the last city he stood totally beaten and at the same moment Jenny became wearied out and unconsciously dropped into the arms of Morpheus and in due time, the spark burnt down and left John in darkness. He raised his head from the book and riveting his eyes; not upon a sleeping Venus, but upon sleeping Jenny Brown, and roared with a voice like a sudden crash of thunder 'Snipe the speal in a devil to ye! What's the muckle taupie aboot!! ['Stop your sleeping, the devil to you. What's the great scatter-brained woman doing?']

Jenny was so unceremoniously roused that she was on her post in a twinkling again, but not before John had closed the book and commenced railing against his sister for her neglect, alleging that she had been the sole cause of the reading being sticket.[18]

We then retired to rest. I slept little and was up early next morning, when my worthy master accompanied me round his boundary and pointed out the little duties which I should have to perform and although I utterly detested everything around me, the kind treatment which I met from with honest John Brown and his sister soon reconciled me to my new abode. I became so much attached to them both that in a very short time I was quite at home. I was indulged even beyond my boyish desires, until I had served them about six months, the period of my engagement, when I again began to think of seeing new places. My

---

16. Scottish – for large.
17. Scottish – from the recess.
18. Scottish – for ended.

master used every encouragement he could think of to prevail on me to fee [serve] with him again but without effect, and I left him, bearing with me his best wishes, as well as those of his sister, who crammed my pockets with barley bannocks[19] and cheese for my journey on the morning of my departure.

I had gone but a little way across the moss when I unconsciously turned round as if to take a last look at the lonely farm of Howfaulds, which had changed its aspect very materially in my eyes, from the time I had first seen it. My first glance fell upon my good old master standing by his bee skeps in the stack yard, looking after me over the feal dyke and nearly on the same spot where he stood to receive me, when I first went to live with him. I immediately withdrew my eyes and with a heart rather full, trudged on my way.

I proceeded to Stirling where I engaged to serve another farmer about two miles from that town. This family had more pride and less happiness than the unassuming & contented inhabitants of Howfauld's. They supported a dignified distance from the society of their servants and paid a greater attention to the cultivation of a haughty disposition than to the cultivation of their farm and no doubt, had a greater burthen on their minds as rent day drew near, than my old respected master John Brown, was ever loaded with.

This place, although in a situation happy for its romantic and beautiful scenery; I never enjoyed and therefore longed for the expiration of the term for which I had engaged to serve them. That term at last arrived and off I trudged as light as the wind that fanned the heather on the adjoining braes[20] of Logie. I now bent my steps towards the City of Palaces, Auld Edinburgh and I leave to the imagination of the reader what I must have felt on approaching the metropolis of my native land of which I had heard so much and long'd to see from my earliest recollections. My father had now removed to the neighbourhood of Auld Reeky and I once more spent a few weeks at his homely hearth, however I had no desire to be at home and he soon found me a situation in the service of a gentleman whose country seat lay on the banks of Loch Lomond in Dunbartonshire and I prepared with high spirits, to take the road for what I considered another new region.

---

19. Scottish – a round flat cake cooked on a griddle.
20. Scottish – for hills.

I proceeded to Edinburgh on the morning on which I was to take my departure, accompanied by my father and my heart was lifted to a height beyond conception when I mounted the coach for my journey. I had never before ridden so high and the anticipation of being thus conveyed to a country I had never before seen, pleased me beyond measure.

I travelled to Glasgow this day & next morning prosecuted my journey along the beautiful banks of the Clyde, charmed with a variety of enchanting views, till I came within sight of the huge rock of Dumbarton[21] rising from amid the waters of the bussy[22] Forth and overlooking like a guardian angel, passing angels careering with their loads of treasure to the flourishing city I had left in the morning.

I proceeded up the north side of the Leven water[23] through Bonhill to Kilmaronoch[24] and at last arrived at the entrance of the old avenue which approached with an unbending line to the front of the Ross house.[25]

The sun had just gone down behind the stupendous Ben Lomond[26] and the fine summer evening sky was glowing with radiance around its towering summit as I entered under the shade of the stately beeches & elms mixing their luxuriant foliage from either side overhead, formed an arch of the most delightful effect, the landscape around teemed with all the fruits of a bountiful harvest and the woods which extended themselves far along the shores, reflected their proud foliage, now assuming an autumnal hue in the pure waters of Loch Lomond. I gazed with wonder on this delightful scene, while the air was charmed with the various notes of the feathered songsters in every grove. As I neared the ancient mansion, a luxuriant lawn surrounded it, favoured by the help of the combined hand of nature and art. Various clumps of trees bending beneath their gaudy and changing livery dotted the green park; and the dark tone of the venerable yews rearing their heads in many

---

21. Dumbarton Rock on which Dumbarton Castle stands.
22. Scottish – for busy.
23. The Leven River joins the Clyde at Dumbarton.
24. Kilmaronoch Church stands one mile east of Gartocharn.
25. This refers to the Ross House which stood where Ross Priory does today. The present house was completed in 1812 and is now owned by Strathclyde University.
26. The southernmost mountain of the Munroes.

forms among the lofty holly hedges which enclosed the gardens and the pleasure-walks which led from thence and were lost at the entrance of some leafy thicket on the shore of the lake. On the glassy surface of which, a fleet of pleasure boats loitered in the parting beams of the glorious orb of day.

I was now received into the excellent family of Hector McDonald Buchanan esquire of the Ross,[27] as an assistant gardener, where I spent the happiest days of my life; and too, in one of the most beautiful situations in Scotland; or in any part of the world I have ever visited. What could have induced me to leave it; and often too, when my only covering was the worn soldier's cloak; and my bed the cold ground, shared by the noble steed which had carried me during the past day; and under the midnight sky of a foreign land, as my mind wandered to the banks of Loch Lomond.

However, leave it I did! For youth will have its way, as well as old age, I left it to be enjoyed by some wiser striplen [stripling] than myself; nor did I ever forget the morning on which I took my departure, accompanied [by] the best wishes of my superiors and equals. While yet within sight of the old and venerated mansion where I had spent days of delight, often I looked back and waved, a sigh (yet knew not for what) as I lost sight of my favourite groves of venerable oaks, under whose spreading boughs I used to shelter from the sultry sun beams and the sharp pelt of winter's blast. As I lost sight of the far expanse of the waters of the loch, on the clear bosom of which I had so often whiled away the time in the family pleasure boat; and when many miles distant, the lofty & stupendous summit of Ben Lomond caught my returning glance.

Dull and lonely I trudged along, for I had left attractions not easily effaced from a youthful mind, however I continued my journey and reached Glasgow the same night; where I engaged to serve a gentleman at Ayr. I proceeded thither, but found all barren, the house of Castle Hill newly built & the gardens & pleasure grounds in an unfinished

---

27. The male heirs of the Buchanan family who owned Ross had died out at the end of the eighteenth century. Two female heiresses made claim on the estate, the case for the eventual successful claimant Jean Buchanan was made by one Hector Macdonald, an Edinburgh lawyer and friend of Sir Walter Scott. Hector eventually married Jean, taking the further surname of Buchanan and he later built Ross Priory.

state,[28] a cold room to live in and no society but that of another young man (my fellow gardener) rendered every object to bear a barren, cold & cheerless look and my mind unconsciously borne back to the woods, walks, lake, islands and mountains which were always in sight at the Ross.

However, I hoped that time might reconcile me to my new place and therefore determined to make myself as easy as possible. My companion was a merry fellow in whose company I frequently strolled to the town in the evenings and by this means contracted some new acquaintances & when opportunity served us, we visited Alloway kirk[29] & the far-famed Brig of Doon, where, in the words of the immortal Burns:

> Nancy far afore the rest
> Hard upon noble Maggie prest.

As well as many other places rendered famous by the merry ditties of the Ayrshire poet.

Many months passed, but none brought the pleasure I longed for, I could not dispel the gloom that always clouded my mind towards my situation; and to get rid of it, I knew not what step to take, I could not go home to my father's before my term of engagement was out and in this unhappy dilemma I spent day after day without any hope of relief.

One day I had been musing on my uncomfortable plight, which my companion observed, and with a view of rousing my drooping spirits, at the close of our hours of labour, invited me to take a walk with him to the town. We walked slowly along and on our way met an old man whose silvery locks played in scanty traces on his temples and furnished his countenance with a hearty shake of the hand, while he accosted us as follows 'Guid e'en lad, guid e'en te ye, there's a bra' e'enen' ['Good evening lad, good evening to you, it's a fine evening'] 'Guid e'en, Gilbert' replied my companion, 'hoo's a' wi' ye the night?' ['How's it with you tonight?'].

'Troth Jamie, I'm but atween the twa' ['Truth Jamie, I'm but between the two'] continued the old man, 'I'm getting uncofrail man, aw downa

---

28. The new house on the Castlehill Estate was only completed in 1804. It was built for a Mr Patrick Ballantine, an Ayshire banker, and was knocked down in the 1960s.
29. Alloa in the text but it is certain that he meant Alloway, another village near Ayr then. The Brig [bridge] o'Doon lies nearby, near Burns' birthplace.

bide to come out ouer the door unless a bonie night like this draws me oot, I have had a hanlle o'troubles to fecht wi' this whyle high sirs, it's a weary warld this!!' ['I'm becoming a strangely frail man, I have too much pain to come out over the door, unless a beautiful night like this draws me out, I have had a handful of troubles to deal with this while, sirs, it's a weary world this!']. Then addressing himself to me, made some remarks on the fine weather, the beauty of the country, the mildness of the evening &c. For the sun was setting and the glorious bleaze[30] tipping the clouds from his red orbit which was yet only half hid behind the blue mountains in the distant west.

I agreed to his remarks being just, but stated that, I being a stranger; these pleasures did not present themselves to me in the same glowing colours in which he painted them, especially as my mind was not always present with me, but continued to stray back loaded with admiration to the unequalled scenery which gilded the face of the country in which I last lived, 'therefore' said I, 'this neighbourhood may yield you a thousand charms that are totally invisible to my eyes!!'

'Faith man that's true enough' replied Gilbert 'I think I coudna live awa gin I wur to gang frae hame noo, I haena been sax miles frae Wallace Tower sin this auld pow o mine made its first appearance in this queer warld.' ['I think I couldn't live away if I was to leave from home now, I haven't been six miles from Wallace Tower[31] since this old head of mine made its first appearance in this queer world.']

'Well Sir' said I, 'I doubt not but you have acted wisely in spending the long train of years which must have passed over your head, in comfort under your own vine and fig tree, instead of running yourself in the way of the troubles and crosses that are daily met with abroad and also enjoying the satisfaction of never being told that a rolling stone gathers no moss.'

'Aha lad' quoth Gilbert, 'I haena been sae deevelish comfortable, I hae had a pantle o' crosses, although I ne'er gaid far frae hame to seek them and gin ye'l just pay attention a wee, I'll gee ye a sketch o some o'them that will astonish ye.' ['I haven't ever been so devilish comfortable, I have had a number of problems, although I never went far from home to seek them and if you'll just pay attention a while, I'll give you an idea of some of them that will astonish you'].

---

30. Scottish – for breeze.
31. Wallace Tower stands on High Street, Ayr. The original ancient tower was replaced by the current Gothic one in 1832.

We advanced slowly towards the town and Gilbert continued thus, 'Ae bonie morning about twa towmonts syne, I like a gouk gaed aboot five miles ayout that know there, to spear aboot some family affairs that I thought demanded my presence. This was the longest dreighest journey e'er I had travelled a' my days' ['Yes a beautiful morning about two years since, I took a long walk about five miles where no one knew me there, to think about some family affairs that I thought demanded my presence. This was the longest, wettest journey I had ever travelled in all my days.']

'Weel sir; and what do ye think I gaed aboot? No to see the country, or any sic nonsense as that, no sir; it was to see aboot some siller that I thought to hae come at by the death o'an auls sister o'mine.' [Well, sir; and what do ye think I walked about? Not to see the country, or any such nonsense as that, no sir; it was to see about some silver that I thought I was to have come into by the death of an old sister of mine.']

'This sister' continued Gilbert 'was an auld worthless piece o'deformity that I ne'er keepet ony correspondence wi; her spirit was sae laigh, that she danner'd frae hoose to hoose among the neebours like a beggar, and whae'er had a heart that melted wi' the force o'her pity fue tale, gied her something; and sae sir, she was encouraged to hand at her begging trade and brought muckle disgrace on a' her kin; and at last sir, this poor crazie creature had the impudence to come sighing and nashing her teeth to me. She tried monie a wylie gate of softening my heart (as she ca'd it) and getting into my affections; but a' she coud do had nae affeck; diel a in I wad let her get; but drove her aboot her business wi a positive order that she was ne'er to show her auld withered face to me mair.' ['was an old worthless piece of deformity who I never kept any correspondence with; her spirit was so timid, that she sauntered from house to house among the neighbours like a beggar, and whoever had a heart that melted with the force of her pitiful tale, gave her something; and so sir, she was encouraged to keep at her begging trade and brought much disgrace on her family; and at last sir, this poor crazy creature had the impudence to come sighing and gnashing her teeth to me. She tried many an attempt of softening my heart (as she called it) and getting into my affections; but all she could do had no affect; the devil I would let her get in; but drove her away on her business with a positive order that she was never to show her old withered face to me again'].

'A gay twa three hearsts gaed o'er but my sister Jibby ne'er troubled me, till aboot twa years syne she fell suddenly sick, and Lord sir, it

spunket oot that she had seraped a hantle o' property and siller the
gather; Gas sir, then I began to see the damned blunder I had made
by forbidding Jibby to enter my door. Ay man, I saw it, I saw it at once
Sir, and flew to wark wi my wits, but what could I doo? To gang till
her then wad only been geeing her the satisfaction o' ordering me oot
o' her house & sae I determined to let her e'en slip awa oot o' the road
afore I gaed near the place. Weil sir, she diet sure aneugh; I heard of late
at night; sleept unco little wi thinking o' the siller, sprang oot o'bed e'er
the Laverocks began to whistle neist morning; and clapping my blue
bonnet on my pow, my Rauchin round my sheuthers and wi my cudgee
in my neive, aff I gaed.' ['A pleasant two or three harvests passed over
without my sister Tibby troubling me, till about two years since, she
suddenly fell sick, and Lord sir, it turned out that she had gained a
large property and gained some silver; God sir, then I began to see the
damned blunder I had made by forbidding Tibby to enter my door.
Yes man, I saw it, I saw it at once Sir, and flew to work with my wits,
but what could I do? To go to her then would only have been giving
her the satisfaction of ordering me out of her house & so I determined
to let her even slip away out of the road before I went near the place.
Well sir, she died sure enough; I heard of it late at night; slept a little
strangely with thinking of the silver, sprang out of bed before the sky
larks began to whistle next morning; and clapping my blue bonnet on
my head, my plaid round my shoulders and with my cudgel in my
clenched hand, off I went']. 'The morning was very fine, I hurried on
and monie [many] a scheme I thought on to insure my success, before
I got to the place.'

'The house lay in the how o' a glen, just in the bield o that bit height
ouer by there, sae snugly hidden that I coudna see't till I was amaist
on the rigged at; but Lord, as soon as I came near and saw the taps
o the lums, my heart began a louping and dunting to sic a degree wi
fair anxiety that I verily thought it wad hae floun oot o the very mooth
o' me; however sir, composing mysell as weel as I coud, I met a'my
friends weeping and wailing about Tibby's bed. I was obligated to put
on a mournful face too; do you understand me?' ['The house lay in the
valley of a glen, just in the shelter of that bit of height over by there,
so snugly hidden that I couldn't see it till I was almost on top of it;
but Lord, as soon as I came near and saw the mess of the rains, my
heart began a leaping and pounding to such a degree with such anxiety
that I verily thought it would have flown out of the very mouth of me;
however sir, composing myself as well as I could, I met all my friends

weeping and wailing about Tibby's bed. I was obligated to put on a mournful face too; do you understand me?']

'Perfectly sir' said I.

'Weil then', continued Gilbert, 'I set mysell til't and I sigh'd and sabb'd and turned up my een and roar'd and grat as wiel as the best among them in spite o' their teeth till the first gush o'grief was ouer, then they a sat down and fell a cracking about the property she had left i'this warld. Ye ken; for ilka ane was expecting something, less or mair.' ['I set myself to it and I sighed and sobbed and turned up my eyes and roared and cried as well as the best among them in spite of their teeth, till the first gush of grief was over, then they all sat down and fell to talking about the property she had left in this world. You understand; for everyone was expecting something, less or more.']

'My auldest brither [oldest brother] then plied oot [pulled out] a kind o' a will which Tibby had made; this, after demanding attention to hear their names mentioned and how do ye think it ended? Damme the baubee [Damn the silver sixpence] she left me, but had disowned me a'the gitther [altogether], just for that confounded mistake I had made in discarding her frae [from] my house.'

'There was I, left in the lurch, but I found I coudn'a mend the matter and therefore seem'd as careless as possible about it; though Lord, man I was absolutely like to split wi' downright vexation and danner'd [strolled] awa hame again dowie [dispirited] eneugh.'

'I lamented my ill fortune, nae doubt; however, I manfully determined not to harbour a thought aboot it after I gat hame. But weary fa them.'

'Misfortunes are eternally at the heels o' ane anither [of one another], wicked luck stack [stuck] to me; the disappointment I had me wi wasna the warst, for while I was awa some o'the diels [devil's] infernal gang wha [which] are ne'er satisfied wi their ain [own] had broken into my shop & plundered it o' the maist feck [total value] o what I was worth in the warld.'

'There man; there was a thunder stroke, wasen it? I'm no sure to a pennie or tippnee [penny or tuppeny], how muckle siller [much silver] they took; for I was in sic guid [such good] spirits when I gaed awa [went away] that I hadna counted it, a thing I seldom neglected to do daily for thirty years afore.'

'How unfortunate' exclaimed I, 'that was indeed a thunder stroke, after such a disappointment, to be robb'd in that manner.'

'Rubbet' [thieved], quoth Gilbert, 'Faith I was rubbet, o a' the valuables I had in my shop, I tell ye. For beside a' my siller [silver] which I had wi muckle [much] trouble and anxiety harl'd [pulled] the gither [together] and watched ouer; & aboot which, monie [many] a night I was deprived o' my sleep. They made fearful ravages among my claes [clothes], my yearn [earnings], my chees [*sic*], my butter, my snuff, my oatmeal, my barley, herring, tobacco, pepper and saut [salt]. Was sic [such] misfortunes as thae easy to bide [endure], think ye? Ma Lord no! Their weight added thousands to thir [those] gray hairs o'mine. Lang I dammer'd [stumbled] aboot like a daft man; and let me tell ye, very little mair wou'd have gar's [forced] me put haun to mysell [commit suicide] and had it no been prevented by the guid advice [of] a neebor, I belive I wou'd hae left this warld a thieves a thegither [all together], but as I tell ye, this friend remonstrated wi me aboot acting sae daft like aboot the loss o' a trifle o warls gear [few worldly goods] (as he term'd it) but it was nae sic a triffle in my estimation. However, he advised me to take to my shop again, which after a guid deal o thinking aboot it; I did, and wi a degree of fortitude scarcely to be described; I forbade a single thought on the subject from entering my breast. But for a'my [all my] endeavours, my resolutions and determinations, it was a lang lang time indeed afore I got the better o' the weight o'grief that crushed me to the ground. But noo the gloom is by degrees dispersing, and as fortune has been kind enough to help my ain, never ceasing industry to scrape as muckle thegither [much together] again (gin [if] I can keep it oot o' the gate [way] o' rottens [dirty] and yeuky [itchy] fingers) as I think will keep a wee pickle [grain] meal i'the bink neuk [on the ledge in the alcove] till my auld pow [head] slips its wa's aneath [way beneath] the yird [ground]; I maun e'en let it dee a thegither [die all together].'

'Good God' said I, 'I am astonished how you could support yourself under such a train of mischances as seem to have combined themselves against you; but it affords a degree of pleasure to hear that you have so far overcome them as to be enabled to carry on your business again.'

'Aye', answered Gilbert, 'I hae recovered mysell sae far as that; and my goods is unrivalled in Ayr, either for price or quality; nae doubt ye'l use a hautle [bunch] o'things in my way yourself, and as I can supply ye cheaper and better, ye may as weil deal wi me as ony ither body. I'm sure I'se be muckle obliged to ye for ye'r custome, and for butter, cheese, tobacco, snuff, pepper, saur herren [pickled herring] and spelderus [dried fish], I'll no hurkle [bow] to man born.'

'Jamie there' alluding to my companion, 'kens [knows] me brauley [finely] and aften used to come and crack [talk] a while at e'en [evening], but I haena seen my auld acquaintance this monie [many]

17

a day; step as far and see my dwelling noo.' So, with Gilbert leading the way we trudged onto his house. On arrival at his low thatched cottage, Gilbert opened a door at the gable end which admitted us to the interior of his abode, it was lighted by one little solitary window, well stenchered [grated] by iron bars. The counter, or patchwork of old boards, on which stood the bulk of his merchandise, was barely visible in the background of the gloomy scene. Two rickety chairs; a kind of table propped up to the wall, a wooden luggie[32] and a large horn spoon stood on it; a broken iron pot in the attitude of a ship on her beam ends lay on the floor, and a very lean cat looked with eager attention into the pot; these composed the principle objects in the foreground of our picture.

On entering I cast my eyes around to discover where Gilbert had his goods stored, but was at last obliged to conclude that all was in sight and consisted of a lump of butter, a part of a cheese and an enormous large bladder of snuff standing on the counter, over which were suspended a pair of old worn out scales and a barrel of herrings stood in the corner of the sorry shop.

As the darkness gave way, I perceived Gilbert's bed obscured in a recess at the further extremity of the place; and a board nailed against the dusky wall on which was clumsily written Gilbert Yettinheart, grocer &c &c, also these lines by some half-bred wit *Bring siller [silver] wi' ye gin [when] ye can. For Yettinheart will trust no man.*

When we first entered this dowie [dismal] abode Gilbert hastened to a little cupboard or hole in the wall, and after opening and examining it he returned seemingly satisfied that all was right; he then desired us to be seated; added a few pieces of turf and succeeded after a good deal of puffing to make a kind of fire, by which we spent some time with our venerable host, who had begun in the kindest manner, to express his friendship towards us, begging as we took our leave that we would repeat our visits and spend a dull hour in the evenings in his house.

These visits we continued and although I found some amusement in Gilbert's stories, yet they were not sufficiently amusing to divert me into a love for my situation; every morning gave birth to some new and more unpleasant idea till I could no longer endure the reflection of being bound in a place in which I enjoyed no happiness.

---

32. A bowl with two handles.

On this I mused day after day, but could not fix upon a substantial method of altering my condition, till one day I being in town, heard a drum beating in some distant part of the streets and accordingly followed the crowds of country farmers and others who attended the market and flocked to meet the sound of the drum, and who as the recruiting party of a favourite regiment advanced, praised their fine appearance and applauded them with hearty cheers. I continued to follow the military party into several streets, admiring the manly figure of each individual as they paced the causeway, their gay scarlet habiliments and lofty snow white plumes nodding in the air, and their broadswords glittering in the noon day sun, so filled my imagination with such a flood of delight that I fancied I should be at the very summit of my wishes if I could but become one of these noble warriors. I made many enquiries about them and was informed that they belonged to a regiment which stood very high in popular favour. I signed and sealed the resolution I had made of offering my services at all hazards; I hurried home and informed my companion of having seen these fine fellows and that I had determined to enrol myself among them immediately.

Poor Jamie, who had as little comfort in his situation as myself, was no sooner made acquainted with my attention, than he sprung from his chair and with a look of inquisitive doubt, coolly asked whether I was joking. I declared I was not, but had fixed my mind so firmly that no advice could alter my resolution; adding that his endeavours (which I expected he was about to offer) would therefore be totally fruitless.

Jamie smiled and seizing my hand exclaimed 'No, no, my boy; I do not intend to offer any advice against the step you are about to take, but you may believe me when I tell you, that it gives me in that way of thinking; particularly as my own mind has for the last fortnight been bent on the same method of relieving me from this dull hole, but could not muster courage enough to tell you of it.'

'This is glorious news, unexpected; now for a wooden leg or a golden chain', and without farther hesitation off we marched. As we proceeded, Jamie informed me that he was a little indebted to Mr Yettinheart, who notwithstanding the friendship he professed to us a few nights before, had attacked him that morning for it in the most abrupt manner, and this step he rejoiced to think, would immediately put him in possession of the means of paying the small sum, which only amounted to nine shillings.

I was not a little surprised to hear this relation, as I had formed an opinion that Mr Yettinheart's friendship to us was unchangeable; and to prove this, proposed calling and informing him of our intention to enlist, that Jamie might be released from that encumbrance.

This retrograde being agreed upon we went to Gilbert's house, where we found him sitting before the fire watching the slow progress of a salt herring roasting on a few dying embers for his dinner. He received Jamie with such indifference as showed an evident abatement of the flame which on former occasions seemed to fill his heart and gladden his countenance when they met.

However, I advanced and informed him of what had brought us to the town; but instead of remonstrating against it (as I expected he most certainly would) he hastily erected his long figure and after pulling up his breeches and rubbing his elbow, exclaimed, 'Very weil lads, very weil, by the conscience o me, I'm glade to hear ye hae sic [such] spirits. Ye ken Jamie, it will put it i ye'r power to pay evry bodie their ain; dishonour and dishonesty are twa things that a Scotsman detests. I see ye are a true Scotchman yet Jamie; honesty will gav a man's name shine forth frae behint the darkest cloud that fortune can spread ouer't; like the very moon when she keeks [peers] frae behint the blackest that traverses the face of the midnight sky, man.'

Our professed friend thus harangued; regardless what became of either of us, if by the sacrifice his nine shillings were secured. He readily proposed accompanying us to the rendezvous to see (as he said) that we were fairly dealt with by the party to whom we intended offering ourselves 'for' continued he 'the sodgers are queer chields [boys] and wou'd ablins [perhaps] tak an advantage o'lads like you gin [before] they warna weil looked after; but I'll gang wi ye and see ye knighted. I'll mak the bargain for ye; but ye maun tak particular care that a' the oots and ins o'their wimpled [convoluted] meanings are clearly understood afore ye haud [hold] oot your haun [hand] to receive the shilling; for as soon as the glittering treasure dabs [pushes] the print o'Geordies [George's] head on ye'r loof [palm]; I' the king's name; the bargain is settled; ay unalterably settled; and farther words rendered of nae uteelity [utility] but ye maun [must] wait till I gee ye the signal, and then ye may wi safety take the siller [silver].'

Gilbert having now finished his preparatory drill, marched off and we followed our venerable leader to the tavern. In a short space, we arrived at the rendezvous, which was easily distinguished from the other alehouses in the town, by the clash of warlike music; the drums, fifes, trumpets, bugles and bagpipes lent their undistinguishable aid to the unremitting din which deafened the passing ear and shook the antient [*sic*] fabric under which they seemed to contend for the mastery.

Mr Yettinheart took the earliest opportunity of communicating his business to the corporal of dragoons and informed him that upon condition of him becoming answerable for the nine shillings which Jamie owed him, as well as insuring him of the bringing money, which was then allowed and amounted to three guineas for each recruit, we should both enlist with him.

All this the vetrain [*sic*] readily agreed to, but was not a little surprised (as he afterwards expressed himself) to see a man of Gilbert's years & appearance, for the sake of the trifle arising from it, so busily employed in getting us fixed as if to the highest bidder.

However, all was amicably settled; I had accomplished my wish, being accepted by the party which had so much taken my fancy in the morning but my companion being too low in stature for the dragoons was, compelled either to return home again or enlist with a party of foot. This circumstance rather damped our spirits, as we had cherished a hope of still being companions to talk over the scenes which at some future period would by distance be made more dear to us; but poor Jamie, who could not brook the idea of returning home, had no alternative left but to enlist with the other party which he rather reluctantly did and the hours passed merrily away till late in the night with many a fair good health to our Royal Master King George the 3rd from the often filled goblet of genuine Campbeltown mountain dew,[33] which was proclaimed by the hollow drum and brazen trumpet, to a multitude who filled the street to gaze upon the local scene.

The corporal with whom I had some conversation respecting Mr Yettinheart, informed me that he regarded him as one who would sell his nearest and dearest friend to satisfy the craving thirst he had for gains 'but in this instance' continued he, 'he shall meet with a disappointment which he little anticipates and which will fall far short of satisfying his expectation', adding, 'I'll play him a trick tonight yet', so saying he gave orders that his party should retire to their quarters and after settling the bill, desired Mr Yettinheart to call on him the following day to receive his money. This being all agreed to, we took a friendly good night of the old man and departed.

---

33. Campbeltown whisky was a great favourite at this time, with no less than thirty-four distilleries in operation.

My worthy commander desired me to follow him, the sergeant of the foot and Jamie joined our party, however we had not proceeded far when a post chaise, which had been ordered for the purpose, drove up; into this we were expeditiously huddled and off we went to Glasgow and joined the party of recruiters there.

Here I parted with my faithful and much esteemed companion in whose affectionate eye a tear unconsciously gathered itself as he stretched forth his hand for the last friendly grasp.

The corporal being appointed to conduct the recruits to their destination and the order being received for our departure, we accordingly took the road & the drummer proclaimed Mr Yettinheart's and all other claims settled, with a merry peal on his sheepskin as we passed through the Gallowgate[34] on our way to Edinburgh.

---

34. The Gallowgate is a long road running for about a mile in Glasgow which had eighty-six public houses on it at one time.

Chapter 2

The Scots Greys

We remained in Edinburgh a few days during which time I used the best generalship I was master of to evade my relations, as the bulk of them resided there; however, an order to embark relieved me from that anxiety & in obedience to this order we proceeded on board a vessel at Leith; she was bound for London and we sailed to join the regiment.

This was the first time I had turned my back on my native country and although my heart exulted in my departure, yet my bosom filled with a kind of regard before unknown to me, when I viewed from the Firth of Forth the ancient turrets of Edinburgh gradually gaining a more distant appearance and the summit of Arthur's seat reflecting the last beams of the evening sun. I gazed on them as I stood on the deck till the twilight melted away and these objects, now rendered dear, vanished in the gloom of night.

I continued on the deck during the night and gazed on the seeming quick passage of the moon from cloud to cloud as they were driven before the increasing gale along the face of the heavens. The wind increased with dawn of day and before the second evening arrived a fearful storm overtook our little bark. The gathering clouds like those of dark December approached with night and the winter like tempest roar'd o'er the tumbling current of the foaming waves; the wind still increased & the howling hurricane tossed the vessel to and fro on the mountains of the watery element. The deep roll of distant thunder approached nearer; the lightning played around us and gave to the awful surge, as it boiled round and dashed across our creaking deck a glowing tinge.

The passengers were all ordered below to give to the mariners a better opportunity of exerting themselves in saving the vessel in this disastrous situation; but I having previously crawled on all fours behind a huge cable which lay coiled near the bow, was not discovered till the hatches were secured. Here I might have shivered unnoticed long enough had not an awful mountain of water overwhelmed the deck and swept with it every moveable article that lay in the way of its furious passage, however being quite buried by this pitiless visitor, I clung to a spar which was lashed to the side of the vessel but the cable by which I lay lost its neatness and was scattered in disorder towards the mast, my heart now gave way, I thought all was lost sure enough. I threw my terrified eyes along the deck and faintly beheld the sailors clinging to the shrouds and different parts of the whistling rigging. I squalled out some inarticulate ejaculation which was heard by one of the crew who was nearest me, he hastened to the spot from which my despairing cry proceeded and discovering me still sticking to my hold, exclaimed, 'Halo my hearty; what the divel brought you here? Get below 'n bedamn to ye.' And seizing me by the arm assisted to raise me on my trembling legs. I staggered along with him, shivering with cold and dripping wet, to a little hatchway, through which he stowed me into the dark forecastle and dark I anticipated it was to continue for I never expected to view the sun's fair face again.

Here I panted the remainder of the night in darkness and in dread as the oft repeated peals of thunder burst through the clouds; or the seas dash with rustling fury passed o'er the deck of our little tide toss'd bark and the wild shouts of bustling sailors over our heads, invariably accompanying the seeming approach of the destruction which I thought completed in every succeeding struggle the vessel made.

I now leave you to judge what I thought of my first trip from home when I conceived it was surely to have put a period to my soldiering and quartered me in the arms of death till the blast of the last trumpet called me to my post again, however the vessel being new and strong, braved the tempestuous night, and the wind having greatly abated; the passengers were allowed to ascend from the dark regions below to the deck next morning.

The approach of the rising sun was marked in the eastern horizon with grey and vermillion streaks and over the face of which still sped the distorted remnants of black clouds, or scattered followers of the storm. No land was visible to the eye, for we had fortunately been driven to sea in the hurricane, which our vessel bore evident mark of. The rags of her torn main sail fluttered in the wind, the boat was gone and the deck cleared of every movable material.

This day proved very cold and as we had no inducement to remain on deck; the corporal desired me to accompany him into the forecastle, where he said he could form a comfortable nest for two. We occupied the greater part of the day in making a kind of couch (or in the words of my worthy commander, nest) to repose in among the lumber in the forecastle. We had now entered Yarmouth roads and as evening again approached, we posted ourselves in this snug retreat. The storm was quite gone by, the night serene, the moon's beams descending from a cloudless sky and the heavy swell which invariably follows the storm, frequent turning our creaking deck towards the great luminary of night, from whence a wandering gleam occasionally visited us. We thus mused on the serenity of the night and talked over the horrors of the preceding one with much satisfaction; when the corporal remarked that he had experienced many such changes since he had been a soldier and comforted me by adding that I might also expect to have some rough marches, both by sea and land, before I reached his term of service, 'but cheer up my hearty' continued he 'and let not these thoughts discourage you, for a good soldier and the difficulties he overcomes never fails to magnify the honours which are lavished on him by his grateful country. What a gratifying reflection fills the soldier's breast when his country's applause is thus called forth, as he returns from a foreign shore crowned with the laurels he has dearly won and exulting with his countrymen in the vanquished pride of the enemies of his dear, dear, native land. The very thought almost makes me wish I was young again, to share in the glory of drubbing these haughty frog eaters, for war is now again declared[1] and no doubt our good old regiment will have their thumbs in the pie as usual; for many a bloody business they have assisted in; their deeds may be traced as far back as the wars of King William 3rd in Holland; Marlborough's wars under Prince Charles of Lorraine; the 7 Years War under the Duke of Cumberland and Prince Ferdinand of Brunswick and latterly under His Royal Highness the Duke of York in Holland; with a train of exploits including the Battles of Blenheim, Ramillies, Oudenarde, Malplaquet, Denain,[2] Sheriffmuir,[3] Dettingen,

---

1. The Peace of Amiens which had ended the 'Wars of Revolution' failed and Britain declared war on France on 16 May 1803, which marks the beginning of the 'Napoleonic Wars'.
2. Fought in 1712 during the War of the Spanish Succession.
3. A little-known battle fought in 1715 during the Jacobite Rising.

Fontenoy, Rocoux, Lauffeld, Bergen, Hilbeek and Langensalza;[4] with as many skirmishes, bivouacking in frosty nights, smotherings among snow and drowning in floods and rivers as would fill a volume and do an old soldier's heart good to read it.'

The worthy veteran thus entertained me with his enthusiastic stories till Morpheus spread his soothing mantle and folded us in his peaceful arms. We again mounted the deck as the bright messenger of day rose over the eastern horizon and guided the rippling ocean to the bow of our vessel as she glided into the mouth of the Thames. We landed at Gravesend about noon; and I considered myself no mimic traveller when I set my foot on English ground.

---

4. Fought in 1761 during the Seven Years War.

Chapter 3

Joining & Initial Training

Here our commander determined to rest all night for the whole of his forces were much fatigued with their voyage and for my own part, my head was so jumbled by this first sea excursion, that my brains [*sic*] were still swimming. I imagined the streets with every other object possessed a motion similar to that of the rocking bark we had left and to prevent being upset, was frequently compelled to prop myself against the walls along the line which led to our quarters.

The corporal had chosen me for his comrade and I followed him to the public house in which we were to remain for the night; here we arrived, but met with a reception that, in my inexperienced mind; had almost established a bad opinion of old England at first sight. For no sooner had we entered and presented the billet to our landlady, than she burst into a fit of passion which furiously overshot the bounds of her government. She flitted indignantly about the house, fixed her fat form in the lobby to prevent our advance and exclaimed 'What the divel, more zoulgers again, damn such warmint, for we are never done wi um.'

'I say Popjoy', addressing her husband who rolled like a rum cask on a kind of sofa in the bar. 'Get off that there sofa you drunken brute and mind your business. Mizzle [Leave] ye your old Willan [duty], if you'd do that there instead of craining [lifting] your paunch and running a'ter the wenches it would be better for you. Come out o' this you old rogue ye and look after the rights o' your family. Snigger [Catch] me if I stand any more o' your imperence [impudence].'[1]

---

1. This is Old English.

The social son of Bacchus with some difficulty raised himself from his delicious couch and in a manner which indicated unfeigned submission toddled towards his stormy spouse, muttering 'Lord, love your soul Dolly; what is the matter? I'se sure I always attends ven you vants me.'

'Vats the matter' continued Dolly 'Vy don't you see vats the matter. Another parcel of souljers come'd a tormenting us, I'll be damn'd to um all.'

'You don't zay so! My joy.' Answered the jolly landlord as he staggered forth. 'Lawks! Vat a precious row will I kick up, wi' that there brandy faced villan o' a billet master o' ouren ater I see um. My eye Dolly, I'll make him stare.'

'Vel there' said Dolly 'Do you go ater him too, for vat I care, for they shaunds [shouldn't] be here.'

While this business was going on between our host and hostess; my commander who was better acquainted with such scenes than myself, told me to follow his example as he posted himself by the fire, coolly observing to the landlady that he was determined to maintain his position till her passion subsided. 'I am aware' said he 'that you are often put out of the way by the visits of we kingsmen! Yet your appearance tells me that you are a lover of your country! Your face is not formed like one that could long be the messenger of an angry heart and from these appearances alone I sit down convinced that the storm is nearly blown by.'

These coolly deliberated sentences from the veteran had their effect, for the jolly dame's face began to divest itself of the detested contractions which passion for some vile purpose had formed in the agitated muscles and again to assume the smooth surface and lovely dreadful smiles of the British fair. In the influence of which alone, the hero bends the knee and humbles his dear bought laurels.

She immediately followed us with a pot of ale and some bread and cheese which she placed on the table before us, and made a pithy apology for her want of civility. She said that she had been put out of her usual temper by a set of rood [sic] watermen who had been drinking in the house and as her husband, who was always willing to take pot luck with his customers; had filled his belly amongst them; they had found an opportunity of stealing on and leaving him to pay the reckoning. She then invited us to partake of the refreshment she had placed before us, by way of put off till dinner should be got ready and left us in perfect good humour.

The corporal smoked his pipe in the corner, while I sat mute enough; scarcely daring to look round, fearing I should not look like the folks in England, till the smoking dinner made its appearance. It consisted of a large piece of beef with accompaniments which would have done honour to the table of an alderman, but I unacquainted with dining in such public places, was so bedaubed with modesty, that it was sometimes with the utmost difficulty I found the way from the plate to my mouth, especially as every boor who entered made some uncouth remark which accompanied their longing eyes as they played with seeming delight over our well-furnished board. One of John Bull's true breed entered just as we began to eat, he fixed his eyes on the table, laid one hand on an enormous belly he carried about with him & raising the other to an attitude of astonishment exclaimed, 'Vell to be sure! That there is a picture.'

Another simpered from under a rueful countenance 'Who would not be a zoulger', while staggering came a groggy boatman and squaued aloud 'By the timbers of me, it warms the cockles o'one's heart to look on't! Huzza for Old England my hearty's!' &c &c and some similar remark was the messenger of the greedy appetite of everyone who entered and gazed with seeming ferocity on our table till we had finished our repast. I succeeded but with great pain; in making a kind of meal, yet it fell far short in point of enjoyment to the social rules of my own country where we would have been allowed to dine in some apartment un-annoyed by such a motley group. However, we passed the evening among them & I bore with as much fortitude as I could the unpolished compliments which they lavished on me as a fine young soldier &c not daring to venture upon lengthened answers least I should blunder in attempting the English language.

We retired to rest early in the evening and marched next morning for Sittingbourne, where we halted all night and next day gained the ancient city of Canterbury where the corps was stationed[2] to which we belonged. The regimental band met us at the entrance of the town and led our van [advance] through the streets to the barracks in which the regiment lay.

---

2. The Scots Greys had arrived at Canterbury in June 1803 and remained in garrison there for nearly two years, ready to face Napoleon's invasion if it ever came. With the renewal of the war, the regiment was augmented from eight to ten troops. The regimental establishment was now fifty-one officers, ten quartermasters, fifty-four sergeants, ten trumpeters and a thousand rank and file. William arriving the following month indicates that he was part of this augmentation.

This day was extremely fine. It was the month of July & I shall never forget with what admiration my heart was filled as we formed in front of the barracks. When I beheld the fine manly appearance of the old soldiers who flocked round us dressed neat and clean in their white stable uniforms. I saw no summit to which my wishes could aspire, equal to that of arriving at the character, honour and dignity of a veteran warrior & I beheld those men with a degree of veneration & respect which I do not in the whole course of my life remember to have lavished on any [other] of my fellow creatures.

Our commanding officer having inspected us, we were appointed to our respective troops and each given in charge of an old soldier, whose duty it was to instruct us in the different introductory branches of soldiering in the barrack rooms and stables. We were clothed and accoutred without delay; sent to horse and foot drills and every possible exertion used in getting us sufficiently disciplined to join the ranks in case of the regiment being called on foreign service or more active service at home; for apprehensions of an attack from the French coast were entertained and every night expected to be put to trial.

Our duties were consequently laborious and fatiguing, invariably turning out for horse drill, or riding school, at five in the morning. Returning at eight and after cleaning the horse accoutrements, arms &c, attending foot drill at ten, returning at one, dining and attending stables at two, drill again from half past three till half past six and closing the toils of the day with the evening stable hour from seven till eight o'clock. We were by this time fit for our beds, for the season was extremely hot and the field in which we were exercised had no cooling shades to afford a refuge from the all-powerful beams of the sun; but such was the garrison of Canterbury at this time that even nightly rest rendered so necessary by the fatigues of the day was but little enjoyed. Almost the whole of the old buildings in the city had been converted into barracks for the reception of troops concentrated there in readiness for such an emergency as the one which seemed then to threaten the adjoining coast. These unwholesome habitations were filled with tormenting insects, which, together with the loathsome heat arising from the breath of the men who were crammed into the room totally destroyed the seasonable remedy for daily fatigues which is experienced in the cherishing arms of unmolested sleep.

These evils blended together soon began to make an impression upon me. My spirits dropped and weakness, youthful debility &c began to attack me. However, I bore all in silence hoping that when I had learned my exercise I should at the same time arrive at the enjoyment of more comfort.

A few months passed over and those of our recruits who had made sufficient progress in their several branches of discipline, to befit them for it, were put on duty in their turns with the old soldiers. Mounting guards, picquets &c and patrolling the vicinity of the garrison during the night.

I happened to be one of the few who was first considered fit to make a beginning with these more important duties and the task which then fell to my lot was mounting guard. I exulted while I prepared for my first guard, in the cherishing idea that the time was fast approaching when I should turn my back with the confidence of a well-disciplined dragoon on these harassing drills which had made so serious an impression on my health and so heavily crushed the spirit which alone kept me afloat. I exerted my utmost skill which was also aided by the assistance of my comrades in cleaning my arms, clothing and accoutrements that I might make my first start with (what I considered) something like real soldiering creditably and when I appeared in my full uniform arm'd and plumed, I flattered myself that there was no room left for improvement. I accordingly came on parade, my appearance gave great satisfaction to my superiors and I took my share of the duties connected with the guard I mounted.

It so happened that one of the posts belonging to the guard on which I was placed, had from its lonely situation fallen so far into dislike among the soldiers as to be considered the haunt of a ghost or within the prowling boundary of some supernatural midnight wanderer. This report had so far gained ground as to draw the men on (although they disdained to confess any want of courage) to reckon whether this post might fall to their lot or not and if at night, would rather have missed than hit upon it.

However, fate seemed to have reserved this favour for me at half past eleven at night. The post was near the outlets of the town, on the southern ramparts or decayed city walls. The ruins of a Gothic tower, which in former ages had reared its proud head above that part of the stately fortification which secured Dane John[3] from feudal assaults, was the point on which the sentinel formed his walk.

---

3.   Dane John Gardens in Canterbury is the site of an ancient Roman graveyard which was converted into a motte and bailey castle in the eleventh century, Dane John being thought to be a corruption of 'donjon.'

I was posted and the supernatural inhabitants of the old tower which was said to pay its unsocial respects to the sentinels, occupied the heavy end of my attention, such tales however little credited, has sometimes the power of agitating the mind of man so far as to bring all the stories relative to them fresh before the imagination, particularly when the gloom of midnight surrounds him on the spot which is said to be the scene where such visions make their appearance.

I began my walk, occasionally looking over the wall upon the dark expanse of flat country which presented itself covered with heavy unvarying prospects of hops, gardens &c while a glance to the other hand fixed my eyes on the venerable tower of the ancient cathedral rearing its head above the poplars which skirted the public walks of Dane John field. The night was still, the almost impenetrable breath of wind unheard save when the restless leaf of the poplar trees, stole a gentle flittering march upon my attentive ears and filled my imagination with the torturing doubt that the lady of the old tower was on her way towards me; however my fortitude was sufficient for the task it had to perform, for nothing put it to trial; nor was I annoyed with any of the wailings and songs of sorrow which were said to have been heard at this place, unless they were the songs of the numerous sentinels posted round the garrison proclaiming at the end of each revolving hour, the well proven war song, 'All's Well!' whose varying voices in the stillness of night bore through the air a warlike echo till it melted away in sublimity and the extreme distance.

As the hour of my deliverance from this doubtful situation approached I gradually gained courage and was marching about with a firm regardless step when the relief came round, with which I proceeded to the guard room; but although vigorously interrogated respecting the ghost and my aun [own] courage, I disdained to confess I had harboured the slightest degree of uneasiness on my part.

Chapter 4

Recuperation at Reculver

I had now been with the regiment about twelve months and my
health getting daily worse, insomuch that apprehensions began to be
entertained of me being in a consumption; on that account and hoping
that a change of air might be of service, our medical officers proposed
sending me home on sick furlough. This, however I declined, for my
parents were not yet acquainted with my fate and would probably
have met with no small surprise on my appearing suddenly before
them in the character of a soldier. I could not therefore brook the idea of
returning home until I had broken the ice with them, in a more delicate
manner. Fortune however here for once in my life seemed to have
pitied me; for as I crawled about unconscious to what remedy I should
have recourse for the recovery of my health, an order was received
specifying that several parties were to be detached to stations on the
coast, for the purpose of conveying despatches express from the signal
posts, if occasion should require it during the night and as one of the
stations named in the order, was unlikely to be productive of hard duty,
it was agreed upon that I should be sent to it with a steady old soldier.
Having thus received our orders, we got ourselves in readiness and I
marched next morning with a light heart, to the ancient but pleasant
little village of Reculver situated on the summit of a high white cliff
on the coast between Ramsgate & Margate. We arrived at the sweet
hamlet and took our quarters at an alehouse[1] where we were received

---

1. The original Hoy and Anchor public house fell into the sea around 1808
    and the original vicarage was converted into the new Hoy and Anchor,
    which was then rebuilt and renamed around 1840 as the King Ethelbert
    which still exists today.

with the greatest kindness, for scarcely had we got our horses into the stable when the landlady, a motherly looking old woman, called us into the house for the purpose of partaking of some refreshment after our march and having noticed my delicate state, made some remarks to my comrade on my extreme weakly appearance.

The old veteran embraced this opportunity of describing the nature of my complaint as well as informing the landlady that I had been sent there for the recovery of my health and the statement seemed to fill the good woman's heart with the tenderest feelings towards me, who as she placed our repast on the table pathetically ejaculated 'Poor lad! What made the[e] go asoulgering? I doubt [not] thy poor mother has a sorrowful heart if she be alive now' and as she uttered the last sentence she fixed her eyes upon me, they were full with tears and she turned from the table unable to utter more.

To the future attentions of the worthy woman I believe I was indebted for the restoration of good health, nor could the tender feelings of a mother have urged to acts of greater kindness than those I daily experienced from her unremitting exertions to restore me to my wanted vigour and bodily strength. And to my inestimable happiness she was successful, for I had only been about five weeks in her house when I began to recruit and to assume the appearance of the returning blessing.

Her first duty every morning was to visit my chamber with an air of kindness which could not fail in its good aim. Her expression on entering used to be 'Well, how is my lad this morning?' and being answered satisfactorily would continue 'Well cum the ways down to thee breakfast.' For this repast she invariably had something nice, which she expected would induce me to eat, which being over she would continue 'Now thou must walk on the heights an hour or more if thou canst and our dear Dick shall go wi' thee.' Then jocularly driving Dick and me out of doors exclaiming 'Now don't let me see the faces o' thee again these two hours.' We were therefore obliged to perform this task along the top of the stupendous chalky cliffs, overlooking the British Channel, which with the passing vessels continually loitering in the mild breezes of a fine summer season, combined the good effects of strengthening the body, cherishing the mind and delighting the craving sight with the various beauties continually unfolding themselves and sublimely playing round the wondering spectator.

We again returned to the little but hospitable alehouse where my worthy hostess had something in readiness by way of repast. After this I usually accompanied my comrade on horseback a few miles along the beach, or occasionally to vary the scene, directed our course into the country; these healthful excursions together with the unequalled kindness and attentions of mine hostess began gradually to show their good effects. I daily recovered and by no slow degrees was nerved with all my former strength & vigour. My officers viewed the progress I made for the better with pleasure and gave orders for my continuance in this happy retreat beyond the time limited for these parties, who were regularly changed every month.

The family where I was quartered consisted of Mr B[rown] the landlord, a man of three score, Mrs B[rown] the landlady who was perhaps eight or ten years younger.[2] Their son Richard and his amiable sister Mary who officiated as a servant in the house. I had also now become like one of them and enjoyed no pleasure equal to that of being in the happy group when they encircled the clean hearth in the evening and joined their utmost efforts in amusing each other with their simple unvarnished country songs or pleasing tales of 'auld lang syne.'

Mary B[rown] was a girl possessing a remarkably agreeable disposition, the delicate sweetness of her features, her graceful manner and figure of finished symmetry, with an enchanting voice were accomplishments which (clad in the modesty of this unassuming girl) would have done honour to the fairest of her sex; but kindled not the flame of vanity in her mind, which only grasped at the enjoyments due to the station of life in which she was placed.

I had long viewed her person and actions with admiration, without anticipating the result, nor imagined that by cherishing that regard, it might in time penetrate deeper into the chambers of the heart, than those constructed for common friendship. My esteem was of a growing nature, I admired, but feared to inform her, lest she might treat my solicitations with indifference. However, as she had always been attentive to me, I sometimes dared to believe that I might in safety tell her my mind, yet could not muster courage enough. I grew daily more unhappy,

---

2. Reculver was a very small community. The one family we can discover that lived here with a surname beginning with a 'B' were the Brown's. William and Mary's home was actually not the public house 'The Hoy and Anchor' but it is quite possible that they ran the pub but lived nearby. They certainly had a daughter named Mary (although known locally as Molly) who was baptised at Reculver in 1790. Later the Browns received rent for letting a row of cottages to the Revenue men. I must thank Mandy Boxall for her help in uncovering the history of the Brown family in the local archives.

particularly when she was out of my sight and being unable longer to bear in silence, the impression made upon my mind, I determined at all hazards, the first opportunity that offered itself, should see the cause of all my uneasiness put to trial. I therefore watched every chance of speaking to her and followed her into a little arbour in the garden to which in her leisure moments she used to retire with her needle. I had seated myself near her and in the absence of courage to broach a more important subject; began to make frivolous remarks on the beauty of the flowers which were unfolding themselves in endless variety around us, the honeysuckle that overshadowed the arbour, in which we sat and charmed the senses with its exhaling odour and the serenity which accompanied the declining sun to the western horizon; when she who was by nature innocent, addressed me as follows 'Perhaps you will forgive the liberty I have been prompted to take with you, by observing you more pensive and low spirited than you used to be. What is the matter? Has any of us offended you; or from what quarter has the ill tidings come that are capable of depressing your spirit? You used to lead the way in the sports of our village but of late we have all remarked a visible change and would be glad to know the cause.'

This interrogatory address was quite unexpected, I paused for a moment in deep thought and at last being assured by her tender manner, that a fair path was open for me in which I was to meet with no obstacle answered 'Perhaps you may have guessed the cause before now as I think my attention to you for some time past has been sufficient to explain so tender a question.' A smile, clothed in the snow-white garment of virgin modesty, instantly spread itself over her flushing countenance, she fixed her eyes upon the ground and in a tone scarcely audible, assured me that the development of the mystery was no more agreeable to me than herself.

Most of men are capable of judging with what pleasure a youth like myself would hear this declaration from one so much esteemed! I was happy indeed and continued so (unnoticed) for a considerable time, meeting in the same solitude every evening and joining in a conversation which alone seemed to be an earthly enjoyment to either party. However, it would have been presumption in either of us to have hoped that we were to enjoy such pleasures for time without a limit; it would have been enough for those in the highest sphere of life whose gold might even fail in making the great purchase; but individuals so humble, who were to journey through life in the most difficult paths dared not even to hope for its continuance, and so it was, for a few weeks had only glided past when Mrs B[rown] began to suspect that something more than common friendship existed between us. She accordingly charged her daughter with the supposed offence, who being unacquainted with guile or duplicity, remained in dutiful silence which confirmed all suspicion and filled the old lady's mind with the most appalling doubts. She often shed tears and chided her daughter for cherishing a regard for one whose situation in life could never afford her that comfort with which they (some future day) hoped to see her blessed. The life 'of a Soldier' said the good old woman 'is a life of misery! And let me beg that you will not now give me and your time worn father cause to approach our last tenement in sorrow!!'

Mr B[rown] was not yet informed of the alleged ill conduct of his daughter and the mother, (with a promise of concealing it from his knowledge) one morning required her to promise that she would never again speak to the soldier! This the daughter considered too severe a request and remained silent. The old lady next had recourse to threats but finding that neither foul nor fair means could extort such a promise, disclosed the whole budget to Mr B[rown] who after admonishing his daughter, called me into the parlour and accosted me as follows. 'Hah W[illiam]! Is it true that thow art turned a snake in the grass? Impossible! Well what can attract or bind the faith or gratitude of any man after this?!! Dame thy power is too weak to bind one bosom to thee! All thou hast done is disregarded! W[illiam] I was not prepared to meet such a blow as this from thee! Is this the gratitude of the man who has been cherished under our roof? Is it with this sort of villainy he repays our continued exertions in restoring his lost health? Oh man! I little expected that thou could have been an instrument which was thus to pierce me to the heart! Are we so deceived? A lad on whom we looked as scarcely having an equal? O, how worthless thou hast now proven thyself. Could any man have so far forgotten the ties of duty, gratitude and honour by which he was bound to us.'

Mr B[rown] was so much affected that he could proceed no farther, and I myself being much impressed by the manner in which he had harrowed up my feelings, remained silent; hoping that when his agitated feelings were a little calmed, I should find an opportunity of setting his mind more at rest and convincing him that his fears were unfounded; I turned to withdraw, but Mrs B[rown] whose eyes were swimming in tears, exclaimed 'Nay do not turn away without a word and thus add further unkindness to the insults thou hast already heaped upon us!'

I now found I could not escape and therefore summoned the slender powers I possessed to my aid; I faced my much-respected friends once more and blundered forth in broken accents 'Mr and Mrs B[rown] I do not know that I have been guilty of any such crime as you seem to charge me with; your daughter I esteem too much to have been the author of injustice to her, nor am I ungrateful to you for the many marks of kindness I have experienced under your roof. The only offence I consider myself guilty of is (I hope) pardonable, having no deeper stain attached to it than a pure regard for your virtuous daughter. However, I shall endeavour to set your minds at rest, by making an application tomorrow to be removed from the house and should it be so ordered that I may never see one of your family again; even that shall not obliterate from my mind the gratitude which I owe to you, but the many favours which you have lavished on me shall have a place in my memory wherever I roam while life remains!'

I then hastened from the room and passing through the kitchen found their amiable daughter absorbed in melancholy meditation, I approached and enquired why she wept; a question to which I required no answer.

'Do not ask me' she replied 'for I fear to run myself into further mischief. Away to Canterbury and I will see you there, whatever be the consequences. Here it is forbidden! Farewell!!!'

The following day being that on which either myself or my comrade went weekly to Canterbury to receive our pay &c afforded me an early opportunity to join my troop and on the other hand I was so fortunate as to have me request granted without hesitation, another man being ordered to replace me and I withdrawn from the spot which of all others on earth I valued the most.

Some time elapsed after my removal to head quarters without bringing the satisfaction I so earnestly wished for, either of a visit or some other communication from Reculver. I could neither account for the cause of her silence, nor dared to write lest my letter should fall into the hands of her parents, however after waiting some days (I cannot add with patience) I determined at all hazards to risk a note & sent it by the carrier, a man well known to me and whose integrity I could safely rely on, who came daily from the favoured village to Canterbury.

On the following day, I received an answer, by the same conveyance, requesting me to meet her at St Peter's,[3] a small village situated between the points of attraction, adding that an opportunity offered itself by the absence of her father and mother on a visit to some other relation. This

---

3.   St Peter's is now an area of Canterbury.

was too valuable an opportunity to be allowed to pass unembraced and I availed myself of it. I obtained leave and we met at the appointed place, where we contrived to see each other; once or twice every following week till her parents were again informed of our lawless meetings, who to do away with all further doubt and to eradicate from her mind a passion which they were determined to suppress and which they feared might lead her to some imprudent step if not effectually crushed; sent her into Worcestershire where she was placed under the care of some trusty friend.

I was informed of her banishment by Thomas the carrier and when she had been a few weeks absent a letter from her, stated that her parents were determined to oppose our wishes to the last extremity and as it was only to be a source of misery to her, she begged that I would think no more of keeping up a correspondence to be attended with such grievous consequences; adding that she was now resolved to yield to their wishes and to break forever that tie of friendship which was only to disquiet our lives.

I read the letter and although I saw the propriety of her resolution, I experienced an uneasiness which the cultivated minds of others may judge with more truth than my pen will attempt to describe! However, I had no alternative as she kept her address a profound secret, by which means I was compelled to yield to a resolution of endeavouring to bury all remembrance of her in oblivion.

I was aided in my struggles to forget these scenes (so pleasing to youth) by the duties of the summer being extremely harassing. The troops which were encamped on Barham Downs[4] and those of the garrison of Canterbury, which were six miles apart, frequently assembled for exercise on that extensive common as early as 5 or 6 in the morning, where our drills were sometimes spun out to such a length that our return to Canterbury was as late as three or four in the afternoon and many having gone out without a breakfast and during their absence, been unable to procure even a drink of water, came home also most exhausted; however these fatigues we were compelled to bear and prepare ourselves to meet new ones every hour, for in many instances we had barely time to get some refreshment after these field days and clean our horses and appointments when the approach of night, again summoned us to arms for the purpose of patrolling towards the coast or some other sleepless duty.

---

4.   Just over six miles south-east of Canterbury.

Chapter 5

Storms, Shipwrecks & Smugglers

However, previous to the breaking up of the camp I again got a release from these harassing duties, by being sent to a small village named Whitstable[1] on the Smuggling Service.[2] This place was situated on the coast about six miles from our headquarters, where (on our arrival) I with my comrade, was quartered in a house kept by an old infirm man, whose three sons (fine young men) had given up all legal employment to follow the hazardous and dangerous profession of smuggling. These men had acquired some degree of eminence among their associates in the lawless profession they had chosen, they had raised themselves to the name of daring fellows and the tale even ran so far in their favour as to allege that they could face the devil; they had become accomplished masters of all the low, cant, slang, of coasting watermen and in short, were sufficiently depraved to fill a situation in a canal drag.[3] Their father was proprietor of some fine fishing wares on the shore about two miles from the village and the duty of attending with a horse and cart, to bring away the fish at every ebb tide; fell to the lot of some one of the family. The winter season had set in and the piercing winds had an uninterrupted sweep along the open beach and rendered the fishing excursion a dreary task (particularly in the night). It however very frequently fell to the lot of the old infirm father, for

---

1. Whitstable is a small village on the coast two miles to the west of Herne Bay.
2. The Army, particularly the cavalry, had regularly been used to aid the Customs officers in preventing smuggling. During the Napoleonic Wars smuggling between Britain and France/Holland was at an all-time high.
3. A dredger on the canals.

the sons had become so inhuman by continued drunkenness & rood habits, that he only had the most unfeeling abuses heaped upon him by requesting either of them to go to the wares in his stead.

One night, which shall cease to have a place in my memory only when I cease to live, these young fellows came home from one of their smuggling enterprises in a state of intoxication; their father begged that they would go for the fish, the night being so extremely dark and storming that he dreaded to venture out by himself; the request, they however refused to comply with and after many abuses forced him out to brave the blast on the dreary strand, a task very unequal to his years.

My comrade, who was at all times a warm defender of insulted age, proposed to me that we should go to the wares instead of our landlord, this I readily agreed to and after, rigging ourselves out in great rough coats and fishermen's boots, off we set!

The same evening, great anxiety had prevailed in the village concerning some small vessels which were in the bay and particularly a passage vessel from London to Margate, which seemed to be unable to keep under way off shore.

It was after twelve when we set out and the storm seemed to increase (as we descended on the beach) with redoubled fury from the north-east; it blew so violently that we began to despair of being able to reach the wares, having lost the track by which we used to be led to them and our horse almost unable to force his way against the wind and rain.

We continued however to struggle with the tempest and frequently heard signals of distress from the vessels in the bay; but it appeared utterly impossible that the slightest assistance could be rendered to them; and an idea striking us that to all probability, some of them were drifting on the shore; we determined to approach the water's edge in hopes of giving our aid in the case of such an event.

We approached the raging flood, which broke with tremendous violence along the gloomy beach, just as a small bark had struck; our ears were immediately assailed with the most appalling cries from the hopeless crew and in a few minutes we discovered a boat dashed towards the shore; it was overturned and two men endeavoured to save themselves by clinging to the keel; a sharp shreek at the same moment issued from among the surge which drifted towards us like tumbling mountains of snow; it was the voice of a perishing woman! My comrade who saw her floating on the swell of a heavy wave, leaped from the cart and plunged into the water determined to exert himself in saving her, even at the risk of his own life. He was several times repelled by the fury of the waves and buried in the dreadful tumult; the sea was carrying her body nearer the shore and he at last succeeded in getting hold of her clothes and dragging her to the beach. She appeared to be lifeless, however with the assistance of some other people who had now arrived at the spot, she was wrapped in our rough coats and with one of the men who had been saved from the boat conveyed to a cottage about a quarter of a mile distant.

The people were now assembling on the shore from all quarters; many more impressed with a desire to plunder the wreck than to render assistance in saving the sufferers; which was made manifest as soon as the wreck began to be thrown on shore, in short, the scene quickly assumed the appearance of a hoard of savages who were deprived of all sense of feeling towards their fellow creature and with this impression I followed my comrade & those who had been saved to the cottage.

I found on my arrival however, that all the inhabitants of these shores were not of the same vile stamp, for by the humanity of the good matron, who was spinning out the thread of life in this lowly dwelling the two unfortunate strangers were in a fair state of recovery; they informed us that there had been three other men onboard with them, who must have perished in the watery element.

We left them here & proceeded home with the cart, where although we brought no fish, the old landlord was glad to see us make our appearance, having begun to fear from our long absence, that we had met with some accident, however the cause was fully explained in our account of the wreck; when the old gentleman informed us that two small vessels had got safe into the quay at the other end of the village and that some of the passengers from the Margate hoy[4] (which was one of the vessels he alluded to) were now in his house to remain till the storm abated. We had changed our clothes and were ushered into the room in which the strangers sat for the purpose of taking some refreshment which our landlord had ordered to be prepared for us and on entering a little parlour, it may be allowed that I had some ground for being a little surprised, when the first two objects who caught my eye were no other than Mary B[rown] and my much-esteemed friend, her brother Richard.

I stood thunderstruck for a moment; however, the strange meeting had so agreeably surprised all parties that after we had pledged each

---

4. A hoy was a sloop-rigged boat or heavy barge, from the Dutch *hoey*.

other in a few bumpers we began to allege that the tempest had been sent for the precise purpose of blowing us together.

After the first flow of pleasure had gone by, I enquired what in the nature of fate, had brought them to Whitstable or the cause of them being on sea on such a night, when Dick replied that some months before, his father had been informed that I had left Canterbury and being warmly interested in the welfare of his daughter could not compose his mind till he had her again at home. 'I was' continued he 'about a week ago, sent into Worcestershire to conduct her home, I reached the place where she was living on Sunday last and on Monday returned to London for the purpose of spending two days with an aunt who resides there. On the third day, we left London in the Margate hoy and proceeded down the river with a fine breeze, but in the afternoon the wind gradually arose and before night overtook us, the wind had veered round to the north-east and baffled all the skill of our hands to bear the vessel against it. We were thus tossed about till midnight, apprehensive every passing minute of being driven ashore. However, by a happy chance, a pilot was brave enough to put out to our assistance, who, after getting safe onboard ran us into the quay below, where the vessel now lies in safety and she will remain till we have more favourable weather to complete our short voyage.'

My friends remained two nights in Whitstable and although the attachment which had formerly existed between us had been dwindling out of remembrance, it now received so salutary a refreshment as to place it on a lasting foundation and a regular correspondence followed in which Dick filled the office of a faithful mediator. In such cases, there is hope while there is life, let the distance or inconveniences be ever so great, but alas! It at last fell to the lot of this young man to communicate to me the sorrowful news of his sister's death!! The news was sorrowfully received, for occurrences of this nature makes an impression on the mind of some men, of such a weight, that they are ready to believe the foundation of all their earthly hopes given way and the fabric which is raised thereon hurled headlong into ruin.[5]

---

5. If William's Mary was Mary Brown (see Chapter 4), then there is a serious twist in the tale. Mary did not die! Presumably William was told she had died to put him off pursuing her. Mary carried out trading in contraband throughout her life and she regularly walked the 18 miles to Canterbury, carrying her wares. Molly lived until 1870 and never married, perhaps

Our party was very often called out on night duty after the foregoing occurrence at Whitstable; the dark nights of winter were most suitable for the purposes of the enterprising smuggler and we were consequently compelled to prowl about the coast and battle with the inconstant elements, oftener returning home drenched to the skin than otherwise. These events seemed to afford great pleasure to the sons of our host who in their disordered state of mind, used to sneer at our weather-beaten appearance and frequently in the braggart style exclaimed that they would not hesitate to blow out the brains of any soldier who might dare to molest them; adding under the seal of a vulgar execration that we might depend on getting a sound drubbing if they ever met with us on any of these nightly excursions. These threats served only to amuse us, yet we heartily hoped that some night we might have the good fortune to fall in with them and their gang; nor were we long waiting the arrival of fortunes favour, if this could be called one of them, for we were one night, called upon to accompany the Revenue officers in order to make a seizure of some goods, which they were informed were to be landed a few miles down the coast. We proceeded by a circuitous route which gave the appearance on leaving the village of our destination being quite in an opposite direction to the point for which we were intended. This was a necessary precaution to dupe the villagers who invariably had a watch upon the party and never failed to give their friends timely notice in the event of its taking a direction leading to the point at which they were to land their illicit cargo.

After scouring the by-roads a considerable way into the country, we again approached the cliffs and descending to the beach took refuge from a heavy shower of snow, as well as from the observation of the smugglers, in a cave which had been work for the waves for past ages.

Here we remained in silent ambush upwards of two hours and at last our lookout informed us that the boat was in sight and hovering off land; we mounted our horses in the greatest silence, a light flashed no great distance from our den, as a signal that all was safe and the smuggler shot into a creek, from which the light had issued.

---

still pining for William? But one other intriguing question arises. James Abernethy, an engineer, was once a customer at the Hoy and Anchor and had a strange encounter with her. He found that she often gave him drinks on the house and when he queried this, she replied that *'You are just the image of my only son, drowned at sea, and it's quite enough for me to see you.'* Was this William's child?

Now, it was our turn; we sallied from our ambuscade and came upon them with such a rapidity that left them no time either to put the boat to sea again or to save any part of their goods by concealing or carrying away and the whole was instantly captured. There were about 12 or 14 men in the boat and in waiting for the goods, among whom I recognised at first sight, two of our old friends, who had promised us so sound a drubbing at our first meeting; I rejoiced that chance had at last given us a meeting with these pretended desperados and putting spurs to my horse, I dashed into the water alongside the boat, exclaiming 'Ho, ho my hearties, you are here, are you? How stands your courage tonight? I hope you have not left it at home, where you make so common a hack of it! I should think you cannot have forgotten your often-repeated promise, we are now quite prepared for the drubbing you know! But you braggards are invariably the most courageous over your hot pot by the fireside!!'

The two young men stood absorbed in thought, without uttering a single sentence and a moments reflection opened a way to the more tender chambers of my breast! I felt sorry that I had acted a part so unmanly as to chide those who were already conquered; and I saw no rule, if they had done wrong, why I should have followed their example.

Some of those who were waiting to receive the smuggled goods made a feeble attempt to escape with two carts and horses which they had in readiness, but were followed and brought back. The cargo was unloaded and deposited in the carts for the purpose of being conveyed to Whitstable. It consisted of 37 tubs of Hollands gin and a considerable quantity of tobacco. The boat was boarded by one of the Revenue officers, who with the assistance of two other men conveyed it also to Whitstable where the whole of the seizure was safely lodged by six o'clock the following morning.

Chapter 6

Change of Quarters

The party to which I belonged was soon after this withdrawn from the coast duty and I remained in Canterbury with the headquarters of the regiment till the spring following, when the route was received and the corps marched to Ipswich.[1] The regiment crossed the River Thames at Gravesend and the day on which the division I belonged to marched to Billericay I was left behind in Gravesend for the purpose of carrying forward some orders which were expected to arrive with the billeting party of the following division. There I waited their arrival, received my dispatches and followed my troop; but had only crossed the river when the sable veil of night began to spread itself over the face of the country before me; and as the road by which I should have proceeded was unfrequented and across the country; I had not gone far till I lost my way, having taken a wrong road soon after I left Tilbury Fort.[2]

By this road I travelled about an hour and a half without dreaming of having committed any blunder and was jogging on by a narrow lane which wound its way along the margin of a thick wood, when I perceived at some distance in my front, a light glimmering through the brushwood, from which at intervals a blaze ascended & reflected a bright glaze upon the scattered and time worn trunks of some decayed trees that reared their hoary remains in different parts of the thicket

---

1. The regiment had its quarters moved to Ipswich and Colchester in May 1805.
2. Tilbury Fort is an artillery fort on the north bank of the River Thames. The first fort had been built here in the reign of Henry VIII, but it was greatly enlarged and strengthened from 1670.

as monuments of the once stately oaks that had in past ages inhabited it. At first view, I conjectured this to be some of the farmers clearing their land of fuzz bushes, or some other unprofitable branch of nature's variety and felt convinced that I should meet with a house of some kind at no great distance, where I might make some enquiry respecting the road and distance to Billericay. And with this intention, I pushed on till I came to a vacant green recess which penetrated the boundary of the thicket, similar in size and equality to a bowling green. But to my surprise instead of meeting with a farmhouse, which I thought most likely here; in a few seconds I stood in the presence of the gruff & tawny master of a numerous gang of gypsies, who having heard the sound of my horse's feet, waited my approach at the front of his portable pavilion, with the dignified air of an Indian chief. The trees and bushes which surrounded the retreat in which these wanderers had established themselves so completely hid them from the notice of anyone who might approach their temporary residence that I was close upon tents e'er I perceived my situation. However, being thus taken at a nonplus, I considered it best to show no surprise and so marched boldly up and enquired of this king of the brown race,[3] how far it was to Billericay, but my words were still lapped in the moorland accent and before I had made him understand my question, the whole legion (consisting of about thirty) flocked round and their chief accosted me as follows without paying the smallest regard to what I had said.

'Holo, you fighting fellow; where the devil are you from? What wild wind has blown you to this country? Thief catching, I suppose! Where is the rest of your red crew? In ambush no doubt hard by?'

'No, no' said I 'you are mistaken! I am on my way to Billericay and will feel obliged if you will be good enough to direct me the right road.'

'Billericay' exclaimed about a dozen of them in a volley, and the old man continued 'Why soldier, this is not the road to Billericay! You are 26 miles from Billericay! You are going a strange way for Billericay however! Where have you come from soldier?'

'From Tilbury Fort' replied I, 'From Tilbury Fort!' continued brownie, 'Thunder bolts and back doors! What an article you are to come here seeking Billericay! By the Lord, my hero, you have come above a round dozen miles out of your way. And let me tell you, the devil himself could not direct you how to get into it again in the dark.'

---

3.   He means that he was of a swarthy, weatherbeaten hue.

I was almost confounded at this information for instead of being (as I expected) almost at the end of my journey. I proved to be at a greater distance from it than I was at starting my march. The gypsies, however, observed the consternation I was in and seemed to partake in my disappointment. They made many enquiries respecting the regiment to which I belonged, admired the beauty of my horse &c &c, while the old man drew near and said 'Come my young fellow! The job is now done and cannot be helped by any other means than that of getting right again as soon as possible, but you cannot, nor must not think of trying to find your way before you have daylight again to aid you. I therefore would have you to get off and we'll tie your horse to one of these stumps among our kiddy's[4] till you rest yourself a while. We will find you something to eat; and as all soldiers can drink; your spirits shall be kept afloat for we have plenty of good Hollands for you and here is a variety of fine young brown faced lasses. Among these you may choose a sweetheart if you like! There my buck is a sketch of the manner in which we entertain strangers, but should you require more, give it a name and you shall enjoy it if in our possession or to be procured by my rangers, who seldom fail in the object of their researches; providing our forest or its neighbouring fields, farms or lordling's hall contain it! At all hazards you shall have what you wish to enjoy, if you make reason your guide! Will that sort of hospitality please you? If so, dismount and I will see your horse taken care of.'

I hesitated; not altogether from a fear of entrusting myself in the power of this covey of brownies; but from a desire of getting up to my troop; however, a moment's reflection convinced me of the impropriety of attempting to pursue the unfrequented path by which I was to be led to it and which was totally unknown to me at the solitary hour of midnight. I without further deliberation, dismounted and fastened my horse to a scraggy bush as the gypsies directed. The whole corps of woodlanders now flocked round and warmly invited me into one of their tents. I had yielded to their entreaties and was preparing to follow them; when one of those who generally bear the appellation of the fair sex (but who the sunbeams had almost deprived of any right to that name) approached me, drew my sword and flourished it round her head as she skipped before with a display of inviting gestures to follow her. Another bounced on the green turf, exhibiting all the flaunting

---

4. Goats.

fooleries of a Morris dancer, decorated with my huge bearskin cap. Another paced the green sward with the mimic dignity of a duellist taking his ground on a point of honour, armed with my pistol, which she had driven from the holster of my saddle and a fourth took refuge under the wing of my red mantle and cheerily chanted as we scanned the wild structure of the tent we were about to enter 'I long to be in a sentry box, lapp'd up in a soldier's cloak.'

I entered the tent rather embarrassed, not only by the unbearable compliments which were loaded on me; but by the difficulty I found in answering them for as they all spoke at once, I knew not how to acknowledge their volleys to give general satisfaction. However, by the old man's direction, I seated myself on a green sod and was immediately supported on right on left by two of these forest Venuses, who notwithstanding the nut-brown colour of their faces, were by no means disagreeable companions; for a smile of satisfaction had spread itself over their well-formed features, which displayed itself to advantage on their seeming free open and guileless countenances.

The old man ordered the banquet to be got ready while he himself drew from the pannier which stood in the middle of the tent, doomed to bear the weight of the viands which were preparing, a large jar or earthen bottle of liquor from which he filled a copious goblet and presented it to me. I found it contained genuine Holland gin and partook, while some of the happy crew busied themselves in covering the pannier with various kinds of provisions. They all joined me at supper and after it was over, kept the gladdening goblet in quick circulation round the festive board, till the stores of all hearts were opened and the pleasing sensation of purest friendship defused itself among the merry corps. I was entreated to eat, pressed to drink and compelled to be happy amongst the jovial woodlarks; who drank deep, danced and sang merrily and spent their time in the most convivial manner till day began to peep in the east, when the chief addressed himself to me as follows. 'Now my dear friend, I see your time approaching, the grey and vermillion streaks, bright Phoebus's[5] messengers begin to dance over the eastern horizon to remind us of our duty towards you. We will now see you right and satisfy you that although our manners are unpolished we have hearts like other folks.'

I proceeded to thank them for their kindness but the old man interrupted me by adding 'Peace, peace my young friend, you owe us

---

5. Phoebus the Roman God of the sun, known as Apollo in Greek mythology.

nothing, your company has sufficiently replaced us and we shall all be proud to treat you in the same manner if we ever have the pleasure of meeting you again.' He then turned to his son and desired him to take my name and that of the regiment to which I belonged. 'My name' continued he 'is Wentworth, I have served my king and country before you was born, but as it is now time for you to pursue your journey, I will reserve an account of my military career till we meet again. I shall see you at Ipswich soon', and then addressing himself to his son he said 'bring the dragoon's horse, Ambrose! And we will set him a little way on his road.' I mounted my horse and after taking a leave of my new acquaintances, which a past age of intimacy could not have raised to a higher pitch of friendship. I followed the old man and his son who proceeded on the choice of their stud of asses before me, they accompanied me about four miles on the road and after exchanging promises of a continuation of friendship, they returned to their camp and I pushed on to Billericay where I joined my troop previous to its march for Chelmsford.

We continued our march to Ipswich where the regiment was brigaded with another corps which was quartered in the town and one from Woodbridge Barracks[6] which met us on Rushmoor Heath[7] on the exercising days. The whole was under the command of Lord Paget[8] during the following summer. The ground on which we manoeuvred was excessively dusty owing to the dryness of the season and the hot summer sun beating upon the black moss and such was the effect on the troops that on their return from the field, men, horses, accoutrements, clothing &c wore alike a dark hue and rendered it impossible to distinguish the features of one man from another.

We were one day returning from the heath in this sable state and passing a small piece of waste ground which lay on the road in our way home, it had been occupied (between the time of our going to the field and that period) by the same troop of gypsies who had entertained me on my way to Billericay. I had advanced opposite their tents when I saw Wentworth posted on the wayside attentively eyeing each passing individual, frequently turning his head away in a fretful manner and looking as if much disappointed by the dust having rendered the task

---

6. Woodbridge Barracks was home to the cavalry and the Royal Horse Artillery during the Napoleonic Wars.
7. Actually Rushmere Heath.
8. Major General Henry William Paget (1768–1854).

of recognising me among the rest of our soldiers too great for him. However, his countenance was familiar to me as well as those of many of his followers who looked on as we passed, but I felt somewhat satisfied that I myself was so disguised for the few sparks of pride which I had about me seemed to allow no entrance for such an idea as associating with a gang of gypsies, I therefore passed unnoticed! Ruminating in my way home how I should be able to visit them, or receive their visits without the knowledge of my comrades, for I loved the old man's conversation and only feared their scoffs for corresponding with his profession. However I resolved to see him that night at all hazards and during the stable hour, after we got home, I ventured to inform my comrade Sandy B[orland][9] of my intended visit to the gypsies camp & to request him to accompany me, Sandy, who was a merry fellow readily agreed with my request and to secure ourselves against the danger of not returning home in due time, to which the approaching happy evening might have exposed us. We obtained the commanding officers leave for the night and impressing the minds of our brother soldiers with an idea that we were going to spend the evening with some friends in town, we directed our steps towards the camp of this wandering troop.

---

9. Sandy being a Scottish nickname for Alexander, this leaves only two possibilities in the regiment Private Alexander Borland or Private Alexander Blackadder. However, Blackadder did not enlist until 1806 so this has to be Borland. Alexander Borland, was born at Glasford, Lanark and had been a weaver before he enlisted. He had served with the Lanark Fencible cavalry from 1795 to 1800 and then joined the Scots Greys in 1800. He was 5ft 8in tall. He served at Waterloo but he was not wounded and he retired in August 1818 due to chronic rheumatism. His conduct is recorded as having been very good.

Chapter 7

The Gypsy King's Tale

We took our way through some enclosures where the sultry beams of the declining sun fell refulgently on the surrounding corn fields, which were speedily partaking of an autumnal hue and as we came within sight of Wentworth's camp, the bright rays reflecting from the grotesque tents attracted the notice of my comrade who exclaimed 'Halo mate! Yonder appears a camp, are these the tents of your wandering acquaintances?'

'Yes' replied I 'and here comes my particular old friend by the margin of the corn. We shall just meet him, he is a worthy fellow although he be a gypsie.' Wentworth who was on his way to the barracks in quest of me, met us and after the forms which mark the meeting of old friends were gone through, he conducted us to his pavilion and I had no sooner made my appearance than the whole troop flocked round and gave me a hearty welcome into their lines. I introduced my comrade and we were hurried into the commandant's marquee where the operations of mirth and jollity were immediately set on foot. The board was again covered with abundance of provisions and the cheering goblet set in motion round it. My former supporters took their stations right and left and my comrade who had taken his post on the opposite side of the tent was attended in like manner by some of their fair (or rather brown) companions, while we partook of viands which would have been no disgrace to the tables of some of the finest lordlings of the land.

The evening went merrily on and each seemed to strive for the name of making us most happy, till night enveloped us in its murky mantle and the lamp was suspended from one of the spars which supported the canvas over us and every other arrangement made for a convivial night. I now took the liberty of reminding Wentworth of his former promise to relate some particulars of the period of his life he had spent in the army. He acknowledged he had made such a promise and requested that I would walk round the adjoining corn field with him by which means he would satisfy my curiosity without putting a stop to the enjoyment for which the rest of the party had made preparations. To this I readily agreed and after we had taken a turn round part of the field, we seated ourselves under the silvery beams of the moon on a dry bank by the hedge side and Wentworth proceeded as follows. 'My friend' said he 'you may think it strange that the story which I am now about to tell you has never before been allowed to stray beyond the threshold of my own breast. I have kept a prisoner for the long space of 52 years, the cause of my being what I am, as well as the cause of many a day of sorrow and sleepless night. My life which might have been one of the most happy ever enjoyed has (by the malicious disposition of my youth) proved to be one of the most miserable, but of this you shall hear anon; when you may judge what portion of happiness fate has allotted to my share. I will relieve my mind by opening it to you, for I am now old and maybe may soon require a tenement in the clay. My parents resided in the south of England, they were wealthy, generous and beloved by all who knew them. Myself and an only brother were the whole of their care. Their estate was bounded on one side by that of a Mr F. . .[1] a gentleman of exalted character whose family were on the most friendly terms with that of my parents. Their frequent visits to each other had founded an intimacy of the most sincere & lasting kind and they were equally looked up to as examples worthy of imitation and their neighbours were proud to follow the moral and benevolent path by which their past lives had been led forward in unsullied happiness. So forcible were the ties of friendship which existed between these two worthy families that they were seldom found separated and at a ball which my parents gave to a select party of their neighbours. The presence of the family of Mr F. . . was of course indispensably desirable to complete the joyous celebration of the anniversary of the day which gave me birth.'

'I was called from Cambridge schools to attend the festival, I had only arrived the evening preceding the happy occasion; having scarcely sufficient time to salute my aged parents and to admire the magnificent preparations they honoured me with, when the hour arrived which was

---

1.   It has proven impossible to identify Mr F. . . with any certainty.

to call our splendid guest together. Mr F. . . had an only daughter who possessed all the charms that captivate and rule the heart of man, her all powerful attractions had on former occasions commanded much of my attention, but I had not seen her for the space of fifteen months previous to this period, which elapse of time had so matured her perfections that this night completed the work which her peerless form had long founded in my breast. I welcomed the company on their arrival and delighted my eyes with the splendour which was every moment unfolding itself in our hall of mirth, till the arrival of the family of Mr F. . . was announced. At this agreeable summons I hastened to pay my respects to the much beloved friend of my father, but alas, when I approached the presence of the fair Eliza. I was struck with astonishment, my senses wandered from the business on which I hurried thither and I became lost in a labyrinth of admiration; no language is sufficient to describe what she was, her many charms were beyond the power of mortal description, she was all perfection & I gazed with wonder on nature's choicest production as I led her into the presence of the admiring assembly. The appearance of the company, which (previous to Miss F. . .'s arrival) had afforded me much delight, now lost its lustre, nor did I any longer pay the slightest attention to any one save the lovely Eliza and I dreaded the arrival of the hour at which she was to depart.'

'However the night passed over, but I failed not to visit at the house of her father next morning. I endeavoured to have an interview with Eliza, but this she seemed to evade and I was compelled to return home fired with disappointment and almost mad with jealousy against someone who I concluded must have been in possession of her heart and thus the cause of my addresses being shunned. However, I repeated my visits daily, yet they still fell short of producing the happy results I aimed at & still I returned to my father's house in deep meditation on some new scheme of gratifying a voluptuous disposition. All my endeavours to gain an interview proved fruitless and I began to despair of ever enjoying that happiness. This reflection led me frequently into solitary and private walks where I could enjoy my own contemplations and indulge in my extravagant thoughts uninterrupted. I one evening loitered in this manner, in the walks of a little wood which ran along the outline of my father's domain & divided it from that of Mr F. . . no great distance from his house, when I saw Eliza seated under an arbour of shrubs, in earnest conversation with a man whose face I was unable to recognise in the dull shade, which the stealing evening had already spread over the laurel grove in which they sat. I fixed my eyes upon them, my breast filled with indignation against a man who had not injured me. I knew him not, yet I burned for revenge and a base design upon his life immediately laid its accursed foundation in the very innermost dens of this black heart. I could then have rushed upon my victim, but was in possession of no instrument of destruction wherewith to complete my horrid resolution.'

'With my unhappy mind thus fermented, I crept unnoticed, near enough to hear some passages of their conversation in which my supposed rival appointed a meeting with the lady at Portsmouth for the purpose of proceeding to spend a few weeks with some friends in the Isle of Wight. This arrangement was agreed upon and he drew a card from his pocket on which he gave her instructions respecting the time and place of meeting. They departed but Eliza left the card behind her on the bench on which they sat. I was soon in possession of it, found it contained matter enough to suit my purpose, returned home & with a heart elate with mischief, prepared to follow the lovers to Portsmouth, who I learned were on the point of being made happy for life. I accordingly next morning, took leave of my parents and loving brother on pretence of having a promise of meeting one of my fellow students at a neighbouring town to perform that day. A servant who had only been about ten days in my father's service, was ordered to accompany me. This man proved useful, although they little dreamed that I had such services laid aside for him.'

'I shall never forget, when we were ready to proceed, the looks of tenderness which my aged father's mother cast upon me, when I stretched forth my hand from the carriage window for the last grasp. They craved the blessing of heaven to accompany me on my way thither and its unbounded protection to guide me again in safety to their affectionate arms. Alas! It was indeed the last grasp. The blessing of heaven could not be upon such a wretch, nor could the all governing power have sanctioned the return of so hideous a monster to the presence of unsullied virtue.'

'I proceeded without delay to Portsmouth and previous to the day on which Eliza and her intended husband were to arrive, I had formed a connection with a band of characters little better than midnight assassins. With these I had made an arrangement respecting the destruction of the man she loved, while I myself was to be employed, him to wait on the lady, under the colours of a messenger from her friend, with instructions to repair immediately on board a vessel which was about to sail for the Isle of Wight, where he would meet her from another port to which he had unexpectedly been called on urgent business. The vessel above alluded to was an American, she was to sail the same evening. I had procured passage on board as well as by a sufficient bribe, embodied the master in my train of deceivers and he waited on the lady as she came on board, conducted her to the cabin with due respect and immediately put to sea. I had hitherto concealed myself from Eliza's eyes, she yet knew nothing of her destiny. Night came on and she was kept close in her prison, but previous to being visited by the captain's wife (who was likewise an accomplice) she began to be apprehensive of some foul design, having been put in action against her and begged to be made acquainted with her situation. She was however, kept as much in the dark as possible and spent some days in her prison overwhelmed with grief and despair.'

'Several days passed and Eliza's misery still increased, for she was kept close in her prison, till overwhelmed with melancholy, she was seized with an alarming fever, which impaired both her strength and reason to such a degree that her life was despaired of. This circumstance awoke in my mind a feeling of deep remorse and I determined to see her whatever the consequence might be. For this purpose, I sent the captain's wife to break the mystery in the most gentle manner she could devise and desired that my name might be mentioned to her, lest she might have been too suddenly surprised by my entering her apartment. Those tidings were no sooner communicated than she declared 'Great God is it George D. . .[2] who had reduced me to this misery? Impossible! Oh, no it cannot be the brother of my dear Edwin who has been guilty of so cruel an act! Oh heaven, can it be possible that he would drive to the deepest degree distraction his own tender parents and mine who doted on our childhood, who taught us all the rules of justice to each other and every good principle which adorn the human mind. I cannot believe it, but I can now bear aught and long to know the worst. I entreat you to summon him hither that I may know who he be, who thus scoffs the dictates of humanity and the vengeance of heaven.' I was accordingly called to the cabin & trembled as I approached the door for I dreaded to meet the eyes of her I loved to madness. I approached her bedside and her countenance which was flushed with the burning disease, turned pale, she riveted her penetrating eyes upon me, exclaimed in great

---

2.　It has proven impossible to identify George and Edwin D. . . with any certainty.

agitation 'Yes it is he' and sank breathless upon her pillow. The organs of life seemed to yield for a time to the feelings of her troubled mind, ceased to break & I went over the deathlike form of her, who at a period, not long gone past, was the pride of the gay circle in which she walked and the admiration of all who beheld her.'

'I stood in sad suspense, when she again opened her eyes and calmly murmured 'Oh George D. . . what must now be the feelings of your amiable brother? You are little aware of the nature of the deed you have committed. Surely if you had known that I was the lawful wife of your brother Edwin, you could not have been guilty of so horrid a transaction. What is your design, or what has prompted you to treat me in this manner? Oh George! If you prize your own future peace or that of those who are by the most tender ties allied to you immediately relinquish your accursed resolution and conduct me back to the arms of my loving husband and tender parents.'

'My extreme emotion now interrupted her, I started as she pronounced the name of my brother, who to all probability was ere that period in eternity by the bloody hands of hiring assassins which I had fee'd for the horrid purpose. My limbs shook under me and I stood almost deprived of every rational faculty. 'Oh' said I 'Eliza, what unexpected tidings have I heard, why was a matter of such importance concealed from me? What have I done?' I was unable to utter more and endeavoured to withdraw that I might give full vent to my torturing grief, but she entreated me to stay and give her the satisfaction she implored.'

'She continued to weep bitterly, while I with a flattering voice related to her as much of the cruel transaction as I judged her tender situation fit to bear; and promised to return by the 1st vessel we might fall in with, but my inwards struggles I can scarcely now describe. The murder of my dear brother cried aloud for revenge and the name of Edwin seemed to assail my ears in the howlings of the increasing storm and stung my inmost feelings with deep remorse and horrible reflections. The wind for two days previous to this had been gradually increasing and the ship's crew began to be apprehensive of a storm overtaking us. The vessel was bound for Quebec and we kept under weigh 32 days under a westerly wind, but on the night of the 19th November it veered round to the north east and still increased. The weather at the same time intensely cold and the vessel discovered to be so leaky that she made water to an alarming degree. In consequence of this discovery a pump was put to work and kept constantly going, however the water still gained so fast that on the 4th December they were under the necessity of rigging another pump and keeping both constantly playing. A heavy fall of snow accompanied by intense frost, fraughted the gale with such fury as to cause a depression of both strength and spirits among the seamen and all on board began to despair of ever reaching a haven of safety. We were now approaching the Gulf of St Lawrence with four feet water in the hold and the sailors so much overcome with cold and fatigue that they began to show great indifference respecting their fates. They refused to work at the pumps, the hurricane increased and the snow fell so thick that we could not see the mast heads or from the stern to the head of the ship. We were in this hopeless plight when night came on with the sea running mountains high which soon added to our distress by breaking upon the ships quarters with such force that the dead lights were stove in and the cabin filled with water. I was attending the injured Eliza and lamenting to see her suffering under the malady already mentioned, when the sea burst in and she was swept from her bed by the pitiless waves. The alarm which this circumstance created was great, however I seized her senseless body in my arms and removed her to a place of greater safety. But all hopes of safety was now nearly lost and I saw the vengeance of heaven in every sea that broke over our shattered vessel. The gale continued with unremitting fury and about an hour after the sea so materially damaged the stern of the ship. The main mast went overboard with a dreadful crash, it gave way about seven feet from the deck and dragged along with the vessel, for the men were so benumbed with cold that they had no power to disentangle it and thus we continued between hope & despair for the four following days and nights. The foremast also gave way, the gale still increased, the captain thought we could not be far from land, but knew not into what latitude the fearful hurricane had driven us till about 11 o'clock on the morning of the 16th. The sea was observed to assume a muddy colour, the waves to grow shorter and break higher, these were convincing proofs of our being no great distance from some shore and in the space of three more hours a cry of land echoed from all quarters of the ship. We were within a hundred yards of the beach before it could be discovered and the ship running direct upon it. Now was the time for the most dreadful apprehensions the vessel every moment expected to strike and to all probability that moment to go to pieces. Some ran to the boat which we had still preserved, others stood in motionless astonishment while regardless indifference marked here and there a countenance and many a glance of wild despair sped from eye to eye as the weather-beaten bark rushed on the shore. At length, she grounded with a prodigious concussion & the only standing mast went overboard, sweeping five of the seamen with it into the raging flood. The vessel struck a second time and parted in the middle, the surf now broke over the vessel in all quarters and the intenseness of the cold froze the water that fell on our clothes and immediately covered them with a sheet of ice.'

'I leave you to judge what must now have been the sufferings of the fair, the tender Eliza and the effect they produced on my own harassed feelings, for situated as I was, I could have welcomed any fate to remove me from a world in which I was never to enjoy another happy hour, but I felt myself bound to prolong a detested existence for the purpose of employing it in her safety & perishing in some daring attempt to save her life. The most active of the crew exerted themselves in getting the boat out, which was at last accomplished with great difficulty, for they were nearly deprived of the use & feeling of their limbs by the cold and after this task was accomplished, there were but few who did not prefer, even the hopeless situation they were in onboard the wreck to that of entering the boat for the sea ran so high that it appeared impossible for anything to live in it for a moment. The mate of the ship however and eight or ten more had got onboard when I approached the side on which the boat was put out with the almost expiring Eliza in my arms. She was also, with great difficulty got on board, I followed and the boat was instantly shoved off towards the shore. We had scarcely cleared the wreck when a heavy sea dashed the boat with such violence upon a rock that she was severed to pieces in a moment. The lovely Eliza who was already insensible of her situation perished. Nor did providence even allow me an opportunity of endeavouring to save her. I was to be foiled in all my schemes and saved to be punished; but the innocent, the angelic Eliza's sufferings were ended.'

'Two of the boats crew succeeded in gaining the shore, where I was also, without the slightest exertion miraculously thrown by the waves. I emerged from the raging element with reluctance for Eliza was left behind. Oh God! To what a state was my mind now wound up! I gazed around me with mad emotion in quest of the object which on earth I only regarded. I ran from rock to rock regardless of my own safety and from the rugged side of one of them again plunged into the tide at the sight of an object which I supposed to be her body. I recovered from a state of insensibility and again found myself lying on the beach and near me lay the lifeless bodies of many of the ship's crew, who had been thrown on land by the fury of the waves. The tide was receding and some of the ship's timbers which still clung together marked the spot of her dissolution within twenty yards of the water's edge. The desert shore was covered with the wreck of the noble vessel and the lifeless corpses of her once gallant crew lay strewed in promiscuous irregularity on either hand, for only four of the seamen had escaped with me.'[3]

'These four seamen were using their utmost endeavours to recover me when I opened my eyes on the melancholy spectacle. I was by their assistance raised and my eyes again wandered over the death like waste in search of her whose memory shall never be obliterated from mine, but alas! She was no more! Her troubles in this world of woes were ended!'

'The sailors accompanied me in search of her, but we were unsuccessful and night overtaking, obliged us to quit the scene of destruction, to go in search of some place wherein we might better shelter ourselves from the severity of the weather, for we were convinced we could not exist during the night on the beach; being already much exhausted. We accordingly turned our steps to a forest which appeared to be about a mile from the shore. This cover we reached with great difficulty for the snow had fallen to so great a depth that we frequently sank in it to the armpits. We could discern no signs of the country being inhabited and on our arrival at the wood could find no other shelter than that afforded by the trees and bushes and on the lee side of a thick clump we trod down the snow and sat down close together, this afforded us considerable relief and screened us during the remainder of the night, from the piercing north east wind, but when morning arrived and we endeavoured to raise ourselves on our legs, we found ourselves so benumbed that it was with the utmost exertion that four of us accomplished it and our companion who did not move, and we imagined was asleep, we found on examining him to be quite dead. As we had it not in our power to pay a sweeter tribute to his remains, we covered them with snow and returned by the same difficult path to the wreck. On our return to the beach, the three sailors immediately set themselves in search of such provisions as they could pick up among the wreck, for our future subsistence, while I sauntered from one spot

---

3. The shipwreck described could be the loss of the *Duke of Cumberland* which foundered off Newfoundland in December 1755.

to another in diligent search of the body of Eliza, but all was in vain, the night again approached, the wind had now considerably abated and the moon broke its way through the gloomy sky. I continued to explore the recesses among the rocks on which I was now more capable of maintaining a footing after the fury of the sea was a little soothed and while scrambling down the icy shelves of a rugged precipice, the moon sent down a bright ray which disclosed to my view the object of my painful enquiry. Her body had been washed upon a bed of sand under the hanging projections of a wild cliff; I approached and wept bitterly as I viewed the cheeks which had so lately charmed all around her, lie snow white and cold on a foreign and desolate shore. The gloomy hour of midnight brought my companions in search of me, who assisted me in carrying the body to a hut they had made during the day with pieces of planks &c from the wreck and next day we made a grave under the shade of a large pine, some distance from the shore, in which her bones to all probability rests in peace till this day.'

'I spent the following day at the grave of Eliza and cut her name deep on the trunk of the tree, also the name of the ship and date of her dissolution. Our minds, up to this date (being the fourth day after the vessel was wrecked) were occupied in such a manner as to preclude any consideration respecting our future comfort, or the nature of the shore on which we had been cast. For my part I continued absorbed in her plight and regardless of my fate, indeed I longed for the setting of that sun which my eyes were last to behold and welcomed frost, famine or any other means of drawing my life to a close. I shuddered at the sight of my own shadow, for it seemed to have a deeper and gloomier cast than those of my companions, being more detested in heaven and I wasted no consideration on trying to prolong an existence that was ever to be miserable. However, the sailors began to think it time to look forward for some inhabited spot as that on which we now were, seemed totally unfrequented by the human race. Nothing came within the reach of their enquiring eyes, save a vast country covered with snow, wild mountains towering to the dim clouds and dark forests extending themselves in wild irregularity on either hand. No appearance of any habitation, nor the traces of a human foot, could be discovered, save where we had ourselves trod and where even the print of my own foot attracted my attention, as bearing a disagreeable appearance among the foot marks of my fellow sufferers.'

'My three companions, observing my unhappy condition and probably conjecturing that it would be prudent to remove from this place, for I continued to spend my time at the grave of Eliza and was continually overwhelmed with grief, concluded that a march into the interior of the country would be advisable and after we had all consulted on this subject it was agreed upon that we should commence this undertaking the following morning and immediately began the necessary preparations for our journey. We first applied ourselves to the making of four bags of sail cloth (being one for each) something similar to a soldier's knapsack, for the purpose of carrying our provisions and such other necessaries as we had saved from the wreck & next morning after I had bedewed the tomb of Eliza with heartfelt tears, we commenced our march accoutred as above carrying with us an axe, a saw, a tinderbox and a small camp kettle. We had also a musquet & some ball cartridges which my friends selected from some barrels of ammunition which had been on board and each armed himself with a cutlass.'

'We proceeded through the forest in which we had sheltered the first night, but this was so extensive & so thick in many places, that it was with the greatest difficulty we could force our way. We perceived by the rising sun that we had been cast upon a north shore and considered that by steering southward where the sun was visible, it would be our guide. We followed this rule during the first day, being clear, but as the snow was a great depth and the wind piercing, we were very much exhausted before the approach of night. We could see no prospect of getting out of the forest and therefore looked out for a proper place in which we might shelter till daylight again returned. We accordingly chose one well shielded from the wind by brushwood & after beating down the snow, we struck a light, made a fire, boiled a small quantity of our salt beef in melted snow and spent the night in warming our benumbed limbs; in turns keeping a sharp lookout against an attack from the wild animals whose feet marks we could trace in all directions and whose unpleasant roarings and howlings assailed our ears from all quarters of the wood. When day again appeared in the east, we packed up our apparatus and set off on our journey. This day we saw some birds, which we might have killed, but considered it imprudent to make such waste of our ammunition before necessity called for it. The cold still continued unabated and we pushed on for the space of nine days without any appearance of getting to the other side of this immense forest. We saw many animals of different kinds; but they invariably seemed inclined rather to evade than molest us. 11 days had now elapsed since we took to our journey & our provisions began to get so scanty that we were compelled to subsist on about three ounces of salt beef without any other food, except when we killed a bird of any kind, for we had cut up some of our balls of which we made a kind of small shot for that purpose and when we had the good fortune to shoot a bird, we had a day of rejoicing. Twenty-six days had now passed since the dissolution of the ship, during which time we had suffered so much from the effects of the intense frost that I & another of my companions were scarcely able to continue our journey; our limbs were frozen in many parts and began to break into sores of unbearable pain and that night my afflicted friend died in a state of derangement. I envied the dead man of his happy change and heartily prayed for the speedy arrival of such fortune to myself; for my situation was now so miserable that it seemed scarcely possible for any new distress to make a sensible addition to it and I considered it would have been rather a happiness than a misfortune to be deprived of life. The pain arising from a perpetual sense of hunger and cold. The agony I was in from the sores occasioned by the frost; every party of the body covered with vermin and under such sufferings not daring to lift my eyes to heaven where I fancied my guilt recorded and my name stamped for the vengeance of the almighty ruler, at whose hand only I could obtain relief.'

'Next morning, I found myself quite unable to proceed and lay down near the dead sailor, in hopes of ending my sufferings in the same place. My surviving companions however, were unwilling to leave me in this situation and determined to halt a day or two to give an opportunity of recruiting more strength. They betook themselves to cutting branches from the trees and bushes with which they made a hut or kind of arbour to screen us from the cold, they also had the good fortune to shoot a very large wild cat, which was a timely supply of provisions, for our old stock was quite exhausted and here we remained five days. Our stay in this place together with the nourishment derived from our fresh food revived me surprisingly and on the morning of the 17th January we again set off. Proceeding slowly southward we arrived about noon at a river covered with ice, where to all appearance the animals of the forest had recently held a meeting for the snow-covered ice was marked with the feet of numerous & various kinds. We followed the track of the river and saw beautiful deer and other animals frequently issue from the forest on either hand, in which they again speedily took refuge on seeing us as we moved along on the ice. We loaded our musquet with ball in hopes of getting within shot of some of them, but were unsuccessful and night again coming on, we lighted our fire in a well sheltered recess on the left bank of the river. The light from the fire seemed in a short space, to have attracted the notice of the inhabitants of the woods, for our ears were so appalled by the manner in which they rustled, roared, barked & howled round our place of rest that we were obliged to be under arms, watching with the eyes of sentinels in front of the enemy, till near daybreak, when we were suddenly alarmed by something resembling a number of these unwelcome visitors rushing upon us. We instantly sprung to our feet; the two sailors seized their cutlasses and I had scarcely time to grasp the gun in my hand; when a fine deer appeared flying from the furious attack of two huge animals which were in close pursuit of it. I immediately fired a random shot amongst them, not with a view of making a prey, but in hopes of frightening them and thus saving myself and companions from being devoured. However, fortune here seemed to have bestowed on us a kindly glance at least, for the ball was directed through the head of the deer, which fell dead in a moment and its two pursuers, with a roar that made the forest echo again, redoubled their speed into the thicket. We were immediately in possession of a fine fat buck, which prolonged our stay in that place for the day.'

'This prize was one of no common value to us; however, we exercised judgement enough to abstain from eating too great a quantity, at once although our appetites could have welcomed much more, of so delicious a feast as it afforded, even without salt, bread, vegetables or any substitute for them. We replenished our sailcloth bags and next morning betook ourselves to our journey. The spirits of my companions were now raised to a height far above the level of their expectations, but I was to be unhappy under any fortune, yet continued to conceal my unpleasant reflections as much as possible from their notice, that they might not also be discouraged. We pursued our way up the track of the river three days after this without any extraordinary occurrence and as we still proceeded one of my companions observed a tree divested of a piece of its bark, as if by the cut of a hatchet or some sharp instrument, as if by the cut of a hatchet or some sharp instrument and although trifling, the hopes which we could in reason derive from such a discovery, it gave great encouragement to persevere, for we were convinced that it must be the work of some human hand and that the country must have been inhabited no great distance from this appearance.'

'This was the fourth day after we had killed the deer and being afraid of again running out of provisions, we put ourselves on a small allowance and in the evening we cut a quantity of pine branches which were very abundant in the place and by making a couch with some and covering our hut with others, we spent the most comfortable night we had enjoyed since the commencement of our journey, even on our small allowance of about a quarter of a pound of venison. Next day on our journey one of the sailors was seized with a fit of vomiting which compelled us to make a stay, in hopes that he would with a little rest recover, however the malady continued upwards of three hours when the poor fellow began to evince marks of extraordinary terror & temporary derangement and finding it necessary on his account to establish ourselves for the night, we erected a shield from the weather and made a bed of pine tops for our sick brother. We laid him on the couch & proceeded (with our musquet) into the wood in hopes of shooting some birds for his relief. We were unsuccessful although we had been in the forest about an hour, but on our way back to our hut we had the good fortune to fall in with some bushes covered with berries of a bluish colour, these we gathered and hastened to the hut, rejoicing over our having it in our power to present some refreshing fruit to our sick companion. We entered the hut, but looking round, were not a little surprise[d] when we found our friend gone! We hastened in search of him, imagining that as he was almost in a delirious state he might have sauntered into the forest. We also fired a shot which we intended to serve as a signal in the event of him having lost himself in the woods, but all was to no purpose and night coming on we were compelled to abandon all further enquiry for the night. We spent this night in great anxiety for a thousand doubts & fears were awakened in our minds by the disappearance of our unfortunate comrade. We renewed our researches next morning and continued them until noon, when we concluded that he must have been devoured in the wood by some ferocious animal. We were now reduced to two in number and continued our march refreshing ourselves at intervals with a few of the berries; for our venison was nearly exhausted and what remained in so putrid a state from the length of time it had been carried that our appetites, keen as they were could scarcely receive it. My body was, by this time, liberally covered with painful sores, reduced to a perfect skeleton and so weak that I could scarcely crawl along. My only surviving companion, who was a hardy, robust fellow; had none of these pains to endure and encouraged me to persevere by carrying all our camp equipment except my canvas bag. One day as we proceeded slowly, I begged my friends to allow me to sit down a few minutes to rest. He agreed and we were seated on a rotten trunk which lay among the trees, when to our inexpressible joy, an Indian made his appearance among the bushes. He did not at first perceive us and was approaching at a pace similar to a dog's trot, but had no sooner cast his eyes upon us than he uttered a yell which made the woods ring again, sprung back and vanished from our sight in an instant. My companion followed him in hopes of making up and craving his guidance to some inhabited part of the country, but returned unsuccessful. This was a circumstance which, although we had lost our object, gave us great encouragement, for by the appearance of the Indian, we were assured that we could be no great distance from some inhabited region and after taking a few berries to refresh ourselves pushed on with renewed spirits. But alas! It was hope alone that lured us forward, it indeed performed its part and kept us from sinking for the five succeeding days. Our putrid venison was quite spun out and we had tasted no other food for the space of three days, save the few berries we had in our bags and were so weak that on taking up our resting place in the evening. We gave up all hopes of being able to proceed any farther. The spot we had chosen to end our troubles in, was more open than any part of the desert we had hitherto seen. We applied our last spark of strength to the kindling of a fire, which with difficulty we accomplished, but were unable to go in quest of materials to build a hut and consequently suffered much from the cold, not alone on account of being without a hut, but as we were unable to gather or cut wood for our fire. We made several excursions on our hands and knees to procure pieces of wood or rotten branches, for we were totally unable to stand on our legs; and in this deplorable condition we survived four more days, having no earthly nourishment for the latter two, except some green leaves which we discovered under the snow; our berries being exhausted. All hope being thus vanished, my companion consigned himself to his God; but my guilt, which I looked up to as the cause of all our sufferings and which continually hovered round my soul, forbad me to ask forgiveness or to hope for mercy. Oh heavens; how shall I describe the nature of the torture I experienced in body and in soul when unsolicited relief presented itself to us; for I was afraid to live and afraid to die. This relief was brought by the appearance of two Indians, who as we lay by the dying fire issued from a thick part of the wood no great distance from us. They cast their eyes upon the spot where we lay and stood for some time in an attitude of amazement, but seemed afraid to come any nearer. I for my own part, was unable to raise my body from the ground, but my friend who first saw the Indians, sat up and made signs for them to come forward.

They at last seemed to understand his meaning and advanced with great precaution, they took several circles round us and approached a little nearer at the termination of each revolution, betraying marks of great surprise and horror every time they cast their eyes upon us. My companion exerted his skill in making the Indians acquainted with our situation and in a short time succeeded in drawing them close to us, when they both winced a deep concern for us. They viewed us minutely from head to foot, felt our tattered garments, touched our faces with their fingers, handled our cutlasses and musket which they seemed to admire, but laughed violently at our axe and saw. We made signs for food and after a short consultation together, one of the Indians departed towards the part of the forest from which they had issued and the other showing marks of great compassion for our distress, busied himself in bringing rotten branches and making a good fire. This greatly revived us, for we were drooping under the effects of the cold as well as the hunger. About an hour had elapsed when the other Indian returned, accompanied by three more. They brought with them some boiled meat, of a very soft white substance, of which they gave each of us a small quantity and a draught of liquor which they carried in a bladder. The whole seemed much affected to see us in so wretched a condition, but ceased not to examine us in so curious a manner that notwithstanding the low state of my strength and spirits, I could not avoid smiling.'

'After we were a little refreshed, the Indians assisted in raising us from the ground, but perceiving that I was quite unable to walk, placed me on one of their backs and the whole proceeded towards the forest, where they entered and after journeying slowly through a winding footway, arrived at a few huts which were occupied by their families. Here the women prepared couches of a kind of grass, on which we were laid and treated with the greatest humanity. The news of our arrival at the habitation of these people had spread among their neighbours and many visited us during the following day, who pestered us with their curiosity and compelled us to sit or stand up for their inspection as they individually entered. They gave us, very sparingly a kind of soup made from venison and seal oil till we gained a little strength, when they also gave us of the meat. In this manner we were around fifteen days, at the termination of which we were so much recruited as to be able to walk about. We knew not to what turn of fortune we were now to be indebted for an end of our stay among these savages and began to imitate and conform with their manners, as far as we understood them, with a view of making ourselves agreeable and the kind of life we enjoyed, although under any other circumstances, it might not have been altogether congenial to our feelings, after our late miseries made us exceedingly comfortable till we found our constitutions beginning to come round again, for they were so much shaken that they were not easily to be repaired. They subsisted entirely on venison and hunting in the woods to procure the wild deer for the use of their families, was the whole of their occupation. We remained here five weeks during which time the treatment we received from the Indians, in point of kindness and humanity, far exceeded our expectations and would have been no disgrace to the most civilised nation in the world. We again began to assume the appearance of returning health and strength and when so far recovered as to enable us to do so, we accompanied our benefactors to the woods on their hunting excursions, that they might be satisfied. We were not inclined to idle our time away and impose the trouble of providing for us upon them after we were ourselves able to do so. We knew not by what means we were to recompense them for the trouble they had already experienced by our presence. I had a few English guineas still left in my purse, 'tis true; but did not dream that they could be of any service to us in our present situation and therefore looked upon them as a useless encumbrance. One day we went a hunting in company with several Indians from our little hamlet and in the wood met with another party of hunters among whom was an old man whose long white beard descended in beautiful ringlets on his breast; he fixed his eyes upon us and quickly advancing to me, enquired in broken English, to what country we belonged and what misfortune had driven us into that island. It was no small gratification to us, at last to hear something like the language of our misfortunes; I begged he would acquaint us with the name of the country we were in and how we might get into some cultivated part. He accordingly informed us that we were on the island of Breton[4] in the Gulf of St Lawrence and by travelling to the coast we might by some chance get a passage to Halifax or some other port on the continent of America, but the undertaking would be attended with considerable danger as the journey would be upwards of seventy miles through the desert frequented by all manner of wild beasts and over several lakes and mountains which were often times impassable at that season of the year.'

---

4. Cape Breton Island, inhabited by the Mi'kmaq Indians.

'We walked together a considerable time and the old man enquired whether we had not saved any valuable articles from the wreck of our ship, as they might now be of great service to us. I answered in the negative and with a disapprobatory shake of the head, he observed that, that was not good for us, for we might be conducted to the coast in safety if we could remunerate our guides for their trouble. The guineas I had in my purse, struck my memory & I informed him that I had some English money, but feared it could be turned to no advantageous service in that country, however on hearing this, the old man's countenance brightened and he hastily requested to look at it. I pulled out my purse and gave old white-beard one of the guineas in his hand; he seized it eagerly and in a loud fit of laughter exclaimed 'Tat is te coot tings.' This called the attention of the rest of the hunters who immediately flocked round and each requested a similar gift. I reflected on the probable consequences which might attend a refusal and immediately complied with their request. I presented one of the pieces to each of them which they received with loud shouts of laughter, this I was afterwards informed was the only method they had of expressing their gratitude for any favour conferred upon them. The Indians were so much delighted with the sight of the money, that they immediately offered their services to conduct us anywhere we had a mind to go & I embraced the offer by choosing the old man and another to accompany us to any part of the coast, from which we might procure a passage to the continent. Next morning, we accordingly prepared for our departure, furnished ourselves with some provisions and such necessaries as we could procure and two days after we took our leave of the rest of our old friends and set out on our journey. This day we had a heavy fall of snow which obliged us to remain all the following day in a comfortable well shielded hut which our two conductors built of pine branches with amazing expedition and neatness. The 3rd day, being then 11th March, we again set forward and made considerable progress being accoutred with snow shoes which our guides had taken care to supply themselves with previous to our taking our march and with which we travelled with much less fatigue. Thus we continued our journey nine days, during which time our conductor contrived to kill a fine buck and several birds, which always kept our haversacks well supplied. On the 19th March we arrived at the banks of an extensive lake.[5] A few Indian habitations presented themselves along the wooded shore, from whom we purchased some fish which afforded us a delicious feast. The lake

---

5.   The huge Bras d'Or Lake in the centre of Cape Breton Island.

was some parts free from ice and we engaged two Indians with small canoes, in these we proceeded till we came to shoals of ice, then got out and walked, while the natives carried their canoes on their backs till we came again to the unfrozen parts of the lake. This part of the country was exceedingly wild, the lake bounded on the one side by a range of stupendous mountains covered with snow and rearing their winter heads into the still more wintry clouds that hung over them. We continued to proceed by the lake all day and having lighted a fire on its banks we rested all night, went a hunting in the woods next morning, killed a few birds and again set off on our journey and about noon quitted the lake, took to the woods and in the evening got into a country considerably populated. Among the inhabitants were some French families, we proceeded to a small settlement called Vengula; here we were kindly received into the house of a gentleman, whose treatment for the space of two days was highly honourable, when we bear in mind that he was a French merchant & the nation to which he belonged at war with England. On our departure from this good man's house he loaded us with a stock of bread (which was then a great luxury to us) and other provisions, we then set forward on our journey; and after proceeding two days in a more thinly populated tract, arrived at another little town named Delotta. Here we remained all night and next day reached Narrastote where we were again very hospitably entertained by some French merchants. Here we discharged our Indian conductors and remained with the merchants of Narrastote, who informed us that at the expiration of a fortnight; one of their vessels was to sail for Acadia[6] in which we should have a passage, accordingly at the expiration of that time we took our leave of the French merchants, embarked in their vessel and sailed on 9 April. We touched at the harbour of Canecaw and proceeded to Halifax where we landed and were received into the house of an English gentleman who had amassed a fortune in that country, among this family we spent six weeks during which time my companion looked out for a vessel in which he might procure a passage to Quebec where his family resided although they were English. He often expressed his impatience to get off and his anticipation of causing an agreeable surprise when he reached home, while I answered only with sighs drawn from deep reflections on my own situation, for I had no home, I dared not to turn my eyes on my

---

6. Acadia was a province of New France which covered the area around modern-day Maine up to near Quebec.

native land and silently suffered the pangs of a diseased conscience. At last an opportunity offered itself and my companion left me to mourn my loathsome time alone and to medicate in private to what use my remaining days were to be applied; but alas it was hard to bring my mind to any fixed determination, my earlier life had been spent in a manner which precluded all chance of getting my bread by the sweat of my brow. My purse had already yielded the last of its yellow store! And I exclaimed 'Oh that I had sprung from some of the happy peasantry of Old England and been taught to drudge in obscurity; with such accomplishments I might now have turned my hand to some labour whereby (even in this place of exile) to procure food & raiment for this wretched body, but here am I an outcast on a distant shore! Farthingless and forlorn! With no other probable prospect than that of eternal misery. Sad hope! Oh to bid a last farewell to that bright sun that bends his way to the western horizon. Yet I tremble to meet the author of his glory.' Thus, I often spent my mournful hours on the sea beach where my laden eyes stole along the surface of the boundless deep, in the direction of Old England and discharged their load of sorrow. Three weeks I thus spent in solitary sadness after the departure of my companion. The gentleman with whom I lived soon became interested respecting my unhappy manner and frequently drew me into strict interrogations, however they proved only productive of evasive answers. He at length concluded that my uneasiness arose from being disappointed in getting a passage to England and exerted himself in procuring me one.'

'He made an arrangement with the captain of a large merchant ship lay in the harbour and was to sail for London in a few days and on his return home informed me what he had done. He desired me to prepare for my departure and furnished everything necessary for my comfort while on [the] sea. I reflected deeply on receiving this friendly information, for I knew not what to do, I could not reject his offer nor dared to accept it. I saw no prospect of escaping the dreaded punishment due to my crime if I returned home or the most degrading misery if I did not do so, however I feigned as much satisfaction on hearing his orders as I could master courage to counterfeit and thanked him for the interest he took in my welfare, after which I spent the remainder of the day in a solitary walk on the sea shore. The two following days passed over without inventing any experiment to prevent my return to England and the vessel being ready for sea and a prosperous gale blowing, my worthy friend accompanied me to the ship's side & bid me farewell. Our ship was well armed and manned, yet (being only a merchantman) the crew had no desire of trying their powers against any of the French cruisers, who at that period were looking out for such prizes and while they wished to escape them, I earnestly prayed for the appearance of the French flag, nor dreaded the worst of fates should my prayers be heard. They were, indeed heard at last, for we had only been ten days at sea, when the news of *a Frenchman in sight!* was proclaimed from the main top. This caused great consternation throughout the ship & although preparations for action were promptly made [for] the enemy's visit, as she bore down upon us, seemed only acceptable to myself. All sail was crowded but the Frenchman gained rapidly upon us; the elapse of three hours brought us within reach of their guns and a brisk cannonade was opened & continued till the enemy closed alongside, when a bloody contest followed. I now embraced the opportunity I longed for and exposed myself where the danger seemed greatest, in hopes that some agent of destruction would sweep me from a world of misery and close my grief swollen eyes for ever. However, all my hopes were frustrated, I was doomed to suffer more lingering tortures for my crimes demanded them. The engagement continued upwards of three hours and although I exulted in observing that the Frenchmen were not to be beaten, I viewed them as the enemies of my country and fought with a maddened courage till our deck was covered with the slain and the gore of my countrymen flowed profusely from the scuttles on both sides. I paused, I beheld the horrid scene and shuddered as the idea struck me that the blood of so base a wretch as myself, could not be suffered to mingle with the pure life streams of the sons of my native land and again dashed into the thickest of the fight where the enemy had boarded our ship, but all my efforts were vain; I could not meet with a man who was able to withstand the force of the cutlass I wielded and more than one bowed to the superior strength of this time worn arm. We were however, in time and by superior numbers overpowered and I (as if awaking from a dream) found myself lying on the deck to which I had at last been levelled by repeated blows and where I to all probability had lain in a senseless state for some time. I saw we were conquered and in possession of the foe; the dead and dying strewed around me, the ship dismasted and the deck literally covered with blood & destruction yet I smiled on the sad scene which was to prevent my being landed in England. All was now over, our ship a prize in the hands of the victorious enemy, one half of our crew killed, I (like many more) severely wounded and in this situation triumphantly towed into Brest. Here we were put on shore and those who were able to walk driven along on foot while the wounded were tumbled into carts; the whole conducted to Rennes and cast into prison. I lingered long under my wounds and within the gloomy walls of that prison I spent the three following years. During the above-named period, my mind was haunted by the most appalling reflections, I had a country and dared not to own it, tender parents who (if not sunk beneath the sorrows with which I had loaded them) were pining away in a slow and painful progress toward that cold mansion which affords rest to the afflicted and virtuous. I dreaded a release even from the bondage I was in, was detested by my fellow prisoners and all around me; had no social manner; no place of rest and my hours were worn away in lonely dread & deep contemplation. We had completed the above term in Rennes when it was whispered that we were to be removed to another district, but our destination we were unable to learn, till placed under a military escort, who commenced a march towards the interior, during which we were compelled to humble ourselves to the most ungenerous treatment from our conductors and the peasantry as we passed through the country. However, after a tiresome and long march we reached Dijon in Burgundy where we were again secured for a few weeks and conducted to Vesoul,[7] here we remained two months and at the expiration of that time were forwarded to Metz, a considerable town on the Moselle, where we were put on board a small vessel and sailed to Cologne. At this place, we became acquainted with our destination by the appearance of an equal number of French prisoners under a British escort. An exchange accordingly took place and we sailed immediately for Battenberg, which was then in possession of the allies and the sailors of our party who chose to go home were put onboard a transport which was about to sail for England with sick and wounded men and those who had a desire to be in the service, were put on board the ships of war. In this arrangement, I knew not how to act, going to England was no good speculation, nor did I much fancy offering myself to serve on board a King's ship and therefore determined to join the army which was then in the country. I accordingly offered my services, was readily accepted, sent off with a party which was on its way to join the army, put into military uniform and sent to drill immediately.'[8]

---

7. A town in Franche-Comté.
8. Wentworth undoubtedly joined one of the six regiments of foot with the army.

Chapter 8

He Fights During the 7 Years War

Ihad only been three weeks at my new trade when the regiment to which I belonged was called into the fields. I was a young soldier indeed; nevertheless I was harnessed, armed and posted in the ranks of the company; nor murmured when the fatigues of long marches, bad roads and scanty provisions extorted discontent & complaints from the hardy veterans who were long inured to the fatigues of war. The war had taken its rise from disputes concerning our American possessions but it was transferred to Europe by the French invasion of Hanover,[1] in defence of which the Duke of Cumberland[2] took command of an army of Hanoverians, Hessians and Brunswickers; but after a disastrous campaign, was forced to retreat & sign a convention which was not ratified[3] and immediately Prince Ferdinand of Brunswick[4] taking command of the same troops, soon relieved Hesse and drove the French over the Rhine, which he also crossed himself and defeated their army under the Prince of Clermont[5] at Krefeld, bombarded and took Dusseldorf, but the French threatening Hanover from the Upper Rhine and also to insure a junction with the British forces which were ordered to Germany; he

---

1. The French invaded Hanover in 1757 as part of the Seven Years War.
2. Prince William August (1721–65), third son of King George II, best known for commanding the English army at the Battle of Culloden.
3. The Duke of Cumberland was beaten at the Battle of Hastenbeck and signed the Convention of Klosterzeven which removed Hanover from the war, but the Convention was revoked the following year and Hanover rejoined the war.
4. Ferdinand, Prince of Brunswick-Wolfenbuttel (1721–92).
5. Louis, Count of Clermont (1709–71).

re-crossed the Rhine and marched to Coesfeld in the vicinity of Munster where on the 19[6] August 1758 the British reinforcement under the Duke of Marlborough[7] joined the Allied army. It consisted of the six following regiments of horse & six battalions of foot.'

> 'The Oxford Blues (Lord Granby's)
> The 1st Dragoon Guards (Bland's)
> The 3rd Dragoon Guards (Howard's)
> The Royal Scots Greys (Campbell's)
> The Inniskillings (Cholmondley's)
> The 10th Light Dragoons (Maurdaunt's)
> 12th Regiment of Foot
> 20th Regiment of Foot
> 23rd Regiment of Foot[8]
> 25th Regiment of Foot
> 37th Regiment of Foot
> 51st Regiment of Foot
> With a suitable proportion of artillery'

'After the British troops arrived, the army advanced to Dulmen where they lay for some time, but intelligence having been received that the Hessian General Oberg[9] had been worsted in Hesse. Prince Ferdinand in order to make a diversion in Oberg's favour, marched the main army to Warendorf, crossed the Lippe, marched to attack the Duke of Choiseul[10] at Soest and came so suddenly upon him that he had no time to form. The allied cavalry charged (if chasing a mob of people among their tents & huts can be so called) by which a great number were killed, wounded and made prisoners. The French then retreated to Werle, where the British troops dislodged them next day much in the same manner and the French fell back, broke up the campaign and went into winter quarters, which the allies also did and thus closed the campaign of 1758.'

---

6. Fortescue says they arrived on 21 August.
7. Charles Spencer, 3rd Duke of Marlborough (1706–58).
8. The 23rd did proceed to Germany this year, but is omitted by Fortescue in his work.
9. General Christoph Ludwig von Oberg commanded 9,000 men to protect the Hessian provinces. He was defeated at the Battle of Lutternberg in 1758.
10. Étienne-François de Choiseul, Duke de Choiseul (1719–85).

'The British Army was preparing to take the field & commence the next campaign when I joined my regiment, for Prince Ferdinand had received information that the enemy were collecting in great force near Frankfurt with a design to invade Hesse and had collected his troops and begun a march upon Fulda.'

'The regiment to which I belonged commenced its march with the rest of the division on the 15th February and during the advance were daily engaged in skirmishing & a great number of prisoners were made and many magazines taken or destroyed and when the army arrived in the neighbourhood of Fulda, it was halted a few days to recover the men and horses from the fatigue of their rapid advance. This respite, the French general made good use of in strengthening his position, however the allies considering it an imprudent measure to delay long, again began the march by Freiensteinau and Budingen to Windecken which they reached on the 10th of April.'

'The village of Bergen,[11] halfway between Frankfurt and Hanau is situated on a height which terminates abruptly on the east towards Hanau; but the approach from the north is a gentle rise till the ridge is gained. Then appears a deep wooded glen, through the hidden bottom of which a stream murmurs which after taking its unequal course about a couple of miles terminates in a marsh. This ravine runs southward from the village of Bergen towards Frankfurt, the ground on the south side, rather highest. It was possessed by the French and furnished with several batteries of heavy guns drawn from the ramparts of Frankfurt.'

'When the Allied Army had arrived within a mile of this ground, the whole of the cavalry were moved quickly on and formed in line on the summit of the opposite height, in front of the French Army. The enemy's line appeared full in their view, formed in fine order, with a large reserve behind and the town and vineyards of Bergen, filled with their best troops; they remained steady till they observed the prince forming his line of infantry behind the squadrons; then opened a dreadful fire from the whole of their artillery. The allied cavalry retreated through the intervals of the foot, who instantly occupied the height. Where it was wooded, strong reserves were posted and where free from wood, the cavalry supported in a second line.'

'The allied generals considered the only chance of success was confined to obtaining possession of Bergen, by which the enemy's

---

11. Bergen-Enkheim.

right would have been turned into a narrow ground where they could scarcely have changed their front. Accordingly, the town was assaulted in the most gallant manner by the Hessian and Hanoverian infantry, who succeeded in entering it, but the immense numbers powered in upon them by the enemy's right wing, prevented them from maintaining possession.[12] Three attacks were made but unfortunately, without success and at the third of which; General Prince Isenburg[13] commander of the Hessians and director the attacks, was slain, 4,000 men also fell in the village.[14] The enemy's loss was much greater as they were so crowded in the town, that two guns which they could never dismount, raked the principle street the whole day and dealt destruction at every round. About five p.m. I received a ball through the right thigh, which I bound up with a handkerchief and endeavoured to conceal, under the pretence of the wound being slight, till I was unable to stand longer in the ranks; and as I tried to make my way to the rear, I sunk to the ground. Here weakness arrested me till night came on, for although the allied generals saw that they must retreat, they did not consider it a prudent measure to show any preparation for retiring from the height in daylight and the wounded were allowed to lie on the ground till it became dark, when the whole army fell back about three miles and bivouacked. I was put into a wagon with other wounded and removed to the rear. Thus ended that sanguinary action and next morning the allied troops, being a little rested, began their march & continued it unmolested till the 19th, but the enemy's light troops then appeared and by the capture of an orderly officer, made prisoners some squadrons of Prussian cavalry, molested the rear of the Allied Army, took a great number of prisoners and killed about fifty or sixty Hessians.'

'I lay in hospital about two months, during which time the army continued in cantonments at Zugenham. At that period some regiments were ordered to join the Hereditary Prince's corps, which marched towards Fulda to expel the Wurtemburgers who did not wait their approach. However, they took and destroyed some magazines at Hosenfeld and occupied Fulda on 10 May, but the allies were called from this quarter in consequence of the French under Contades &

---

12. The Battle of Bergen, 13 April 1759, at which the French were victors, the Allies falling back on Minden.
13. Prince Johann Isenburg, Landgrave of Hesse-Cassel.
14. Each side lost around 2,000 men killed and wounded, but not all would have occurred in to town.

Broglio[15] advancing to the [River] Lahn. Contades though he had then a good opportunity of attacking the allies and about the end of July, the whole French army consisting of 90 battalions of infantry & 95 squadrons of horse formed in order of battle on the plain of Minden, by five o'clock on the morning of the 31st [July]. Prince Ferdinand not being apprised in due time of the enemy's movements, did not put his army in motion before that hour! However, he advanced with his right towards the plain and reached it about half past seven, when the battle began and continued from that time till noon with the greatest gallantry and firmness on both sides. But the enemy, after this began to give way and were soon forced to retire in the greatest confusion, leaving behind them 6,000 men killed and a great number of prisoners, cannon, standards and colours captured.[16] The loss of the allies on this occasion amounted to little more than 2,000 killed.[17] The British infantry and cavalry of the left wing gained very great applause for their gallant conduct. The regiment to which I belonged suffered severely[18] but I had the fortune to escape without injury. This action was rendered more decisive by the Hereditary Prince at the same time defeating the Duke de Brissac[19] at Coveldt and destroying the bridges on the Werra [River] by which means the retreat of Contades between the mountains and the Weser was prevented and the whole were obliged to defile through Minden on the night of the 1st of August, where the Hereditary Prince entered on the 2nd, commenced his pursuit of the flying enemy and took a great number of prisoners, cannon and baggage wagons. The flight of the French was by [Hessisch] Oldendorf, Haslinbeck, Einbeck, Gottingen etc and on the 11th they assembled near Cassel where D'Armitures[20] joined and posted them near Wolfhagen. Here both armies kept moving from camp to camp but could gain no advantage

---

15. Louis Georges Erasme Marquis de Contades (1704–95), who was made a Marshal of France in 1759, commanded the Army of the Rhine. He was later superseded by Victor François, 2nd Duc de Broglie (1718–1804).
16. The French admitted to losing between 10,000 and 11,000 killed and wounded, 17 standards or colours and 43 guns.
17. It amounted to 2,600 killed and wounded.
18. The brigade that suffered most severely included the 12th, 23rd & 37th Foot, it is probable that he served in one of these regiments.
19. Jean Paul Timoleon de Cosse, 7th Duke of Brissac (1698–1784) was made a Marshal of France for Minden.
20. Actually General D'Armentières.

over each other till about the 8th of September, when Prince Ferdinand caused Count Buckeburg[21] to invest the citadel of Marburg [an der Lahn] which surrendered in a few days. The Hereditary Prince was detached with 20,000 men to the assistance of the King of Prussia and joined him near Dresden on the 28th.

Broglio soon after this quitted his camp and marched back to cantonments at Freiberg, leaving 2,000 men in Giessen, which notwithstanding the severity of the weather was immediately blockaded by the allies. But the consequence was that a great number of the videttes and sentinels lost their fingers and toes with the frost. These two fingers which you see missing from my left hand, was my share of the losses sustained at that time.

Broglio observing large detachments sent from the allied army to Munster and Saxony & concluding that their position at Croysdorff would be thinly occupied, called in his detachments and raised the blockade of Giessen. This took place on the 25th December and on the 27th he meant to have attacked the main army, but seeing good fires blazing from right to left of the allied army's lines, he concluded that they were too well prepared for him and retired to Freiberg, thence into winter quarters. The Allied Army also broke up on the 7th January, returned to near the same place they had left in March 1759, went into winter quarters, about the beginning of February 1760 and thus ended the campaign of '59.'

'Early the ensuing spring, considerable reinforcements from England joined the British army, which now consisted of the following corps, viz:[22]

Cavalry
➢ Oxford Blues
➢ 1st Dragoon Guards
➢ 2nd Dragoon Guards
➢ 3rd Dragoon Guards
➢ Scots Greys
➢ Inniskillings
➢ 7th Light Dragoons
➢ 10th Light Dragoons
➢ 11th Light Dragoons

---

21. Frederick Wilhelm, Count of Schaumburg-Lippe-Buckeburg (1724–77), who fought with the Prussians.
22. This list is not as full as Fortescue's.

Infantry
- ➤ 3rd Foot
- ➤ 8th Foot
- ➤ 11th Foot
- ➤ 12th Foot
- ➤ 20th Foot
- ➤ 23rd Foot
- ➤ 24th Foot
- ➤ 25th Foot
- ➤ 33rd Foot
- ➤ 37th foot
- ➤ 50th Foot
- ➤ 51st Foot
- ➤ With Keith[23] & Campbell's Highlanders

Which made a total of 14 battalions of infantry and 24 squadrons of horse, also other necessary accompaniments for the field.'

'The French army was also strongly reinforced & Broglio determined to make every exertion to penetrate through Hesse. However, Prince Ferdinand prepared to oppose him at the position on the Ohm [River], viz Schweinsberg and Kirchhain with a strong corps at Wetter. Prince Ferdinand advanced a strong corps under the Hereditary Prince and General Gilsoe to Fulda, they dislodged several strong detachments of the enemy at Horschfeldt, Hosenfeld and Tulbach, in which places many prisoners were taken and several magazines and baggage wagons captured.'

'Some time, after these operations, Prince Ferdinand gained the strong position of Sachsenhausen; here the Hereditary Prince surprised five battalions and Berchin's Corps of Horse. He had with him six battalions, with Luckner's Hussars[24] and Elliot's Regiment[25] to which the enemy at last surrendered. The corps employed on this service was led by Major (afterwards General) Sir William Erskine[26] Bart and lost 124 men & 168 horses. The number of the enemy which surrendered to

---

23. Both were reduced at the end of the war in 1763, they were designated as the 87th and 88th Foot respectively.
24. This was a Hanoverian unit.
25. Elliot's Horse became the 15th Light Dragoons.
26. Major Sir William Erskine 15th Hussars.

them was (besides killed & wounded) their leader Baron Glaubitz[27] & 2,000 men with six pieces of cannon &c &c.'

'Prince Ferdinand after having maintained his position at Sachsenhausen for near three weeks, found that St Germain's[28] Corps intended to turn his right and prevent his communication with Paderborn, but to prevent this he quitted that position on the 25th July and marched towards Cassel by Wolfhagen and the wooded hills above Cassel. This was called the retreat of Wolfhagen and allowed to have exhibited a very grand military show. The Allied Army of 90,000 and the enemy of 136,000 manoeuvring over a large plain from morning till night, with all the precision and regularity of a review. The allies continued their retreat to the plain of Cassel when the enemy gave up the point and next day the allied army encamped at Korle near Cassel, but Prince Ferdinand being informed that St Germain's Corps of 35,000 men had crossed the Dymel and marched down its left bank to Warburg and there posted themselves, that Broglio was advancing on his front and Prince Xavier[29] on Cassel. He therefore considered it the safest measure to get out of this corner as soon as possible; for he was then confined between the Dymel [River] and the Fulda and delay would have exposed his communication with Westphalia to being cut off; therefore on the 29th the Hereditary Prince, with two battalions [of] British Grenadiers, two battalions of highlanders with Cope's[30] and Conway's Dragoons[31] marched to reinforce Sporcken[32] who was posted at Korbecke. They crossed the Dymel and took a circuit to attack the enemy's left, while the main army attacked their front.

The French Army was posted on the ridge overlooking the Dymel, their right at Warburg (into which they had thrown part of Fischer's Corps[33]) and their left on a high hill above Ossendorf and as the night and following morning was extremely foggy, the allies crossed the Dymel without being discovered by the enemy.'

---

27. Marechal de Camp von Glaubitz
28. Commanded by Lord Sackville.
29. The second son of the King of Poland, commanding a force in Saxony.
30. Sir John Cope's Dragoons became the 9th Light Dragoons.
31. Lieutenant General Henry Conway's Dragoons became the 4th Light Dragoons.
32. Major General von Sporcken commanded the Westphalian army.
33. Brigadier General Johann Fischer commanded a corps of chasseurs.

'At the appointed hour, the Hereditary Prince commenced on the extremity of the enemy's left and notwithstanding the steepness of the ascent and a stout resistance. Maxwell's grenadiers stormed the hill and drove their left in upon their centre. Meanwhile the main army was making the greatest exertion to get up, but many of the infantry dropped from heat and fatigue. The cavalry led by General Mostyn[34] was ordered to proceed in as expeditious a manner as possible and after advancing about five miles, at a very quick pace, each regiment as they reached the height, charged individually the troops opposite to them. This plan of attack was adopted as the enemy was already disordered by the Hereditary Prince and would probably have escaped had the cavalry ceremoniously formed the line.'

'The British artillery under Captain Phillips,[35] who had advanced with the cavalry, were employed with great effect on the enemy's line; which had now left the height in confusion and were endeavouring to re-pass the Dymel on their bridges, fording and swimming. In this attempt a great number were drowned. The French retreated precipitately and the allies marched down the left bank of the Dymel and encamped near its junction with the Weser. The headquarters at Buhne, leaving under the Hereditary Prince a corps sufficient to occupy the strong position at Warburg.'

'The good consequences of this victory were incalculable, the communications of the allies secured and those of the enemy endangered if they advanced through another country into Hanover; but the main events of this campaign may be said to have terminated here. However the allies kept their position till late in the season and some excursions of inferior importance took place, which will be mentioned in their order of dates.'

'On the 5th August Prince Ferdinand being informed that the enemy were to forage towards Geismar, crossed the river with a corps of artillery, which he posted in such a manner as totally to prevent them though covered with 20,000 men; and on the same day the Hereditary Prince learned that the Volontairs de Dauphine & Clermont[36] who occupied the town of Zierenberg, conceived themselves in perfect security; being within three miles of the French camp; and determined to surprise them. For this purpose he ordered five battalions, viz

---

34. Lieutenant General John Mostyn.
35. Captain William Phillips commanded the artillery at Minden.
36. Both regiments were in de Nortman's Brigade.

> ➢ Maxwell's Grenadiers[37]
> ➢ Kingsley's[38]
> ➢ Block's[39] & two battalions of Hessian Grenadiers, with 150 high-landers under Major McLean; with eight squadrons of cavalry, viz.
> ➢ 2 of the Greys
> ➢ 2 of the Inniskillings &
> ➢ 4 of Bock's[40]

'The whole of these left their tents standing and passed the Dymel at eight o'clock at night. Maxwell's, Kingsley's and the highlanders led the column and at Welzen met the light troops under Bulow, who were to intercept the communication between the town & the French camp.'

'At the entrance of the wood at Malzberg, the Greys and Inniskillings were posted with a battalion of grenadiers, Block's infantry and Bock's Dragoons at their proper stations to support in case of a repulse and when drawing near the town, Maxwell's & Kingsley's took different roads but contrived to reach the gates together, where they immediately attacked, killed the guards and drove everything before them. The enemy attempted a fruitless defence by firing from the windows of the houses which were instantly stormed and all within put to death with the bayonet, as none of the attacking party had or were suffered to load.

'The troops entered the town on this enterprise at two o'clock and at three by signal of bugle, every ad had left it, bringing with them Brigadier de Norman commanding the Volontaires de Dauphine[41] and M. De Comeiras,[42] colonel of those of Clermont,[43] with about forty officers of inferior rank & 300 men.'

'As this surprise took place within two miles of the left of Broglio's army. Bulow's light troops guarded their rear while they returned to their camp, which they reached about nine or ten o'clock next morning, 6th August.'

---

37. A combined battalion of grenadier companies.
38. Colonel William Kingsley commanded the 20th Foot.
39. A Hanoverian battalion.
40. Bock commanded a Hanoverian cavalry regiment.
41. Composed from a number of small units in 1758 of six companies of forty infantry and thirty mounted dragoons each.
42. Lieutenant Colonel Marquis de Comeiras.
43. The Voluntaires de Clermont was raised in 1758 and consisted of 1,800 men in 16 companies of dragoons and 11 companies of infantry.

'On the night of the 21st August, Broglio's army quitted their camp opposite Warburg and marched towards Cassel; the Hereditary Prince's Corps of 12,000 men crossed the Dymel early on the 22nd to follow them. They commenced the pursuit with the light troops skirmishing in front till they came within a short distance of Zierenberg and were then ordered to encamp. They had just begun to pitch their tents, when information was received that Broglio's whole army had entered the entrenched camp at Cassel, leaving only a rear guard at Zierenberg. The whole of the Greys and one squadron of the Inniskillings, with Beckwith's Brigade[44] and the other battalions of British grenadiers were ordered to march immediately to attack them. They moved expeditiously and when they arrived near the town, they saw six squadrons of French cavalry drawn up on a flat piece of ground ready to receive them. The Greys and Inniskillings immediately charged and were received with a volley which the French dragoons fired from their pistols. However, this had no other effect than alarming their own horses, but it afterwards proved to be a signal for a body of infantry who were ambushed behind a hedge, who instantly sprung up and discharged a volley of musquetry through a thicket on their right flank. This killed about a dozen of men & horses and wounded a considerable number of each. The charge was nevertheless completed with great success, upsetting the French dragoons by divisions together and chasing those who could effect their escape as they fled in a confused rabble towards the town; the Greys & Inniskillings followed them to the gate which they endeavoured to bar, but was prevented by a dragoon of the Greys riding his horse into it; however this brave fellow was immediately shot from within.'

'When the enemy's fire was seen proceeding from the hedges by the British grenadiers, they advanced rapidly, attacked and drove them with great loss to the other side of the town, from which the whole of the French withdrew; and it being considered unsafe to remain long so near their main army, the British (as soon as they could be collected into some order) retired a few miles and bivouacked all night and next morning returned across the Dymel to their old position at Warburg.'

'The French cavalry opposed to the Greys & Inniskillings in this affair were the Dragoons Royaux & the Regiment De La Ferronnays.'[45]

---

44. Major General John Beckwith commanded the brigade of grenadiers and highlanders.
45. A French dragoon regiment.

'Many other skirmishes took place previous to the closing of this campaign, which took place on the 10th December when the army went into winter quarters. Our regiment were quartered at Barentrup four miles from [Bad] Pyrmont, a village belonging to Count la Lippe Buckeburg, who having been an officer in the British Guards, spoke English fluently and seemed to delight in paying more than common attention to both officers & men. In this comfortable situation, we could not expect to remain long and so it was; for in the space of two months Prince Ferdinand perceived that Broglio was actively employed in the fortification of Cassel, Gottingen, [Seeheim] Jugenheim &c and in collecting great magazines, by which means he might have taken the field before the allies were in any readiness; the prince therefore resolved to proceed against and destroy these preparations. Accordingly (although not recovered from the effects of the last long campaign) in the beginning of February 1761 he put the whole army from the frontiers of Saxony to those of Holland, in motion, the Hereditary Prince marched from Munster by the upper Dymel to Fritzlar, Sporcken from Saxony (where with the aid of the Prussian cavalry he had gained several advantages and advanced to Fulda, the very middle of the enemy's cantonments.'

'Broglio finding himself thus annoyed, although he had strengthened Cassel and other places, was compelled to retire upon Homberg, Herschfeldt, Giessen and at last to Bergen; where he ordered all his troops, with those of the lower Rhine to assemble.'

'The Greys, Bays and Mostyn's Dragoons, under General Webb marched to Fritzlar where they met General Gilsoe's corps of Hessians. The whole were put under the orders of Lord Granby and marched to the support of the Hereditary Prince, who assaulted the garrison of Cassel on the 14th, but being without cannon was repulsed. they however bivouacked all night in front of the town to prevent the enemy from leaving it and were (e'er next morning) nearly frozen to death. Next day some artillery came up and were posted; scaling ladders procured from the nearest villages and every preparation made for taking the garrison by storm. However, just when all was ready a dreadful hurricane of snow and wind came on and increased in fury, till at last cavalry, infantry, artillery and all descriptions mixed together were driven to take shelter in the nearest place of cover.'

'The next day being a sharp but clear frost, the British cavalry and Prussian Black Hussars under Colonel Jannerel crossed the Eider at Neidermollerich to observe the garrison from the south. The town was cannonaded for some time when the commandant Mons De Narbone capitulated to march out his men with their army but not to serve till next campaign. His strength was 1600 men, the greatest part of which were Irish. Next day Lord Granby offered the commandant of Gudensberg the same terms, which were readily accepted and the allies continued their advance.'

'Broglio left Hirschfeld after having set fire to a great magazine which he had collected. The Greys & Bays with a considerable corps of Hessian infantry marched rapidly on and succeeded in saving a great part of it. The magazine contained 80,000 sacks of meal, 50,000 sacks of oats and a million of rations of hay. On the arrival of the British cavalry the town was occupied by some French dragoons and hussars which the former chased out and took prisoners.'

'Lord Granby then marched to Frillendorf and Neuenkirchen and General Sporcken engaged and beat the enemy at the same time at [Bad] Langensalza in which action they sustained a loss of 5,000 men.'

'The Allied army marched to the neighbourhood of Annenburg, where they bivouacked several nights notwithstanding the severity of the weather and about the 15th March their cantonments concentrated between Schwelm and the Ohm; here a position was marked out to the troops, in which it was said that Prince Ferdinand intended to give battle, but the want of subsistence in a place already exhausted by friends and foes; forced him (if such was his intention) to relinquish it. He therefore sent orders to raise the sieges of Cassel and Jugenheim and the Hereditary Prince to join the army, which he did on the 22nd, but he having been attacked the day before near Grimsberg, Closen, whose large body of cavalry had beat the few Hanoverian cavalry which were with the prince and flanking his infantry made prisoners 1,500 men.'

'When these corps had joined the army a fresh arrangement took place. The Greys, 7th & 11th [Dragoon] Regiments were again put under the orders of the prince and marched towards Fritzlar. They met with no annoyance till the 26th; this night they bivouacked on the heights of Wildengen, where they found a considerable number of troops assembled to avoid which, at day break the following morning the allied infantry began their march from the heights, the three above mentioned regiments of British cavalry, with some Hessian Hussars forming the rear guard. They kept the heights till the infantry had reached the enclosed country on the plain; but no sooner began to move, than they were beset with a swarm of Berchin's and other hussars. The British cavalry made several attempts to disperse them, but their immense numbers more than once repulsed their attacks and so vigorously did they follow up the rear guard, that the Hereditary Prince, Captain McLean of the highlanders and his German aide de camp were literally obliged to cut their way through the enemy, sword in hand.'

'The whole army passed the Eider at Fritzlar and its neighbourhood and as the French could not advance any further for want of subsistence, the allies (without further annoyance) continued their march to their quarters of refreshment where they arrived about the beginning of April and cantoned in the countries of Munster, Paderborn and Osnabruck, while Broglio returned to the Rhine and the Maine.'

'Our regiment went into quarters at Grohnde on the Weser about twelve miles from Barentrup and so ended the campaign of 1760.'

'The secret of this winter expedition had been so well kept, that the enemy had not the least idea of being disturbed and when the allies quitted their quarters, their movements were so well combined and directed on the points where the enemy was to be dislodged, that they were totally surprised; and although the sieges of Cassel and Zeigenhain failed from deficiency of troops, yet they were raised without loss and the allied army after destroying several large magazines and subsisting on their stores for the space of three months, retired without sustaining any essential damage; but occasioned so great a loss to the enemy, that Broglio's army were effectively prevented from taking the field till such time as green forage was to be obtained. However, the magazines and territories on the lower Rhine, having escaped the devastations of the allies in their winter expedition, enabled that army of the French (which was strongly reinforced) to be put in motion about the beginning of June following, under the command of the Prince de Soubise.'

'The intentions of the enemy, with this army, amounting to 90,000 men, were to take Lippstadt and Munster and to move through Munsterland and Paderborn into Hanover. To frustrate these intentions Prince Ferdinand sent a corps under General Conway to Soest and General Howard with some battalions & cavalry proceeded to secure Ham; these were to communicate with the Hereditary Prince, who covered Munsterland from the camp of Nottelen & the main army to be in readiness, at the same time to march from Munsterland & Paderborn.'

'Soubise accordingly crossed the Rhine at Wesel on the 14th June with 109 battalions & 108 squadrons and Broglio's army (daily expected) consisting of 88 battalions and 89 squadrons, forming a total of 141,000 men.'

'The allied army was composed of 68,500 infantry, 15,160 cavalry, with 8,000 light troops forming in all 91,660 men. This was really a prodigious superiority in numbers but the allies had a man to direct, who (in the course of a few weeks) proved that his head was of more avail than many thousands; for by his superior judgement, this enormous mass was dispersed like a cloud, without succeeding in any measure.'

'This great French army advanced to Dortmund and encamped there on the 18th of June; this obliged the Hereditary Prince to move forward to the Lippe and encamp near Hamm. The main army assembled on the 19th, in high spirits, in camp at Paderborn, leaving Sporcken to watch the motions of Broglio at Warburg.'

'In order to observe and counteract the operations of the enemy, Prince Ferdinand marched from Paderborn on the 21st to Stadt Geske, but learning that Prince de Conde's reserve had driven the Hereditary Prince from Kamen &c, they advanced next day to Ale Geske and on the 24th, very early in the morning, to Soest and encamped; here they were joined by Conway's Corps which had been posted on the Lippe; Lord Granby advanced on the 25th with his six battalions and six squadrons of cavalry on the left of the army to Wipperenhausen and the Hereditary Prince crossed the Lippe and encamped at Hamm.'

'On the right of the 27th, the infantry of the allied army who occupied the garrison of Werl Castle were vigorously attacked but repulsed the enemy and next day the allied army advanced and obliged the enemy to withdraw their advanced posts and abandon several villages on the river, which were afterwards occupied by the allies.'

'The whole French army being now assembled in one camp, it was necessary to approach them with caution; accordingly the allied army marched on the 29th from the camp at Werl to that of Lundern, and Prince Ferdinand occupied the 30th and 1st July in reconnoitring the enemy's position while he cannonaded his, but with little effect; however the Prince having minutely examined their position, found it by nature so forfeited, that he considered it impregnable in front, but being determined to attack them, changed his own position with a view of getting to their rear, which by forced marches he accomplished, but a dreadful deluge of rain, had so retarded their march that the artillery were delayed at least twelve hours later than expectation, a circumstance which prevented them from immediately attacking the enemy, although they were observed to be in great confusion. And when at day break on the morning of the 4th they advanced upon Soubise's position at Unna they found he had struck his tents in the night and marched upon Werl. The Hereditary Prince immediately followed the enemy, and with his van drove their rear from hollow to hollow till they formed behind the Landwehr from Koer to Budrick. Soubise finding his rear so roughly handled returned and encamped between the Castle of Werl and the woods. The heads of the allied columns marched close up to them but finding them strongly posted and supported by the whole army, fell back and encamped at Hemmerde.'

'A circumstance was observed on entering the camp which the French had evacuated at Unna strongly expressive of French gasconade. A fine camp kitchen composed of turf &c was seen with a piece of paper secured to it containing compliments from Prince de Conde's cook to Lord Granby's, with a request to preserve the kitchen as his master would have occasion for it in a few days again. However it is probable he was a better cook than prophet, as his master returned no more that way.'

'On the 5th at five in the morning the allied army received positive orders for the attack of the enemy. This was the only time during the war that orders were issued to that effect; however, the attack did not take place, for although the army advanced in the finest condition till the heads of the columns were within cannon shot of the enemy and a few fired on each side; but were then halted, sentinels & videttes posted, the infantry allowed to pile their arms and the cavalry to dismount and link horses. Meanwhile the Prince assembled his generals to consult on the state of affairs and having received their counsel respecting the strong position held by the enemy; relinquished the attack & the army again fell back to the ground they had left and on the 7th in the morning marched to the camp at Hilbeck.'

'At an early hour on the morning of the 15th Broglio marched from Ervitte and succeeded in getting so near, without discovery as to enable him to drive in the outposts of the allied army, which he followed up and briskly cannonaded their camp before a man was under arms.'

'No sooner were the allies thus alarmed, then the infantry flew to their arms, and after forming as well as time would allow (some accoutred, some partly so and some displaying their courage in their shirts) inclined to the left to align with the highlanders who had occupied a small landwehr[46] and were already engaged with the enemy in the wood.'

---

46. His use of 'landwehr' is unusual – the term normally referring to a militia unit trained for home defence. Here he seems to indicate the line of a river or other defensive positions.

'The cavalry were immediately posted at certain extremities of the wood with orders to charge any of the enemy who might attempt to turn the line of infantry, as also to observe the motions of the enemy on the plain towards the Lippe and about seven o'clock Prince Anhalt[47] with a corps of Hessians entered the wood on the right of the British infantry and with three loud cheers opened a tremendous fire, rushed on and drove the enemy back. Meanwhile General Wutgenau with a considerable corps turned the enemy's right in conjunction with the other troops, forced them into the woods and kept his ground and this may be said to have been the last effort of the day, for as night approached the action died away and dwindled into popping shots which continued here & there during the remainder of the night.'

'During the night Prince Ferdinand greatly reinforced the left and as the armies were only separated by the hedges of some enclosures and a small landwehr, all were anxious to begin the task which awaited them next morning.'

'Accordingly at daybreak Broglio began his attacks on the posts occupied by the allies, extending from the heights of Dunckern, by Fellinghausen to the Lippe; but such were the difficulties of the ground and gallant conduct of the allied army that his repeated attacks made no impression. The heights where the army was formerly encamped, were now occupied by a numerous artillery under the Count La Lippe Buckeburg,[48] who kept up a destructive fire on their columns. The count could not see through the thicket, but was directed in laying his guns, by Lieutenant Alexander Stuart (afterwards general)[49] of Maxwell's grenadiers.'

'This brave officer ascended a huge oak, from which he had a full view of the French army and this with other batteries were so well directed by his signals from the oak, that they literally destroyed a whole column advancing from Lancerod. This strong column of the enemy intended to have deployed, but was so completely checked and thrown into confusion that they could advance no farther. The sight of the spot on which they stood (and to which the allies afterwards advanced) shocked every beholder, so great was the carnage & destruction, guns, carriages, horses and men, dashed together in promiscuous heaps so that it was impossible to distinguish them.'

---

47. Prince Moritz of Anhalt-Dessau (1712–60).
48. Count Frederick La Lippe Buckeburg.
49. General Alexander Stewart (1739–94).

'This check to a column intended to support his principle attack and the resistance Broglio had met with at other points rendered his efforts very languid; this Prince Ferdinand perceived and learning that Sporcken had crossed the Lippe at Hus Haven and was on his flank with six battalions and six squadrons of horse, ordered (about ten o'clock) the whole to advance upon the enemy.'

'This movement was decisive, for when the infantry and cannon of the allied army commenced to fire with double vigour, the enemy's retreat (which was already begun) became a complete & irregular flight. A considerable body were however surrounded and surrendered to the amount of four battalions of the Regiment de Rouge and besides many other prisoners, nine sixteen pounders of artillery with a number of smaller guns and several stands of colours fell into the hands of the victors.'

'Soubise (at the time this action commenced) had also made an attack on the right of the allied army, but could never get across the Saltzbach, nor enter Scheidengen, being there so baffled by some picquets in an old redoubt and at the same time learning of his colleague's defeat, retreated to Soest.'

'The French were pursued to Heintrey, but the country being impracticable to cavalry, the troops were recalled, the tents ordered from Hamm and the army encamped precisely as they were on the 15th and thus terminated an action which (when the immense superiority of the enemy's numbers are considered) was most glorious to Prince Ferdinand and the allied army. The skill of the prince in the choice and defence of this position appeared more evident when it was known to extend seven miles from right to left and the communications so well established to render the approach of the enemy so difficult as one corps not to be able to assist another or act in conjunction. Their efforts were thereby reduced to partial attacks of points which were so well defended that they made no impression.'

'The forces under Broglio & Soubise were now joined together, they crossed the river and came out in the low countries near Wessel where they had begun the campaign. Here they continued till reinforcements from France again enabled them to take the field and Broglio being thus strengthened marched back on Paderborn, so transferring the seat of active war to a new part of the country. The allies immediately advanced to Borgelen, Givette, Storenede and Wangenheim [and] encamped. Broglio next intending to attack Hamilton had posted different corps behind the Dymel; at Stadtberg and the hills and woods of Paderborn and getting his artillery ready at Cassel.'

'Prince Ferdinand to render the scheme abortive, marched on the 10th August by his left to Delbruck, Stuckenbrock, Detmold and on the 13th to the strong position at Blomberg which protected Hamilton and obliged Broglio to relinquish his design and cross the Wesser into Hanover. But his rear was closely pressed and cannonaded by Captain Duncan Drummond, by which the enemy sustained a considerable loss. The Hereditary Prince also rapidly advanced to Bergen and greatly contributed to the annoyance of Broglio's army by many spirited attacks on his rear.'

'The enemy were much extended to secure a communication with the upper Rhine, but Prince Ferdinand kept them in continual alarm by holding a central position near the Dymel, ready to move on my part of the enemy. This gave rise to an almost continual scene of skirmishing and Broglio having at last collected some scanty supplies, made an effort against the Electorate of Hanover, but was repulsed with great loss.'

'It was however, discovered that Broglio was strongly fortifying Einbeck to make it a point of appuye to invade Hanover the ensuing year. Prince Ferdinand therefore resolved to march against them to prevent their assembling and to relieve Einbeck. Accordingly he ordered General Luckner joined by the garrison of Brunswick, to march on the 3rd & 4th November and to be opposite Stainville on the 5th, to keep him in check and follow his march. The Hereditary Prince's corps to cross the River Leine at Coldingen and to proceed so as to get possession of Einbeck on the same day. Lord Granby[50] to march by Coppenbrugge and Dusen and to force the enemy's post at Kappelenhagen and on the 5th to be at Wickensen to block the defile which leads from Eschershausen to Einbeck. He accordingly after a smart action, forced the post above mentioned and arrived at Wickensen at daybreak in the morning of the 5th. However, the French burned their camp & effected a retreat by marching due south through the pass at Stadtoldendorp, the only way left them and which without an accident, they would also have found blocked and their retreat entirely cut off. But General Hardenberg who was ordered to have passed the Weser on the 4th and to have been early on the 5th at Ametunsborne on the road to Eschershausen was prevented by the pontoons overturning in a hollow way, which delayed

---

50. Lieutenant General John Manners, Marquess of Granby (1721–70). He became commander of British forces in Germany after the resignation of Lord George Sackville.

him from reaching Bodenwerder till seven o'clock on the morning of that day.'

'The enemy having thus escaped and joined another strong body at Have, prevented the Hereditary Prince from getting possession of Einbeck and after one assault he found it so strongly occupied, that he desisted from close attacks, but kept up a brisk cannonade till night.'

'Next day, the 6th, there was much skirmishing on all hands. The Hereditary Prince marched to Junnenson and Lord Granby to Forwhole, Broglio followed the prince but did not attack.'

'The 7th was a dreadful night of snow, in which between five and six hundred men were lost during the march and those who had strength to support them through the storm, so exhausted that they were unable to proceed. However, the ground was no sooner taken on which they were to encamp and the men began to exert their little remaining strength in pitching their tents &c, then Count Broglio attacked and drove in the rear guard. It was often remarked among the army, that at this crisis a dread of a reverse began to prevail throughout all ranks; as officers, men & horses were nearly worn out, no meat, no forage, nowhere dry to set a foot and the men sulky almost to mutiny. However, the moment some guns were fired in front and the cry of 'turn out' was heard. Everything was altered and every man was under arms in a very short time. They formed, advanced and routed Broglio in an instant, he was driven to the Huve and Prince Ferdinand finding it unattackable in front, marched on the 9th at three o'clock in the morning to the heights between Mackenson & Lithorst and when the allies began to move their left was again attacked by the enemy, who was routed as before, but with greater loss.'

'Broglio now found that the allies had turned his flank and were getting in his rear; had his choice to fight or run; he chose the latter and after blowing up the gates of Einbeck retreated to Gottingen &c where he went into winter quarters.'

'The allies were immediately cantoned in the neighbouring villages, but marched soon after and went into winter quarters at Holtershausen within twelve miles of Osnabruck. This was about the middle of December and so ended this campaign which terminated with glory to the allied army and particularly to Prince Ferdinand whose superior abilities had rendered all the plans of the enemy abortive although they took the field with a superiority of 50,000 men.'

'We lay in our winter quarters from this period till the beginning of May without either of the armies disturbing each other, but the French then collecting an army of 100,000 men in Hesse and about 30,000 on the lower Rhine; the first under the command of Marshal d'Estrees[51] & Soubise. This the allies considered a good exchange as Broglio, notwithstanding reverses in the last campaign, was an excellent general and had the first year he commanded forced the allies to change their ground above fifty times. The Prince de Conde commanded on the lower Rhine.'

'About the middle of May the allied troops were drawn closer together and on the 4th [of] June the infantry and artillery encamped at Blomberg; the cavalry cantoned in the neighbourhood till the 17th when they joined the infantry and encamped.'

'On the 8th July Lord Granby's reserve advanced to Brackel and was followed by the Grand Army of 46 battalions and 48 squadrons who occupied Brackel, Lord Granby moving to Pecklesheim & the light troops occupied the passes of the Dymel. However, information was received that the enemy were assembled near Cassel and on the 22nd their army under d'Estrees and Soubise encamped at Grebenstein in front of Wilhelmsthal, about half way between Cassel and the Dymel. This position was in a plain, but with gentle risings and woods intervening. On their right ran the Weser skirted by the woods of Sababourg and on their left a chain of wooded hills.'

'Prince Ferdinand having resolved to attack them, began to take measures to prevent their escape from this, their own choice of ground. Luckner who was near Einbeck was consequently ordered to march with six battalions of grenadiers, four squadrons of horse and his own hussars. On the evening of the 23rd he passed the Weser at Bodenfeldt and was ordered to proceed on the 24th at daybreak to Marienberg and to form between that and Udenhausen.'

'Sporcken passed the Dymel at Sielen about four o'clock in the morning, with 12 battalions and part of the cavalry and marched on Monbrexen and Udenhausen with orders immediately to attack d'Estree's corps at Carlsdorff in flank, while Luckner charged their rear.'

'Prince Ferdinand crossed the Dymel at different places at three o'clock with 12 battalions English, 11 battalions Brunswickers & 8 battalions Hessians; with the English and part of the German cavalry; the picquets formed the vanguard on the left and the chasseurs and Scheiter's Corps that of the right under Lord Frederick Cavendish who was to seize upon the Longenborg.'

---

51. Marshal Louis Charles d'Estrées (1695–1771).

'The Greys, Inniskillings and Mordaunt's Dragoons[52] were ordered up as expeditiously as possible to occupy the heights which formed the valley of the Dymel. These they soon gained and had an extensive view of the plain towards Cassel with the whole of the French camp, which was perfectly quiet. They discovered a small corps to their right rear which they imagined to be that of Debastrie's who might have quitted their tents to save their troops; however it afterwards proved to be Luckner's who also perceived Sporcken's large body debouch from the woods on the enemy's right front and the picquets still more in their front.'

'A great bustle was instantly perceived in the enemy's camp. They struck their tents and the troops moved off towards their left rear, leaving a considerable body of cavalry formed to give a little time for their infantry and baggage. However, they were furiously charged and routed by Luckner's, who defeated Fitzjames's Horse,[53] made three hundred prisoners and captured their standards.'

'A column of Hanoverian artillery, covered by the British cavalry, gained the heights and opened a tremendous fire upon the woods to the enemy's left, which they were obliged to file through. Count Stainville[54] finding that the grand army of the allies has arrived, saw that if he did not make a grand effort to stop their rapid progress, the French might be cut off from Cassel; he therefore occupied the woods with the Grenadeers de France, Grenadeers Royaux, Regiment de Aquitaine[55] and some others of their best infantry. Lord Granby, who was destined to act against the enemy's left; attacked these troops most vigorously and after a determined resistance the enemy found that the grand allied army was already up and a retreat impossible, being so surrounded. Some of their cavalry indeed debouched from the wood and endeavoured to escape; but were charged and driven back by the Oxford Blues and Royal Dragoons.'

'The whole of the troops which occupied the wood were compelled to surrender. They were accordingly brought out prisoners, while the light troops continued the chase of the enemy till they reached their entrenched camp at Cassel and captured a great number of prisoners, cannon and baggage wagons.'

---

52. 12th Light Dragoons.
53. FitzJames' Horse was a regiment in the French Irish Brigade.
54. Lieutenant General Jacques Phillipe de Choiseul-Stainville was command-ing inspector of the French Grenadier Regiment.
55. Formed in 1756 as the 19th Regiment.

'Thus, the great achievement ended, in the defeat of the two French Marshals who were never dreaming of any danger. They sustained a loss of 6,000 men killed, besides a great number of prisoners, cannon, baggage, colours and standards which were captured during the action. The loss of the allies were upwards of 3,000 men and the army encamped on the field of battle behind Wilhelmsthal all night.'

'In this action I considered myself extremely fortunate, for our regiment was almost cut to pieces by a body of the enemy's cavalry who unexpectedly attacked us in the wood, however, I got off with the loss of my right ear, which (no doubt) had been sliced away by some of the French dragoons during the bustle of the charge and although I knew by the blood trickling down, that I had received a wound of some kind I was not aware that I was an ear deficient till the battle was over.'

'On the 25th the French crossed the Fulda at Cassel and encamped. The Saxons were on their right near Munden and Rochambeau[56] on their left at Homberg with posts on the Werra, Fulda &c to cover their communications with the Mayne.'

'Prince Ferdinand extended to his right and Lord Frederick Cavendish,[57] on the 26th marched to Fritzlar which was taken and Gudensburg also surrendered on the 29th.'

'On the 1st of August, Lord Granby and Lord Frederick Cavendish marched to attack Rochambeau, who had retired for fear of Luckner, who was advancing to surprise him. General Conway had also taken the Castle of Waldeck and about the 12th the enemy began to take alarm for their communications with the Mayne.'

'On the 15th a large corps of the enemy crossed the Fulda and took post on the Heiligenberg and woods of Meloungen, which movement had drawn them considerably to their left. However, General Zastrow[58] (notwithstanding difficulties) crossed the Fulda and at Lutterenberg, attacked the Saxons in front, while they were assailed in the rear by a corps from Uslar and defeated with a loss of 1200 men and 13 pieces of cannon.'

'On the 24th and 25th the enemy's main army marched to its right, but the French marshals fearing being turned quitted their strong post

---

56. Marshal Jean-Baptiste Donatien de Vimeur, Comte de Rochambeau (1725–1807).
57. Major General Lord Frederick Cavendish (1729–1803) commanded a cavalry brigade in 1761.
58. Lieutenant General Christian von Zastrow (1705–73).

on the Heiligenberg and his light troops took Fulda. The French generals finding their affairs in such a bad plight, called in the aid of the Prince de Conde, who marched from Heltern on the 17th July and reached Grunberg on the 7th August. The Hereditary Prince accompanied the armies of the of the lower Rhine, like their shadow and marched on the other side of the mountains by Weller, Kirkhayne and on the 7th arrived at Homberg on the Ohme, not far from Conde's corps.'

'Prince Ferdinand wishing to profit from the success of the late battles, prepared for a general attack; this took place on the 9th on several points, especially on the enemy's left which was vigorously assailed and turned by Wangenheim, who was detached from Lord Granby, but some troops who got in the enemy's rear, forced their position to be so very strong, that it appeared necessary to exercise great caution in approaching it. The allied army was therefore newly arranged and Luckner joined the Hereditary Prince at Alfeldt.'

'The French marshals now began to retreat in good earnest. On the 13th the Saxons retired, two days after the garrison quitted Gottenberg and Munden and on the 17th leaving a great garrison at Cassel, their whole army marched to the left upon Bergen &c.'

'On the 28th the allies leaving a strong corps to observe Cassel, marched by Homberg, Schwarzenborn, Grebenau, Maar, Ulrichstein, Schotten and Nidda, where they arrived on the 29th and was sufficiently near on the 30th to prevent any evil consequences from an untoward event about to be related. The Hereditary Prince being reinforced, advanced on the 21st to the heights of Homberg, dispersed Levies Corps, took his camp and above 500 prisoners and on the 28th marched towards Grunberg, to attack Conde, who retired to Gruningen and was followed there by the prince, from thence to Waldersheim near Friedberg, beyond which Conde had joined the marshals. The allies at this time understood that the French Grand army was at Bergen (which unluckily was not the case). However, on the 30th the Hereditary Prince ordered Luckner to occupy the heights of Johannesberg which is a strong position, while he was marching on Assenheim, a village to the south east of Friedberg, but being informed that Conde had attacked Luckner, he immediately marched to support him; the prince arrived, but in place of finding Conde's corps only, he found himself opposed to the French marshals and their whole Grand Army. The event was as might be expected; the prince's troops defeated, with a loss of 2,000 men and obliged to retire on Wolfersheim with their gallant leader (the Hereditary Prince) severely wounded.'

'The Grand Army of the allies was within sight at the close of the action, they were immediately drawn up along the skirts of an immense wood, the infantry ordered to ground their arms and lie down; the cavalry to link close to the forest and in this situation, they expected to wait, unobserved by the enemy, until they had followed up the prince's corps, within reach of their ambuscade. But the French generals contented with the advantage they had gained, advanced no further.'

'On the 31st Prince Ferdinand marched the allied army to Bingen-heim and Staden in the face of the enemy and even advanced considerably to the left towards Bergen, but the French generals were not disposed to be bullied and so began to extend to their left towards Geissen.'

'On the 7th and 8th September, Prince Ferdinand marched towards the strong position of the Ohne, intending to pass it next day, but from the excessive rains & bad road, his artillery and rear did not arrive till the 11th when the army was posted as follows.'

'General Luckner at Longenstein; the main army at Schweinsberg and Hardenberg. The Hereditary Prince's Corps occupied the heights of Homberg, Lord Granby's reserve, those of Maulbach and General Bock with the troops that formed the rear guard, were on the left of the whole and on the heights of Burgemunden. But in consequence of the enemy moving towards Wetter, the allies again marched on the 13th to Kirchheim and next day to Schwartzenborn. Luckner and Conway were pushed on to Einhausen to cut off their communication with Frankenberg by which they meant to force a passage and relieve Cassel. Lord Granby's reserve joined them and part of Hardenberg's and Bocks, with the light troops of the left occupied the heights of Homberg.'

'The enemy's main army was now between Neiderwetter and Marburg; Conde's corps on the heights of Gros near Wetter and Levie's light troops occupied Wetter and the heights behind it. Prince Ferdinand being determined to oppose any progress from Wetter, ordered Luckner and Conway to march by Amonau and Schwartzenbeck, while the main army occupied the heights of Ober & Neider Rosa where they were formed in order of battle; however the enemy moved to their right which gave reason to suppose that they meant to force the passage of the Ohme, but it afterwards proved that their determination was to take Amoneberg which place the allies occupied with Kruse's Battalion of the British Legion and 200 volunteers.'

'Accordingly on the night between the 20th and 21st September, they attacked it three times but without success. The darkness of the night was observed by both armies to be excessive and the fire of the cannon and musquetry of the assailants and defenders displayed an awfully brilliant firework round the hill.'

'The morning of the 21st being a very thick fog, gave rise to a mistake which occasioned one of the most bloody conflicts of the whole war. A small rivulet divided the heights on which the hostile armies were posted. On the French side, at the end of a narrow bridge stood a mill, which gave the name of Bruckner Muhl to the place and on the side of the allies a small redoubt occupied by 100 men. The French having posted some guns at the foot of the hill about 300 paces from the redoubt. Their intention was to prevent a communication with Amoneberg only; but the thick fog and the fire of their cannon gave the appearance of a design to cut or separate that corps of the allied army from the main body, for they had above 20 pieces of heavy cannon, against which the allies brought all the Hessian and half the Hanoverian artillery, the whole of which continued a most destructive fire from daybreak in the morning till dark at night. The redoubt was exposed to the enemy's guns at 300 paces and to their musquetry at 30. The men in the redoubt were constantly relieved after firing their sixty rounds and in the reliefs going & coming they were exposed 400 paces in a clear range of the enemy's cannon with grape shot. The mill yielded the enemy rather more shelter. The allies however maintained the redoubt and the French the mill in spite of the utmost efforts on each side.'

'The loss of the allies engaged on that spot was 638 men killed and that of the French rather greater. I received a musquet ball through the left shoulder while I was running with a relieved party to the rear, after having fired our sixty rounds in the redoubt. After I was wounded I was unable to continue my pace to the rear with my comrades and two of which, who were (by ties of former friendship) unwilling to leave me behind in this situation, laid hold to assist me along. However, the next shower of balls numbered my two friends with the dead that lay around us and again wounded me through the thigh. I fell to the ground and lay till nearly exhausted by the loss of blood and as the dusk of evening approached, another of my comrades who was passing and saw me endeavouring to crawl towards the allied position, got me on his back and lugged me along with him. My wounds were now examined and amputation of my right leg found necessary; so without further ceremony my good old servant was lopped off and this stump which you see, only left to keep me in remembrance of the event. However it might have been much worse, for I expected I should have lost my arm too; if not my life altogether and knowing that I merited greater punishment I bore all with as much fortitude as my weakness would allow me to call to my aid; but I suffered long under these wounds.'

'The enemy next morning took Lunenburg and both armies began to fortify their respective positions and while war was thus carried on so furiously on the left, things seemed to have a different and more civil aspect on the right. A butcher from one of the French regiments came over to Conway's Corps with 100 sheep, Conway retained the man as a deserter, but sent back the sheep under an escort, with a card to the Prince de Conde, who returned a polite answer with a present of wine and an intimation that some French wine merchants (if permitted) should supply the British officers with some of that article which he heard was scarce in their camp, at the same rate as they sold it in his own; the offer was accepted and they brought a quantity of good wine, some Paris snuff, wax candles &c &c at a very reasonable rate. On the 16th October Prince Frederick being reinforced with 26 battalions and 10 squadrons, commenced the siege of Cassel and on the 1st November forced it to surrender. In this interval of waiting the event of the siege, Conway's Corps being far from forage were withdrawn, leaving only strong posts on the heights above Wetter. This was observed by Conde who thought if he could occupy these heights by a sudden eruption he might have a chance of doing something important by turning the right of the British and opening a communication with Cassel, his army was accordingly ordered to be in readiness to march and only waited the return of an aide de camp & engineers who were sent in the night to reconnoitre and to return and conduct their columns. However, the allied army had received information of the design and was under arms at midnight, with orders to light no fires, nor to smoke or make any noise and these people who were sent from the enemy to reconnoitre were not a little surprised to find themselves nabbed by Conway's Corps who were on the ground previous to their arrival. The French after waiting in vain for their return found at daybreak their attempt frustrated. So correct and speedy was the intelligence of Prince Ferdinand, that the orders concerning this matter were delivered to the allied army, before it was generally known to the French themselves.'

'This was the last military event of the war, for on the 7th November at gun firing in the evening, the allies heard a prodigious shouting among the whole of the French army, which they conjectured to be a rejoicing for some success in another quarter, but the advanced posts learnt next day that it was for peace. However, Prince Ferdinand had received no orders to that effect and commanded the siege of Zeigenhein to begin; doubled many posts and ordered that no communication should be had with the enemy's outposts, but on the 14th a courier from England arrived and the cessation was signed at Bruckner Muhl.'

'Next day many of the French came over to the camp of the allies to make merry, buy horses &c &c but as neither parties were overburthened [*sic*] with cash, their bartering chiefly terminated in swapping horses, watches, snuff boxes, pistols &c &c.'

'On the 16th the French marched to their winter quarters after giving their camp and its contents of forage &c to the neighbouring inhabitants and thus ended the war, glorious to Prince Ferdinand and his army, who had made head for six campaigns against a superiority of seldom less than two to one, but their confidence in his superior abilities and his in their strenuous exertions & bravery in the field surmounted every difficulty.'

'On the 19th November 1762, the allied army separated with esteem and good wishes for each other, the British marched to cantonments on the frontiers of Holland, through which they passed in February, following on their way to England.'

'I was (with many more wounded men) left in a hospital at Cassel, where I remained till the 17th April 1763, and being then sufficiently recovered of my wounds, I was presented with a new timber leg to supply the deficiency of the old one I had left at Bruckner Muhl; this wooden supporter I fitted on, the first morning in May and took my march for England in company with nearly 50 maimed veterans, amongst whom there were only nine who had not left behind them a leg, an arm, an eye or some other member. The old officer who commanded us was, like myself, divested of one of his main pillars and having, besides been severely wounded in the face, wore a large black patch on one of his thin cheeks, which completely finished the once dashing Lieutenant O.N. for the command which now devolved upon him & a more grotesque company has seldom been seen than the above appeared when we took our departure from Cassel. However, with the old lieutenant at the head of his motley corps, whose garments were now become a patchwork of many colours and with one solitary wooden legged drummer Row Dowing in front, off we limped towards the frontiers of Holland.'

'Our march was continued by short and easy stages till we arrived at Nijmegen from whence we continued our route by Graves, Bois le

Duc &c and reached the neighbourhood of Breda about the end of June. Here we rested a few days and proceeded to Klundert near Willemstad, where we embarked on board a ship which was about to sail for the Thames and after a fine passage of five days landed in London. Here we soon after passed a board of generals and I was awarded a handsome pension of one shilling per day as a reward for my services and the loss of my fingers, ear & leg. I received my discharge and independent of all danger determined to visit the south and learn the fate of my parents. Accordingly, after receiving some prize money which was due to me, I set off. My countenance was much changed, my cheek bones high, a limb deficient and what was now left of what I once was, lapped up in old tattered regimentals and limping along without the least dread of being discovered by the most intimate acquaintance. I arrived thus incog! In the neighbourhood of my father's former residence and soon learned among the neighbouring peasantry that my parents were long dead, that my brother (whose life, I was happy to hear, had at the time of my departure, been saved by some chance or other) had sold all our family's possessions and as the report ran, gone abroad in search of a younger brother, who had gone off with his wife and has never been heard of since.'

'The father and mother of Eliza were also dead; and finding all gone, I turned my back on the spot which my own misconduct had marked with desolation and wandered from place to place till I fell in with a strong corps of gypsies, whose manner of living and lodging seemed so nearly to correspond with the kind of life I had spent in my late campaigns & their society seeming so suitable to me I without hesitation enlisted in their social squadron, soon married one of the old general's daughters, who has since blessed me with plenty of young brunettes and in the space of two years by the death of our old leader, the command devolved upon myself and from that period I have been their conductor and have enforced among them such order and discipline as will bear me through and accompany my name down to posterity without another blot.'

Here Wentworth finished this interesting history and the night being far spent, we returned to the tent and found the merry corps as jovial as plenty and contentment could make them. I again joined in their happy ring and we continued the merry dance upon the green sward till the face of bright Phoebus appeared above the eastern horizon and warned us that the hours we had dedicated to Vitula (or the [Roman] goddess of mirth) were expired.

We therefore prepared for our departure and with promises to visit them again, we set off accompanied by two of the fairest of their fair sex, one of whom my comrade Sandy had grown particularly intimate with, during the time I had been hearing Wentworth's narrative we parted with our female friends for this time, but often after (during their stay in this neighbourhood and when leisure hours were on hand) we visited them at their camp.

Chapter 9

Garrisons in the North

Nothing worthy of notice occurred during the remainder of this season and in the following spring the regiment marched to York and occupied the barracks there, detaching one troop to Beverley.[1]

The troop which was sent to the above-named station was that to which I belonged and after our arrival at our destination, I (with my faithful comrade Sandy B[orland]) was ordered to Hull for the purpose of acting as orderlies to General Cockburn who commanded that garrison.[2] We found the general at the Head Inn, in which house we were in compliance with his orders also put up.

In the event of changing our quarters, in those days, it used to be no bad movement to make as speedy an inroad upon the favour of the female servants as possible. My comrade therefore (who being oldest soldier and consequently claimed the presidency) lost no time in making his arrangements for the forwarding of this important object and observing that as our success would greatly depend on our appearance, it was in the first place, necessary that we should make ourselves as smart as possible. Our boots were accordingly made as black as sloes! The sheen of our spurs attracted all eyes as we paced the courtyard of the Neptune Inn.[3] All other parts of our dress were

---

1. The Scots Greys marched into Yorkshire in the spring of 1806. William fails to mention it, but in January 1806, two squadrons of Scots Greys went to London and took part in the funeral procession for Admiral Lord Nelson. As William does not mention it at all, it is almost certain that he was not one of those who went to this momentous occasion.
2. Major General George Cockburn (1763–1847).
3. The Neptune Inn stood at 49 Neptune Street until demolished in 1985.

made as clean as hands could make them and put on so as to improve (as much as possible) the proportions of the gay figures they decorated. Thus, with our hair well powdered, whiskers well frizzed, cap set tastefully over the right ear and the snow-white plume with which it was surmounted, nodding true time as the feet were alternately placed upon the causeway, we advanced to the attack.

Operations being now about to commence, my comrade (who was a cunning comrade) informed me that he had resolved to pay his addresses to one of the chambermaids, who was a pretty little girl, but fearing our larder might fall short of supplies, in the event of both making our advances on beauty alone, strenuously advised me to make a vigorous attack upon the kitchen, to which I agreed and accordingly directed my attention to the scullery maid, who was the only object in that department for my choice; the cook being an old woman and consequently against such attacks.

The young woman which my crafty companion had selected for me (although he described her as a very bonny and agreeable lass) was prodigiously clumsy. Her face although not extremely disagreeable, possessed no attracting feature. Her cheek bones were high, her nose flat and her eyes squinted furiously to either flanks; her shoulders were broad and as square as those of a grenadier while the glance of the sun beams from her large red elbows was almost too powerful for the naked eye!! However, the work was set a going and this Dulcinia was kept in play as a barrier against any scarcity during the approaching summer, which we spent very agreeably and experienced no little regret when ordered to join our troop at Beverley. However, the fatal order was received about the end of September and we were removed from this comfortable station and continued at the headquarters of our troop for the space of the two following months, after which I again proceeded on detachments stationed at Patrington, Hedon[4] &c where I remained till the regiment received orders to commence its march into Scotland. This took place on the 6th January 1807[5] and being in the depth of winter we had a very unpleasant march to Edinburgh Barracks, which the regiment occupied on its arrival there.

I rejoiced in again visiting my native country and as good luck would have it, soon after our arrival my exultation was still more heightened

---

4. Both villages lay to the east of Hull, near to the coast.
5. This is confirmed by the Regimental History.

by being promoted to the rank of corporal.[6] This was for more than one reason a matter of great interest to me; for having thus gained the first step toward preferment, I was at once armed with courage, boldly to face my relatives; while it also pointed out to them that my conduct had been such as to be worthy of the notice of my officers and I had no sooner got the badge (of two silver stripes) on my right arm than I set off in high spirits to visit them.

I proceeded to Lanrick Castle[7] near Doune and there added another fortnight to the years of happiness I had spent under the peaceful roof of my parents, returned to my regiment much satisfied with the pleasure I had enjoyed and made my time more pleasing during the year, by consigning, at intervals, a few days to their social society or that of some more distant relations; or after our field days which were usually on the exercising sands at Portobello[8] repairing with my faithful crony Sandy B[orland] &c on a pleasure party through the magnificent streets of Edinburgh, to the top of the Calton Hill, from whence to feast our eyes on the unequalled architecture of modern Athens, the ancient Palace of Holyrood &c and at other times we were drawn by their wonders to the wild summit of Salisbury Crags or the towering crest of King Arthur's seat; from which station among the clouds, our eyes were again exercised by a ramble over the dark expanse of the German Ocean[9] & circling to the left, over the blue turrets of the Ochil, Grampian and Cheviot Hills, returned to a place of rest on the fruitful plains of the far famed Lothians to muse on the magnificence of nature's works and the beauty of the happy land which surrounded us.

The regiment (which had not been in Scotland for upwards of 30 years previous to that period[10]) was in such esteem among the inhabitants, that a degree of favour was lavished upon them by all ranks and Piershill Barracks[11] seemed to be a spot which attracted a mass of visitors from all parts of the Scottish nation. Here friend met

---

6. It was whilst at Edinburgh that William became a corporal, but his record shows that this occurred in 1808 near the end of their term here.
7. Near Stirling.
8. Now a suburb of Edinburgh.
9. The North Sea.
10. This is an error, the regiment had last been in Scotland in 1791, so had actually been absent for sixteen years.
11. Piershill Barracks were built in 1793 for the cavalry. They were demolished in 1938.

friend daily and many who had never seen each other before saluted with heartfelt warmth, although in some of their countenances could be read a degree of uncertainty whether or not the parties were the identical blood relatives, each expected to meet till some far sought sign, which was only understood by their own clan, was given to remove all doubt, at which period of the interrogatory conference, a new meeting generally took place. Their faces assumed a more lively covering; a more vigorous squeeze of the hands followed. A gill & a bottle o'yill [ale] came after that and the tail of the evening brought up by the care drowning shouts of 'Should auld acquaintance be forgot.'

There were scarcely any merry making at which the presence of a group of our jovial fellows was not considered necessary to enliven the scene & as the war with France was going on with great spirit, they had an unbounded liberty of mixing with their countrymen, for the purpose of getting as many recruits as possible while the regiment remained in the country and for this purpose the commanding officer also frequently sent mounted parties to parade the streets of Edinburgh or the neighbouring villages when any particular holiday or amusement had congregated the inhabitants to a greater than usual number.

An occurrence of this kind which took place at Dalkeith about the middle of August, although of no particular moment, is not unworthy of notice. As a good deal of sport was anticipated from a carter's race in that part of the country; a party consisting of two sergeants, two corporals, two privates and the whole of the band were selected to attend it. We mounted on the morning of the day on which this amusing spectacle was to take place and our gay train proceeded towards Dalkeith where we arrived amid the congratulatory shouts of auld & young. The streets were crowded to excess as we paraded through them with our splendid musicians playing the most favourite national airs and the attention of the whole congregated mass was soon drawn from the carters, as they exhibited themselves in their braid blue bonnets, headed by a kind of patchwork band, to our dashing cavalcade and its martial music, which carried such magic in every bang, as to place many an auld wifie at the sunny end o'her biggen [pregnancy] and bring to light many a flannel toy, which had to all probability been in darkness for years before. The joy increased as the day advanced & the holy water was never more profusely thrown about the aisles of Rome's St Peters than was the streets of Dalkeith watered with the native mountain dew as the hour approached at which the great fate of winning a saddle was about to be achieved by some one of fortune's sons among the blue bonnet tribe.

It had been announced that the race was to take place about one o'clock in the day and when that hour arrived, a crowd rushing towards the starting post served as a signal that the fun was about to begin. We followed the waving multitude till we arrived at the spot where the uncouth squad of competitors were assembled and rolled awkwardly about on their heavy heeled coursers till a saddle and bridle was reared on the top of a long poll as a trophy of emulation and revelry. The carters were all dressed in large flat bonnets (or the scone of Scotland[12]) decorated with ribbons of various colours, some booted and others to gratify an admiring concourse of spectators displayed a well turned calf in a guid greymash [stocking], or blue stocking of home manufacture, each furnished with a whip of immense longitude which he flourished and cracked round his head as a token of his independence and disregard to all his rivals; and when all was in readiness, the horses were placed in a row across the road and only waited the signal to start when a half exhausted voice was heard bellowing at a considerable distance 'Bide awee, bide awee, Jamie Carnes is coming! Bide awe for Jamie Carnes! gin ye dinna bide for Jamie, I wudna gie a bodle[13] for ye'r race.' Wait a while, wait a while Jamie Carnes is coming, wait a while for Jamie Carnes, if you don't wait for Jamie, I wouldn't give a bodle for your race.'

The cry which was immediately taken up by the crowd, flew from mouth to mouth and the disorder which followed compelled the racers to postpone their start till the throng opened and a little old man forced his way into the ring. The grey mare on which he was mounted, appeared to be well stricken in years, by the deep cavities which time had formed over her eyes, her hanging under lip, clothed in a whisking beard of snow white bristles. The naked stump from which her Lillie [beautiful] tail flowed when she was a fillie & her weather-beaten bones which had now ceased to carry a load of superfluous flesh. The rider in spurring her up to the middle of the jostling troop, cast around him a look of genuine sagacity; he took his place with an air of great consequence and the again prepared to start. I could not help fixing my eyes on this droll figure, for he was truly an oddity. His habiliments of the oldest fashion, his mighty bonnet set so judiciously ajee [to one side] over his little red eyes, his long necked spurs flashed the reflected glance of the sunbeams

---

12. The scone cap was a large flat cap, also known as a 'bunnet.'
13. A bodle was a Scottish coin worth one sixth of a penny.

into all eyes as he applied them with his cutty [stumpy] legs to the ribs of his auld mare, yet a degree of respect seemed to prevail throughout the motley gathering for him; and the wise wives frequently exclaimed 'Weil doon Jamie Carnes, Weil doon Jamie, we needna be wondering who'll take hame the prize noo! Huzza for Jamie! Jamie Carnes for ever Huzza,' and so continued till they were marshalled and completely ready for a fresh start.

The road on which the race was to take place, led out at one end of the town and by taking a circuit came in at the other; however all the roads were covered with dust, the weather having been extremely dry for some weeks before and consequently the following cavalcade might have anticipated a glorious smothering; but every mind seemed to be filled with anxiety for the success of some individual among those who were to contend for the prize and left no room for such trivial matters.

All was now ready and Jamie Carnes who had the prayers of a great majority of the spectators on his side; flang a smile of confidence over his shouther [shoulder] among them as the town's drummer gave them the starting *Row de Dow* with his crazie drum (which to all probability had been in the prime of life about the time of Marlborough's wars). The signal was no sooner given, then, off gaed they, & monie a skreigh gaed [off they went & many a horse went] after them for the better observation of Jamie Carnes. The spectators burst from all quarters wi' a 'God gang wi' [God go with] Jamie Carnes, for a yellow Geordie [a gold guinea coin]', 'he'll win, gin the muckle bruits disna ding him ower! Whaur is he noo, poor bodie? The Lord guide us, I've tint him althegether among the stour! Preserve us, sicken a stoor, the vera sun's gaun dark among't' [he'll win if the great brutes don't knock him over! Where is he now poor man? The Lord guide us, I've lost him altogether among the struggle! Preserve us from such a struggle, the very sun's gone dark amongst them'].

The racers were now heard in the distance hobbling along, but no one could tell who was the best man; for the clouds of dust that rolled from under the broad feet of their heavy steeds, had totally enveloped the face of the earth all round them & the train that followed them, for monie a braw lad, on their ain or faither's shalties [many a fine lad, on their own or father's Shetland pony] were at their heels.

Our party, who also followed in their train, were scudding along under tight reins and guarding against the danger of running foul of the heavy craft in front, who were by the thickness of the dust rendered invisible, but notwithstanding all precautions, disorder soon began to creep in among those who formed the van and frequently showed itself in the shape of some honest country farmer or laird o' a mailen [lord of the rents], scrambling among his cotters [cottagers] in the ditch or flying from the wrath to come by boring his head through the hedge which separated the dangerous road by which he was travelling from some peaceable field into which he longed to force his way.

Our horses seemed to have a great dislike to their station in the tail of the charge and so imperceptibly made ground towards the front, that in a few seconds the whole of the following cavalcade became tumbled with the racers and the confusion was completed by the upsetting of Jamie Carnes and several of his fellow travellers, who were (in a twinkling) run down and placed in the unpleasant situation of stumbling blocks for those who were yet behind and bewildered in the dust. Many tumbled over them in their hurry and many a black eye and bloody nose were begotten. Man and horse, auld and young, scrambled in a promiscuous heap together besmeared with sweat; blood and dust; blue bonnets flew in all directions; whips and cruppers[14] cracked and the wild cry of despair issued from the obscure recesses of the hedge covered ditch on either hand.

Hegh Sirs! What a scene of disorder was here; how profusely did the life streams of monie a braw fellow, trickle o'er his haffets and beard [the blood of many a fine fellow trickled over his cheeks and beard] and how quickly did the intelligence of the sodgers having killed them all find its way into the town again. All was done in a moment and so loudly resounded the threats of the angry populace against our party who were loaded with the blame of all the mischief that on our again entering the town, the whole moving mass of men, women, auld, young, little & muckle [many] were up in arms against us. Here we were in a pretty scrape! Ay in an unpardonable hobble [confusion], surrounded by thousands of inveterate enemies, powering the very essence of their reproaches out against us, as we struggled to effect a passage through them to The Sun[15] which we had chosen for our rendezvous during the day.

Our ears, as we thus pushed forward, were assailed with loud & threatening execrations from all quarters, on one hand buzzed in our ears 'O ye scounderalls!' on the other, 'My bairns murder't, my bairns

---

14. A strap buckled to the back of a saddle and looped under the horse's tail to prevent the saddle or harness from slipping forward.
15. The Sun Inn still stands a mile and a half outside Dalkeith on the A7. It is now a gastropub.

murder't!!' While a somebody's grammie, an auld wee wifie, wi' might & main [strength], craved the vengeance o' the powers aboon [above], to come doon on our devoted heads wi' a crack [strike] for our misdeeds and squalled aloud 'O the loons [rogues], what brought them here to massacre honest Jock? We want nane [none] o' their cursed red coats here! Lord I could see their vera een riven oot! I wonder what you men's made o' that, ye dinna plaister [didn't plaster] their harns athort [brains across] the causeway! O' gin [if] I were but a man mysell for their sakes.' Then raving like a maniac she continued 'Oh Sandy poor fellow, whaur are ye? He's lying dead on the highway nae doot, for Jolly's com'd [come] galloping hame without him! O my bairn! O Sandy muckled [much] in, hae they silenced ye for ever? Ay tweel [truly] hae they, who wud hae thought my poor Sandy was to come to sic [such] an end as this? Hegh Sirs, I thought that something was to befa' our toon [town] this day! Anybody might a kent [known] it! Ay might they! It wasna for naething that a' you corbies [ravens] cam croaking sae soon aboot the dukes yeth [ducks gate] this morning!'

And so on went their complaints & wailings while we with a deal of difficulty weathered the storm of wind and stones which opposed us on our way to the inn, which at length however, we reached with all our heads on.

We now saw the impossibility of pacifying the raging populace and considering it imprudent to provoke them by continuing to parade the streets, put our horses up and made ourselves merry within doors; where, after all the wounded were brought in and matters cleared up more favourable to us; we were joined by a number of the inhabitants and kept the house alive till a late hour. We then prepared for our return to Piershill, mounted our horses and set out, but had not proceeded far from Dalkeith when the fumes of the whisky kindled a dispute among our Germain [German] musicians and a scuffle ensued, in which many of their instruments suffered so severely, that some of them (upon inspection) were declared unfit for further military service and the time required to put others in a fit state for duty again; to all probability, outstripped that for mending the broken heads of the unfortunate carters who were the founders of all the disasters which happened.

Soon after this period, the troop to which I belonged was ordered to Hamilton.[16] Here we had a few months indulgence which bordered on

---

16. A small town near Motherwell.

illness; having no duty but that of looking after our horses to perform & consequently had time enough on hand to rove in pleasure where our inclinations led us, which was sometimes to the groves in the Duke's park, grounds and woods adjacent to the town,[17] or towards Blantyre cotton mills[18] situated about two miles from our barracks.[19] These mills abounded with bonnie lasses, which was a kind of commodity ever in requisition among us and very often had power enough to draw us into the road which led thither; it soon became the favourite route and begot many a fair acquaintance. It was a magazine of female beauty which was but a short time discovered when all who had any share of gallantry were supplied with sweethearts and the light hours of each revolving evening were hailed with joy; for they brought to each hero a term of delight which could be derived from no source but the society of his heart's companion.

This mode of amusement which was pleasing to both parties, grew so rapidly that in a short time our female friends seldom allowed an evening to pass without repairing to Lucky C. . .'s[20] change house in Hamilton, which had now become the place of meeting and the scene of many a care-scoffing ditty and merry dance, where toasts went round and hearts melted beneath the all-powerful blaze of love and whisky.

Night after night were thus spent in Lucky C. . .'s till the hour arrived when the sound of the bugle called us into barracks; but the obeying of this sound was in time, so reluctantly yielded to, that we seldom mustered all our forces within the walls at the appointed time. However, the merry corps always broke up at ½ past nine o'clock and those who were not inclined to ramble in pleasure all night and occupy the black hole in the morning, made the best of their way home and tumbled into bed ruminating on the state of their finances and the probable means of rising the wind for the following evening.

---

17. The grounds of Hamilton Palace were very extensive. The house was demolished in 1921 and the grounds formed the major part of the Strathclyde Country Park.
18. Blantyre Cotton Mills employed about 2,000 workers at this time. The buildings have been demolished.
19. The Cavalry Barracks were built in 1794 and later became the home of the Cameronians until demolished in the 1960s.
20. This would appear to be the Cross Keys Tavern which was in Muir Street, the crossed keys being a symbol of good luck.

It so happened that one night a few of us had spent two or three delicious hours at the rendezvous, with our smiling cotton dearies and having no mind so soon to part with [them] resolved that after we had as usual, made our appearance in barracks, we should scale the walls and conduct them home. We laid our plans accordingly and no sooner was all quiet within, than we stole over the walls into the woods behind, through these we steered to the point at which the lasses were to be in waiting for us. We enjoyed the remainder of the night with them & as day began to peep in the east, returned in hopes of being able again to enter our fortress unnoticed; however this hope was frustrated by our elopement having been discovered during the night; and consequently a way was paved for us from the point at which we again made our entry to the black hole. This was a grievous disappointment to us, and no less felt by Lucky C. . . & her Blantyre customers, for being kept some days in the prison and afterwards confined to barracks and sent to drill for the space of a fortnight, it had nearly put the business of the favourite festive den to stand and kept several grey beards, still groaning under the weight of their contents, which would otherwise have had a happy release some time sooner.

I was severely reprimanded for the above offence and ordered to drill the rest of the refractory gang, to whom I was said to have shown so bad an example; till the expiration of the fortnight. This was not only the first, but the only time I was confined in the black hole during my whole servitude. I do not flatter myself, nor deceive others by asserting that I never merited a repetition of the same mode of correction, but always found forgiveness for any offence which might have subjected me to it. And I do not hesitate to say that a soldier's own misconduct too often draws upon him that unpleasant life for which the tyranny of his officers very often and very falsely stands accused.

Our troop was soon after this removed to Edinburgh and from thence to Haddington[21] where we remained[22] till an order was received for the march of the regiment to Ireland.

---

21. The town lies fifteen miles east of Edinburgh.
22. The regiment had its establishment reduced by 100 horses at this time.

Chapter 10

Ireland & Smuggling

The first troop accordingly proceeded from Edinburgh on the 21st June 1808 & continued its march to Dundalk; where it had no sooner arrived than a party was called out to aid the Revenue officers in making a seizure of some smuggled goods of which they had received an information. A party consisting of one sergeant and six men, mounted and proceeded to Ardee[1] where they seized a large quantity of illicit malt, but as they proceeded along the road with it, in the direction of Dundalk, a sudden attack was made upon them by a gang of desperadoes, who had waylaid them by ambushing behind the hedges. These ruffians were armed with military musquets & without hesitation, springing from their cover, when the moment was favourable for their purpose, fired upon the unsuspecting escort and killed the sergeant on the spot. The excisemen immediately fled and the attacking banditti embraced the opportunity of surrounding the remainder of the party by hundreds; five of whom, who saw their leader killed, their directors fled and they themselves threatened with instant destruction if they did not immediately quit the seizure, proceeded to Dundalk, but the sixth man, who was the sergeant's comrade, a faithful and daring fellow, regardless of their oft repeated threats to blow his brains out if he persisted in continuing on the spot, stuck by the dead body of his master till the troop arrived from Dundalk to their assistance.

Many of the offenders were then taken into custody and afterwards suffered the lash of the law for their unwarrantable proceeding; many were hanged and among others were three brothers, many of them belonged to the volunteers and would appear to have been

---

1.   About ten miles south of Dundalk.

very improper subjects to be entrusted with government arms in their possession.[2]

The troop to which I belonged marched from Haddington a few days later and took its route for Londonderry where we arrived about the middle of August and found abundance of sport during the following year chasing the Inishowen whisky manufacturers,[3] for smuggling was carried on to such an extent that our assistance was rarely a night dispensed with, nor dared the revenue officers to stir from their own threshold without a military party at their heels. However our labour was seldom lost, for the fruits of our nightly prowlings through the neighbouring country cabins & the mountains of Inishowen, was generally a seizure of some kind; and it was invariably the fortune of some poor son of Hibernia, previous to our return home, to see the apparatus which was now become dear to him, from its so often having

---

2. This incident has been written about extensively in *The Journal of the County Louth Archaeological and Historical Society* in Vol. 25, No. 3 published 2003. In an article entitled 'A poteen affray at Ardee in 1808' by Larry Conlon there is a very good account of this affair. An escort of a sergeant and six men (Conlon says twelve, but provides six names, which agrees with William's statement) were sent on 25 June 1808 to collect a large supply of materials used in the making of illicit poteen discovered at Ardee with the local Revenue man William Kilpatrick. Having collected ninety barrels of material, they were loaded on carts and the whole marched towards Dundalk. Having left Ardee, the convoy came under continued attack from a group of seven local men who fired their muskets at them and then closed to recover the barrels. Sergeant David Forbes (his records state Daniel, but his gravestone at St Nicholas Church, Dundalk, where he was buried on 29 June, clearly says David), aged 36 was shot and died instantly and Private David Hunter was wounded in the leg, the rest (Privates Thomas Symms, William Lochead, Andrew Marshall, William Young and Thomas Phillips), were forced to surrender and the carts were driven off. Eight local men were named as having been committed for trial but there is no evidence that two were ever tried (Andrew and John Pepper). Of the other six, three were found guilty of the murder of Sergeant Forbes and were condemned to death (Thomas Pepper, Joseph Gunnell and James Maclean). The other two were found not guilty and acquitted (Leslie Marino and Henry Porter). The three men were executed on 1 August 1808.

3. The area was rife with distilleries of both whisky and poteen. Aeneas Coffey (an excise officer at the time) estimated that there were over 800 illicit stills in operation in Inishowen, County Donegal alone.

assisted him in making a drop of the creature to keep his heart warm, triumphantly carried off by a ferocious exciseman who durst as soon have carried off the mountain on which Barney's cabin stood as to have appeared in its vicinity without a military protection. These heroes of the revenue were not unaware of the hatred which existed among the peasantry towards them, which at times, roused their tyranny to such excess that the act of destroying their all and rendering them destitute, seemed to be their purest earthly enjoyment, consequently the utensils they had for illicit purposes were not all that underwent destruction; but too frequently did their little abode undergo such injury as to be left nearly a total wreck.

The proceedings of these excisemen who made themselves so extremely busy on such occasion by beating the occupants of the forlorn habitation with their sticks and pulling down all before them, often brought to my mind the words of the immortal Burns:

> A damn'd exciseman in a bustle
> Seizing a still,
> Squeezing the sides of like a muscle,
> Or lampit shell.

This duty however was by no means disagreeable to us, for it was attended not only with much amusement, but also with a more interesting property in the shape of an additional allowance of pay, each private being allowed one shilling & eight pence[4] and the non-commissioned officers more in proportion to their several ranks, per day, from the board of excise, over and above their regular pay, when out.

We only mounted a corporal's guard at our barracks and one night when I happened to be on it, an express arrived for a party; it was required to turn out as expeditiously as possible for which reason I (being in readiness) was ordered to proceed with it & my comrade corporal who should have gone to take command of the guard in my stead. I accordingly mounted and with four men followed two of the gaugers [excisemen] by unfrequented paths towards the mountains and a little before daylight in the morning entered a wild glen in which we ambushed ourselves behind the rocks to wait the arrival of a band of

---

4. A cavalry trooper earned 1 shilling and 3d per day, so this more than doubled his pay.

smugglers, who were (by an information received) to pass through that glen at an early hour; the spot in which we took post, was surrounded with scenery truly romantic. A narrow path led up the hollow between two craggy mountains, which appeared (when day unfolded their impending precipices) to be almost inaccessible and a look back on the rugged path or hollow way by which we had advanced, caused us to wonder how we had scrambled up in the dark.

We remained concealed in this retreat upwards of two hours and at length one of the excisemen, by peeping through a cavity among the rocks, saw a fellow make his appearance at the top of the glen, with two cags [kegs] under him on horseback, however this being only a decoy proceeding a considerable distance in front of the main body of smugglers, which they allow to be taken after making a faint effort to escape and thus leading any party that may come upon them off the road by which the rest of the gang are advancing and thus affording them an opportunity of escaping. However, this method had so often been practised previous to this, that the excise officers were now awake to it & this solitary merchant was allowed to pass on unmolested. We still kept a sharp lookout and in the space of fifteen minutes 17 or 18 men and horses loaded in a similar manner entered the glen. It was previously arranged that the whole should be permitted to pass our ambuscade before we sallied out, as they by that means, would be forced into the low country and prevented from baffling us (as they had often done before) by scrambling among the hills with their wicked little ponies, which were well trained to such wild paths and could maintain a footing where our horses had no chance of following them. We therefore stood fast till they had all gone down the glen and no sooner had we secured the defile between them and the top of the pass, than we mounted and dashed out upon them. However, they had no sooner discovered us than they took to their heels and the hunt began. We followed them down the glen with as much speed as the rugged path would allow; some of the smugglers scrambled up the side of the hill like as many cats, others made the best of their way down the hollow before us; this was the only division we could follow, but so rugged was the path and so difficult to pass that even these were leaving us rapidly & before we got to the outlet of the glen, my horse in making a spring over one cluster of large stones came in contact with another and being unable to recover himself, fell with such violence to the ground, that I flew over his head and was stunned to such a degree by the force with which I alighted among the rocks which set their stubborn heads up through the surface of the ground, that I lay motionless for some minutes! However, I soon recovered from the dormant state into which I had been hammered by the fall and sat up looking round me, when I discovered that I was posted alongside four tubs of whisky which some of the smugglers, who were probably on the point of being captured, had thrown off with a view of saving their horses. My own horse had followed the chase and I was left alone among the crags. I felt myself dreadfully unhinged by the fall; however I got up and staggered down the remainder of the glen in the best manner I could get my foundered supporters to work, till I came to an opening through which I could see the level flat below as well as the road which the smugglers were compelled to take; I saw the party had got possession of a number of them and two of my men still chasing the rest. I hurried on and at length saw one of the party coming back; he was returning in search of me, I mounted his horse and sent him on foot to take charge of the lugs [hidden recesses] that lay in the glen. I then proceeded to the party who had captured 4 men & 7 horses with their loads; the rest of the smugglers had directed their course into a bog where one of my party in attempting to follow them, plumped into a black mire, from which, with some difficulty, he weltered out himself, but could not extricate his horse, he having sunk so deep that his head and neck were only to be seen above the flimsy surface, four of the smugglers had thus escaped into the bog and baffled all our skill and efforts to get near them. We succeeded after a great deal of labour, in entreating the horse which had got into the bog. However, the poor animal was so feeble with struggling in the mire that we could count no longer on his services but even despaired of getting him home. My own horse never stopped to see how the business went, but galloped to Derry, a distance of about 18 miles, through fields and by-lanes, of which he could know nothing more than what he retained on his memory of our dark passage out the night before and marched into his own stable in less than two hours from the time he left us.

We were compelled to relinquish the idea of following the smugglers any farther into the bog as there was no hopes of catching them in so perplexing a situation and therefore proceeded on our way home with the seizure we had secured which consisted of 7 horses and 162 gallons of genuine poteen. We arrived at Derry late in the evening and set the minds of the troop at ease, who were in a state of alarm concerning the party from the time that my horse had made his appearance at the barracks, fearing we had had an affray with the smugglers, hence my horse returning home without his rider.

Soon after this period I was detached in command of a party of six men to Strabane; here we were stationed for the space of two months during which we were kept almost continually scouring the neighbouring country and hunting the poor whisky mongers like their shadows. I was quartered in a little public house, which was kept by a Micky M. . ., our landlord was famed for selling the best whisky in Ireland and the neighbours used to describe him as having, at one period, been possessed of considerable property, but being a man of great wit and humour, his society had at an earlier age, been courted by all classes, by which means he had been led into so expensive a life, that his property vanished and he became a bankrupt. He was soon after compelled to betake himself to smuggling, in which line of getting a livelihood he continued for some years, but at last, fortune, even in this uncomfortable business began to knit her brows upon him & during the last year that he had followed it, he could not get a cargo turned safely over to a purchaser but was invariably seized on his way from the country cabin in which he lived, or after he arrived in any town where he disposed of it.

It appeared that he had been in the habit of serving a spirit dealer in Strabane with this sly article; and after a long train of bad luck and misfortunes he resolved to make one more voyage to his friend and Strabane; which hazard was either to set him on the way of being a gentleman again or complete his ruin. He accordingly started with a load of genuine stuff, steered clear of molestation into the town and immediately applied to his old merchant who he expected would take it off his hand without delay, but his friend knowing the misfortunes that he had lately met with, as well as the jeopardy he was then in, by being exposed with his whisky on the street, determined to have a good bargain from poor Micky, who he supposed would be happy to sell it at any rate and therefore offered him so low a price that Micky disdainfully refused it and determined to sell it to greater advantage or lose it altogether.

The merchant being thus disappointed, resolved to play Micky a most barbarous trick in return and calling him back after he had gone out, he directed him to the Principal Excise Officer's house, who he said was a particular friend of his and wanted a supply of good poteen, for which he would give a good price. Micky not suspecting anything to his injury, went to the house as directed and after being introduced to the excise officer, informed him of the business which had brought him to his house & the gauger [exciseman], who in this instance seems to have been more susceptible to humanity, than Micky's old friend the spirit merchant, enquired who had sent him and other particulars which he answered without hesitation and gave such an account of what had transpired as made the Excise officer at once acquainted with the diabolical trick which his feigned friend had framed against him. He shuddered at the base design, but still kept Micky in the dark and at last for some unexplained reason, desired him to go back without delay and inform his friend that he (the exciseman) was not in the way and fearing to have it any longer in danger, was thus forced to return and make a sacrifice of his poteen for the money he had offered, to be expeditious in receiving his cash and returning to his house where he should receive a further sum, to make up the amount at which he valued it. He was at the same time cautioned against putting the dealer up to any part of this arrangement; which they at last completed and Micky again appeared at his old friend's door with his cargo.

Micky's tale was no sooner told than the merchant rejoicing, took in his good bargain and after receiving his cash &c Micky returned to the house of the exciseman, where orders were left for him to wait the master's return, who was said to be called out on some business. He was indeed *out* on business! For Micky had no sooner turned his back on the spirit merchant's shop, than he walked in and made a seizure of not only the smuggled part, but the whole of his stock, which was rendered liable to forfeiture in consequence of the illicit goods being found on the premises. The merchant's loss was great, but the gauger had no mercy. He lodged the whole in the excise office, returned home and disclosed the intrigue to thunderstruck Micky; who would (as soon as informed of it) fain have made a retrograde movement to disentangle himself from the perilous situation in which he supposed himself placed; a doubt having shot into his mind, that the gauger intended also to seize upon the small sum he had already received for his whisky. However, his escape was prevented by the exciseman, who (after setting his mind free from any doubt of that nature), advised him to discontinue so hazardous a traffic and having obtained Micky's promise to be a good boy and do so no more, paid him the promised sum and home came he, rejoicing and lavishing praises on old dame fortune for the kind smile she had once more deigned to cast upon him, for he feared (before this occurrence) that she had totally forsaken him. He also ruminated as he trotted along, upon the most advisable method of laying out his little all. But the smallness of his fortune rendered it impossible for him to fix upon any new line of life till he had received the counsel of his friends.

However, next day the news of his success and the curious manner in which it was brought about spread through the neighbourhood & Micky who made a merry theme of the matter was resorted to by his old companions, who (after learning that he was desirous of trying his luck in a small public house which was then to let in Strabane) were prompted by some kind spirit to assist him and he was, without delay, shoved into it and commenced retailing ruin among his fellow creatures, without a fear of being run foul of, having pledged himself, by the cross, to be true to the king. Thus did Micky hop step & leap into fortune, which a few days prior, he little anticipated; for having had a good knowledge of mankind in general, he of course believed his friends and had sunk himself into the cold abyss of poverty and want, he therefore looked up to them no more, knowing it to be a general rule for such friends to neglect, forsake & even shun such as him. His wit & humour was no longer profitable & consequently no longer to be courted and he anticipated that he was left, as many had been before him, to gnaw his nails in solitary and deep reflection. However Micky was more fortunate, for the old acquaintances in whose entertainment he had exhausted a great portion of both his fortune & humour, were the very men who now set their shoulders to him. They did not only put him into the above-mentioned house but also furnished him, with a good stock of whisky & penny wheep [whistle], by which Micky was set fairly afloat once more.

My landlord used frequently to entertain me as he sat quaffing a little black pipe in the corner of his bar (which was also bed, dining & drawing rooms) with an account of his struggles through life and however melancholy the groundwork of his tale might have been, he never failed by interweaving a few of his own care defying expressions, to give it a gloss, which at intervals commanded a hearty laugh. These tales he invariably concluded by helping himself to another drop of the creature, by way of drowning the remembrance (as he said) of the gloom he had struggled through, to reach the fair sunshine, which he at last, had gained and would exclaim with enthusiasm 'By the powers corpulars [corporal], I have never looked behind me, since these decent gentlemen set me up, but have been scudding before one of fortune's prosperous gales ever since and let me tell ye, corpular it would be work for one of her nor-westers to sink me now.'

Micky's company was so attractive that his house had become a place of resort for the nobbs of the town; he posted himself among them each evening with his usual amusing powers and reminded them that there was no disgrace in thus receiving a solid reward for the entertainment he afforded them. He paid great attention to his business, was extremely polite to his guests, particularly to strangers whom he never addressed without sending an advance guard composed of the words 'Yer Honour' before his speech, whatever might be their rank or appearance, for said he, 'Sure I get as mich profit from the beggars naggin, as I do from the barons; and ye's are all gentlemen to me.' He would boast of the respectability of his house and when a stranger called at his door, usually approached it blowing up the waiter, cook or some other imaginary office holder under him. Although, God knows! He himself filled the situation of landlord, waiter, boots, cook and scullion [servant].

I remained in this curious fellow's house for the space of two months and was then sent to Omagh on the same duty; here we had only been a short time stationed when an order was received for the removal of our troop to headquarters and we were recalled to Derry previous to its march.[5]

---

5.   At this time the regiment was ordered to cease plaiting their hair and powdering it, maintaining short hair instead.

Chapter 11

Dundalk Bathers & More Smugglers

We left Derry about the middle of April [1809] and marched to Dundalk where the headquarters division of the regiment was stationed;[1] our spring drills immediately commenced on the sands by the river side about two miles distant from the town, which with the smuggling duty was very harassing to our horses.

Our barracks lay close to the banks of the navigable rivers which communicated from Dundalk Bay to the town. This was a place to which vast numbers of the peasantry resorted from the surrounding country, to take the benefit of the salt water in the summer season and fine groups of men and women were at all hours to be seen bathing indiscriminately together. The fair sex of this part of Ireland did not seem to be encumbered with much of the modesty which so highly distinguished the character of the fair of their sister kingdoms, for it was no singular thing to see the women appear as Eve did in the Garden of Eden before she plucked the ruinous apple; plunging in the strand among their brethren, nor had the approach of two troops of dragoons to the water's edge for the same purpose, the slightest impression on the feelings of the country peasantry, who appeared nearly as uncultivated as the rest of the animals that inhabited the neighbouring mountains. They deliberately performed the task of scrubbing each other in the water and when fully satisfied with the time &c they had been in, retired without ceremony to the beach and became

---

1.   Dundalk Cavalry Barracks were established in 1798 and still exist although renamed Aiken Barracks.

spectators, while they leisurely dressed themselves; they inhabited the by-lanes and hedge backs during the night and again infested the shore in the morning, which at certain hours of the day was literally covered with hordes of both sexes basking in the sun and exhibiting in endless numbers along the shore, ocular proofs of their having freely partaken or perhaps overloaded their social stomachs with repeated and copious draughts of the briny waters they invaded.

Smuggling was also carried on here to a great extent and our aid was called for almost every night, and many parties were kept out for several days and nights together, which invariably pleased the parties so employed, for although the duty was fatiguing to both man and horse, yet it was always attended with some amusing occurrence which softened the labour and gave it rather an appearance of pastime; which their duties at home never could be converted into. Although much more deserving of the term, than our midnight prowlings among the hills & bogs on a smuggling excursion.

One night at eleven o'clock I was roused to go out with a party to assist the excise officers in making some seizures, as they had received information where illicit distillation was going on. Myself and six men were speedily mounted and being headed by Messieurs McCrum and Donahue[2] off we set. We proceeded in the direction of Carrickmacross,[3] but before we reached this place took off to the right and after scrambling our dark way through corn fields and peat bogs arrived at the edge of a little wood. Here our leaders commanded a halt and after we had drawn up our forces in a place of concealment, Donahue informed me that on the opposite side of the wood was the house of a great smuggler named Barney O'Brien and that a still was then going in the glen behind the house. 'Now corpular' said Monsieur D[onahue] 'You's must make a great attack, because if you's give them time they will drive us off and sure, we's must not be beaten. We will soon be masters of a great prize, for they cannot escape us at all at all. You's must go first to terrify them at once, by St Patrick the sight of your great swords will frighten them to death.' He then conducted me through the thicket to the crest of the height behind which we were ambushed. From this situation we overlooked Barney's cabin and saw in the recess of a hollow behind it, the little mud hut which contained the still, with Barney and his gang at work.

---

2.   Excise officers.
3.   Carrickmacross is a town situated twelve miles to the west of Dundalk.

Mr D[onahue] showed me the path which would lead us to the spot. We then returned, mounted our horses and prepared our formidable squadron for the great attack. We rushed upon the smugglers, sword in hand, three of our party blockading the little fortress to prevent escape, while I with the other two, dismounted and took possession; all was vanquished in an instant and our generals ventured forward to share in the glory of the great achievement. No sooner did Mr D[onahue] enter, than he opened a dreadful cannonade in poor Barney's ear. He exclaimed 'By the book Barney, your sold again. Blazes to my soul Barney but the gallows will be your next trip. Now Barney ye may swear by the cross that ye's will never do the like again for by the Holy Ghost ye'll be hanged. What scoundrels have ye got wid ye's Barney?' &c while in the same interval the other hero (Mr McCrum) addressing himself to me, exclaimed with the dignified voice of a Caesar, 'Do you see what I'm after saying to ye sergeant,[4] if one of these raskells [sic] speaks a word, by the holy father, run him through, blow his brains out if he stirs a finger. Look at that vagabond, sure that's a notorious scoundrel, scatter his brains if he lets an angry look. There's another gallows rogue, that villain's look would hang him' &c &c while the poor fellows who seemed to have no intention of offering the least resistance, were obliged to bear the greatest insults without daring to murmur and with a trembling heart and sorrowful countenance look on till all their utensils were destroyed before their eyes, their still pulled down and beaten together, thirty gallons of whisky and 5 sacks of malt loaded on Barney's 'own car' and ready to be transported to Carrickmacross. They were then brought out to march rank & file behind the prize while poor Barney was himself forced to drive off their lost all and bear as he went the oft repeated abuses, which the canes and tongues of these two mimic heroes were productive of.

We arrived with the triumphant prize, amid the many lamentations which were made by the populace for poor O'Brien and his five companions as they passed through the street on the way to the excise office, where the seizure was lodged.

We put up at one of the inns and the smugglers were kept in a stable, to be scoffed [at] by these unfeeling excisemen during the remainder of the day, however they were set at liberty in the evening by making a solemn promise to manufacture no more poteen. The party was

---

4.   He was only a corporal at this time.

then ordered to prepare for another nightly prowl among the cabins of the surrounding peasantry and about 8 in the evening we started in another direction from the town, proceeded about 10 or 12 miles without making a stop, through cross and almost impassible roads. The night, by this time had become very wet and stormy and frequently compelled us to take shelter in the thickets which lay near our dark route, from which as the heavy clouds had successively vented their vengeance, we issued and splashed on through trackless bogs and deep rutted lanes, unknown to Mr Macadam[5] or his ancestors.

The storm still increased and we advanced to the edge of an extensive forest, here we again took refuge, but could not long bear the pelt which fell from the lofty trees on our devoted heads and assailed our ears with howlings less prone to pity than the open fields. The gaugers consulted whether we should return to Carrickmacross or proceed to the spot at which they expected to fall in with their prey. They were loth to abandon their enterprise, yet every object was now so completely enveloped in darkness as to afford them little hopes of finding their way to the place they so earnestly strove to reach. However, they determined like sons of Erin to persevere and again led on.

We had not long left this cover when our leaders lost their way and became totally unconscious whence they conducted us, we could now see no human dwelling nor did we know where to steer in search of one. We perceived our horses moving under us but where or how we could not tell, sometimes sinking to the belly in water and sometimes with difficulty maintaining a footing as they scrambled along the unknown way, till a faint light descended through the battling elements and indistinctly presented to our view, the narrow lane branching off in two directions. Here another council of distress was held and as the footing seemed a little firmer we were induced to conjecture that some place of cover must be near. However, which of the branches to follow was still a perplexing mystery, till it was unanimously agreed that we should divide ourselves into two parties and each take a separate road. The firing of a pistol was to be the signal when either division made a discovery, but in case of failure both to return and meet at the same spot where we separated.

I with two men accordingly accompanied Donahue and the other four followed McCrum. We plodded on a considerable way, meeting

---

5. John Loudon McAdam pioneered his new road surface from 1820.

with several turnings which afterwards proved very unfavourable to us and at last heard a shot from McCrum's division. We instantly wheeled about to make the best of our way back. The two men being then in front of us and the lane too narrow to admit of our passing them to take the lead, I desired them to make as much haste as they could. They pushed on to a considerable distance and through some unhappy chance, Mr D[onahue] and me turned from the proper path and after riding in this dilemma God knows where, in hopes of arriving at the division of the roads and joining our friends, we found ourselves again bewildered on the verge of the forest in which we had before screened ourselves from the storm.

Our situation was now become deplorably hopeless for the night, we fired our pistols several times but no answer from the party, we called aloud in hopes of attracting the notice of some friendly aid, but all the signals of distress which our joint judgements could devise were without effect.

Here the diligent officer of excise and me stood cold and wet under the battering of the unabaiting rain and wind, till fate threw a glance of pity upon us and directed the eyes of shivering Donahue through a clump of trees that overshot the boundary of the wood and riveted them on a light no great distance from our cheerless situation. This glorious discovery was no sooner made than he exclaimed, 'Thunder an' wind corpular, here is the great north star at last! Look this way boy and tell me, was ye'r eyes ever as glad before?' So saying he bent his way towards its glimmering motion, which resembled that of a will o' the wisp through the brushwood and agitated trees.

We soon reached a little farmhouse whose inmates had been alarmed by the firing of our pistols and had turned out with a lanthorn to endeavour to discover the cause. We informed them of our situation and having lost our way when a robust fellow advanced exclaiming 'Is it your way ye's lost? Shure ye's might been kilt wid such a starm. Such a night to be out, father bless us! Come in and ye's welcome to such fare and shelter as our little cabin can afford. Hey Pat, take the benighted gentlemen's horses into the t'other cabin there and d'yu hear me now, clean them well and give them some meat, poor beys, shure they are starved.'

'Come this way ye'r honour, come this way, clear away ye'r praties [potatoes] and stuff Judy and make a great fire! Stir now! Heaven bless ye'r honours, but ye's are as pale as death! D'ye hear me Judy, get some meat ready for these poor gentlemen in a crack; by my soul they're perishing, blessed virgin who ever saw such a night as this' &c &c.

As soon as the kindness of our host had got full vent, which was not till we had filled our skins with bacon, eggs, potatoes, butter &c which was cooked for us in great abundance, I took the liberty of asking whether he had any whisky in the house and assuring him that we would take no advantage, if he sold us a little, but would consider it a great favour. 'Is it whisky?' replied he 'troth an' by St Patrick I'd swear by the book, that we's never had a drop of the creature in this little cabin, this many a month and it's just the little spot that we's had plenty in long ago, but it was destroyed. For one night I was distilling a small drop to keep us alive when one of the king's excisemen came upon me wid a troop of horsemen and took all I had and more. That the Almighty may forgive him for he's a bad man and never did a good turn to poor Ireland.'

I enquired who the exciseman was who had thus frightened him from making poteen, to which he replied, 'His name is Donahue faith and he lives at Dundalk, he took every beast I had and every car and left myself and my helpless family destroyed. That he may not be abroad the-night to perish in the storam, for the divel a man in the County Louth would harbour him under the roof of his hut. Many's the poor man that raskel has destroyed and many's the child who wishes for the curse of God upon his head for the injury done to their fathers,'

'And the divels luck to him' says I 'wherever he be.'

'Well sir' said I, 'you are not now in the power of such men as Mr Donahue and we shall be very grateful if you will even let us have a small quantity to warm our stomachs after the ducking we have got.'

'Oh the divel choack me' replied our host, 'if we's have as much as would wet ye'r tongue suppose it were in bleazes! But, d'y hear me Pat, throw ye'r trusty upon ye & just make a trot wid Teddy to Galacher's beyond and get a drop of the creature for these dying gentlemen.' So off went Pat through the wind and rain, as cheerful as doing his fellow creature a service could make him and soon returned with a bottle of whisky under his trusty. Of this we heartily partook, but my companion could not make himself happy, even with all the comforts that fortune was lavishing on us, as our host still harped on the villainous actions of Donahue, little thinking that the man against whom he so bitterly railed then shared his hospitality and was frequently obliged to join his nod of ascent to reproaches which were fired in volleys against himself, to prevent his being suspected.

Poor Donahue now became much prejudiced against the farmer and saw in his every look something that soon filled his own mind with the most horrible suspicions, he was besides reduced to great depression of spirits from the fatigue he had endured and became strongly possessed with the notion that he was known and that the retreat which dire necessity had compelled us to take shelter in, was nothing but the assembling post for some gang of his mortal enemies, the smugglers. This idea had taken possession of his imagination and everything around him assumed a fearful appearance, while the retired situation of the house and the gruff look of its master, as well as the bitter exclamations he had uttered, concurred in strengthening the horrible doubts which crowded the mind of the trembling gauger.

Mr D[onahue] had whispered several times to me that he considered it very imprudent in us to stay there and advised that we should make a retreat as soon as possible, but that could not yet be accomplished, for we were stripped almost to the skin, while our clothes dried round the fire and our landlord insisted on us going to bed until they were fit to put on again. He promised he would attend to them himself and bring them to us as soon as they were sufficiently dried. My fellow wanderer long resisted this other offer of kindness, but seeing me inclined to yield to the persuasions of the honest farmer, at last complied and with a palpitating heart followed Pat who lighted us into the better apartment.

The farmer, previous to our arrival, having made an arrangement for killing some of his pigs the following morning, went to the door and was in the act of giving directions to some of his inmates concerning these operations as we passed on our way to the adjoining apartment & the situation of Mr D[onahue] may be more easily conceived than described when he heard the farmer conclude his sentence with 'we'll stick the little divel first, shure, he's as plump as a turnip.' This expression struck to poor Donahue's heart like a knife, it bore an exact description of himself and he immediately concluded that he was to be murdered in spite of fate.

We entered the room, Pat retired and the exciseman stared around him with a heart fraught with dread [&] anxiety, he eyed me with a glance bordering upon contempt, as I jumped into bed evincing no apprehension of danger, but stretching myself to enjoy a short space of repose and exclaiming 'this is glorious luck at last, Mr Donahue.' To this my friend answered as he stood like a motionless post on the floor. 'Is it luck you mean? Do you see what I am going to say now, by my soul corpular, if we's don't get out of this like a flash, our luck will be in the other world before morning and that ye'll see.'

I laughed at his ridiculous fears and endeavoured to convince him that the notions he had harboured against the inhabitants of this humble abode, whose kind attentions to our comfort could in no way have been exceeded, were very erroneous, but all I could say had no effect in pacifying the mind of the terrified gauger, who passionately resumed 'Thunder an' winds corpular, de ye think that I'm a fool? See now by the powers, I could swear by bell, book and candle light, that if we's don't fly directly we'll be as dead as that turf in the corner there before daylight and that's all about it.'

'Fly' said I, 'where the divel can we fly without clothes?.'

Zounds' resumed Mr D[onahue] 'we's can better fly without clothes than wid our throats cut!'

However, I protested that I would not stir till I saw or heard something to strengthen such an opinion and the gauger paced the room pouring forth many a bitter lamentation of his hard fate.

I now feigned drowsiness and began to snore, leaving my companion to his own ruminations, which were certainly not of a very agreeable nature. Nearly an hour had glided away and my friend still sitting on the bedside, so fraught with horrid apprehensions that he dared not to lay himself down. Yet nothing had occurred to justify his fears and the influence of Morpheus commenced a gentle march over his senses, to envelope in the veil of oblivion the remembrance of all his cares; when a sound, as of persons conversing in a low but earnest tone, roused him from his dormant state. His heart fluttered as he held his breath endeavouring to catch their sentences. The voices of the speakers were gradually raised and as there was only a thin partition between the room in which we were and that from which the voices issued, many of their words were distinctly heard and Donahue discovered that there was an animated dispute between two or more persons who talked of throats, catching blood & succeeded by the whetting of large knives, by which he was fully convinced that his fears were at last confirmed and that his days in this weary world were nearly at a close. His very soul was ready to freeze within him, the cold sweat gathered on his forehead and trickled over his face, his limbs trembled and the hair stood like bristles on his terrified head with the horrid idea. He reached into the bed for the purpose of awakening me, muttering 'Oh corpular! We's are murther'd! What shall we do? If you had taken my advice sooner, we's might have got away wi's our lives, but sure it's all over now, the Lord bless us!'

I was still convinced in my own mind that his imagination had misled him and being much fatigued, determined to pay no farther attention to his importunities. I endeavoured to give way to sleep, but being continually disturbed by his heavy sighs and half articulated ejaculations as he crept from corner to corner of the room in search of some place of concealment from the imagined approaching attack of the assassins, or a hole by which he might creep out and save himself by flight. I only fell into restless slumbers and saw my friend at last succeed in forcing his way through a little window into an outhouse where the cows and pigs were kept. However, fate was still against him & his schemes pregnant with destruction, for he was now no more secure than in the chamber, he could neither go back nor yet further out, but was compelled to remain a prisoner and blend his sighs and lamentations with the pitiless gruntings of his companions as he groped among them in order to discover some place by which he might escape into the wood, whence he flattered himself his deliverance might be effected, at all events any fate was preferable to the horrible one which now inevitably awaited him if he continued in his present situation.

The storm still continued, the fury of the elements seemed to be suspended over the lonely habitation. The rain fell in torrents and was heard tumbling its rushing deluge from the roof, while the wind howl'd through the surrounding forest and seemed to threaten tearing everything that opposed its fury from the surface of the earth. Still unmindful of the hurricane without my unfortunate friend continued his anxious search for a place of egress and at length to his inexpressible joy, discovered a door to the opening of which he diligently applied himself, but alas, this was secured in such a manner that the utmost efforts of his strength proved ineffectual and oh what mingled feelings of disappointment, hope & despair must have pervaded poor Donahue at this critical moment. But so it was, and believing all to be now certainly lost, humbling himself among the swine, bade adieu to this transitory state of existence, the world and all its vanities & applied himself to the study of the affairs of the other world during the remainder of the night.

Thus my friend spent a night of sorry apprehensions which were not yet at an end, for as the morning began to gleam, the door was suddenly opened and the precious figure of the farmer made its appearance. Mr D[onahue]'s heart had almost burst its prison, he beheld the intruders eyes flash with murderous fury as he stalked towards him with a fearful knife in his nervous grasp. This weapon attracted the gauger's attention as the instrument which was to realise all his doubts and fears. He could no longer remain in silence and as the farmer groped about for the pig he intended to kill Donahue roared aloud 'Holy father, have mercy upon a poor sinner.' The unexpected volley so alarmed the supposed assassin that he flew towards the door screaming out 'Oh by the powers! The divels among the pigs.' My friend at the same time making a last great effort to save himself, ran out with the swiftness of a fox roused from his cover and in trying to make a spring beyond the power of human capability, came in contact with the flying farmer and both were tumbled with great violence into the dunghill pit. The whole family were now alarmed by the uproar and ran to the yard, where I also appeared and gave some explanation of the mistake for the two combatants stood in breathless agitation, beyond the power of speech, covered with mud and each possessing the same mysterious doubt of his opponent's intentions.

I being in possession of a full and correct knowledge of the affair, unravelled the whole mystery, to the no small amusement of all present, except the mortified Donahue who anticipated being made the theme of ridicule and merriment should the adventure gain a passage into the open world.

The gauger's anxiety to get away now increased for his name or character was not yet developed. We therefore recompensed Pat, who had taken care of our horses and presenting our acknowledgements to the farmer and other members of the family for the hospitality we had enjoyed with them, departed and in a few hours, reached Carrickmacross where our companions had arrived during the night and the remainder of the day was spent in talking over the mischances of our unsuccessful excursion.

We remained at Carrickmacross seven days longer, sallying out every night in quest of the smugglers, from which rambles we seldom returned without bearing some poor fellow's fortune with us, after which we returned to Dundalk.

A few days after our return I was sent with a party to escort three prisoners from Dundalk gaol to Armagh where they were to take their trial, one for stealing a cow & the other two for highway robbery. The former was a stout, robust young fellow, but a notorious character; he had often been in custody before & had as often contrived to effect his escape. The Governor of Dundalk prison informed us by way of caution, that he was well known in the country through which we had to pass and that to all probability many of his associates would be on the road to aid in liberating him, as they had formerly done. We were therefore enjoined to be strict in preventing any of the inhabitants from coming near him or ourselves.

We had got our three heroes mounted on a car, accompanied by a constable, during this cautionary drill and all being proclaimed ready we set off on our journey. Our cow stealer continued as gay and full of humour as the most happy situation could have made him. Every house and tree we passed he gave a name to, nor was any living creature that came within a reasonable distance of us, unknown to him. All who met our fettered vehicle seemed to feel or feign much sorrow on beholding the situation he was in, but he himself made very light of the matter by laughing and joking with all who passed. Nobody seemed to feel any concern about the other two, for nobody knew them & they sat in pensive silence.

When we had proceeded about ten miles, our hero pointed out to us at some distance on the road in front, a few irregular cabins. 'There' said he, 'is where all my family lives; sure ye'sll let me drink wid my good aull mother.' However, this request was rejected and on arriving at the houses we were surrounded by upwards of thirty men, who in a very suspicious tone hailed the prisoner and pressed forward on pretence of saluting him by the hands. This proceeding however was opposed and the bandit like squad was informed that if a man attempted to force themselves upon the guard in the slightest manner, we should immediately fire upon them, but notwithstanding these threats, as well as our car-man driving as fast as the horse could go, we were besieged nearly five miles of our journey. Repeated threats had however, the effect of keeping them at a respectful distance, where they followed wishing their friend good luck and he returning the compliment by exclaiming that he would be back drinking whisky with them again in a few days. He might have been a better whisky drinker than prophet, for his ever returning was prevented by being hanged a few mornings after.

We remained in Dundalk till the 9th of June,[6] when the regiment removed to Dublin and occupied the Royal Barracks[7] there. In this fine city we spent the following year and although our duties were

---

6. In June 1809, the quartermaster in each troop was removed, being replaced by one regimental quartermaster. The troops were then each given a troop sergeant major.

7. The Royal Barracks at Dublin were built in 1701 and were one of the largest barracks in Europe. After Ireland gained independence in 1922 they were renamed Collins Barracks after Michael Collins. In 1997 the buildings were converted into the National Museum of Ireland.

generally hard, we were very partial to the station, the gay town and affable manner of the Dublin people so far surpassed anything we had yet seen of Ireland and the scenes that daily presented themselves,[8] had so much changed to enliven the mind, that even the wearied soldier felt a delight in being called to the Phoenix Park to mix in the splendid trains of a Grand Review, sham fight and adding his endeavours to those of his comrades in trying to bear off the laurels from a rival corps by a display of superior discipline. The time passed pleasantly on for some months, in November I got married,[9] after which the regiment remained in Dublin till 24th June 1810 on which day we embarked, sailed for England and after a fine passage, landed on the 26th at Liverpool.

---

8. Whilst in Dublin the regiment was further reduced by another 100 horses.
9. There is only one marriage recorded in Dublin in 1809 between a William Clarke and Isabella Manders, but see the Foreword for reasons why I believe our William may have married a Mary Macavity.

Chapter 12

The Midlands in Revolt & Prisoner Escorts

The headquarters marched to Manchester, leaving the troop to which I belonged in Liverpool, where we remained till the month of October, when it also moved to Manchester. The regiment continued in the counties of Lancaster & York during the following year,[1] moving frequently from place to place, occupying during the time, the towns of Ashton under Lyme, Rochdale, Bury, Blackburn, Oldham, Huddersfield, Halifax, Leeds, Tadcaster, Market Weighton,[2] Beverley, York &c &c and again took station in Manchester at the time of the Luddite disturbance in May 1812.[3] Here we remained during the whole of that disagreeable period and until tranquillity was again completely restored among the inhabitants.

---

1. During 1811 the regiment was bolstered by an additional 100 horses added to the establishment.
2. A small town situated halfway between Hull and York.
3. On 20 April 1812 several thousand men attacked Burton's Mill at Middleton near Manchester. Emanuel Burton, who knew that his policy of buying power-looms had upset local handloom weavers, had recruited armed guards and three members of the crowd were killed by musket-fire. The following day the men returned and after failing to break into the mill, they burnt Burton's house down. The military arrived and another seven men were killed. Three days later, Wray & Duncroff's Mill at Westhoughton, near Manchester, was set on fire. William Hulton, the High Sheriff of Lancashire, arrested twelve men suspected of taking part in the attack. Four of the accused, Abraham Charlston, Job Fletcher, Thomas Kerfoot and James Smith, were executed. The unrest continued well into the summer.

On 22nd October we marched for Birmingham and occupied the barracks there.[4] Here I had the good fortune to be promoted to the rank of sergeant and was appointed to a troop which was stationed at Coventry. This I joined soon after and continued in this place a considerable time, but we were often harassed with escort duty, as deserters were very frequently passing through on their way to the Isle of Wight and other places. Some part of the regiment moved frequently during this season and occupied Derby, Chesterfield, Sheffield, Mansfield, Newark, Nottingham &c &c. On the 13th December 1813 I was sent with a party to escort two deserters to the Isle of Wight, for no troops being in our direct route to whom we could turn them over, we were compelled to proceed the whole of that distance, with such as came to our station without deviating from their direct line of route from where the prisoner was apprehended to the place of his destination. Our march on such occasions occupied upwards of three weeks from the time of our departure till that of our return home. The weather proved very wintry and disagreeable, cold winds with frequent blasts of hail, rain & snow, by which one of the poor wretches we had in custody was nearly frozen to death, for he exhibited a figure little short of nakedness; yet notwithstanding the intensity of the cold & the scanty covering with which they were to repel its attacks, every day, on our arrival at the end of the stage, they were thrust into some miserable dungeon in the town's gaol, their unhappy bodies sheltered only by a scanty allowance of straw in addition to the rags they wore and in this doleful plight forced to weep the night away till the hour arrived each revolving morning at which they were claimed by the escort and again put upon their journey. The sorry allowance of sixpence per day provided their subsistence and they proceeded during the day, shackled with cold iron handcuffs & frequently during the night fettered with heavy irons to prevent escape from the gaoler's custody who was answerable for their bodies during the night.

We had proceeded on our march till we arrived at Andover within two day's stages of Southampton and owing to some repairs which the prison was undergoing, the gaoler refused to take our prisoners in charge and we were thereby compelled to go to the landlord on whom we were billeted for the night and request his permission to keep them in the room which he had allotted for some soldiers as might at various times be quartered on him. He granted our request and we took post all

---

4.   This was Great Brook Street Barracks built in 1792, where it is confirmed that two troops of the Greys were quartered during 1813.

together, determined not to leave the prisoners, although we had secured them with leg bolts which we carried with us, for such an emergency. We retired to rest in good time, intending to get on the road early next morning & make up for the former day's confinement by arriving earlier and having a longer day to spend at Winchester. We occupied two beds & to ensure safety, each two of my party stowed one of the deserters in the middle and thought that all was perfectly secure; however about midnight when all (except himself) were profoundly wrapped in the arms of Morpheus, our ragged rascal stole from between his cautious guard and had effected an egress from the room with his legs closely locked together with irons and had also forced a door at the bottom of the staircase, by which only he could gain a passage into that part of the house through which he must have passed, to work his way into the street; when one of his keepers awoke and found his charge decamped. He sprung out of bed and uttered a yell which placed us all on the floor in the clap of a hand. We all rushed to the door (except one who I commanded to remain in charge of the other prisoner) and descended the stairs with such hurly burly, that the whole family were alarmed and rushed down stairs in their shirts. The landlord on being informed of the cause of all the uproar, promptly examined the doors and declared that the fugitive must yet be in the house, as no one could escape by any other means than the doors he had tried. Lights were procured and a strict search made, when our customer who had no hope of long evading discovery, crawled from a kind of box which formed one of the window stools in the taproom & surrendered himself.

I was now determined to be under no more anxiety, nor any further trouble to the house and immediately got ready and took the road for Winchester, where we arrived early in the morning. We lodged our heroes in the prison and spent the whole of the day and following night in comfort. The next day we reached our destination and gave up our charge at the depot in the Isle of Wight. We commenced our march back and continued it till we were within three stages of Coventry, when we were informed that our regiment had marched on the 23rd of December for Canterbury,[5] to join in an expedition which was ordered to embark from the Kentish coast for Holland.

---

5. Eight troops of the regiment had indeed marched to Canterbury in December 1813. It is possible that they were destined to join Sir Thomas Graham's force in Holland, but the failure at Bergen op Zoom caused this move to be cancelled.

Chapter 13

Canterbury Again

On receiving this news, I was put to all my generalship to know how to act, but as we had received nothing official (being only informed by the guard of a coach), I determined to proceed to Coventry, hoping that some orders would be left there for our guidance and above all some money, as we had merely a sufficiency to carry us back to that place. We accordingly continued, but found on our arrival at Coventry, neither money, orders, nor any friend to advance upon the name of the regiment, which was supposed by this time (being now the 5th January 1814) to have gone abroad and that much difficulty might be in the way of recovering it again. We were consequently compelled to set our faces to another march of about 13 days, with our hearts and purses about a level and hope, which always lends her aid on such occasions, encouraged us to persevere for the first four days, each subsisting on the small sum of six pence per day. The turnip fields were indeed hailed with a hearty welcome as they intruded on our sight during our march every day and although they were but cold food for a winter's day, yet they were seasonable to us and we took care to supply our scranbags with a few to sup upon in our bedroom. We had arrived on the 4th day at Aylsborough[1] and after we had unencumbered ourselves of our accoutrements, we went out to look through the town, 'not' as Dr Goldsmith[2] says 'to create an appetite, but to try to make us forget we had one.' We strolled along the street when a coach drove up to one of the inns on which (to our great joy) we descried a sergeant belonging to

---

1. He means Aylesbury.
2. The Irish novelist Oliver Goldsmith had had some training in medicine, but did not really apply himself to the profession.

our regiment and hastened towards the spot. We now rose a sufficient supply to carry us to Canterbury and as the coach did not stop many minutes, we bid our comrade prosper, returned to our quarters with elevated spirits and elevated them still more with a good dinner and two or three foaming tankards of good old English ale, smoked our pipes, threw away our turnips and went to bed as merry as those who never knew want.

We continued our march to Canterbury & joined the regiment in barracks. The expedition which they were intended to have joined, [had] for some unexplained reason been relinquished altogether. We continued in Canterbury till the 26th March when the regiment again received orders for service and commenced its march with all expedition to Portsmouth, but on arrival at Chichester, the news of some reverses having taken place with the French army had arrived; which rendered it unnecessary to send reinforcements to the British forces at that time; and we were again doomed to vexatious disappointment. We lay in Chichester (in a state of anxiety, every day hoping that something might turn up to put us on board) from 1st April to 25th, when we were again marched back by the same route to Canterbury, Deal, Dover and other places on that coast.

During our stay in Kent, at this time the revolutionary government of France was subdued, Bonaparte confined in the Island of Elba, a reduction of the strength of the British Army took place. The Allied sovereigns visited England, our regiment attended their landing at Dover, accompanied them to London and were quartered in the suburbs during the stay of the foreign princes;[3] after which we returned to Canterbury, Deal &c &c.[4]

Here we remained till the 20th October when a route was received & the regiment began its march for Exeter; it reached its destination on the 7th November and occupied a temporary barracks till the 22nd of the same month, on which day it was again put in motion for Bristol,

---

3. The Emperor Alexander of Russia and King Wilhelm of Prussia and a huge entourage arrived and proceeded to London to celebrate the end of the war. The Greys formed part of a Great Review in Hyde Park on 20 June 1814.
4. With peace being declared in Europe the regiment was again reduced to eight troops numbering in total 584 officers and men, including 16 dismounted men per troop.

detaching one troop to Trowbridge.[5] This troop (to which I belonged[6]) arrived at its new station on the 29th and took possession of a handsome little barrack which was pleasantly situated no great distance from the town and constructed to accommodate only one troop of horse. We entered it with pleasure, for having experienced so many harassing marches, were happy to get into any place, in which we were likely to enjoy a few month's rest & we were not disappointed, for we remained unmolested till the beginning of April 1815, when we were roused out of this snug retreat by Napoleon Bonaparte, breaking away from Elba.

5. This is confirmed by the Regimental History. Trowbridge Barracks was built in 1794 on Bradley Road, but they were removed in 1815.
6. William was in Captain Robert Vernor's troop.

Chapter 14

Ordered to Belgium

The news of this occurrence arrived one morning when we were enjoying a little relaxation from the regular duties of the soldier, and each employed in such amusements as the delightful morning in spring had tempted us to; I had gone with one of my comrade sergeants to pass a few [hours] in the pleasant pastime of angling in a river which meandered its winding way through the meadows near the town. We had only commenced our sport, when we saw a messenger from the barracks hastening towards us; he was sent to recall us from our pastime & informed us that the troop was to march on the following morning.[1] We of course repaired to the barracks and spent the remainder of the day (the 8th April) in making preparations for our march, which we commenced the following morning for Gravesend, where we arrived on the 14th and on the morning of the 15th embarked at Northfleet; men in high spirits and horses in excellent condition. The transports dropped down the river and anchored opposite Gravesend till ten a.m. on the 16th, when the signal was made for weighing anchor, this was done and the ships proceeded to the Nore, where the fleet was assembled, but in consequence of adverse winds were forced to lie at anchor till the morning of the 19th.

We had onboard with us a young man (a highlander) who had joined with a party of recruits from Scotland a few days prior to the march of the regiment from Bristol; we found him a very young recruit and being aware that such men were invariably kept with the depot till disciplined, some curiosity was created as to the cause of his accompanying the

---

1. Six troops were ordered to make ready for 'Foreign Service', the remaining troops being ordered to Ipswich.

regiment, which drew forth the following explanation from some of those who left Bristol with him.

A day or two before the march of the regiment, Angus McPherson (for such was his name) was numbered among the recruits who were selected to be left at the depot. He with seeming great reluctance, complied with this arrangement till the morning arrived when the regiment was to march off and leave them; he saw the first squadron mounted and parading in the market place, every man exulting in the happy chance which called him on service. His mind was lost in ideas of a strange nature, to be left behind his regiment on such an occasion, he considered, marked him with disgrace and his mind at last became wound up to such a pitch that he could forebear no longer from making a push to accompany his comrades. He ran to one of the led horses and sprung on his back without saddle or accoutrements and formed in the rank, the squadron being then about to move off. This strange manoeuvre drew all eyes upon the young soldier; the officers demanded his meaning and ordered him to the rear, but without effect; Angus was immoveable as a rock, so much so that the colonel at last came and remonstrated against his proceeding and gave him his word of honour that he should be one of the first remount that joined the regiment, but all which they could jointly say was to no purpose. Angus exclaimed that he would never stay behind his regiment to be looked upon as a coward, when it was going abroad and that if the commanding officer did not allow him, now, to go, he would desert and follow it wherever it went. The colonel who could not withhold his admiration of a spirit so truly noble, replied 'Well my brave fellow, you shall go.' And gave orders for his being properly mounted &c to accompany the regiment. Poor Angus was killed early in the action of the 18th June following.[2]

About six a.m. on the 19th, the wind veered and the signal was given, from the agent to put to sea. The fleet got under weigh about seven o'clock and although we had a high wind and heavy sea, got into port at Ostend without any accident at four on the morning of the 20th remained on board all that day, disembarked on the 21st, taking from the ships, one day's rations for men and horses. The whole regiment (except those on board one transport which was obliged to wait a spring

---

2. Private Angus McPherson was from Moidart (a remote area to the east of Fort William) and had been a labourer before he joined the Greys. He was indeed killed at Waterloo.

tide to enable her to enter the harbour) marched to Bruges, a large town on the Brussels road.

22nd. Marched through Maldegem to Ekloo, which being only a village, could merely accommodate the commanding officer and staff of the regiment and the troops found quarters among the farmers round the country; I with my comrade was billeted on one about three miles from the village. We searched out our resting place, by presenting our billet to any of the peasantry we chanced to meet with. The rural mansion at length appeared within view, it was situated in the middle of an orchard & nearly hid among trees of various kinds immaulted in such livery as bespoke the approach of a fruitful season. We were received by an old man who assisted in putting up our horses and then invited us to the house where such refreshments as the humble dwelling could produce were placed before us, which we heartily partook of, for our meal was made more delicious by the unceasing attention of our hostess, who gaily pressed and adorned the homely abode by the smile of welcome which wantoned over her long-matured countenance. The family was about seven or eight in number, who used their joint endeavours to make us comfortable till we retired to rest; we preferred the stable in which our horses were for our bed chamber and after rolling our blanket round us and stretching ourselves on some clean straw which was laid in a corner for us, we indulged in the arms of Morpheus, till the sun's glare on the white blossom around us was seen through a little lattice on the opposite side of the stable & reminded us of the hour, at which we were again to take the road. We accordingly took leave of our hospitable entertainers and proceeded to the village where the regiment again assembled in order of march.

23rd. Marched through Waarschoot to Ghent, but the town was crowded with British & Belgic infantry, previous to our arrival, which compelled us again to take refuge, under the cloud of night, in the farm houses around.

My next host was a joiner and in his house we experienced more kindness (if it had been possible) than that which had been lavished on us the preceding night; the best, the country could produce was considered insufficient for the British soldier and we were therefore pestered with their repeated endeavours to raise us above what we ourselves considered the summit to which a soldier's comfort (under such circumstances) could mount.

We remained here four days and on the 27th I with my comrade moved to another farm house near Ghent. The headquarters for the regiment was at Drongen, a small village a few miles from it, in this house we were also treated with the utmost degree of kindness. This was a part of the country which had suffered much from the ravages of the French army in their passage to & from their ill-fated invasion of Russia, who had pillaged all that lay in their way; nor had the Russians or Prussians been better ruled by the dictates of justice or humanity, for in addition to the excesses which they had committed in plundering all before them, they had in many places, wantonly destroyed the property of the defenceless inhabitants, particularly the churches and valuable appendages with which the Flemish people take a pride in profusely adorning their places of worship.

The particularity of the people to the British troops was not to be wondered at when we consider the difference of their behaviour from that of other nations in a foreign country, whatever the British had occasion for from the country, was paid for; whereas the French did not only force the youth of their neighbours into their ranks, but also supplied themselves with provisions, horses, waggons or anything they were in need of which they carried with them without making any remunerative allowance for them. Often did the old man on whom I was quartered, with bitter lamentations, exclaim against them and describe to me, how his two sons were forced to accompany them after they had divested him of all his waggons, horses & in short everything that was of any service to them. His sons, he never more heard of, and many hundreds who were torn from their homes in the same manner, were ever after in oblivion; no doubt they had fallen in Russia, victims to the sword, famine or frost and the country thus drained of its youth. There were very few young men to be seen, the work of husbandry &c carried on in the fields by the young females and that generally allotted to them in England by the enfeebled branches of both sexes.

The brigade which was composed of three regiments, was now formed and put under the orders of Major General Sir William Ponsonby. The other two regiments were also in the neighbourhood, and about the end of the month, the general received orders to move from the station for the purpose of affording quarters for other troops who were on the advance from the port of debarkation.

1st May. The brigade marched from Drongen & its neighbourhood, but being detained in drawing rations at Ghent, did not leave that place until 7 in the evening & took the march in the night through Alost,[3] a

---

3. Now Aalst.

considerable town on the road leading to Brussels, it was occupied by the French Garde du Corps. Here we left the great road and continued our march by a route to the right till we arrived at a small village named Denderhoutem, it was situated about two miles north of Ninove, where the Marquess of Anglesey,[4] had established his headquarters. We reached Denderhoutem at four in the morning, 2nd May and General Ponsonby, with the staff of our regiment took possession of such quarters as it afforded. The remainder of the regiment was scattered among the neighbouring farmhouses as heretofore & the other two regiments occupied the most adjacent hamlets.

4.   This is slightly anachronistic as Henry Paget, the 2nd Earl of Uxbridge, did not become Marquess of Anglesey until July 1815.

Chapter 15

Denderhoutem

The men now received orders to put their arms and accoutrements in the best possible order for service, as well as to be attentive to the care of their horses in order to get them in the best condition for the field, as it was anticipated their services might soon be required. Nothing particular till the 6th when the regiment was received by the Earl of Uxbridge who was pleased to express his entire satisfaction with its appearance and discipline. It was again inspected on the 9th by General Sir William Ponsonby who was also highly pleased with its appearance.

It was now the 10th of May, the troops lying at ease; horses getting in excellent order, men in high spirits, experiencing no want, nor any wish, more ardent than that of getting within arm's length of their country's foes. The evening was approaching and the sun hastening down on the western horizon, when its enchanting allurements unconsciously drew me into a grove which covered our rural abode from the blaze of the summer's sun and the fury of winter's blast. I was charmed by the feathered legions which surrounded me and lent their notes in the completion of the sublimity with which nature seemed to have covered the vast expanse that came within the search of the inquisitive & wandering eye, in the fine view commanded by the flowery bank on which I sat. My mind was at once filled with the majesty of nature's great author and could not withhold the homage which was evidently due to the deity whose wonderful work overspread the face of the surrounding country. The part through which we had already advanced was a levee, flat and the view uninterrupted as far as the human eye could perform its office, of beautiful plains covered with abundant crops of wheat, barley, rye, rapeseed, tobacco &c interspersed with orchards & clumps of fruit trees by the waysides, rearing, their forms enveloped in white blossom, the gaudy livery and forerunner of a fruitful season.

At this time an augmentation of two troops to each cavalry corps was ordered to take place and a proportional addition on non-commissioned officers appointed. This caused considerable promotion in the regiment and as a custom prevailed of making the newly appointed non-commissioned officers pay their footing and be initiated into their new rank, over a few convivial bowls of punch, we assembled for the purpose (on the 13th) in an orchard a short distance from the village;[1] a table about fifty yards in length was erected among the fruit trees & spread with the best viands which the season & country could produce, here we enjoyed a good dinner and when night stole upon us, lamps & candles were suspended from the branches which bent their silvery tops over us and joyous manner, passing many a hearty, appropriate & loyal toast and song hailing the morning's dawn and driving care like a coward from the presence of our social hearts.

Nothing extra occurred till the 29th on which day a Grand Review of all the British cavalry took place, on the meadows of Schendelbeke, a beautiful and extensive plain near the village of that name. This was the most superb sight of that kind, I had hitherto seen and may with some justice add, that there were (perhaps) but few on the ground who had seen so large and so fine a body of cavalry together. The plain was sufficiently extensive to admit of 27 regiments, as well as a strong body of horse artillery, forming in one line and were assembled for the purpose of being seen by the Duke of Wellington, who came on the ground accompanied by Prince Blucher,[2] The Prince of Orange,[3] the Earl of Uxbridge, Lord Hill and a multitude of both British & foreign

---

1. The regiment was ordered to be augmented to ten troops again with an establishment of 946 officers and men, but this would take some considerable time to achieve fully.
2. Gebhard Leberecht von Blücher, Fürst [Prince] von Wahlstatt (1742–1819), commanded the Prussian army during the Waterloo campaign.
3. William Frederick, Prince of Orange (1797–1881), was the son of the newly-proclaimed King William I of the Netherlands (Belgium and Holland having been made into one kingdom by the Congress of Vienna in 1815). He commanded the main Netherlands army in the Waterloo campaign although he served as subordinate to the Duke of Wellington. He is often blamed (often unfairly) for the disasters to certain units that occurred at both the battles of Quatre Bras and Waterloo.

officers of all ranks, who passed down the front of the line after the general salute and returned by the rear to a station on the right, where the line marched past in a column of half squadrons & saluted.

We were now getting very intimate & friendly with the inhabitants of the places wherein we were quartered. Our landlords frequently gave parties to which they invited the neighbouring farmers and the soldiers who were quartered with them, that their acquaintance might become more general and those who were thus entertained felt it a duty upon them to return the treat in the same manner on some future evening. One of these good people, one evening invited a few of our men to accompany him to the village, where they enjoyed themselves till a late hour and again commenced their walk home. They had a church which lay in their way to pass, at the entrance of which stood a stone Virgin Mary which the inhabitants superstitiously imagined possessed the power of healing any disease with which any part of their bodies or limbs might be afflicted and for this purpose they had a model of the diseased part cast in wax and hung upon the virgin to keep her in mind of their condition. The men approached the statue and seeing so many of these appendages dangling about it, thought a pity they should not be applied to some more useful purpose. Wax being an article with which they gave a superior gloss to their saddles and other horse equipage, they dismantled the virgin of all the hands, heads, fingers, toes &c, which they carried with them to their quarters, but the sacrilegious act was no sooner discovered, than a general murmur arose and a grievous complaint laid before the general. However, the depredators were not known and the matter ended as might be expected; by the men being cautioned against violating the laws or customs of the people in future.

The weather continued exceedingly fine and the continued blaze of the summer's sun in cloudless sky, had such influence on the teeming fields that they were already begun to assume an autumnal hue and the soldiers became so familiar with the peasantry that they were looked upon as part of the family in each of the cottages which were scattered many miles over the plain and kindly invited to take a share in their rural pastimes and fireside sports.

On the 13th June I went to Alost to purchase some articles for the regiment and being accompanied by two of my comrades, we agreed to enjoy the pleasures of the town for an hour or two & for this purpose went into a schnapps shop, where by chance, we met with some of the fair sex who were pretty easily courted to give us the pleasure of their society during our stay. However, I believe that had the effect of making our stay rather too long and night coming on we were assailed by the French guard[4] and ordered to repair to our respective places of quarters, which order one of my companions refused to obey, alleging that the Frenchmen had no authority over us. There being only a sergeant and two men sent to dislodge us, they retreated to their guard and in a few minutes returned with a party of about a dozen, who were to take us to their guard house; but behold when my obstinate comrade saw them, being a wonderful, powerful man, seized his stick[5] and dealt such blows as made a way & we cleared our road to the end of the town, took into the cornfields & lay quiet till their search ended.

One evening, being in the village of Denderhoutem I met with the farmer on whom I was quartered and two other neighbours, with whom I remained till a late hour, for my landlord loved his schnapps most dearly. The other two who accompanied him were his nearest neighbours at whose houses Peter[6] and me had been several times entertained, we were getting merry together and I (without considering the state of our larder at home) by way of returning, in a limited degree, the compliments which I had repeatedly received in their houses, invited them to dine with us the following day. The schnapps by this time, had considerably elevated our notions and the warmth of friendship began to defuse itself over the happy group, when the little cuckoo clock proclaimed from a dark recess in Jean Vandermann's best parlour the hour of midnight, which rather hastily raised us on our legs and put us in motion toward our country quarters. However, my invitation was readily accepted by the farmers and we parted each directing his steps towards his own place of abode.

I thought nothing more about my friends that night, but when next morning arrived, I began to think something seriously about the jeopardy I had placed myself in, for our store was so completely cleared out that I knew not how to raise a dinner for myself and comrade, much less to what experiment I could have recourse in order to furnish our board with viands fit to be placed before the guests I had invited. I ruminated on fifty schemes but could think of none that reflected the

---

4. The Army of Louis XVIII, consisting of royalists and deserters from Napoleon's army, was forming at Aalst.
5. His sergeant's cane.
6. The only Peter in his troop was Private Peter Wotherspoon, who came from Paisley and who died of wounds sustained at Waterloo on 29 June 1815.

slightest possibility of being able to perform the duty I had encumbered myself with. I again thought there was a chance of my friends forgetting their promise altogether and as they were all rather groggy at the time the invitation was given, I was willing to make myself believe it really was so.

However, I told my comrade, Jock [Wise][7] about it, who was a shrewd fellow and possessed in an eminent degree the inestimable quality of an excellent forager, he smiled and said I had no occasion to be to put myself to so much uneasiness about that, adding that I would excuse him from attending parade (being Sunday) he would manage the matter whether the farmers attended or not. I readily agreed to Jock's proposal but could not conceive in what manner he hoped to save me from disgrace. However, I left him at home and proceeded with the regiment to hear prayers in the village, but my mind was so loaded with the foregoing matter, that it frequently marched back to Jock strongly impressed with a mixture of hope, doubt and fear.

The family, who rigidly attended Mass, had left the house previously to my departure for Denderhoutem and after I had gone Jock sallied forth on a foraging excursion. His first object was to twist the windpipes of two fine fowls from the flock which bask'd in the sunny side of our own barn. These he plucked and made ready for cooking with great expedition, carefully concealing the feathers and fragments, placing them, in case of the farmer's family returning home previous to their being cooked, in the market basket, as if so brought from the village. He next bent his hasty strides through an orchard which separated the house of Mynheer Rulant, one of the farmers whom I had invited, from our own and on reconnoitring the premises found this family also attending their religious duties. Jock got through a window into the house and found the large pot on the fire boiling; he hastily examined it and to the sacrilegious invasion of the kitchen and real pot, his conscience became reconciled by the savoury smell and agreeable appearance of a huge lump of fine beef which he found it contained. This, which was intended for the family after returning from Mass he dislodged and after pausing a few seconds until the contention (which had arisen in his mind as to whether he should make a prize of the whole or only part) was decided, he divided it into two fair halves, the one he again consigned to the seething pot and the other to the

---

7.   Identified by a later entry.

The ruins at Dane John in Canterbury where the Scots Greys feared to patrol at night.

A typical smuggling operation which the Greys spent so much time trying to capture or disrupt.

The Scots Greys in a Bivouac, a painting by James Howe.

A typical Irish whiskey still set up in a woodland clearing to avoid detection.

The Dawn of Waterloo 18 June 1815, by Lady Elizabeth Butler

The Scots Greys by Giuseppe Rava.

The 92nd Highlanders join the Charge, a painting by Stanley Berkeley.

'Scotland Forever', by Lady Elizabeth Butler.

The Greys Charge the French Infantry by Norrie.

Sergeant Ewart captures the Eagle, by William Holmes Sullivan.

Sergeant Ewart leaves the Field with the Eagle, by Simpkin.

Eagle of the 45e Ligne
Captured by Sergeant Ewart.

The Battlefield on 19 June 1815, by Matthew Dubourg.

The National Monument to the Dead of the Napoleonic Wars, Edinburgh.

George IV Entering Prince's Street 1822, by William Turner.

The Procession of George IV 1822, by John Wilson Ewbank.

durance of the haversack which he was so accustomed to carry across his shoulders when our stack of provisions were nearly spun out, that the state of our larder was generally conjectured by the presence or absence of Jock's scranbag.

Having thus arranged matters, he effected his escape unobserved save by the venerable turkey cock and his play fellows who had been enjoying the sunny end of the house and set up the shrill alarm or death song, which Jock was no stranger to, having often raised it on former occasions in his nightly prowlings among the feathered tenants of the neighbouring hen roosts and poultry yards, as he lightly leaped the old mud rampart that surrounded the house and shipped across the orchard to his own citadel.

On reaching his quarters, Jock (whose mind was always pregnant with matter sufficient to confute suspicion) got on his cooking kettle, cut his prize beef into mincemeat and made an excellent mess with plenty of soup, which he knew the natives of the country were very partial to. Thus, together with plenty of vegetables and his two fowls, he had an over abundant supply for the occasion.

Meanwhile I contemplated the improbability of Jock's undertaking being accomplished and turned the affair frequently over in my mind while at prayers. This being over I hastened home where I found the farmers waiting my arrival. I gave them a doubtful welcome and handing forth the bottle, was in the act of inviting them to partake of a small quantity of schnapps by way of laying a foundation, when Jock began to place his dishes on the table and in a few minutes our board displayed a sight which might have cherished the eyes of a German prince. The bottle nearly dropped from my hand with astonishment, however I contrived to conceal my surprise and we set to work, each extoling the delicacies of which we partook, as being beyond our reach in common. My worthy host declared that he never had polished the joints of a more delicious fowl and our neighbour Francis Rulant joined the other members of the company in praising the quality and cooking of the meat of which the other dishes were composed.

We enjoyed our schnapps after dinner till a late hour in the evening, when the farmers took their leave impressed with an idea that they lay under a particular obligation to me for entertaining them at so much expense, unaware of their having contributed so materially to our feast themselves.

A few days passed over and our worthy Dame Mynheer Debrucras

Vrow, who had missed two of the choice of her feathered legion, began to question Jock concerning them, however my comrade (who was never short of an air in his manner to stamp with the resemblance of truth any of his counterfeit declarations) threw himself into a dreadful fit of passion and protested that immediately on my arrival home, he would report the circumstance of her having impeached him with dishonesty. 'This is an offence' said Jock 'which when brought home against any man before a court martial, is punishable by death, but in the event of the accuser not being able to substantiate the charge; he or she, so offending is liable to be punished at the discretion of the same court! And I shall not' continued Jock 'quietly submit to this accusation with which you have endeavoured to stain my character, which is beyond all other considerations most dear to a British soldier.'

The honest vrow shuddered at the sound of a court martial, for as such, she had often heard fearful tales and trembling, begged that Jock would not tell the waughmaster of the matter, as she would not appear before a court martial for all the fowls in Flanders; to which, with seeming great reluctance and the weight of a promised reward he agreed and the stolen fowls were no more spoken of, but even the very remembrance of them ordered to be buried in oblivion.

Chapter 16

The Bugle Calls

On the evening of the 15th June, the men had retired to rest in their barns and stables (for where his horse was, there did the dragoon sleep) and when the calm solitude of midnight had lulled the troops to sleep; a messenger arrived from Brussels bearing the orders of the Duke of Wellington to Sir William Ponsonby.[1] The bugles were instantly ordered to sound to arms, but so extended were the cantonments occupied by the cavalry that a considerable time elapsed before the signal could be carried round. However, it was no sooner heard than every man sprang from his straw couch to obey the call for which they had most earnestly prayed for some weeks past. I shall never forget the night! I heard with delight, the oft repeated call of the war horn sideling over the plain & no one could experience greater satisfaction than I did, at the prospect before me; yet in spite of all this, my mind at intervals rambled back to the spot where they lived, who were most dear to me and waited in melancholy anxiety to hear the sequel of the event which had parted us. My comrade, who was a hardy resolute & excellent soldier, hastened to accoutre our horses and in the space of fifteen minutes we were mounted and on our way to Denderhoutem, our alarm post, accompanied by our landlord and his two daughters who seemed as loth to part with us as if we had been their dearest relatives, leaving them for a similar purpose. The good man soliciting us to return to his house again if we survived, awoke in my mind many

---

1. This order was sent by Lord Greenock and was discovered on the battlefield after Waterloo. It is simply dated 15 June and said 'The brigade will assemble with the utmost possible expedition.' It is annotated 'Received 1¾ hours 16 June.'

strange thoughts; father, mother, sisters and brothers crowded upon my imagination and the parts of my native country which were the dearest, seemed to question me whether it was probable I should ever visit them again. The chances (I thought) were against it and as I loved my relatives and my country, it was impossible for me to avoid a pang of regret at the idea, that to all probability I should behold them no more.

However, the gloom of these ideas were dispelled as we approached the village by the noise of the troops hurrying in from all directions. The brilliancy of twilight appeared in the eastern sky as we entered, but a thick fog had taken possession of the village and low grounds about it; which rendered objects so indistinct to the eye, that our ears were assailed for some time, with a confusion of voices, trampling and neighing of horses, clattering of swords & canteens and loud words of command; but on a nearer approach, we beheld the troops as they hurried together, forming their ranks and surrounded by multitudes of men, women and children, who had gathered themselves together to witness the departure and cheer the soldier going forth to battle with a last kindly farewell.

The regiment were on parade to a man by four in the morning and the trumpets struck up a complimentary tune to the inhabitants as we moved off in the direction of Ninove, at which place on our arrival, the other two regiments composing the brigade joined us and the whole was led on by Sir William Ponsonby towards the frontier. We continued to pursue our route till the day was getting far advanced and although none were strangers to the cause of the movement, yet all were ignorant as to the distance we had to go. We passed through Enghien late in the afternoon and soon after heard a distant firing of cannon and on gaining the summit of a small eminence which lay before us, the rising of the smoke, still far distant, pointed out the scene of action. General Ponsonby immediately increased his pace to a brisk trot which was continued upwards of seven miles, leaving a number of horses behind that were unable to keep up. We passed through Nivelles, a small town about five miles from the plains where the battle was raging.[2] Night

---

2. The left wing of the French army commanded by Marshal Ney advanced up the Brussels road from Charleroi. They came into contact with a Dutch/Belgian division at the crossroads of Quatre Bras, where Wellington's troops arrived at various times throughout the day. The troops were immediately thrown into the fighting as they arrived and the British infantry suffered heavily from the French cavalry because the British cavalry did not arrive

now began to lower her black curtain upon the face of nature and as we approached nearer the field, the din of war was apparently lessening, subsiding about the time we formed in rear of the infantry, into the stillness of night; except now and then, a popping shot in various parts of the field, the neigh of the warhorse, the groan of the wounded or dying soldier, or the half uttered shriek of many a brave fellow suffering acute pain from wounds which had laid them in some undiscovered recess by the hedge backs or among the long grain.

We had met in our way between Nivelles and the field of action a great number of wounded, seeking their way to Nivelles; some limped along on foot, some on horseback & some officers were carried by a party of their men, while others who were unable to proceed farther, sat or lay by the wayside and implored assistance from him who gave them existence. Many of them were of the highland regiments, who had suffered severely from the attacks of the enemy's cavalry.

On arrival at Quatre Bras (which was a straggling village on the road) General Ponsonby led the brigade to the right and formed in a bean field, some distance in front of the village. The men were then dismounted with orders to stand by their horses during the night. The plains of Fleurus and eminences all around were in a short space illuminated by the watchlight fires of the two armies, who had each maintained their ground. The weather was mild and all was awful stillness except the protruding murmur of the wounded men, who were frequently carried along our front by parties of their respective regiments for the purpose of being placed somewhere under cover to evade the damp of night in the open fields. Their complaints were grievous and none else knew how to complain, for gentle is the dead & gentle the hero after victory.

During the night the dragoons busied themselves in plucking grass for their horses with a view of refreshing to an appetite for their oats, which the most of them refused, owing to the fatigue they had endured in the advance, having travelled about fifty miles that day, at a very harassing pace, encumbered with baggage, arms, accoutrements and three day's oats and hay. The action was expected to be renewed with daylight and as they knew that a dragoon cut but a poor figure in such

---

until darkness. The Battle of Quatre Bras was effectively a draw, with both sides suffering about 5,000 casualties each, but is seen as an Allied victory because they held their ground, whilst the French eventually retired for the night.

a place, without his horse, they were diligent in making the best use of the time they had in recovering them.

The men had not lost their appetites but had not [the] wherewithal to silence their cravings, as no rations had been drawn for them previous to the march and no appearance of the commissary department coming up that night, I longed for some refreshment and was thereby induced to accompany two of my comrades to the village [Quatre Bras], for the purpose of trying to purchase some liquor or bread, but on our arrival there, we found the houses wholly filled with the wounded, the dead and the dying, and their former inhabitants fled with all except the bare walls. Every cottage we entered, presented a scene sufficient to have shocked the most hardened heart, on the floors were stretched as many as they could accommodate, some dead were intermixed with the wounded, whose cold earthen beds were clotted with their blood and frequently was our eyes drawn to some miserable being struggling with the last pangs of death.

In one of these cottages a highlander[3] lay on the floor, with his blanket spread under him and his head (which was bound with a handkerchief) reclining on his knapsack. The blood from a wound on his head found its way through the handkerchief & trickled over his cheeks; I after expressing my sorrow for his hard fate, enquired how the day had gone, at which question he turned on me, a contemptuous frown & replied. 'Ye might a-been here to see how the day gaed, I think! And keepet the French horsemen frae gaun inthrough and outthrough among our poor fellows as they did.'

'What' said I 'Did they break your ranks?'

'Our ranks' replied the veteran 'I've been in monie a battle, but ay got something like fair play afore, it's a wonder they didna ca us a' to the deevel the gither, for feint [not] a horseman o' our ain came near, either to save or help us.'

'Were none of the cavalry up during the action?' replied I.

'Oh no, di'el a one, but a when fellows wi' white faces and black claes, wi' a dead man's skull & marrow bones.[4] On the foreside o' their doolful caps!! But Lord mon! Gin they had been awa too, it wad hae been a hantle better for us, for we lippened [looked] to them doing

---

3. He was a soldier of the 42nd (Highland) Regiment of Foot which later became the Black Watch.
4. The Brunswick Hussars wore black uniforms with a silver skull & cross bones badge on their shakos.

something among the French dragoons; but they nae sooner came on than off gaed the black chields [children] as hard as they could scoor [scoot] and left us to make the maist of an ill bargain ourselves. The French horsemen gaed through our line, for we hadna time to run into square and killed an awful heap o' us!! Ane [One] o' the hanget [hangman] like scoundrels, gied sic a skelp [strike] awa and I canna tell what happened till I came to mysell again. But we ne'er saw mair o' our black hussars; our colonel was killed[5] and sae monie o' the men that the general spake o' surrendering what was left to the French, but Captain Campbell grippet the King's culler [colour] and swore, not as long as we had one man on his shanks [legs].' The veteran again sunk upon his hard pillow and we returned to our lines as empty as we left them, for we found it utterly impossible to procure, even a drink of water.

We were informed that the Duke of Brunswick was killed, with many officers of meaner rank and men, particularly of the 42nd, 69th, 79th & 92nd Regiments who had suffered the most.

---

5. Lieutenant Colonel Sir Robert Macara, commanding the 42nd Foot at Quatre Bras, was wounded and when being carried to the rear in a blanket by four of his men, they were attacked by the French cavalry and slaughtered.

Chapter 17

Retreat to Waterloo

The whole of the cavalry and horse artillery came up during the night and waited with anxiety, the dawning of morn. The infantry were seen lying in battalions by their piled arms, in which situation, many, from the fatigue they had undergone the preceding day, fell into uneasy and restless slumbers, from which they were aroused by every popping shot that was fired; while the dragoons stalked in groups about the fields in search of green forage for their horses, that they might next day be enabled to go through the work, which appeared to be cut out for them and as the hour approached at which daylight came in, every man was at his horse's head.

The long looked for moment at last arrived, the new day began to brighten the eastern sky and the lines were formed in order of battle, in this situation we stood for the space of half an hour, which was half an hour of awful stillness; not a motion nor a voice was heard, but every soldier in painful anxiety for the commencement of the work of death. The light at length overspread the plain and opened to view the hostile lines of the enemy which were no sooner clearly discerned than the firing began.

The Forest of Ardennes skirted the rear of the enemy's position and formed a complete fortification against any attack which might have been made by the British cavalry, as their infantry had nothing to do but retire into this cover and open a more destructive fire, had any such attack been made.[1] This circumstance (I think) limited the action to a

---

1.　Almost every British memoir of Quatre Bras mentions that the French army retired in the morning into the forest, many claiming that this was a ploy to ambush the British as they advanced on the French. It is totally

brisk fire of artillery & infantry, at which the cavalry (without moving) looked on till ten o'clock, when the whole French army retired into the wood and the firing ceased. The men were allowed to pile their arms and the cavalry dismounted that both man and horse might benefit as much as possible by any interval of rest which could be allowed them. Parties of the cavalry were ordered with their leather buckets, to a stream, which wimpled through a hollow some distance to our left rear. I accompanied a party of the troop to which I belonged and by the time we reached the rivulet, for it was invested by hundreds who panted for water, some prostrate on the ground, drinking greedily from the stream, while others were forcing their way with the greatest eagerness into the middle of it, to fill their canteens and leather buckets; and had the waters (as heretofore) actually been turned into wine, no greater struggle or desire to obtain a portion could have existed. We however, with great difficulty accomplished our task, but after each man had filled his bucket & canteen it was no less difficult to guide the prize we had obtained, back through the crowds who still ran to the water, where many were upset with their precious gains and compelled to return a second time.

The enemy continued in the wood, and the Duke of Wellington (after an elapse of nearly an hour) saw with his usual discerning eye, the necessity of a retreat, not only to draw them from this cover but also to preserve his communication with the Prussian army, who he learned were driven back from Ligny and St Amand. The infantry were consequently drawn off the field and commenced a movement to the rear by the great road leading to Brussels. The cavalry at the same time forming a line to cover their retreat; for this purpose, the two brigades of heavy cavalry, viz the 1st & 2nd Life Guards, Oxford Blues, 1st Dragoon Guards, Royals, Greys and Inniskillings, with a brigade of hussars, a brigade of light artillery and a troop of rocketeers, were selected. But the French had no sooner observed the movement than they sallied from their stronghold and commenced the chase. Their cavalry issued from the wood in immense bodies, upon whom our light artillery immediately opened their fire and kept them in check to the foot had got in regular order of retreat. The village of Genappe was situated in a hollow on the road, about half a mile from Quatre Bras, the little stream

---

incorrect, but being so commonly stated, it is clear that this was a prevalent rumour within the Allied army on 17 June.

above alluded to, ran through and turned two or three miles in[?] it. A narrow bridge was thrown over the drought drained bed of the water, at the point where the road crossed it at this place which the whole of the army had to pass. The passage of this defile retarded the progress of the retreat so that the French were pressing very hard upon our covering cavalry and had opened a brisk cannonade before the situation of the retreating army would admit of our falling back. However, they had no sooner passed the defile of Genappe than the covering division also began to retire. They were drawn from the fine fields teeming with heavy crops of wheat, rye &c which in many places, nearly covered the horses; into the great road, which descended with a gentle slope into the village. We passed the bridge and entered its deserted street, for no inhabitant had dared to remain in it, nor was any human being (who was not of the army) seen, in our march through, except a solitary old man who weeped bitterly as he took a momentary peep with a terror covered countenance, through an attic window.

Many of the wounded men were in this village, who, as well as many who were still at Quatre Bras, must have been exposed to the mercy or cruel treatment of an inveterate and braving enemy; two poor fellows belonging to the 42nd who sauntered in the street, attracted the notice of many of our men as we passed them; they appeared to be in a state of stupor and seemed to evince no fear, but rather a heedlessness concerning their situation, one of them had been wounded through the leg and with great difficulty limped two or three steps at a time, but did not direct them towards the road by which his escape might have been effected. The other was wounded about the head and although very pale, most probably from loss of blood, he seemed to be perfectly capable of walking so as to save himself. However, neither of them seemed desirous of doing so, for when some of our men accosted them in terms which they expected would have encouraged them to get away and even offered them their assistance. They spurned the offer and one of them answered 'O ay, but we maun hae anither [mean to have another] shot at the loons [rascals], yet, for the loondering [beating] we got among them yesterday' and continued to limp from corner to corner, as if waiting the arrival of the enemy's van, which they frequently turned to look for with the greatest coolness. We left them there and what their fates were I cannot pretend to say, but may reasonably imagine that they soon after fell into the hands of the French.

It was now about one o'clock in the day, the sun's beams extremely hot and sultry, we ascended an eminence which overlooked the village we had passed and were again withdrawn from the road and formed a line extending right & left along the summit of the height, with the artillery prepared in proper stations to salute the enemy as soon as they came within range of their guns. About this time, the gathering of heavy clouds began to darken the atmosphere and announced the speedy approach of a thunderstorm. The gentle elevation we occupied, raised us so much above the extensive plains that we were enabled to command most magnificent views of the progress and formation of the clouds as they swam in large black masses towards our station, accumulating in their progress all the smaller vapours, till they at last formed a vast black canopy over the face of the heavens, when tremendous peals of thunder burst forth, lightning flashed, the clouds broke and in a few minutes deluged the fields to such a degree that our horses sunk nearly to the knees at every step.

The enemy had entered the village and the Earl of Uxbridge whose superior skill, saw the necessity of checking their progress, ordered his own regiment (the 7th Hussars) to charge and drive them back; the 7th attacked accordingly but were repulsed with considerable loss. The attack was renewed by the 1st Life Guards, who after a spirited combat with the enemy's van in the narrow streets, forced them to retire and again took their station in good order. The Life Guards lost none of their glory by the above alluded to attack, but whether they returned covered with new laurels or not, I have no hesitation to say that they were totally covered with another material, which I am induced to think they would have dispensed with if they had had a choice. The figure they cut coming up the hill after their charge gave rise to many a hearty laugh, although it was no trifling task to muster a laugh just then. They were so completely bespattered (or rather besmeared) with the mud from the feet of the horses while dashing in the streets, that it was difficult to distinguish even the colour of their clothes; for the rain still poured in torrents.

The infantry were now sufficiently retired to admit of our falling back to the next rising ground. We accordingly retired in two lines, and the enemy gained possession of the height we had quitted. They immediately opened a brisk cannonade which was smartly answered by our light artillery and rocket troop. After the guns began to fire, the rain came down in sheets, the sky was black and gloomy, the thunder rolled in dreadful peals, the vivid lightning flashed in our eyes almost incessantly, the guns rattled and the rockets roared as they sped through the murky scene; which was indeed a scene of awful sublimity, which must have impressed the mind of every reasonable beholder.

The ground now became extremely soft, the horses sunk deep, the cannon shot flew thick, but where they struck they buried themselves and thereby (to all probability) many lives were preserved which might have been lost had the ground remained in the dry state it was in a few hours before and caused the balls to bounce and take a second flight. However, a considerable number fell during the retreat! Every now and then, some one of Fortune's least favoured sons stood in the way of these destructive messengers and a most unpleasant sight it was to see a man struck with one of them. This leads me to a faint description of one who fell close to the spot on which I stood myself, I could not help shuddering at the sight, although they were frequent. He was a poor fellow belonging to the Royals, who was passing the flank of the squadron on which I was posted, on his way to our rear.

A shot struck him behind; it went through his valise (or saddle bags) and nearly severed his body, near the loins; it passed through his cloak in front, and tore away the greater part of the horse's head, laying the whole fabric, a mangled and shapeless heap on the ground, in an instant. When the ball struck his valise, wherein were his shirts, stockings and other articles of necessaries, they were dashed in different directions with such force that the shirts were seen flittering in shreds in the air some yards above our heads. I daresay the warrior was not struck with the idea of his linen being thus unfolded, when he, with all the pride of a soldier was in the act of folding and packing them, so as to call forth the praise of his captain on the neatness of his kit. Nor did the father, mother, or perhaps the bosom friend who edited the letters that were scattered around him; contemplate their destruction.

The retreat was conducted with the greatest regularity on the part of our commanders, we continued to retire from height to height; from each of which the enemy were kept in check, till our infantry had gained sufficient ground to the rear, nor durst they make an attack upon our line during the day.

We at last reached the heights of Waterloo and saw preparations making which convinced us that it was, at least, the ground selected for another battle. We passed the farmhouse, La Haye Sainte, which is situated on the roadside and in the hollow between the elevations on which the two armies were afterwards posted and behind a hedge, which skirted a narrow lane that ran along the brow of the height we were ascending, we discovered a brigade of artillery ambushed [in ambush]; their guns were pointed through the bottom of the hedge and the artillery men were laid down so as to be concealed from the view of the enemy. We moved past these guns and the rocket troop was drawn up where the road was cut through the height, where they were totally concealed till very close approached. Our other troops were all drawn behind the height and the covering cavalry manoeuvring on its summit, as if preparing again to retire. The enemy, as usual, to gain the height which they supposed us about to quit, with all possible expedition made a rapid advance till they were within a hundred & fifty yards of the hedge; the word was given, our artillery sprang to their guns and opened such a shower of grape among them, as sent them reeling in all directions.

The rocketeers were no less effective, for they sent one after another of these frightful things among the enemy; which flew with great velocity, roaring and spewing columns of fire, that, to witness them making ground towards him, were sufficient to have frightened the master of the fiery region himself. Whenever one of these was well directed against a column, it made an avenue and the French could no longer brave the reception they had got. They wheeled about and all that were able to wheel made off, leaving a considerable number of their companions behind, whose wheeling days were terminated. The French retreated precipitately till they got beyond the reach of our guns which ceased firing and seeing our noble commander had posted himself, they made no further attempt to disturb our quiet during the night.

The ground was now pointed out to each brigade, on which it was to take post and they took their station accordingly. Sir William Ponsonby's Brigade covered the highlanders who were near the centre of the line and close to the left of the great road. We were dismounted, between six and seven in the evening, the horses much fatigued and men wet to the skin and sulky with hunger, no provisions having yet been received. If they had come in contact with the enemy in this state, a Frenchman might have called to some other quarter for mercy, for I believe he would have experienced but a small portion at their hands. They exclaimed violently against the commissaries, who had fled with the stores which ought to have been delivered to the men when an opportunity served for drawing them; but their complaints were to no purpose; these fellows were off to save their skins, supposing the army to be in full flight before the French, and those who were to perform the work left in the lurch. However, the large farmhouse, Mont St Jean, was close to our right rear and it may be conceived that it would not have been and easy task to prevent the men (under such circumstances) from making their way into it. They were no sooner dismounted than they ran in all directions in search of green forage for the noble animal which had carried them during the hazardous day and afterwards bent their steps to the farmhouse; the farmyard was a square formed, partly by the dwelling & outhouses and partly by a high wall, there were two gateways facing each other on opposite sides of the square, which on the approach of the storming party, were found shut and strongly barricaded within. However, in a few minutes they were hoisted from their hinges and a free entrance made for all parties and no house ever was more completely ransacked; it contained a great quantity of provisions, wine and fuel, which was carried away as fast as the men could load themselves.

I had not accompanied the first party who went in, but seeing so many returning, loaded with the good things of the land, I imbibed a great desire to be a partaker of some of them and off I set. In a few seconds I arrived at the gate and fixed my eyes on such a scene within, as they had never seen before, the interior of the square was crowded with soldiers of all nations composing the army, some were carrying away faggots of wood, some bundles of straw, some buckets of wine, haversacks full of bread, pigs, fowls, &c &c and many were seen in the motley groups, in a pasture similar to that which the Lancashire country boors put themselves in when about to let fly with a bludgeon at the pins on Kersal moor race ground.[2] Taking a good aim with their swords or some other weapon at the wandering individuals of the feathered legion who had yet escaped and flew with shrill and despairing cries from corner to corner, to save as long as possible, the small spark of life, which mortal terror had only left; the venerable turkey cock was carried off in triumph by a foot guardsman with whom one of the highlanders had disputed aboot the bubbly jock [turkey cock], so earnestly that their victim was nearly torn limb from limb. I met Jock W[ise][3] of the troop

---

2. Kersal Moor, near modern-day Prestwich Golf Club, was Manchester's principal racecourse from 1681 to 1847.

3. Jock is of course a derivative of Jacob or John, making the soldier Private John Wise. He was born in Falkirk and joined the regiment at Glasgow on 27 August 1805 aged 22, having previously worked as a labourer. He was recorded as being 5ft 8in tall, with brown hair and hazel eyes. He served until 10 November 1827 when he was discharged still as a private with a 'good' conduct record. One of the celebrated 'Falkirk 13', thirteen men of the town who fought in the Scots Greys at Waterloo and were called whimsically the 'Falkirk Dozen'.

to which I myself belonged, coming out with an immense old sow on his shoulders. The animal roared most furiously but Jock was deaf to all her complaints and continued his march to the lines 'Where' he said, 'she would be of some use.'

I stared at the progress of this furious bandit-like swarm of marauders for a time, but as things were going very fast, I thought I had better look out for myself while anything remained; and for this purpose tried to thrust myself into the house, and effected it with great difficulty as far as the cellar door, into which I descended and plumped half way up to the knee in wine, there had been an immense quantity of wine in the cellar and the heads of many of the barrels had been knocked in, by which means the whole place was thus flooded. It was, however, with the greatest difficulty I got my canteen filled and if coming in was bad, struggling to get out again was ten times worse; and made me wish heartily I had never attempted such a method of obtaining so trifling a prize. I believe I was a full half hour in this place and was so sick when I got out that I scarcely could stand on my legs; the loathsome heat, the fumes of the wine and the mingled breaths of the crowds that thrust themselves into it, was more than any man could bear and many a cry and ejaculation to get out again was heard issuing from the most remote corners of the sickly dungeon.

I proceeded to the lines with my wine, where the men had several fires already blazing and a general cooking going on. Officers and men crowded round them roasting in the best manner they could devise anything they had got from the farmhouse. The officers who could beg the leg of a fowl from any of the men, did not think their rank at all degraded by turning cook for themselves, but seemed to relish the precious morsel without either bread or salt. I was informed that the method Jock W[ise] had adopted for the killing of his sow, was knocking her down with a piece of a cart shaft which had been burning on the fire. He struck her on the head, as he supposed, often enough to have dispatched the vital spark and to divest her skin of the hair as much as possible, before he cut her up, he with the assistance of his comrades threw her on the fire; alleging it to be no bad consequence if she was thus partly roasted. But poor grumphy [pig], having still a spark left and not relishing the element she had got into, sprung with the most hideous yells from the flames and galloped for her life. But Jock was not to be done in that manner, he could gallop as fast as her, and consequently she was compelled to come back and some of better skill helped Jock in showing her the road out of this world.

The rain still continued to fall and was carried along on the wind, which had arisen to a perfect hurricane. The men had brought everything from Mont St Jean which was of any use to keep their fires blazing, even the plough, harrows, carts, waggons, with the doors and gates from their hinges were captured for the above use and the men huddled round the fires for the night had become extremely cold. Heavy peals of thunder still rolled over our heads and vivid flashes of lightning played upon the dreary plain and flashed their terrific glow on all the apparatus of war. The horses were linked together and from the battering of the storm, became restless and in continual motion, by which means they had worked the ground on which they stood into such a puddle that many of them were sunk above the knees. And the excessive darkness of the night, added to cold, hunger and wet, which seemed to be combined against us on the comfortless plain afforded but a dreary and cheerless lodging.

Our colonel, with a hope of obtaining some rations for the men, ordered a sergeant from each troop to mount and go out in search of the quarter master and commissary. It fell to my lot to go for the troop to which I belonged and after we had received the colonel's orders (which were to divide ourselves by twos and each party to take a separate road and to be directed by such information as we could collect, as to the places where any of these people were to be found) we proceeded, but after a moment's reflection on our situation, we determined only to make two divisions of our number, and accordingly each consisting of three, took a separate road. My two companions and myself resolved to make a trial of going to Braine la Leud, for which purpose we passed along the rear of our army in the direction where it lay. Braine la Leud was a small town situated to the right of the army where (we were informed) many of the commissaries had fled for safety during the retreat. The lights of the numerous fires that blazed on the plain guided us on our dark and uncertain route, till we reached its right flank, where the fires began to decrease in number and left us so exposed to the excessive darkness of the night and the pelting of the pitiless storm, that in a short space, we found we had lost the road which we had been informed, was to lead us to Braine la Leud and were again wading our dreary way through the long corn. We now found ourselves in such a dilemma that we had no alternative but [to] direct our course again upon the fires we had left behind; but so completely were we bewildered that neither of us could positively distinguish which were the English or which were the French fires. However, we moved towards the light, for there were no fences to mar our march, till we came within a short distance of a fire which was a considerable distance from any of the rest, most probably that of some outpost. To this we determined to steer, in hopes of getting some directions concerning our way to Braine la Leud and were on the point of going in among a party of the enemy when we were challenged by an English voice. This proved to be a British officer with a reconnoitring party; he informed us that the fire in our front which we were about to go into, was that of one of the enemy's piquets and put us in a direction by which we again got into the Nivelles road, from which we were to branch off by another lane to Braine la Leud.

How we had not been noticed by any of the videttes, I can account for in no other way, than that the roaring of the storm and the excessive darkness of the night, had enabled us to pass them without being heard or seen.

We were now determined to make another push for Braine la Leud and continued to plod along this narrow lane till we arrived at a hollow way, where the rain had flooded it to such a degree that our horses were in an instant up to their bellies in water, they were still going deeper and when it began to come over the heads of our Wellington boot, we considered it imprudent to venture forward on an unknown track so inundated. We therefore pulled up and after retiring a few yards, groped our way through the hedge in hopes of being enabled to pass the flooded part by the fields. We advanced a considerable time in this manner and at last saw a light moving backward & forward in our front. The glimmer which was tossed to and fro by the dreadful hurricane resembled that of a lanthorn, and filled us with hopes that we were near the village, we accordingly took a direction across the field and plumped upon a foraging party of the French, who busied themselves in filling their canteens with some kind of liquor from a cask under the cover of an open shed by a little farmhouse on the road. The hedge only separated us and although we longed to partake with them, we durst not make our wish known, for they were about twenty in number and two or three peasants, with trembling steps, attended and endeavoured to keep lights burning for the marauders, while they filled their canteens and haversacks with their property.

We were now again compelled to turn back and being thus foiled in endeavours which we knew we could not better, we relinquished any farther attempt to accomplish our design and turning our horses round in the quietest manner, we sneaked off through the long wet corn in the direction of the army again. And after crossing many rye fields and scrambling our way through a number of hedgerows, we by chance emerged on the Nivelles road; this we determined to follow to its junction with the great Brussels road and (if possible) to follow it thither. We accordingly proceeded till we arrived at the village of Mont St Jean, where we hoped to procure some refreshment for ourselves, at least; but without success. The village consisted only of a few straggling cottages on either side of the road, whose inhabitants had fled, with their little property, into the great Forest of Soignes, or some other place of safety. Some of the doors were shut, which induced us to believe that some of the peasantry still remained, but on knocking for an entrance, we were invariably answered by officers of the army, who had taken refuge in them from the storm. We continued our march till we arrived at the village of Waterloo, which is situated on the verge of the great Forest of Soignes or rather embosomed among some straggling clumps of lofty beeches and elms which overshoot the general outline of the forest and scatter themselves on either hand towards the village of Mont St Jean. Here we again renewed our endeavours to obtain some refreshment; we approached the door of a little inn and after calling two or three times, were attended by an elderly woman, who sauntered toward us in tears; she looked as if terror had completely stupefied her, stared wildly at us and muttering some inarticulate sentences, staggered into the house again. The house, yard, stables and other places of cover, were crowded with foreigners and making use of what the place contained at their own discretion, which depredations we saw going on and considered it unsafe to delay long. We betook ourselves to our journey again upon the great road, which we intended to pursue, but had no sooner entered the forest than it became so dark, from the lofty trees which overarched the road and with their thick foliage excluded, even the faint ray of light, which descends from the heavens in the darkest night; that we could see nothing. But our ears were assailed with the most dreadful sounds; the wind howled through the creaking trees and most appalling cries were heard, which we supposed to proceed from the female followers of the army, who were thus exposed to a night of horrors.

We continued to persevere till we arrived at a spot where some of the bat horses[4] were bivouacked and as they informed us, we found that

---

4. Bat horses were those used for transporting equipment rather than for riding. Officers received 'bat and forage' money to pay for their upkeep on campaign.

the farther in we got, the way was the more difficult and at last became completely choked up with waggons, carts, bullocks and baggage animals, also many of the commissaries who were on their way to the army with provisions, but had got so hemmed in here, that they could not effect a movement either back or forward.

We had not got more than two miles into the forest when we were compelled to turn again and although we had found it extremely difficult to get forward; we struggled with much more on our way back. The middle of the road was a pavement of large stones about ten feet in width; between the pavement and the bank on either side, was a space of about four or five feet of nothing but soft clay, which by the continual hurry of horses on the road, were become deep and dangerous ditches, full of mire and water. However, we weathered our way back to where the bat horses were bivouacked and were informed that many lives were lost in these ditches during the hurry of the retreat and that several bodies of Belgians had rushed towards Brussels with such precipitation that they upset a great number of the bat horses by driving them from the pavement and whoever rode thereon was trampled to death in the mire and the opportunity embraced by the marauding followers of the Belgian army, who lurked in the wood and dragged into the thicket, the baggage of any officer which was thus upset, where they disposed of it at their own discretion. They frequently sallied from the wood, when they saw any poor fellow who had lost his horse, endeavouring to save his master's baggage and on pretence of assisting him, drag it amongst the thick brushwood and so ease the poor batman of all his charge. We were met by several parties of foreigners before we got out of the wood and were several times shoved into the clay hole as we afterwards termed it, however we were indebted to the strength of our horses, who, as we found it necessary to make others give way in the same manner; kept their ground with as much firmness as any we came in contact with, till we got out of the dreaded scene.

A feeling mind could scarcely anticipate a scene of greater horror than the one we had just turned our backs on. The rain still poured in torrents and the wind blew with uncommon fury, the drear forest howled and the groaning trees seemed to vie with each other in answering with the most dismal sough [moaning], each fury fraught blast, the frequent neighing of horses, the screams of women and children, loud volleys of execrations bursting forth as if proceeding from some quarter where terror and wrath alike held dominion. And sometimes, from the thicket to windward, the heavy groan of the wounded who had crept therein for safety during the night, was intermingled with all the horrible sounds which invaded the ear.

We found our utmost efforts, to succeed in the duty we had been sent upon, fruitless; and therefore agreed to return to the regiment; however, we determined to make a short stay as we passed the village of Waterloo to make to make another trial of purchasing some liquor or bread to take to the lines with us, we accordingly dismounted and thrust our horses into an open stable, which was already more than full. But so eager were they to get under cover, once more, that they soon made way for themselves.

The stable was crammed with Belgic cavalry & some British bat horses, while under the mangers reposed wounded men, soldiers' wives, officer's servants &c &c and every vacant corner about the premises wherein a head could be thrust, were filled with people of this description; several dead men lay amongst the others, whom (we conjectured) had died of their wounds after lying down and others (we did not hesitate to believe) had, in a state of intoxication been trampled to death among the feet of the horses.

We agreed that one out of the three which composed our party, should remain in the stable, to watch our horses, for many a sham warrior of Belgium, whose brain was heated with wine, swaggered about the inn and yard, who might not have considered horse stealing any crime; and the other two proceeded to the house for the purpose of making a purchase of some provisions, if such was to be had. We entered a large room where the floor was completely covered with weary, wounded and drunken men. The landlady again approached us, accompanied by an old man who seemed absorbed in thought & worn with fatigue, his aged limbs tottered under him. We took the earliest opportunity of assuring them that we were not come to plunder or to use any violence against their property or persons, but wanted some refreshment for payment, at the same time (to ensure success) we showed them our cash. The last motion seemed to have a good effect upon the landlady, for she immediately brought us a measure of Geneva and each a small slice of bread, for which we paid their demand and they seemed much satisfied. We repaired to the stable with what we had got, where we crept into a corner and banqueted like beasts of prey crouching in their caves.

We eat [sic] and drank our precious morsel, after which we again entered the house and having presented our canteens and money together, had them filled for our comrades in the field, departed and joined the regiment about half past 3 in the morning.

The men were now making preparations for the task which they knew was laid out for them; some scraped the dirt from their horses and accoutrements, others adjusted the flints of their firearms and many still sat near the remains of the neglected & dying fires, whetting their swords with a small file, which each man carried for that purpose.

The news had reached the army of the defeat of the Prussians, which being a matter of great interest, every man was anxious to learn their situation. It appeared that dispatches had been received from Prince Blucher's army during the night which gave a slight account of their operations from the commencement of hostilities up to that period, which were as follows.

At 3 o'clock on the morning of the 15th the French General Reille attacked and drove in the Prussian outposts on the banks of the Sambre. The Prussians endeavoured to destroy the bridge by which the enemy must pass the river, to retard their advance and to afford themselves time to evacuate Charleroi, but the injury it sustained was soon repaired by the enemy and their light cavalry passed and took possession of Charleroi. Another corps of the enemy effected a passage at Marchienne au Pont and advanced on Gosselies, a large town on the Brussels road; intending to cut off the retreat of the Prussian column which had left Charleroi. However, the Prussians made good their retreat to Fleurus, where General Ziethen had concentrated the First Corps of their army. The enemy attacked him warmly but he kept his ground until the evening.

The presence of Napoleon and the success with which the first attack of the campaign was attended; had so electrified the French troops and inspired them with confidence, that (in some of their attacks) they rushed with the bayonet upon the Prussians without firing a shot, and charged with such fury that nothing could withstand their first onset and the results of the first day's engagements were, in favour of the enemy, 1,000 prisoners, the passage of the Sambre & possession of Charleroi, where Bonaparte established his headquarters.

The 2nd & 3rd Corps of the Prussian army under Generals Thielmann and Borstel[5] were to arrive on the same day at Sombreffe

---

5.   Thielmann actually commanded III Corps and Pirch II Corps instead of General Von Borstell, who was dismissed by Blücher over the Saxon mutiny and imprisoned for six months. The Kingdom of Saxony had been divided into two by the Congress of Vienna, as a punishment for the King of Saxony's loyalty to Napoleon in 1813. The troops from that part given to

and the 4th Corps under General Bulow on the following day (the 16th) as Marshal Blucher intended to attack the enemy as soon as his army were concentrated.

General Ziethen had fallen back to the same point and although the 4th Corps were not up, nor could not be expected before afternoon, Marshal Blucher resolved to give battle, knowing that the Duke of Wellington had put a strong division of his army in motion to support him, little dreaming that the British division were to be opposed to another corps of the French at Quatre Bras.

Marshal Blucher took possession of the 3 hamlets of Sombreffe, Ligny and St Amand, his right rested on St Amand, his left on Sombreffe and centre in Ligny.

On the morning of the 16th the French advanced with numbers which far outstripped those of the Prussian Army and the battle began.

The first attack was made upon St Amand which after a vigorous resistance was carried by the French. They next directed their efforts against Ligny (which is a large compact village, situated on a rivulet of the same name), here a contest began, which may be considered one of the most obstinate recorded in history. We have heard of villages being often taken and retaken, but here the battle continued [for] five hours in the street continually and the movements backwards and forwards, confined to a very small space on both sides. Fresh troops came up, for both armies, had behind the part of the village they occupied, great masses of infantry which maintained the combat and thus renewed it by reinforcements from the rear. About 200 pieces of cannon from each side, were directed against the town, which scarcely left one stone upon another and set it on fire in many places. The Prussian army was from time to time attacked in other parts of their position, but an unceasing combat was maintained in Ligny.

The battle continued with great fury till the middle of the day, but the issue seemed to depend on the arrival of the Duke of Wellington's division, or that of the 4th Corps of Prussians; but even at this critical

---

Prussia were intermingled with the Prussian army in 1815. Blücher wished to reform them with all the Prussian Saxons in separate specific regiments. The Saxons were very unhappy with this and mutinied. Blücher put the mutiny down with great severity and sent the Saxon troops to the rear as they were not trusted. They were a considerable loss to the ranks of the Allied armies. Von Borstell had criticised Blucher's handling of the entire incident and was summarily sacked.

juncture, a messenger arrived from the Duke of Wellington, informing the Field Marshal that the English division destined to support him, was violently attacked by a corps of the French army and that it was with the greatest difficulty it had maintained itself in a position near Quatre Bras.

This was, no doubt, unwelcome news to the Prussian commander, who was compelled (by the non-appearance of his own 4th Corps) to maintain alone the contest, with an enemy greatly superior in numbers.[6]

Evening was now fast approaching but the battle continued with the same fury and equality of success, all the Prussian divisions were engaged, or had been so, and although night was come, the battle did not cease. But such was the critical moment when Prince Blucher hoped in vain, for those succours which were now become so necessary, that suddenly a division of the enemy infantry, which by favour of the night, had made a circuit round the village of Ligny without being observed, and at the same time, some regiments of cuirassiers forced a passage on the other side and took in the rear the main body of the Prussians which were posted behind the houses.

This surprise was decisive on the part of the enemy, especially as it happened at the moment when the Prussian cavalry were repulsed by another body of those of the French & no other alternative left them but that of making a good retreat.

It however appears that the Prussians did not allow themselves to be discouraged, either by being thus surprised in the dark or by the idea of being surrounded on all sides, as they coolly formed their squares, repulsed the attacks of the enemy and retreated in good order.

In consequence of the sudden eruption of the enemy's cavalry, several pieces of Prussian cannon in their precipitate retreat, had taken directions which led them to defiles where they got into disorder and about 20 guns fell, thus into the hands of the enemy.

The Prussian army retreated about half a league and formed again where the enemy did not venture to pursue them. The villages of Brye and Sombreffe remained in possession of the Prussians all night, where General Thielmann fought with the 3rd Corps, but at daybreak, he began his retreat towards Gembloux where General Bulow had at length proceeded in the morning behind the defile of Mont St Guibert.

---

6. In fact the Prussians were the superior force at Ligny without the IV Corps, Blücher commanding around 83,000 men and 224 guns against Napoleon's 72,000 men and a similar number of guns.

The loss of the Prussians in killed and wounded in this action was very great, however the enemy took no prisoners except a part of their wounded. The battle they lost, but retained their honour untarnished, for they fought with a bravery & courage not to be exceeded. Their gallant chief in leading on a charge of cavalry, was exposed to the greatest danger; the body of horse which he led on were repulsed and while retreating at full speed before the victorious enemy, a musket ball struck his horse, which soon fell to the ground, the veteran general was stunned by the fall to the ground, while his horse lay upon one of his legs in such a manner that he could not disentangle himself and he lay in this perilous situation till the last Prussian horseman had passed. They were closely pursued by the enemy's cuirassiers who followed up the advantage they had gained and also passed the field marshal without discovering him. An adjutant[7] only had remained with him, who had resolved to share his fate, however some kind spirit had taken them both into their protection, for a second attack of Prussians repulsed the cuirassiers, who in their precipitate retreat, repassed the field marshal, where he lay covered with a cloak, without making the discovery & he was disentangled, mounted a dragoon horse & escaped without sustaining any injury except some slight bruises. The horse which was killed from under Prince Blucher was a present he had received from his most gracious majesty, George the 4th, then Prince Regent of England.

On the 17th in the morning the Prussian Army concentrated itself in the environs of Wavre; Bonaparte put himself in motion against the Duke of Wellington and united with the army which had opposed the British at Quatre Bras. Lord Wellington had now taken a position which he was determined to maintain to the utmost of his power. His right wing extended to Braine la Leud, the centre in front of Mont St Jean and his left on Frichermont.

---

7.   Count Nostitz.

Chapter 18

18 June 1815

His grace dispatched a messenger to Prince Blucher, acquainting him that he was resolved to accept the battle in this position, if the field marshal would support him with two corps of his army, which he promised to do with his whole strength and at daybreak on the morning of the 18th the Prussians again begin to move; the 2nd & 4th corps marched by St Lambert where they were to take a position covered by a wood near Frichermont and to take the enemy in rear whenever a moment should appear favourable. The 1st Corps was to operate by Ohain on the right flank of the enemy; and the 3rd to follow slowly in order to afford succour in case of need.

The forgoing is such a detail of the operations of the Prussian army and the latest arrangements between the two illustrious warriors as we were able to collect and rely upon;[1] I shall therefore forbear to enter at greater length upon uncertainty and call the attention of the reader to such particulars as came under my oun eye and those of my intimate comrades after joining the regiment on the morning of the 18th.

At daybreak, the allied army consisting of 95,000[2] men were arrayed in order of battle along the crest of the gentle elevation in front of Mont St Jean, where the dawning of morn opened to their view, the powerful

---

1. It is certain that William would not have known even this much on the day of battle, but much of this would have been learnt much later.
2. The Allied Army under Wellington numbered about 68,000 with another 18,000 covering Wellington's extreme right flank at Hal.

army of France consisting of 130,000[3] men posted in like order on the opposite rising ground, in front of Plancenoit and Mont Plaisir.[4]

The moment was now arrived when every soldier's feelings were aroused. The two formidable armies stood in view of each other; a great battle was now inevitable, in which many thousands must fall; and as slow approaching day still unfolded new masses of the enemy to view; the chance of surviving it appeared to every man to be against him; the arrival of every moment was looked upon as that on which the action was to begin and full day seemed to appear as slow as if nature had been unwilling to lend her light for the bloody purpose. Home, relatives and friends crowded upon the imagination, whom to all human probability we were to see no more, at which reflection, a pang of bitterness, at intervals, could not be suppressed. This might with justice be considered an appalling moment, for no enthusiasm which the heat of battle is capable of stirring up in the breast, aided the courage of those who beheld in calm silence, their inveterate enemy, braving their front with superior numbers and elated spirits from the actions they had already won.

Every man seemed to weigh the danger which stood before him, from the awful silence which reigned in the lines for some time; and I may add, that I have since heard some of the bravest men that Britain's ranks could boast of, confess that at that time they experienced a kind of lowness of spirits, which they could account for in no other way than that of being depressed by the sufferings they had endured from exposure to the fury of the elements; for no want of the best of courage was the cause.

The army, thus stood, in anxious expectation, suffering from cold, hunger and without a dry thread on their backs, or moving from the spot on which they were posted; from daybreak[5] until half past 9 o'clock and as the time passed on, the men grew more impatient for the commencement of the action. The weather had now become more

---

3. The French army at Waterloo numbered about 73,000 men. Many observers of the battle overestimate the French army particularly, being unaware that some 33,000 men had been detached under Marshal Grouchy to ensure that the Prussians could not join Wellington.
4. A farm complex on the French side of the battlefield just to the south-west of Hougoumont.
5. The army was roused one hour before dawn and formed ready for battle until 'a white horse could be seen at one mile' when the opportunity for a surprise dawn attack was deemed to have passed.

moderate, which during the night was tremendous; the rain ceased and the men (who by long suspense seemed to be getting heedless about their fate) as they stood under arms, began to scrape and shake the dirt and mud from their clothes and accoutrements for many were nearly covered with it, in their cold beds on that night of horrors.

It was about half past 9 when some movement was observed in rear of the French army and soon after, Napoleon with his numerous staff placed himself on an eminence from which he must have had a good view of the allied army. In this situation he remained a few minutes, then advanced towards the right of his own line and proceeded with his staff along the front amid the loud shouts of his almost innumerable legions, who blackened the face of the landscape nearly as far as the eye could trace. He continued to move along, with his hat frequently uplifted till he reached the left. The long looked for moment was at last come, for he had no sooner turned the flank and directed his steps towards a station in the rear, than the conflict began.[6] The first gun was fired on the enemy's left flank and as every artillery gunner waited the signal with his match already burning, the whole two lines were eclipsed in fire and smoke, in a space not exceeding one minute. So close were the lines together that the musquetry opened nearly at the same instant.[7]

The destruction was now begun, the atmosphere was darkened with the smoke, the electric flash from the cannon's mouth gleamed through the blue scene and immense quantities of earth were dashed into the air by the striking of the cannon balls.

Our brigade, covered the highlanders,[8] and for the purpose of saving the men as much as possible till they were required in action, were drawn into the hollow a little to the left of Mont St Jean. However, this situation, for the short time we remained in it, seemed equally precarious with the height, for the enemy, whom (it would appear)

---

6. It is generally agreed that the battle commenced at about 11.25 am, although few soldiers had a pocket watch to state the time accurately.

7. The musketry would be that between the opposing skirmishers out in front of the main lines.

8. Ponsonby's brigade stood in line in a hollow behind Picton's division, which was on the reverse of the slope to the east of the Brussels road, with Bijlandt's Belgians in front, actually holding the ridge line at the commencement of the action. Picton's 5th Division included amongst others the 1st, 42nd, 79th and 92nd Foot, which were all Scottish regiments.

considered it full of troops and were actively employed throwing shells into it, by which means we had several men and horses killed in a few minutes after the action began.

We sat in this situation a considerable time and as the sky became darkened by the clouds of smoke which rolled in the atmosphere, the objects in our front became more indistinct and in a short time we could discern nothing but, now and then, a faint glimpse of some part of the bustling infantry & artillery, on the height in our front. The roaring of the cannon and sharper knell of the musquetry were worn into a tremendous medley of sounds and a deafening vibration played in the air, which seemed to rebound from the arches of heaven and shake the trembling earth.

The first attack was made on the right of the British line; the French led on by Jerome Bonaparte made a desperate effort to subdue the brave troops which occupied the chateau and orchard of Hougoumont. The place was filled with Nassau sharpshooters, a Brunswick Regiment[9] and part of the British Guards with a few field pieces.

The enemy advanced impetuously and penetrated the orchard; the Nassau troops gave way and the possession of the post must at once have been lost, had it not been for the desperate exertions of the British Guards and Brunswickers, by which the enemy was repulsed and compelled to abandon the contest, leaving a great number of killed and wounded behind them.

The whole lines were now in hot action, and striving squadrons palely seen advancing and retreating through the smoke in all parts of the embattled field.

---

9. Actually the 1st Battalion 2nd Nassau Regiment, commanded by Major Busgen. This confusion arises because Nassau was once deemed part of Brunswick.

Chapter 19

The Brigade Charges

Napoleon, after witnessing the failure of his first attack upon
Hougoumont, directed a strong body of chosen troops against the
centre of the British line.[1] The left of the great road was the point from
which this coming storm was intended to sweep a line of heroes, to turn
their left and so cut off their communication with the Prussian army,[2] to
carry Mont St Jean and clear a way to Brussels.

For this purpose Bonaparte placed the greater part of his reserve
against the British left centre and with two immense columns
(amounting to nearly fifteen thousand men) advanced to the attack.
They approached the position occupied by Major General Sir Denis
Pack's Brigade of infantry (consisting of the 32nd, 42nd, 44th &
92nd Regiments;[3] covered by Major General Ponsonby's brigade of
cavalry) and had already reached the hollow[4] immediately in their

---

1. It was really the left wing of the Allied line.
2. At this point Napoleon was unaware of the approaching Prussians.
3. William is a little confused here. The first line was Bijlandt's Belgian troops,
    who had taken a pounding at Quatre Bras two days earlier and began to
    crumble and flee in front of these greatly superior numbers. Picton ordered
    the two brigades of his division to advance to the crest line. On the right
    was Kempt's Brigade, nearest the Brussels road were the 1/95th, and to
    their left in line were the 32nd, 79th and 28th Foot. To their left was Pack's
    Brigade consisting of 3/1st, 42nd, 92nd and with 2/44th on the extreme left
    of this division.
4. The trackway running along the crest of the ridge lay between two solid
    hedge lines and was slightly sunken due to centuries of use by farm vehicles,
    the 'hollow' was more pronounced near the crossroads where it crossed the
    Brussels road and was very slight, if not level on the left where the Greys were.

front when the brave Ponsonby received orders to charge them with his horse.[5]

This cloud of Frenchmen, who advanced impetuously with the bayonet, if a spark of courage was amongst them, must have overwhelmed the British infantry opposed to them; yet they kept their ground undaunted and firm[6] and at last wheeled back by companies, through the intervals of which, the cavalry brigade passed and charged to the front.[7] Unfortunately, however, for the British cavalry, a narrow lane with a hedgerow and ditch ran along the brow of the declivity, a short distance in front of our infantry.[8] And while the troops were yet passing through each other, the thrilling notes of the bagpipe suddenly struck the ear & mingled its wild notes in the dread confusion. The war cry of 'Scotland for Ever' with electric swiftness, resounded through the ranks of two of her veteran corps who had thus met; then thistle again shook its head and the soul of every man seemed impregnated with deeds of valour, which were ready under any hazard, to support the glory of their native land and thus full of destructive ire, they rushed forward to the hedge; and the enemy from the opposite height (eyeing what they regarded as a vain attempt of a handful of men, to drive back, or even to arrest the progress of their mighty phalanx), opened a battery which played over the heads of their own masses, upon the hedge. The British squadrons, by getting over and through the defiles of the hedge and by the great number of both men and horses, who fell at the same

5. Ponsonby's Brigade stretched in line, on the extreme right almost touching the Brussels road were the 1st (Royal) Dragoons, to their left were the 6th (Inniskilling) Dragoons and on the extreme left were the 2nd North British (Scots Greys) Dragoons who were behind the 42nd and 92nd Foot.

6. D'Erlon's corps numbered nearly 18,000 men, against Picton's 3,500 and although they fought bravely and appeared to be holding the line, it is pretty certain that if the cavalry had not charged, the British line would inevitably have eventually been overwhelmed by sheer numbers.

7. Wheeling by companies from line into company columns was well practised, but it is unlikely that the passage of the cavalry through the line of British infantry was as smooth as William describes! Indeed a number of Highland infantry describe the cavalry as having simply bowled them over.

8. This tallies with French claims that their infantry, particularly at the eastern end of the attack, where the Greys were, reached and had passed the trackway and both hedge lines before the Greys attacked.

point, by the enemy's shot were literally broken; and although what followed may not have any claim to modern discipline, I do not hesitate to state that it was the only mode of attack by which they had any chance of succeeding in repelling the enemy, or of saving any of themselves from destruction.

The enemy's guns mowed them down so thick,[9] that the gaps became choked up with dead and wounded and retarded the progress of the survivors so much that they could only get over by twos & threes in a body; and in this manner, without delaying a moment to form a line (which expedient they said, was to be attended with almost instant death to every man) they rushed upon the enemy's column and to account for how it was broken is a task which I will not attempt to describe, but broken it was! And very few minutes had winged their passage, when this strong body of the boasting Old Guard[10] were in the greatest imaginable state of confusion, not a rank kept its form[11] and every individual endeavoured to save himself by flight, or by protecting himself in the best manner he could from the sabres of the dragoons, who still powered down upon them like a torrent with shouts that were heard in distant parts of the field, soaring above all the mingled sounds of the engines of death which rent the sulphury air and rolled along the face of the heavens. A most dreadful slaughter followed; the first column was nearly all cut down with the sword; for a report had made its way through the British lines during the morning, that the

---

9. It is very interesting how fierce the cannon fire was at the hedge road according to William. The French had dragged forward a number of cannon to an intermediate ridge to support d'Erlon's attack, but it is extremely unlikely that canister fire from such a distance could have caused such devastation amongst the Greys. It is much more likely that most of the balls whizzing past the Greys were actually fired from the muskets of the French infantry, who were unable to form square in the unusual formation they had advanced in and that their front ranks desperately defended themselves by firing indiscriminately in an attempt to offer a hasty defence against such formidable cavalry.

10. Almost every Allied soldier claims to have faced the veterans of Napoleon's Old Guard, but most are certainly mistaken. The Imperial Guard did not take any part in the advance of d'Erlon's corps.

11. The French confusion was heightened by the fact that they were in an unusual formation which negated all of their training to deal with cavalry attacks. The columns soon disintegrated into a disorganised rabble because of this, offering little opposition to the cavalry, hence its devastating success.

enemy had given no quarter to the Prussians at Ligny. This filled every breast with the same horrid resolution and many a head was cloven and silenced in death while in the act of surrendering or imploring for mercy.

Many of the highlanders left their ranks and seizing hold of the stirrups of the dragoons; descended the declivity bounding like bucks from the mountain, to share (among the enemy) the glory and the danger[12] and when the French soldiers threw themselves on the ground to evade the uplifted swords which hung over their heads, while they shrunk between hope and dissolution. The highlanders were often heard to exclaim, 'Ne'er mind that chield comrade, I'll gie him his fairin [firing]! I'll take care he disna fire after ye'[13] and so the bloody harvest went on till the greater part of the column was laid on the ground either killed or wounded, when the remainder were driven to the rear like a flock of sheep and made prisoners by our infantry, the cavalry who were not yet satisfied with the advantage they had gained, proceeded to attack the enemy's 2nd line;[14] which they did with such spirit, that a great part of it also gave way. And a small detachment headed by Colonel Hamilton of the Greys, by a desperate effort penetrated the

---

12. It is difficult to be certain that some of the Highland infantry advanced with the Greys, but it is certain that the Greys did not advance with any great speed beyond a walk, making it perfectly possible for infantry soldiers to hold their stirrups and to accompany them into the battle.

13. A number of the French infantry feigned death as the cavalry rode by, and some of these then fired on the horsemen from the rear. It is certain that Sergeant Ewart was a witness to exactly such an incident, whereby Ensign Kinchant spared the life of a French officer when advancing, only to die by a pistol ball which entered his back. Ewart who was his covering sergeant apparently looked back to see the French officer hurriedly attempting to conceal the pistol he had just fired. Ewart turned back and did not hesitate to remove the Frenchman's head from his body with one swipe of his sword.

14. Unfortunately no thought had been given to maintain a reserve during the charge and all of the senior officers were so caught up in the excitement of the moment, so that they were in no position to curb the excesses of the charge. British cavalry were regularly criticised for charging as if they were at a foxhunt, without a reserve and ultimately suffering dreadfully at the hands of the French reserve cavalry. It was a scene that was now played out fully at Waterloo.

enemy's position to the brigade of guns,[15] which had dealt so much destruction among our troops at the point of crossing the hedge; and killed every man and horse about them, except a string of the horses which one of our men brought away and with which he galloped back through the panic-struck enemy, like a Yorkshire dealer without meeting with the slightest opposition.

Time was now becoming precious and the delay of a moment of material consequence, for a numerous body of lancers and cuirassiers[16] were impetuously descending the height upon our scattered brigade and in spite of every exertion to make a good retreat, we were intercepted and compelled to cut our way through or surrender. Here a desperate combat ensued and in it a great number of our brave fellows fell, for the lancers flocked in such numbers upon every solitary individual, that few had less than four or five to contend with and many were thrust from their saddles by the force of so many cowardly spears, each at the same moment inflicting a death wound upon their vanquished victim.

One of my comrades who fell here, severely wounded, afterwards described his situation thus! 'I was in close combat with two lancers, whom I should have beaten off, had not a ball which struck my horse, laid him dead on the ground in an instant and also secured me with one leg under him, that I had no means of even longer defending myself. In this helpless situation I was vengefully assailed by these two dastards who now seemed to crown themselves with the honour of having vanquished me, they stabbed me in five places as I lay pinioned to the ground; and although I made signs with my hand (for I was nearly breathless in the contest, before I fell and had no words to crave the mercy which I hoped these motions would have awakened in their breasts, towards one who could no longer oppose them). However, I had none shown me, for they pierced me with deep wounds in five different places of the body and left me (to all probability) impressed

---

15. These were the corps' artillery that had moved forward alongside d'Erlon's troops onto the intermediate ridge and had fired from this much closer position in support of their troops. The remainder of the large number of batteries supplied by Napoleon to weaken the Allied defences before the attack went in, remained on the trackway which delineated the French front line.

16. The French cuirassiers of Travers' and Farine's Brigades and the lancers and chasseurs of Jacquinot's Brigade sought to cut off the retreat of the British cavalry and destroy them.

with the pleasing assurance that they had numbered me among the slain. How long I lay here in a state of insensibility, I know not! However, I was called to recollection by excessive pain! Weak and torpid from loss of blood, with the unbearable weight of my dead horse upon my benumbed leg. I once more opened my eyes upon a scene of such horror and destruction, as precludes anything like a true picture from one possessed of so limited a portion of language, fit for so great a task! I lay steeped in my own blood and saw many of my brave comrades seek mercy from the superior numbers of the enemy, by whom they were assailed and were denied their request; I also observed the fury fraught charges from both sides rolling in different directions through the bloody field; and in one of those I beheld my much-lamented friend and comrade, Peter Wetherspoon,[17] dealing such blows around him, as repulsed the attacks of many assailants! He had a deep sabre cut in the right cheek, from which the blood ran profusely. He seemed willing to escape and directed his steps close past the spot where I lay, pursued by five or six lancers; his eye flashed with wild despair, as his horse began to stagger under him, from a wound he had received some time before in his chest and when making a last great effort to turn his head round, that he might the more effectually defend himself by facing his opponents, who were fast gaining ground on him. His pursuers immediately flocked round and stabbed him in many places, till the vital spark had apparently left his manly form. He then turned on his back, stretched out the arm that could no longer wield the sword in his own (or country's) defence & seemed to cease to breathe. My own sufferings at this moment, were enough for any man to bear, yet I could not suppress the tear that unconsciously overflowed the banks of my brimful eye, when I beheld my intimate, faithful and sincerely beloved comrade meet with such a fate within a few yards of where I lay, unable to render him the slightest assistance. However, this was not yet all, that I was doomed to see him suffer, for the lancers had only left him to continue their waylaying cowardly attacks on our straggling and wounded dragoons who endeavoured to regain their lines; when he slowly raised his body to an attitude in which he seemed to suffer excessive bodily pain, he cast a wild look around him at the moment he saw one of his late assailants galloping again upon him, with his

---

17. Private Peter Wetherspoon or Wotherspoon is recorded as DD (Discharged Dead) after Waterloo.

bloody lance pointed towards his mangled body. The rapid approach of the fell fiend seemed to nerve our brave comrade with new vigour; for he grasped a sword that lay near him, and springing to his feet, struck off the well-aimed thrust of the Frenchman and with a blow of more than human force, unhorsed and killed him on the spot! The mortified companions of Peter's assailant, beheld his dissolution from a distant height; and when with one knee bent upon the expiring body and right arm uplifted; holding in its nervous grasp a part of the sword which he had broken; poor Peter was cruelly attacked behind and the ruthless spears of two more of these blood-hounds, at last found their way through the breast in which the last breath of this matchless hero was stored. At this moment, I felt, I know not how! But the following beautiful passage from an eminent author stole over my troubled mind.'

> O men, if ye be indeed men
> Spare them who can resist no longer[18]

The sequel of this soldier's account of his own sufferings &c will be given in its proper place, as he was found next day, lying in the same place, in a most wretched condition.

Our brigade was again formed behind a little clump of wood some distance to the left of the farm house of Mont St Jean,[19] but so much were our numbers reduced that the whole could scarcely show a front equal to that of one of the regiments, previous to the attack upon the enemy's position; however, advantages of much greater consequence had been gained by the sacrifice. For besides the vast numbers which were killed and wounded, the prisoners which were taken amounted to 6,000,[20] with a brigade of guns rendered useless during the remainder of the day and two of their proud Imperial eagles born triumphantly away by the British cavalry. One of the eagles was captured by Sergeant Charles Ewart of the Greys and the other by Corporal Stiles of the

---

18. From Sir Walter Scott's *Ivanhoe*, Chapter 29.
19. Craan's map of the Battle of Waterloo, which was surveyed just after the battle, shows a small wood some 500m to the east of Mont St Jean farmhouse.
20. This would be one-third of the attacking force and would appear to be too large an estimate. Most estimates make the number of prisoners made after this charge to be around 3,000.

Royals;[21] Ewart was afterwards presented with a commission[22] for this very conspicuous act of bravery. In attempting such an enterprise, he no doubt proved the benefit of being a very superior swordsman.

We had however to lament the loss of our gallant leader Major General Sir William Ponsonby. He was not killed as some writers on Waterloo have asserted, by following his madcap troops and getting into a ploughed field where his horse sunk so deep that he could not extricate himself again and there being surrounded and killed by the enemy's lancers!! But he was killed by a musket ball which entered his breast and laid him, without a struggle, lifeless on the ground.[23] He was in front of the right squadron of the Greys when he received the shot and fell from his horse, which Major Reignolds[24] of the same regiment (who was the General's Brigade Major) perceiving, sprung from his saddle and flew to his assistance, but finding him quite dead, drew the gold watch from his pocket; most probably with an intention of preserving it for the general's family; and was in the act of mounting his horse again, when his progress was arrested by a shot which laid him also, motionless by the side of his master. There were no ploughed fields near the spot, unless an allusion is made to the ploughing of the cannon

---

21. Sergeant Charles Ewart captured the eagle of the 45e Ligne and Corporal Stiles shared the capture of the eagle of the 105e Ligne with Captain Alexander Clark.
22. He was commissioned in the 5th Veteran Battalion but retired from the army in 1821.
23. The 'myth' of Ponsonby's death surrounded by seven lancers has been proven to be false, but there is still some doubt over his death. Almost every member of the Greys states that he was shot, but there is a lot of circumstantial evidence that he was at first captured by Lancer Oban but then killed by a single lance thrust, when there was a danger that he would be rescued by a group of the Greys. Oban certainly retained his sword and a letter by General Pack confirms that his body was discovered the following day with only one lance wound to the body. This would indicate that Oban's story is the truth, but how do we explain this in regard to the evidence of the Greys? I suspect that if Ponsonby was struck by a musket ball during the charge, it may well have been a spent bullet which unhorsed him and knocked the wind out of him. Reignolds, his brigade major, would have gone to his aid and it is possible that Oban captured the pair as Ponsonby got back to his feet after this fall. His death, and that of Reignolds, probably close to each other could then have led to the 'myth.'
24. Major Thomas Reignolds of the Scots Greys.

balls &c. Colonel Hamilton was also killed, which was a loss severely felt by his regiment as well as his country; but his bright example in leading his men into action, was imprinted on their hearts and served as a model to emulate those who succeeded to the command of his faithful followers during the remainder of the day. Seven other officers[25] and a great number of men and horses of the Greys fell with their leader.

The conflict was kept up with the same spirit on the great road, by the first brigade of cavalry, under Lord Edward Somerset[26] and other troops posted there, who repulsed the often-repeated attacks of the enemy with insurmountable firmness, which invariably caused great loss to the enemy in their retreat. Our brigade being again formed and told off, took post on the height, as a strong body of fierce cuirassiers made a desperate effort to dislodge some of our infantry who were posted near a gravel pit[27] on the left of the road which covered their front from assault and consequently enabled them to act with great effect upon the enemy's cavalry when passing or repassing the right or left of their post.

Lord Edward Somerset, perceiving the design of the cuirassiers by the route they were taking to gain the summit of the gravel pit, advanced with his brigade to arrest their progress and render the necessary support to the infantry. The enemy had gained the height, when the Life Guards, Blues and 1st Dragoon Guards, rushed upon them and drove them back in such precipitate confusion, that a great number of them were hurled headlong over the precipice and men and horses tumbled in promiscuous heaps to the bottom and were crushed or trampled to death by one another.[28]

---

25. Major Thomas Reignolds, Captain Charles Barnard, Lieutenants James Carruthers and Thomas Trotter and all three Cornets, Edward Westby, Francis Kinchant and Lemuel Shuldham were killed. The records show that 103 men were killed or died of their wounds at a later date.

26. Somerset's Brigade, consisting of the 1st and 2nd Lifeguards and 1st Dragoon Guards charged in line, with the Royal Horse Guards placed as a reserve. These troops were split by the farmhouse of La Haye Sainte, with half passing either side. These cavalry regiments were not as heavily involved with the deadly lancers, but did suffer severely as well.

27. This small quarry was manned by the 1/95th Rifles until forced out by the French capture of La Haye Sainte.

28. William was not an eyewitness to this event which is another 'myth.' The hollow way was deep here, but horses were able to surmount the obstacle reasonably well, Somerset's Brigade certainly did.

The battle still continued with the same obstinacy on both sides and seemed at many periods doubtful from the unsteadiness of some of the foreign infantry of which the army was partly composed. However, things assumed a more dismal aspect when some of the Belgic regiments actually turned their backs and took flight, and although some of them were (with the utmost exertions of their officers, who were partly British[29]) rallied again, yet others continued to make the best of their way from a scene so truly dangerous, nor dared to turn their eyes behind them till they had reached the gates of Brussels. An occurrence of this kind which came under the eye of one of my comrades, he has described to me as follows.

'About three in the afternoon we were moved to the right of the road and formed (as we supposed) to strengthen a post on which the enemy was shortly expected to make an attack! When we had taken our fresh ground, a regiment of Belgians were marched a little to our right front, formed into square and ordered to lie down on the ground. All near them was going on with a degree of coolness at the moment; but they had scarcely complied with the order, when the enemy opened a brisk cannonade on two angles of the square. The first two or three shots were without effect, but at length a shell was so well directed into the very centre of the corps that it burst immediately on alighting and killed a few men. On which alarm, the whole sprung to their feet and without regarding arms, order or regularity, fled like a flock of sheep; a volley was fired into them by one of the British regiments as they rushed from the field and their own officers cut amongst them with their sabres, to rally and save them from disgrace! However, their endeavours had no effect, they could neither stop nor bring them back and the only way to remedy the evil, was that of posting another regiment in their stead. A British corps was accordingly ordered to occupy it, who moved forward, formed their square and lay down with firm indifference & cool deliberation, seeming to evince as little fear of danger as a field of reapers would have betrayed when placing themselves in order among the corn to partake of a field refreshment; they appeared to regard the shot which was still coming very thick from the enemy's guns, as a mere matter in course and at times jocularly exclaimed to each other "Fire away ye dogs! Death before dishonour".'

---

29. None of the Belgian troops were commanded by Englishmen. Does he mean some of the inexperienced Hanoverian units, which were little more than raw recruits?

'Our now reduced brigade occupied a post on the height and stood under the enemy's fire, ready to oppose any attack which might be made from the dense masses that occupied the opposite rising ground. However, they appeared to have been so completely staggered in that part of their position, by the charge we had already made amongst them; that no further attempt was made for a considerable time and as they were repeating their furious onsets and harassing the troops on the right of the road. It was judged prudent to strengthen that part of the position and our brigade was accordingly moved towards it. On our route thither we were led along the rear of our line of infantry and when passing the highlanders (whom we had not been near, from the time we had passed through them on our advancing to the first charge) a veteran piper of the 92nd Regiment looked steadfastly on our advancing brigade and after having cast a glance of indifference upon the enemy lines; struck up the old favourite national air

Whaur hae ye been a' day!
Bonny laddie, Highland laddie

The sound of the bagpipes (which is a well known and never failing incitement to deeds of valour, when its shrill notes fall upon the ear of a true Scot in the day of battle) had such an effect upon the spirits of the men, that loud cheering followed and all were ready to plunge into the greatest danger without a consideration respecting their own fate; these gusts of enthusiasm must have struck, even the enemy themselves with astonishment and opened before them a ground work of study upon real British courage.'

It is indeed remarkable that the sound of this warlike instrument produces so extraordinary an effect on the Scots in action. However, there can be no doubt of its authenticity, nor that it has even in past ages, urged them to deeds of almost incredible valour. We read of one of those instances which occurred at the Battle of Quebec in 1760 as follows. 'Some of the British troops were retreating in great disorder, when the general, who dreaded the example they were setting might extend to the army, complained to a field officer in Fraser's Regiment of the extreme bad behaviour of his corps. "Sir" answered he, with some warmth! "You did very wrong in forbidding the pipers to play this morning. Nothing encourages the Scots so much in the day of action! Nay even now they would be of great use". "Then let them blow like the divel" replied the general, "If it will bring back the men" The pipers were accordingly ordered to play a favourite national air and the highlanders had no sooner heard their native music, then they rallied again, formed and rushed upon the enemy with such renewed courage that nothing could withstand them.'[30] I wonder what kind of music would have set the Belgians to work again.

The British lines were getting so weak when five o'clock arrived, that squadrons of horse were posted in many places to fill up the spaces which the decreasing numbers of foot left between regiments and brigades. Thus to preserve an entire line; and the attacks of the French cavalry which continued without intermission, were opposed by those of the English; while the infantry were running from line to square and from square to line with extraordinary alacrity, giving a due consideration to the fatigue they had already undergone and although the cuirassiers frequently advanced, almost to the points of their bayonets, when they had thrown themselves into this posture of defence against each approaching storm, they were invariably repelled by the British troops as the waves of the ocean are by the stubborn cliffs of the land that gave them birth. And the moment the enemy's horse commenced to retreat from each unsuccessful attack, they were either assailed by our cavalry or a brisk fire opened upon them from the squares they were compelled to abandon and the scale of advantage turned against them by the fall of no inconsiderable number of men and horses.

About half past five a body of cuirassiers advanced on the right of the farmhouse, La Haye Sainte and made a desperate effort to break a square, which during their advance was formed with such expedition and accuracy as to render it impossible to make the least impression. The cuirassiers confiding in the protection afforded by their armour and dreaming that nothing could withstand them, even dared to ride round the two squares next to each other, in a bravo style, flourishing their swords and cutting at the gallant troops, whose steady and determined courage, rendered the vain efforts of the enemy to reach them, utterly impossible; till the mimic fight was put a stop to by the squares simultaneously opening a tremendous fire from every face, which they were enabled to do, without the danger of injuring each other; by the judicious plan on which they were formed. It was as underneath and they had no sooner opened their fire from the four faces of each square than their besiegers began to reel and were seen tumbling to the ground by dozens.

---

30. This story is still often recounted but is probably apocryphal.

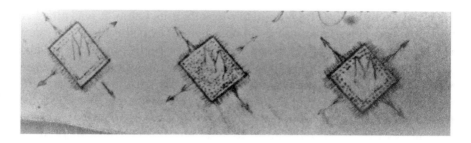

They began a retreat, the firing was ordered to cease and the Life Guards, Blues, and 1st Dragoon Guards furiously attacked them. Lord Edward Somerset and Sir John Elley,[31] who led them on, fought with great courage and their noble examples were eagerly imitated by the men around them, whose deeds announced that their minds were loaded with no other encumbrance but a determination to conquer or die. Sir John was at one time encompassed by the cuirassiers and with sword in hand cut his way through them, leaving several of his assailants on the ground, marked with wounds which betokened no inconsiderable strength in the arm which inflicted them.

The enemy was soon beaten back with the degrading loss of nearly one half of their strength, while the loss of the troops they had attacked, was so trifling as to render it scarcely worthy of notice. About the same time another desperate attack was made upon the troops which occupied the farm house [of] La Haye Sainte. These troops were under Lieutenant Colonel Baring[32] and consisted of the 2nd [Light] Battalion of the King's German Legion and a few others. This distinguished officer bravely defended the post till overpowering numbers obliged him to abandon it.[33] It has been said that Bonaparte became so much elated when this advantage was gained, that he even dispatched couriers to Paris and other places with the news of his being no longer doubtful of the battle terminating in favour of the French.[34] But the troops who had taken it must have been of a very different opinion; when they found that to hold it for

---

31. Colonel Sir John Elley, Deputy Adjutant General. He was wounded at Waterloo.
32. Lieutenant Colonel George Baring, No. 335 in Beamish.
33. The post was abandoned at around 6 pm when the troops defending it ran out of ammunition and were forced to retire.
34. Napoleon did send a messenger to Paris proclaiming a great victory, but he was dispatched early in the afternoon.

any space would cost them a greater loss than its value. It was attacked and attacked again; taken and retaken again[35] and the blood of many nations flowed profusely around its walls; for both infantry & cavalry were called forward from both sides to carry or defend the post. We were led on in one of these attacks against the cavalry of the enemy; several regiments were engaged at the same time, who, when they became inter-mixed with the French troops, displayed one of the most ardent contests that history can produce a parallel to. Nothing could be more terrible, for it became a series of single combats; every soldier assumed the command of himself and seemed (when he had cut his opponent down) to express that he had the glory of his country alone on his mind.[36]

The charges of the cavalry were often renewed and the minds of the men become so engaged that they dashed among the enemy's horse in a manner which evinced a total regardlessness respecting their own fate. Two lines of horse were often seen rushing upon each other and the dreadful clash of swords and clang of armour which preceded their slaughtering struggles rung in the ears of both armies, who now withheld their shot; each line for the preservation of their own troops, who thus combatted in the valley between.

The infantry at the same time struggled to regain or keep possession of the farm house, by a horrid slaughter with the bayonet; every soldier rushed, with hot blood, upon the foe who came in his path and see (by a contemptuous smile) to express his satisfaction when he had buried his steel in the bosom or bowels of his opponent.

Alas! Auld Scotland, full many of thy gallant sons lay cauld [cold] on this part of the famed field! For here it was their lot to have many a furious onset to withstand. Yet when thou mournst their fate; call to remembrance the glorious cause in which they fell; it was in assisting to deliver Europe and mankind from the bondage of a tyrant. Let the name of La Haye Sainte serve as a memorial of their deeds and may thy mighty emblem, the majestic thistle, spring plentifully over their silent beds and point to generations yet unborn. The spot where thy warriors repose, that the stranger who may hereafter be induced to visit that

---

35. Ompteda's 5th Line Battalion King's German Legion attempted its recapture but they were caught in line formation by French cuirassiers and heavily defeated. No other attempts were made to recapture the farm until the end of the battle, when Allied troops found it abandoned.

36. William takes to flights of fancy here, as we will discover later that he was not there at this time.

hallowed field, may view their sculptureless tombs with sacred awe and drop on their grassy covering a generous tear.

The dead and mangled bodies of men and carcases of horses now lay so thick that it was with the greatest difficulty the survivors could maintain a footing and many of the horses from excessive weakness fell to the ground, where the rider was instantly trampled to death.

The infantry who occupied the heights, also continued from time to time to close their files over the dead bodies of their slain comrades to preserve that close array of battle, which experience had taught them, was the only means by which they could defend themselves, in the unequal contest.

The Duke of Wellington was frequently observed to turn his eyes towards the point from which he expected his support from the Prussian Army; but these succours which were (no doubt) now become necessary, he long looked for in vain. The whole army was in hot action and the danger getting every hour greater; the day far spent, the army assuming a weak appearance, yet the battle raging with the same fury from right to left. Frequently did the noble duke witness, with deep anxiety, the storm of havoc rolling along the gory plain upon some division of his decreasing heroes who were fighting and falling in the very uncertain combat; he galloped from post to post to encourage with his presence the brave troops he relied upon; who invariably acknowledged the good effects of his visit by shouting and redoubling their efforts against the enemy.

It has been said that about this time, when the anxiety of our noble commander was wound up to the highest pitch; he exclaimed to some of his staff who were near him 'Would to God that night or the Prussians would come.' However, if he did utter this wish, he was unheard, for neither of them came for some hours after. The excessive difficulties of the passage by the defile of St Lambert had so retarded the march of the Prussians that they were at least three hours later than the time at which the Duke of Wellington anticipated their arrival, which must (under such circumstances) have been a grievous disappointment.

Our brigade was again posted in line on the height, with the 1st Heavy Brigade and Sir J. Vandeleur's Brigade of light troops, consisting of the 11th, 12th & 16th Regiments of Dragoons.[37] We were fronted by

---

37. Sir John Vandeleur's brigade and Sir Hussey Vivian's cavalry brigade were moved from the left wing to bolster the centre when the Prussians began to

a body of the enemy's cuirassiers and others, who, although much superior in strength, durst not venture to attack. We were also reduced to the necessity of assuming a posture of defence and in this situation we looked each other in the face, neither side daring to break their line; till a brave countryman of our own issued from the ranks of the cuirassiers and advanced nearly half way to ours, exclaiming 'Come out the best of you English b[astard]s and I'm your man.' He boldly looked towards us as if waiting for a champion, but seeing no one approach him, fired at our line and flourishing his pistol round his head, retired to his rank. This he repeated several times and several of our men who were getting exasperated by being thus bullied, attempted to go and have a brush with him, but the expedient was forbidden by those of power and better judgement. However, one of the Hanoverian sharpshooters, who scrambled among some long corn a little nearer the spot where he usually posted himself and lay down till he came out again and when in the act of waving his pistol over his head, the German let fly and brought him down. A shout followed from the British line and a yell of discontent from that of the French accompanied their champion to the ground & the enemy then put a strong column of infantry in motion and appeared to be making preparations for another effort against our line. To arrest their progress, an order was given for part of our cavalry to attack them; the Greys were ordered to charge the front of the column and the Blues by taking ground to the right, to fall at the same moment upon its flank; each of these corps accordingly advanced to the charge, but by some unhappy chance, probably not being able to see the enemy through the clouds of smoke which enveloped them when they opened their fire the Blues missed the flank on which they were destined to act and came slap along the front of the column, where the Greys at the same interest arrived. The two corps met with a dreadful crash and many on the point of cutting down their own friends in the terrible confusion which ensued. However, the error being quickly discovered, both corps were obliged to retreat without having gained any visible advantage over the enemy; but themselves having suffered considerable loss.

The Chateau of Hougoumont was situated near the right of the British and left of the French. It was surrounded by a garden and orchard of fruit trees, which, with the chateau and farm yard had been

---

arrive. It is rarely realised that Vincke's Hanoverian infantry brigade also marched to the centre at this time.

taken and retaken many times during the day.[38] It had also been set on fire by the numerous engines of destruction which had from time to time been directed against it. The flames now mounted high over its black turrets and gilded with a glowing tinge, the clouds of smoke that rolled in the air, and sad to relate, it has been asserted by some of the troops who were engaged within its walls, that many of the unfortunate men who were wounded there and had not the power of crawling out, terminated their miserable existence in the blazing straw yard and houses surrounding it. They were frequently seen dragging their slow lengths on their hands and knees, from this scene of horror, willing (although dreadfully shattered) to preserve what remained of life, from the destructive elements which raged within. Some reached a hedge a short distance from the house and crept into the bottom of it, thus to preserve themselves from being overrun by the guns or trampled to death by the horses in their furious charges in different directions; while others in making the vain attempt, fainted on their sad journey & yielded to the stern command of death, that which they had refused to surrender to the enemy of their country.

The French cavalry were again seen charging upon our squares of infantry and the English horse also making their attacks upon some of the enemy divisions and although the cavalry of the two contending powers, in some instances passed each other so close as nearly to bring their flanks in contact; they took no notice of each other but dashed in opposite directions upon the advantages which they seemed to appreciate direct to their front. About six o'clock the battle raged with terrible fury; Napoleon had every engine of death which he could muster at work; and seemed, by a desperate onset, to intimate that he was just about to give the exterminating blow. It is said, he at this time, seemed gay, spoke as if the battle was already won and on seeing his guide La Cost[39] flinch from the hum of the balls which came near him, he said 'Don't turn your back my friend, a ball may hit you in the back as well as the front and wound you more disgracefully.' Then turning to Bertrand[40] said 'We shall arrive at Brussels in fit time for supper.' If these

---

38. It is a recent discovery that the farm/chateau complex at Hougoumont was nearly lost two or three times.
39. Jean Baptiste Decoster claims to have been the Emperor's guide at Waterloo. He certainly made a good living from his claims for the rest of his life.
40. General Henri Gratien Bertrand had accompanied Napoleon to Elba and also accompanied him to St Helena after Waterloo.

really were the ideas of this great general at that stage of the action, I cannot conceive on what ground he decided such an opinion; he saw no failure in any part of the British lines, nor had they lost an inch of ground. Even the breaking of a single square of infantry had baffled all the efforts of the chosen troops he had repeatedly brought against them, which might have taught him, had he never before known what British courage was, that he had a hard task yet before him before they were beaten. The Duke of Wellington, who had been taught by experience to rely on the valour of these brave troops had a very different opinion! There can be but little doubt of his anxiety for the arrival of the Prussian Army; but I am flattered to think that he laboured under no fear of his own maintaining its ground in spite of every effort of the enemy, at least, till night had put an end to their struggles.

A great number of appearances now covered the awful field; in one direction success would smile for a moment, in another some bold effort worsted; with a terrible confusion of sounds from artillery, musquetry, trumpets, bugles, drums, loud words of command, rattle and clash of contending arms and the venerated groans of dying and wounded heroes, which were mingled at times with the horse's neigh and the bitter execrations of contending survivors.

Although the Prussian Army was expected long before the period of their arrival they had lost no time in getting forward, but the roads by which they moved were so deep from the excessive rains that it was with the greatest difficulty their artillery would effect a passage; and Marshal Grouchy[41] believing that Prince Blucher was in full retreat with his whole force, continued to follow them with his corps of the French army; till the Prussians arrived in the neighbourhood of Wavre where General Tauenzien[42] halted with one division to keep him in play, while

---

41. Emmanuel de Grouchy, the 2nd Marquis de Grouchy (1768–1847), who commanded a detached force of 33,000 men, with orders to prevent Blucher's army from joining Wellington at Waterloo. He failed in this mission and has been roundly criticised by those close to Napoleon, but as with everything to do with Napoleon, things are not as straightforward as they may seem. Napoleon failed to provide him with clear orders or to keep him up to date with developments, but Grouchy also failed to show much initiative.

42. William makes an error here. General Friedrich Bogislav Emanuel Tauentzien, Graf von Wittenberg, was appointed to command the Prussian VI Corps but he had not joined before the Waterloo campaign was ended.

the prince continued his march with the body of his army to support the Duke of Wellington at Waterloo; Grouchy immediately attacked Tauenzien, but was repulsed with great loss.

The glorious moment at last arrived, and as the setting sun, which had been obscured during the day, sent from between two dense clouds which hung in a parallel line on the western horizon, his last glorious blaze and tipped the gory implements of war which flashed in glittering grandeur over the death like plain; as if to bear witness to the finish of the great achievement and cheer the spirits of the protectors of Europe and wearied enemies of degraded France; two brigades of Prussians issued from a forest near Frichermont and attacked the right rear of the French army immediately. Their arms reflected the last beams of the evening sun as they unfolded themselves and caught the eyes of a great majority of the Allied army, which were turned to that point when their cannonade opened, with a rapidity that could not now be maintained by the troops which had been engaged all day & were nearly worn out from fatigue! Every soldier gazed with wonder on what they had anticipated long before that hour and the noble Duke himself (the greatest general of the age) could not withhold his grateful exclamation 'There goes Old Blucher at last.'[43]

From some uncertainty which was observed in the movements of the French army, an opinion exists that they were making preparations for a retreat, previous to the arrival of the Prussians. This may have some claim to credit when we consider that, to all probability, the enemy were well acquainted with their near approach.[44]

The first two brigades of the Prussian army, under General Bulow, reached the covered position above mentioned, at sunset! The Prussian general saw there was not a moment to be lost and immediately began his attack. Napoleon turned his reserve against him and another terrible conflict ensued, which seemed to resemble the commencement of a new battle. The Prussian guns opened with a terrible roar and assailed the ears of the British troops, which again nerved them with new vigour and spontaneously, the battle raged with redoubled fury from right to left.

General Johann Adolf, Freiherr von Thielmann actually commanded III Corps which defended Wavre against Grouchy's attacks that day.

43. This description on the Prussian attack would leave the reader presuming that the Prussians only arrived as darkness fell around 8–9 pm, however the Prussians began to launch their attacks on Plancenoit village on Napoleon's right rear around 5 pm.

44. There is no basis for a belief that the French were preparing to retreat.

However, such exertions could not be without a limit & although the French troops seemed to bear these fierce attacks with a spirit that still gave the battle an appearance of uncertainty; It was now evident that the strife was nearly at an end, the first failure that was observed, was some pieces of cannon making their way to the rear, which announced that the glorious and decisive moment was, at last, come.

General Thielman's Corps[45] of Prussians issued, at the same moment, from the forest and thundering upon the enemy's right wing, with a violence which staggered their hopes, spread a terrible carnage among the worn foe! The great Duke of Wellington saw the moment which was good and gave the exterminating word; his victorious arms advanced at his command in awful grandeur. The French army viewed the dread approach of a *wall of warriors* who had defied their utmost exertions to gain an inch of the ground they defended during the day; with terror, their wavering courage gave way, they were panic struck and could no longer be prevailed on to stand another meeting, so their flight began.

Another column of Prussians under General Ziethen arrived and fell to work near the village of Smohain; they charged and broke the right wing of the French in three places.[46] The British army rushed forward on all points, all the Prussians which had come up, followed the example, but the French generals still preserved means of retreating in some regularity. Circumstances however, were extremely favourable to the pursuers, for the ground rose in several gentle heights, one gradually above another, from the summits of which, the artillery of the allied armies could freely open their fire as their own troops descended in safety into the plains or valleys between, formed into brigades in the greatest order. And fresh Prussian columns continually unfolded themselves, issuing from the forest on the height behind.

The French army had no sooner abandoned its position than the great Napoleon had abandoned the army; he left it to its fate. However, the generals who commanded under him, kept the troops in some order till they reached the village of Plancenoit, which was situated about a mile and a half to the rear, on the great road. Here they tried to make a

---

45. He here describes the arrival of General Pirch's II Corps to the south of Bulow, Thielmann continued to defend Wavre from the attacks of Grouchy.
46. The Prussians had initially attacked the Nassau troops defending the Papelotte area, mistaking them for Frenchmen because of their 'French' headgear. Once the error was realised, they drove on against the French and began to roll up the French front line.

stand; and the Old Guard defended the village for a short time with great courage, but after several bloody attacks, it was stormed and carried by the Prussians.[47] From that moment, their retreat became a complete rout and the confusion which followed instantly spread throughout their whole army and they fled in a dreadful disordered mob in all directions, overturning everything that might attempt to stop their determined flight. They now assumed the appearance of a hoard of barbarians & seemed only to vie with each other in fast running, while the perseverance of the pursuers still produced new fears among them and left them no time to contemplate the necessity of preserving order. Discipline was therefore no longer adhered to, the roads were choked up with their guns, tumbrils, cars and all the implements of a fugitive army. They attended to no word but the cry of retreat which had thus spread itself and as they ran, they ceased not despairingly to cry 'Les Anglais! Les Anglais.'

It was now near ten p.m. and the shattered remains of the British army was ordered to halt and indulge their wearied bodies with rest and refreshment, but the Prussians continued in close pursuit with the whole of their cavalry and beset the rear of the flying enemy without intermission or mercy.

At Genappe a part of the fugitives had mustered all their courage and tried to retard the advance of their pursuers by overturning gun carriages &c in the streets and to all probability, they hoped that by opening a brisk fire upon the Prussians as they approached the entrance of the village, they might be allowed to rest there for the night. But their assailants had only answered them with a few cannon shots when they precipitately abandoned it. Here Napoleon's carriage with many other equipages fell into the hands of the Prussians.[48] He had left it here and mounted a horse for his better safety in his flight.

---

47. The defence at Genappe was not as strong as described here. Night had already fallen and the sound of Prussian drums and bugles was enough to drive the French on.

48. The Prussian Major von Keller and his troops captured two of Napoleon's carriages at Genappe. The one was given to Blücher (whose family recently returned it to France and it can now be seen at Malmaison), the other to the Prince Regent, who promptly sold it to a Mr Bullock who ran a Waterloo Exhibition at the Egyptian Rooms at Piccadilly. In 1842 the carriage was sold to Madame Tussauds and was unfortunately lost in the fire there on 18 March 1925 (along with two other of Napoleon's carriages).

Chapter 20

Prisoner Escort to Brussels

Here we shall leave the flying enemy and pursuing Prussians for a time and loiter another day on the awful field of Waterloo. The loss of the British army was very great, but that of the enemy (we had reason to suppose) much greater.[1] The regiment to which I belonged had suffered severely, although we could have no just idea of its real loss when we bivouacked at night. We had (from its appearance) the most grievous doubts, as the number forming the body of the corps only consisted of three officers, two sergeants and sixteen private men! A few (we knew) were escorting prisoners to Brussels and the remainder (it was feared) had perished in the general wreck.

The command of the brigade had devolved upon Colonel Clifton of the Royals[2] and that of the regiment in which I served, upon Captain and Brevet Major Cheney,[3] who was then mounted on his fifth horse, having had four shot from under him during the day.

This small remnant of the good old corps remained a little in advance of the field of action all night. I myself was on the party who

---

1. The Allied army suffered around 16,000 casualties (including missing, many of which were subsequently written off as dead) and 7,000 Prussians. French casualties are very hard to estimate, but it was probably somewhere between 30,000–35,000 (including missing). They also lost up to 9,000 prisoners, who were marched to Brussels and then to the purpose-built prisoner of war camp on Dartmoor.
2. Lieutenant Colonel Arthur Benjamin Clifton.
3. Captain Edward Cheney commanded the regiment at the end of the battle as senior captain. He was a major in the army, but only a captain in his regiment.

conducted prisoners to Brussels, which place we reached late at night and after obtaining some refreshment again began our march to the army. However, before we again turn our backs upon Brussels, it may not be amiss to take a slight survey of the scenes which now filled the streets of that noble city. The wounded which continued to arrive in great numbers seemed to be the principle care of the inhabitants; the hospitals were soon filled, as also the houses of the citizens, who took them in as far as their accommodation would permit and treated them with the greatest attention and tenderness. The inhabitants were also seen carrying to the hospitals, which were established in empty storehouses &c, mattresses, blankets, sheets, linen, lint, rags and bandages of every description, for their use. And much to their honour, ladies of the highest rank were not ashamed to traverse from hospital[4] to hospital in the dead hour of night and employ their persons and property in this work of humanity.

A very peculiar attention was paid to the wounded men belonging to the Highland regiments, who from being quartered with them previous to the commencement of hostilities, stood highest in their favour and commanded a greater portion of their regard.[5] It was no uncommon thing to see the inhabitants exploring every waggon which arrived from the field, for the highlanders who had been previously quartered on them and when anyone was recognised by his host or hostess, he was immediately removed to his former quarters and every care taken of him till his wounds were perfectly well. It is not therefore, to be wondered at, that some of these men joined their regiments some months after, who had been long considered dead.[6]

---

4. The hospitals were largely ad hoc affairs set up in any suitable large building in the city: many were in churches and convents.
5. The Highland troops do seem to have been particular favourites, their national character making them lions on the battlefield and lambs at the family hearth. This characteristic is still evident today amongst the 'Tartan Army' who go abroad with the national football team. They have a very different reputation to that of the English fans.
6. In the chaos, some were shown as 'missing' who eventually recovered from their wounds to return to their regiments in Paris; but a lot more 'missing' never returned, either having fallen in the battle or succumbed to their wounds at a later date and were eventually recorded as presumed dead.

In the squares and open spaces were hordes of French prisoners, guarded by the troops who occupied the garrison of Brussels;[7] many of whom slept profoundly on the cold pavement; others sat in discomfited silence with their heads reclining on their knees, while some with folded arms stalked the boundary of their limited ground, turning, at the completion of every few paces, a thoughtful glance on the waning moon.

Groups of Belgians were seen rolling drunk in every corner;[8] and soldier's wives hurrying from hospital to hospital and from group to group, in hopes of discovering their beloved husbands, even wounded and bleeding among their fellow men. They were eagerly sought and created much joy when found, for something seemed to have whispered to all, that if not so found, they were doomed to see them no more. Others ran raving towards the field of battle, on hearing by some comrade newly arrived from the sad scene, the news of the death of their bosom companions. Waggons entered in a slow and funeral like pace, while others who had left a batch of wounded, thundered the contrary way to receive another load. Men of many nations staggered about the streets and horses neighing, lying on the pavement and stalking from door to door unnoticed; as if soliciting a portion of their humanity, a virtue to which the ungrateful riders had been strangers and had left the worn and noble animals who had carried them during the day (but perhaps not in the field of battle) to pine in the chill of night under the effects of hunger and fatigue while they boozed in the taverns which rung with the empty sound of such characters amid the horrible scenes which surrounded them.

Our party having rested here about an hour & a half, again proceeded towards the field. On quitting the city, we beheld by the light of the moon, which shone with unusual refulgence, the road before us thick with those who still struggled towards the gates. We soon reached the verge of the forest which is no great distance from the town and as we advanced, the numbers of wounded seemed to increase and many sat by the wayside, who seemed to despair of ever reaching any other

7. The 2nd Battalion 81st Foot formed the garrison of Brussels during the Waterloo campaign and were therefore unable to claim the Waterloo Medal.
8. The Belgian troops come in for severe criticism from their British counterparts, although some do some of them justice regarding their role at Quatre Bras and at Waterloo.

place of rest & a dead body now and then, reflected from its pale form, the descending rays of the great lamp of night. But when we had more deeply penetrated the gloomy wood, the dead grew thicker and still thicker, as we advanced to the middle of its dreary precincts.

We were now at the spot where the greatest confusion prevailed the preceding night.[9] The sight was truly horrible; for in the ditches or mires on either side, lay the dead bodies of men, women and even some children, many of them nearly covered in the clay and here and there, a hand or a foot sticking up. Also many dead horses, with broken down waggons, carts, baggage panniers which had been plundered of their contents, where quantities of paper and other materials of similar value, were strewed about the road and marked the tract of the marauders into the thicket.[10]

Commissary stores of all kinds, were scattered on the road; junks[11] of salt beef lay in all directions and large quantities of flour, oatmeal, rice &c &c were trodden among the feet of a horde of Nassau soldiers who had stove in the barrels with their different contents till they had found those which they now regaled upon and which contained, or had contained, gin, rum, brandy &c. They had been rolled into the wood and a group of these fellows stood [a]round each.

On seeing so much good provision wasting in this manner on the road, the officer who commanded us, halted the party for the purpose of filling our canteens and haversacks. For although they were not empty on leaving Brussels, there was still room for more and we knew not how they might be supplied at the regiment. On dismounting, we found plenty of fresh beef & pork, biscuits &c with which we loaded ourselves in an ordinary manner and having discovered a cask of rum, began to ruminate on a method of getting to its contents. This appeared to be a task of some difficulty, which a Belgian soldier, observing from a short distance, induced him to come forward and offer his assistance. We did not reject it and were not deceived when we agreed that he might be a better broacher, than fighter; for he immediately raised his musket and fired through it and so freely did it pour with the liquor on both sides that our canteens were very soon filled, with the greatest ease.

---

9. The 17th, the night before the battle.
10. Many who saw the battlefield very soon afterwards often particularly comment on the vast amounts of paper strewn about.
11. 'Junk' is actually a name for a piece of dried/salted beef.

Having thus got a good supply, we continued our route towards the field; the road continually unfolding new and more shocking spectacles; dead and wounded lay in endless irregularity on the road & on either hand. The hollow groans of the wounded issuing from the thicket, whence they had crept for safety, when their strength could no longer sustain the fatigue of the slow progress they made towards Brussels and frequently did the loud wailings and frantic shrieks of the widowed mother assail our ears as she fondly pressed her now doubly dear babe to her throbbing bosom and sauntered about in a state of stupor, she knew not where.

Arms and warlike wreck of every description lay in our way and quantities of corn, hay &c were strewed about the road. We continued our advance and as the sun, tipped with maiden rays, the tops of the tall beeches, which overhung the road, we reached the outlet of the forest and emerged on the solitary village of Waterloo, lurking among a few scattered clumps, or straggling detachments from the main body of the great forest.

The village exhibited a deathlike scene. It was composed of about seventy or eighty houses which ran irregularly along each side of the causeway, with a handsome little church near the end which rested on the wood. There were very few inhabitants to be seen, and the few which were seen, we afterwards learnt, were fellows who prowled about in search of plunder and that the villagers (with very few exceptions) had fled for safety with their families and property into the forest. We proceeded to an inn near the church[12] and dismounted to feed and refresh our horses as well as to enjoy an hour of rest ourselves, for we were nearly exhausted. The yard into which we thrust ourselves was crowded with soldiers of all the nations who had any share in the recent actions. Some dead; some wounded; and many a weary warrior slept around the pavement.

We looked into a stable, but these were crammed full of horses and many a dead body among their feet; under the mangers slept men, women and children, nor could a foot be set on ground unoccupied. We fed our horses in the yard and curiosity having created a desire

---

12. It is tempting to think that this was the inn 'Bodenghien' which was used by Wellington as his headquarters, but it seems unlikely that the common soldiers would have been allowed to frequent that property. There were at least four inns at Waterloo in 1815 and it is most likely that William and his comrades visited the inn called 'á Jean de Nivelles.'

of looking into the house, I accompanied two of the men thither; we entered the kitchen where we beheld an old man stalking stupidly about on a small space of the floor which remained unoccupied by dead, wounded, lame and lazy soldiers! What could be seen of the floor was clotted with blood and a loathsome smell met us as we crossed the threshold. We passed but little of our time in exploring the secrets of this apartment, but proceeded to another from which we heard voices issue, resembling those of some party making merry. We approached the door of the room and a horrid scene presented itself to our disgusted eyes.

> This was a scene from which we shrunk
> Among the dead, roll'd many drunk.

The apartment appeared to have been a drinking parlour, where many who lay on the floor, as well as four Brunswickers who sat at a table and drank wine from a leather bucket, to all probability, had been carousing all night. There lay three or four dead men on the floor and a greater number grunted in a state of intoxication amongst them. We gazed a few minutes on the detestable scene and drew back, I believe, unnoticed by the Brunswickers, for their eyes seemed to have a defect, which then either rendered it impossible for them to see us at all, or made our numbers greater than reality. We accordingly pushed back to the kitchen and by rousing & adding some pieces of wood to the almost imperceptible remains of a dying fire, we succeeded in frizzling over the blaze, a few slices of the meat which we had brought from the wreck in the forest and some of the rest of our party who were looking about for a dish from which to eat our repast, descended a few steps which led into the cellar, with its door now invitingly open and while groping round its dark precincts found a barrel which the obscurity of the place had concealed from an earlier discovery. The cask was examined and found to contain good wine and a large metal pot (being the only vessel which could be found about the premises) was filled and carried into the yard for the use of our party, who enjoyed themselves over this regaling luxury till the poor old man, who came to the door, saw that some discovery had been made and declared that he was totally unacquainted with its having remained and begged that we would remove or destroy the whole lest it might in the same manner be found by the straggling Prussians or others who prowled in search of prey, by whom he would be considered the concealer and perhaps sabred without mercy. We however, did not choose to comply with the old man's wish, but after having taken a good refreshment, left the remainder for those who might be in need and happily fall in with the prize.

We next visited the church[13] which we also found filled with dead, dying & wounded of all descriptions, the groans which proceeded from all quarters of the sacred mansion, seemed to float on the sun's rays as they streamed through the windows on the melancholy congregation and every beholder who entered felt the weighty pressure of sadness steal over his soul, for awful was the prospect before him! Death in many shapes lay on either hand and the precincts of the sanctuary of peace was dyed with the blood of many nations. Hard indeed must the heart have been which was capable of remaining unmoved in this place! Hence the solemn silence which pervaded all, broken only by the heavy moanings of the suffering objects which lay around and still had a portion of life remaining.

A knowledge of our being unable to render them any assistance, forbid us from tarrying here and consequently loaded with feelings of sympathetic awe we retired. We again proceeded to the inn, where our horses still remained and leading them through the remainder of the dismal village, found every cottage door open and nearly every window broken. The houses were all empty; the curling smoke had ceased to spin its spiral course among the white blossomed fruit trees, nor was the happy peasants' voice heard in their native shades; for they had fled to seek refuge from the rage of man, in the dreary solitude of the vast desert, which we had now left behind.

Dead men and horses increased in numbers as we approached nearer the field and arms of all descriptions were scattered about. We arrived at the hamlet of Mont St Jean, which was situated about a mile and a half nearer the scene of action. We were now completely clear of the great Forest of Soignes and at the point where the roads branched off, the one leading to the right for Nivelles, the other continuing its nearly direct course through the field, to Genappe. On passing the

---

13. The Church of St Joseph is a strangely large and ornate building for what was such a small village in 1815. Completed in 1690, the church was built by Don Francisco Antonio de Agurto, Marquis de Gastañaga, the Governor of the Spanish Netherlands (Belgium then being part of the Holy Roman Empire). It now contains a large number of memorials to the Allied fallen.

barrier[14] and leaving this village (which like that of Waterloo, was a scene of destruction) a fine open country presents itself. It is not a level flat, but composed of large extents of rising grounds then sloping into gentle valleys, without many trees or enclosures, this beautiful tract as far as the eye could trace, was (before the battle) teeming with most promising crops of wheat, barley, rye, beans and tobacco; but it had now changed its aspect. Its black surface was seen afar and the wandering eye caught it like a dark bog surrounded by fertile plains, or the place where some immense fair or market had been held.

No more did the gentle breeze salute the sun's beams with the Olympian wave of the flowing corn! Unheard was the melodies of the morning lark soaring to the downy clouds to cheer the faithful mate whose fond eye followed with delight from their peaceful nest. But all was desolation and destruction, where the feathered songsters no longer had shelter, but had resigned their native plains to the tyrant usurpation of the carrion crows.

---

14. A toll gate.

Chapter 21

The Field of Battle

We having arrived at the farmhouse, Mont St Jean,[1] which is situated on the road in short distance in front of the village of the same name, entered the yard, where a most shocking spectacle presented itself. This house and yard, during the time of the battle, had been occupied by some of the British and Belgic surgeons and in it many amputations had been performed. A large dunghill in the middle of the square, was covered with dead bodies and heaps of legs and arms were scattered around! A comrade who stood near me on entering unconsciously muttered 'Of God. What a sight.' To which I made no answer, but felt as he did, for a great number lay by the sides of the houses and basked in the beams of the sun who had only life's last spark remaining and gasped for relief. Some lay with their heads reclining on the lifeless body of some already departed comrade, who, when we offered our assistance to remove them into the shade, declined being disturbed and murmured 'As their hour was near at hand that they preferred meeting it in peace on the spot they already occupied.

I observed with some warmth of national feeling, several highlander's legs, still wearing the emblem of their country; Auld Scotia's tartan hoe![2] As also the legs of dragoons in boots and spurs and many others

---

1. Mont St Jean farmhouse was owned by a farmer named Berger in 1815, who according to tradition had left before the battle, but his wife reputedly remained in the loft space (where the editor has been lucky enough to have had access) to protect her property, but did not dare show herself throughout the battle. The farm is now a brewery and a museum for the medical aspects of Waterloo.
2. The Highlanders wore kilts and long socks at Waterloo.

which still wore a part of the garment in which they had proudly paced the causeways of their native land and supported the portly figure of a British grenadier whose exalted spirit had ever forbid him to place in the coward's path that well-turned limb which was now consigned to a Belgic dunghill.

The interior of the house was also crowded with dead and dying, lying indiscriminately together. The buildings had not undergone any great damage, there were, indeed, to be seen, a few ball holes through the walls but no part of the premises burnt.[3]

At last we turned our backs on this dreary repository of inanimate bodies and bent our steps towards La Haye Sainte. We reached the height on which the British line had been arrayed; the height on which that line of Britons had determined to baffle the power of France or perish to a man & many were the example which lay around of their determined resolutions.

On ascending the gentle acclivity, we gazed with wonder on a scene in which we had ourselves, been actors and even shuddered to look on a work of such carnage. We beheld spring waggons and other vehicles of conveyance busily employed in different parts of the field, in removing the wounded from among heaps of dead, for the face of the plain was literally clad with dead and wounded, men & horses, arms, clothes, belts, cartridge boxes, steel cuirasses, helmets, hats, shakos, knapsacks, broken down guns, ammunition carts, cannon cartridges, balls, shells and great quantities of paper, as far as the eye could trace; some heaped upon each other and many half buried in the now hardening mud. We descended into the road, which at this spot was cut through the rising ground and in the hollow way lay many a mangled carcass. Here was seen the tender mother's choicest care, the hopeful father's delight or the bosom friends dearest object, in shapeless form, not even retaining a resemblance of the human figure, but crushed by the wheels of guns and feet of horses as flat as a pancake, or like a bundle of rags fallen from a pole in a potato field after having stood its campaign against the invasion of the crows, with the bones squoze [sic] to mummy and their sharp broken ends sticking through many places of the rubbish like bundle, which could not have been recognised as a human body but in such a place.

---

3. Witnesses who lay wounded in the Great Barn here talk of hearing roundshot striking the outside wall every so often.

We now proceeded to the farm La Haye Sainte, which also lay on the road and no great distance in our front. Here lay many a warrior calm'd in death, who had struggled in hottest wrath against each other. The interior of the farm yard was crowded to excess with dead and wounded of the British, French, Belgic & Brunswick troops promiscuously lying together. The buildings which had served as a strong redoubt to both armies in their turns during the battle, was a complete wreck; some part of it had been burnt and some part battered down. The walls which enclosed the yard resembled the front of a pigeon house from the holes which the cannon shot had made through them[4] and a vast number of killed and wounded lay round the outside as well as within; the wounded suffering dreadfully from the scorching beams of the noonday sun,[5] which had now become so powerful that the torrid blaze descended with heartrending intensity on those who lay with deep sabre cuts in their heads and faces, many of whom had swollen from the heat, to such a degree that the open wounds had actually assumed the appearance of pieces of black roasting meat. Yet the poor suffering wretches had no power to shun the torture, but lamentably cried for water and the approach of night; a considerable majority of those who thus suffered from sabre wounds, were of the French; for here several charges had been made upon them by the British cavalry, who frequently carried havoc into the centre of their columns.[6] We however, had the satisfaction of relieving many of them with a little spirits and water, as well as by shading them from the torches of heaven, by sticking a couple of muskets or lance poles into the ground, and hanging a cloak or watch coat upon them; but the relief we thus gave to many of them, calmly conveyed them into eternal rest. For we witnessed many instances of their expiring the moment they had swallowed the draught.

---

4. Because the farm lay in a dip, much of the artillery fire flew over it although some damaged the roof structures. It is often stated that the French did not attempt to break in to the farm using artillery; however, it is clear from a number of witness statements that the walls were breached at a number of points by roundshot during the day.
5. The beating sun would have made the sufferings of the wounded much greater, their wounds already causing them to dehydrate and to constantly implore for water.
6. Many of them were probably horribly wounded during d'Erlon's great attack and had hauled themselves here after the battle.

Two of our party[7] who had strayed some distance from the farm house, employing themselves in the humane office of affording such relief to the wounded as came within the bounds of their power, were by chance, led to the spot where lay one of our own officers in great agony and on making this discovery, one of the two wanderers returned hastily to the rest of the party and desired that we should (without loss of time) repair to the assistance of Lieutenant Carruthers[8] who lay in great distress hard by. We immediately followed him to the spot and found this officer almost exhausted from loss of blood which (during the night) had flowed from several mortal wounds. His look was languid and his countenance pale. He made an effort to raise his eyes upon us, but his now far spent strength was unequal to the task. We applied some water to his parched lips which revived him a little and after several applications of small quantities of spirits mixed with water, his strength seemed considerably renewed and he murmured 'God bless you, my dear friends.' He paused a few seconds and turning his eyes wishfully upon us, earnestly solicited our assistance, which we assured him of, and he seemed to enjoy a great deal of satisfaction. Next enquiring whether any of us possessed any money and begged a loan of a small sum from anyone who might have it in their power to favour him; alleging that if he had had more to offer to the vile wretches who scoured the field in search of booty during the night, he would not have been so cruelly treated. But no sooner was his money gone, when even a touch was more than he could bear in silence, they had rolled him over, torn out his pockets, stripped his dress of its decorations &c without a feeling for his sufferings. The gold lace had evidently been torn with violence from his regimental jacket &c and the cloth in many parts carried with it, leaving shreds of his violated garments hanging to stamp with infamy the vile and dastardly wretches who could thus, under the shade of night, invade the hallowed repose of the dead and wounded for so detestable a purpose.

One of my comrades who stood by and heard the pitiable tale; seemed to exult in the pleasure he felt, when he thrust his hand into his pocket and pulled out seven francs, which was the amount of his ready

---

7. William's party returning from Brussels must have met and joined the burial party sent from the regiment at first light, this detachment was commanded by Lieutenant James Graham and Sergeant Archibald Johnston (according to his own journal – published by the editor in *Waterloo Archive* I).

8. Lieutenant James Carruthers.

money (and but few at that period, could boast of such a fortune). He presented it with a full heart to his dying officer, exclaiming 'Oh Mr Carruthers, I wish I had more to offer, but you are welcome to this, if it be of any service.' The lieutenant took the small sum and enclosed it with an eager grasp in his hand, returning a silent but grateful answer from his fast dimming eye. A little more spirits and water was poured into his mouth and we ultimately obtained his consent to be removed to some shady situation till the means of removing him from the field could be obtained. We accordingly raised him in the most gentle manner we could devise from his blood steeped bed, and our director commanded us to move slowly on to the farm house. The route was indeed short, yet too long for poor Carruthers, who was never to see its completion. For a greater director (he at whose nod nations and empires rise and fall) commanded a halt at an intervenient [sic] stage. Our brave companion in arms expired in the arms of his soldiers, whose silent tears bedewed his clayey countenance as they hung over him, while his untainted spirit soared to the realms of bliss. The men who bore him along, unconsciously stood still and a solemn silence prevailed throughout the party.

It may appear to the reader of such scribblings, a strange thing that soldiers should have tears to spare on such occasions; but so far am I convinced of the right these men had to the name of soldiers, that some who thus proved themselves men, had fought on the very spot where this officer was found with a degree of courage and desperate regardlessness respecting their own fates, that might have been considered (if they imbibed the most trifling wish to escape) an act of madness and now the true colouring of the British soldier had come to light. For what is more ferocious than a Briton in battle; or what more gentle than the hero after a victory.

A few seconds had, however, only elapsed when we were called to recollection that our time might be better spent than carrying the now lifeless body any farther and it was accordingly buried with as much respect as the situation and circumstances would admit of, in the ditch on the opposite side of the road from the door of the farm house, where the words of an eminent writer were observed.

> The sweetest tribute to the fallen brave,
> Were soldier's sorrows on a soldier's grave.[9]

---

9. From 'The Battle of Waterloo' by William Thomas Fitzgerald.

This place had been so often and so obstinately disputed that the appalling numbers which lay within the view, were only realisations of what we might have expected to witness on visiting it; yet the destruction appeared far greater than we anticipated. For besides the vast numbers of dead and wounded men & horses, the wreck of military arms and equipment of every description lay so thick that a foot could scarcely be placed upon clear ground. Cuirasses and steel helmets were (in some places) piled upon each other, with hats, shoes, belts and many broken down and overturned caissons & gun carriages, intermixed with balls, shells, cannon cartridges, knapsacks and great quantities of paper, which had been scattered by the plundering legions who had paid their nightly visits to the sad field and had stripped the dead in search of booty.

A great number of the bodies, particularly those that lay on the road, were crushed in the manner before mentioned by the wheels of the guns and ammunition carts and many still more shocking spectacle presented themselves to our view, in carcases which had been struck by shells or heavy shot & literally dashed to pieces & their very intestines scattered some yards around them. A great number of the dead were stripped of part of their dress and many were naked as they came [into] the world, not even having the shirt left to screen their mutilated bodies from the flies which were now collecting in immense swarms. Those who were stripped to nakedness, had (to all probability) been officers of various descriptions, whose clothes would of course, be considered of some value to the plunderers. However, they had not even considered it beneath their characters to stoop to the dead or wounded sergeants of dragoons and dismantle their gory jackets of their small portion of lace.

We now continued our course along the hollow which parted the heights on which the two great armies had been posted & bent our steps towards the left of the British position. In this direction (we knew) our own regiment had been deeply engaged and had suffered severely; we accordingly proceeded to the spot where many of their bodies were likely to be found. Here we saw many of them, but so disfigured by their wounds that it was impossible for us to identify all in any other way than that of being men belonging to the regiment! Seven officers were among them whom we buried, as well as a considerable number of the men, for any of the party recognising one with whom he had been on intimate terms as a comrade soldier, usually observed 'Here lies poor

A.B.[10] he was a staunch comrade! Let us bury him.' And accordingly, the last tribute was performed by digging a hole with an old spade which we had brought from the village of Mont St Jean for the purpose; to which the body was consigned without further ceremony.

No funeral pall, but marshal vest,
No winding sheet around him.
The warrior sunk to take his rest
Where'er his comrades found him.
How soundly sleeps the fallen brave,
When gory mantle folds him,
How peaceful is the soldier's grave.
The shapeless trench that holds him.
How sweetly blooms the flowers of spring,
Around his grassy covering,
How softly sighs the angel wing,
That o'er his tomb is hovering.

We proceeded to the small farm Smohain, near which had rested the left of the British line, here we found every part of the dwelling house, barn and stables full of dead and wounded, among whom we beheld six of our own men. Five lay severely wounded and one dead; we proceeded to render them such assistance as lay in our power, by administering a cooling draught from our canteens, binding their wounds and adjusting their loathsome beds, when one of our party (who had been reconnoitring among the dead about the outskirts of the field) entered and descried our assistance in removing a fine young man of our regiment, named Alexander McKay[11] whom he had found lying severely wounded among some long corn which still stood erect.

We accordingly attended to the call of humanity and accompanied him to where poor McKay lay, who indeed existed, but so weak from a wound he had received by a ball passing through his body a little under the right breast, that he was unable to speak, yet a glow of gladness

---

10. This may simply be indicative of any initials, but one private with these initials was killed at Waterloo – Private Alexander Black of Captain Barnard's Troop, who originally hailed from Dunfermline.
11. Private Alexander McKay of Captain Vernor's Troop was born in Glasgow and had been a tinsmith by trade. He is recorded as having died at Waterloo, rather than dying of his wounds the following day.

seemed to steal over his countenance as we approached him. We poured a little water into his mouth and removed him towards the house, but like Lieutenant Carruthers he expired in the arms of his comrades and obtained a soldier's burial among the corn from which we had taken him up.

We left a sergeant[12] and two men here, for the purpose of providing some means of removing the wounded men from this desolate place and proceeded over the field towards the right. I with two men, walked along the back of a hedge near which our line of infantry had been posted and were suddenly arrested by the melancholy situations in which we saw many of the wounded infantry lying in the ditch by the hedge side; many of whom we assisted as far as lay in our power and we shaded from the heat of the sun as before mentioned, but were invariably obliged to tear ourselves from them while they lamentably cried for our farther assistance. We led our horses carefully among them, yet many appeared terrified at the sight of them and on one hand were exclaiming 'For God's sake, don't let your horse tread upon me', while from the other resounded in various voices 'Take care, my leg is broken, Oh my head! Keep off my broken thighs for heaven's sake! For the love of God comrade, give me but a mouthful of water; Oh, if I could send this to my poor wife, I am dying.' And such were the sounds which rung in our ears on all sides till we felt our minds so completely overpowered that we resolved to turn our backs on the horrid scene and proceed after the rest of the party. We hurried along heedless of their supplications, but our hearts gave again at the sight of one poor fellow who lay bent together in a seeming painful attitude in the deep furrow or kind of drain where he had fallen. He made a faint motion with his hand for our assistance, which we could by no means refuse. We approached and gently raised him from his uneven bed, while he like all others, continued to murmur 'water.' He had received several ball wounds and had lost an immense quantity of blood from the appearance of the ground where he lay; after we had laid him more easy and shaded him from the sun, we gave him a little weak spirits and water, which he drank greedily, fixed his eyes upon me and murmured 'What is your name sergeant?' I hesitated a moment to reconnoitre his features, but could not trace any that were familiar to me; and therefore supposing the poor fellow in a state of delirium took no further notice. But when

---

12. Probably Sergeant Johnston.

about to leave him to follow my friends, he expressed great anxiety to say something to me and although we were often compelled reluctantly to leave the poor wretches to their fate; something whispered that in this instance I should go back, which I did and he immediately murmured in a low and feeble voice, 'Sergeant is not your name W[illiam] C[larke]? I was somewhat struck at this question and answered in the affirmative; when with a languid look, he continued 'Oh W[illiam], behold your old fellow servant Jamie.[13] This is not the kind of meeting we both wished for when we last parted in Glasgow.' I will here leave to the readers own feelings to judge with what astonishment I met this discovery; for I knew not how to answer, my heart was filled to the brim and I felt all the pains which afflicted my long lost and much esteemed friend. I could not restrain a tear as I expressed my sorrow for his situation and a better pang followed when he in an almost smothered breath whispered 'Farewell.' He could utter no more, for death was steadfast in his now glassy eye, his hands looked withered and their dried veins barely visible through the clayey skin; his eyeballs had shrunken to a ghastly depth and were dimmed in death's hold. His lips white tinged with blue had ceased to move and no sooner was his breathless form still, than the tear that filled my watchful eye overflowed its banks and I exclaimed, 'Be not that sleep disturbed, thy cold and bloodless limbs are now at rest.' The two men who accompanied me, assisted in making a grave for my departed friend, and he was happed [covered] over with more than common neatness to rest in eternal peace.

We now followed the rest of our party, who had again crossed the valley to the left of La Haye Sainte into the enemy's position and were joined with a party of the 42nd Regiment[14] who had relieved a dragoon of our regiment who had lain with one of his legs under his horse from about the middle of the action till that period. This poor fellow's sufferings were truly great; part of his tale has already been narrated, from which as we sat round him on the ground he proceeded as follows.

> I lay in a painful situation with the weight of my dead horse
> upon my leg and unable to struggle for relief till the enemy gave
> way and although I was happy to see the battle our oun [own],

---

13. Jamie had joined the army with William, both introduced to the recruiting sergeant by Mr Yettinheart.
14. Later to become famous as The Black Watch.

yet I wept bitterly when I beheld the small remains of our good old regiment advance in all its glory and join in the conquering shout after the flying foe. They were, however, at too great a distance to assist me and although I implored the aid of many of the infantry who passed me, they in the height of their enthusiasm, either would not see or could not relieve me, but rushed forward & I with many more were left to weep in solitary sadness on the cheerless waste; I turned my eyes several times to the height on which the British army had hitherto stood, but it was now unmanned save by clusters of dead and wounded. I felt my spirits much cast down, for I now considered myself completely lost and as the gloom of night began to overshadow the field of death; I gave up all hopes of ever again looking on the light of day. There was no one near me alive, save a Frenchman who was (like myself) severely wounded and could not move from his comfortless bed which was about fifteen or sixteen yards from me. He, as night approached, began to gabble in his own language, which I did not understand, but failed not to make him some incoherent answer, for it cheered my drooping spirits, nor have I any doubt but it also pleased him to hear a living voice. A heavy swimming cloud at intervals intercepted the moon's silvery rays and veiled the earth-like scene in deep shadow, which again emerging on a clear sky sent down a bright glare on the countenances of the dead that lay around, whose grisly looks as midnight approached, I imagined were fixed upon me from every direction. But my companion continued to call to me & we conversed together with the greatest familiarity, even when a single sentence was not understood be either party. Thus passed the lonely night, till a band of plunderers rushed across the field ransacking the bodies of dead and dying. In the route of these barbarians I happened to lie and one of them approached, who (notwithstanding my imploring his mercy and assistance in relieving me from under my dead horse) desisted not from turning out my pockets and handling me in the most inhuman manner, when the slightest touch forced me to cry out with excessive pain. I was only possessed of a franc and a half, which this prowling wretch deprived me of and left me to my fate without offering the smallest assistance to disentangle me from the perilous situation in which I was placed. He was a peasant of the country and many of the same description, both men and women, were at work all round that part of the field. There were also a great number of Belgic and Prussian soldiers ranging the death-like waste in this diabolical employment, these the peasantry seemed to shun and disappeared as they approached the spot where I lay. I was again visited by three Prussians, who, after discovering my condition and what I was, forbore to disturb me, but paid no attention to my solicitations for assistance. They however discovered my poor companion, the Frenchman, who (having shown some inclination to resist their wishes) received the contents of a pistol from the hand of one of the Prussian soldiers, which calmed for ever that voice which had now become so cheering to me.

I was now more lonely than ever and frequently, in my despairing moments, called to my companion, but alas, he answered me no more. I gazed with fervour on the moon and listened attentively to the cries which, to all probability, proceeded from the maimed objects who were promiscuously, intermingled with wounded horses and suffering from their death-struggles. The hollow groans which floated on the almost imperceptible breath of wind. The vain cries for help in all the languages of the various combatants. The howling of dogs and the occasional shots fired by the wounded at the straggling plunderers, with the terrific screams of those they were attacking, which altogether made an impression that never can be effaced from my mind.

I was frequently visited by the plunderers whose hated clamours, as they approached, were become terrible to my ear, for I was compelled to yield to their cruel handling. Many women were among them diligently employed in the same horrid work.

I sometimes thought I saw hideous figures approaching me and again vanishing before my swimming imagination. The night was long and mournful and often did I turn my wishful eye to the east, murmuring a fervent ejaculation for the coming of day. My wavering mind visited many places in which I had spent days of pleasure and at last settled upon the fair banks of Forth. The fair banks, the lovely plains, on which I had rambled in the days of my youth, were full in my view and I traced with ardour, the windings of the meandering flood to the base of Stirling's ancient fortress.

Oh, exclaimed I, in a frantic moment; my dearest, my bosom's companion, fare thee well! May'st thou never hear of my sufferings. May'st thou never know that man has been so cruel as to withhold his aid under such circumstances! Nor may your spotless mind ever suffer a pang by learning that there is no sincerity between man and man. Here I am doomed to lie racked to pieces with excruciating pains, without a friend to comfort or even to cheer my sinking spirits with one kindly look. Oh my kindest and most faithful; how much do I now need a portion of that soothing care with which thou hast so often sweetened the bitters of my life. Thy willing hand to soften this irony couch, or a single glance of that eye which ever bore the tidings of an affectionate heart. Methinks I see the soft tear of pity with which it would here be loaded quivering over the sad situation of thy long-lost Jamie! Could these my wishes be realised; oh heaven, then could I smile into thy halls of happiness, nor yield a single sigh for ought else left behind.

I had now given up all hope of lasting much longer, but had a strong desire to see daylight once more. I was worn, weak from loss of blood, imagined I saw visionary shadows moving about me or that more plunderers approached whose handling I feared worse than death itself. I lamented that all my comrades had left me and fancied that Duncan Forbes[15] was shaded with the veil of death long before that period.

The glories of the east at length began to drive before them the gloomy shadow of night, which had so long engulfed the dreary plain, and a ray of returning hope seemed to defuse itself over my impaired senses. I praised the great author of light who had now opened to fair view the legions of marauders who infested the ruinous view and who were not even, by the arrival of full day driven from their accursed employment, but continued on all sides, carelessly to turn over the mangled bodies with a lance pole or the end of a musket, tearing the lace from their clothes and even shaking many of them from their gory garments.

O what a sight for a British heart, who could scarcely look on such a scene without feelings of sympathy and remorse. He whose dauntless spirit in battle, draws on him the wondering eyes of nations. He whose unconquerable spirit melts at the sight of the objects by his valour laid low, into the depths of generosity and tenderness. Oh, my beloved country.

---

15. This poor private, who seems to have survived, mentions Private Duncan Forbes of Captain Fenton's Troop who was from Inverie (which is on the west coast of Scotland on Loch Nevis and therefore he could not have spent his childhood on the banks of the Forth) and was a shoemaker by trade. He is recorded as killed at Waterloo.

I lay in this dreary solitude till about five in the morning, when a small detachment of highlanders made their appearance and descended towards this spot from La Belle Alliance; they crossed a part of the field [at] too great [a] distance from me; my heart glowed as they came nearer and I murmured to myself, 'O great God! Hast thou at last sent men of humanity, men who can feel for the sufferings of their fellow men, who can comfort the afflicted and succour the defenceless.'

The tear of heartfelt joy stole from my gladdening eye as they came nearer, as I waved my hand to draw them from a direction by which they would have passed me unnoticed. However, my signal was attended to for an officer and several men immediately came to the spot and with considerable difficulty removed the dead horse, but I remained motionless, for the power of my limbs was quite gone. I begged (and for the first time, not in vain) for a mouthful of water; these Christians gave me water, collected linen rags, bound up my wounds, made for me this bed of soldier's coats, whereon they laid me, gave me some more spirits and water and bid me be of good cheer till their return; they having occasion to visit that part of the ground whereon their own regiment had been engaged. I was then left alone and in a few minutes fell into a profound sleep, in which, I know not how long I remained; but I awoke and beheld your party in the valley to the left of La Haye Sainte; a flood of joy drowned all my sorrows, when I beheld the uniform of my own regiment and I strained my remaining strength in motioning with my hand to draw you to this desolate spot, but alas; all my endeavours were fruitless, my motions were not seen by the party who paused frequently as they passed towards the left to explore the features of some dead comrade which lay in their way and at last I lost sight of my friends and sunk in grief on my comfortless pillow.

The sun became extremely hot and my thirst unbearable; I attentively watched the parties of several regiments come into the field, but none of them observed the signals I made to them till I was again visited by these my first friends, the best and dearest friends I ever had occasion to prove. They have not only saved me from a premature death, but have also brought your assistance to my aid, which may be the means of yet prolonging my existence a sufficient period to enable me to prove my gratitude for the humanity which my countrymen are capable of feeling for the distressed friend or foe. They gave me a draught of water when they returned, which was the sweetest ever [that] passed these lips, for which they shall not fail to express the thankfulness of a sincere heart while life remains with [in] this blighted body.

Here the poor fellow ended his melancholy tale and our officer having made an arrangement for his conveyance, he was placed into one of the spring wagons and with the five from Smohain sent off to Brussels.

After having these poor fellows sent off to hospital, we proceeded towards the Chateau of Hougoumont and on crossing the field were not a little astonished to see such great numbers of naked dead amongst the others; they had been stripped by the plunderers for the clothes which had invested their cold remains, nor had even the shirts of some thousands escaped their unhallowed hands. Several women were seen among the dead who, to all probability, had been shot by the wounded in their plundering excursions.

We reached the Chateau of Hougoumont, which was situated on the Nivelles road, in front of the ridge, which the right of the British line had occupied. A large orchard of fruit and other trees had afforded a good cover to the party possessing it during the battle and consequently its value caused much bloodshed in taking and keeping possession of it; the dead were heaped upon each other. It had been long and obstinately defended by General Sir H Clinton's[16] and General Cook's[17] Brigades of British infantry, with some Brunswickers and Nassau troops, who had loop-holed a long wall which surrounded the orchard and garden, through which they kept up their fire upon the enemy, from whose view the wall was chiefly masked by a thick hedge that ran along its front and against which their fire was directed for a long time without execution. The hedge and trees all round this place were either cut down by the shot or the trunks of the trees stuck full of bullets from every direction.

The wood and house was, however taken and retaken by storm many times[18] during the action and at last set on fire & burnt to the ground.

---

16. It is often forgotten that Henry Clinton's King's German Legion Brigade were heavily involved in the defence of the orchard at Hougoumont from around 4 pm onwards.
17. Cook's Division comprised the Guards battalions, who are most closely associated with the defence of Hougoumont.
18. In recent years it has been proven that Hougoumont farm was broken into for certain two times and possibly three. For further information on this subject the reader is referred to the editor's *Waterloo: Myth & Reality*.

The inside of the courtyard unfolded a large heap of dead bodies, straw, stones, arms, accoutrements and wreck of every description; which still smouldered in one smoky and promiscuous heap. The walls reared their black and ruinous heads and all was desolation within and without.

It has been asserted that Bonaparte stood near this place several times during the action, even when the battle raged the greatest! But this assertion I will not presume to confirm.[19] Seven thousand men were buried in the orchard a few days after; they were buried by the peasantry who were called in from the country around to dig trenches for the reception of the dead throughout the field.

We at length, left these memorable ruins and bent our way across the plain towards La Belle Alliance, a small hotel or public house, on the road leading to Genappe. It stood on the heights near the spot where the centre of the French army rested; its roof was raked by the cannon shot and the gable end which faced the British line full of large ball holes. It had been set on fire late in the day, some part of the walls were black and the remains of a hay stack, which had stood near the back of the house still smoked. It was near this house where the Duke of Wellington and Prince Blucher met after the French army had given way.[20]

The dead and wounded which lay about La Belle Alliance were (with very few exceptions) of the French, nor were their numbers so great as at other places which we had visited. Our attention was however attracted by a French soldier who lay about twenty yards from us and made motions for drink; our officer desired me to go with two of the men & see whether anything could be done for him. We obeyed and on reaching the poor object found him in a condition that we were shocked to look upon. His two thighs were shattered to pieces and his face so disfigured by a sabre cut he had received as to render it without a resemblance of human features. His nose and upper teeth hung down upon his chin, adhering only by a piece of skin to each side of the mouth. He had been a fine stout fellow, which we all observed as he extended his muscular arm and large hand to beckon for water. However, his face and head was swelled to such a degree that we were at a loss to determine how he could receive any relief we could offer & he himself

---

19. This is certainly a myth, possibly being confused with Jerome Bonaparte, his brother, who did command the troops attempting to capture Hougoumont.
20. There is some contention over this claim, many (including Wellington) believing that the meeting occurred further south.

observing our embarrassment, lifted up with one hand the part of his face which hung down and with the other, pointed to the orifice which was to receive the water. We accordingly poured in some from one of our canteens, which were now nearly all empty and after forming a kind of canopy to preserve him from the dew of night; we put what little spirits and water remained into a tin mess can, which lay near him & placing it by his side, were about to leave him, but were arrested for a few seconds longer by his steadfast look. He had riveted his glassy eyes upon us, while we were making the foregoing arrangements for his future preservation and as we walked away he clapped his hand to his breast and a flood of tears ran over his mutilated countenance. The sight was so affecting that a tear quivered in every eye as we hurried from the melancholy spectacle, where to all probability, the poor fellow would in a short time, terminate so miserable an existence.

A little to the right of this place and more retired from the field of battle, stood a framework scaffolding, or observatory. It stood on the margin of a little wood and had been erected by the British engineers at the request of the Prince of Orange, some months previous to that period, but for what purpose I will not presume to say.[21] It commands a view of the greater part of the plains on which the action was fought & it has been asserted by some writers that Napoleon mounted it to observe the battle![22] However, that he posted himself near it some part of the day bears a resemblance of truth; for his staff were seen bearing his orders from thence to his generals who were more advanced. The observatory appeared about sixty feet in height and the spot where it stood well removed from any danger, at least, from where the battle existed.

Night being fast approaching, our officer now ordered that we should proceed after the regiment, having received information that they were bivouacked at Bulleurs[23] near Nivelles. We accordingly mounted our horses & bid farewell to the desolate plains of Waterloo, where we had spent a day, which death alone, can obliterate from the minds of our small division.

---

21. The observatory had been constructed to help with surveying for the production of a map of the new lands recently acquired by the King, quite possibly on William Craan's orders (the surveyor who had been given the task and who produced the first and only map of Waterloo – before the Lion Mound was built, which altered the landscape radically).
22. William was right to doubt this myth.
23. Actually Baulers, a village a mile north-east of Nivelles.

O' May thy sweetest flowers
Sepulchre of the brave
Spring forth in vernal showers
To clothe the warrior's grave
Thy blighted face has told us
Thou'rt ne'er to be forgot
Whatever clime may hold us
Whate'er may be our lot.

*****

William wrote to his parents from Paris with his memories of the Battle of Waterloo and it would seem appropriate to include it here. It mentions both his meeting his brother Mark at Waterloo and also talks of his wife and his two daughters in Dublin, personal details that he omits from the narrative.

> In camp at Natain [Nanterre] near Paris 8 July 1815[24]
> My dearest parents!
> I am not acquainted with the uneasiness of your minds on account of your Willie and Mark,[25] as no doubt but you have heard of the awful conflict of the 18th day of June. This will be a day, which your two sons will keep in remembrance until the last day of their existence here below.
> But I happily write (my dear father and mother) the safety of, or miraculous escape of myself and brother Mark, who has only received a musket ball through his arm, and is getting very fast well. I shall only add here; that I was very sorry to hear of the illness of the tenderest of mothers, by your letter bearing date 13th June last, and come to hand on the 27th. You will excuse my delay in writing when I inform you, that the army was not allowed to send off any letters until the 6th instant,[26] which is always a rule after such an affair as the last. I shall now give you a short detail of our military operations,

---

24. Hampshire Archives: Reference 38M49/1/56/19.
25. The only Mark Clarke in the Waterloo Medal Roll served as a private in Captain Maclean's grenadier company of the 79th Foot.
26. This was to control the information received at home, to prevent anything arriving before the official despatch. Some officers circumvented this rule by putting their letters in the official despatch bags sent from headquarters.

during the three days we was engaged with the enemy. My last letter to you was dated at Denderhoutem.[27]

On the morning of the 16th June about one o'clock, we were alarmed by the bugles sounding to arms; we instantly mounted and hurried to the place of assembly for the regiment when we were informed, that the French army had made an attack on Prince Blucher's brave Prussian army; and that the Duke of Wellington's espitons [sic] were on the advance for the frontier. We marched, and passing over an extent of beautiful country about 38 or 40 miles to the south of Denderhoutem, we arrived at the plains of Fleurus (where the British army had arrived from Brussels at 2 o'clock pm) the infantry had engaged, after coming off a march of 18 miles, and fought until dark; a great number were killed on both sides; but on the arrival of the British cavalry, Bonaparte, drew his army into the forest of Ardennes, where the cavalry were obliged to stand under his fire, and could not act against him. However day bid us farewell, and the black shade of night was again thrown over the face of the earth. We lay by our horses on the plains, surrounded by the lifeless bodies of our dear countrymen, in numbers too many to be accurately accounted for. We anxiously watched the break of day, expecting the awful, but necessary labour to begin the second morning. I term this an awful scene, because it is awful to the thoughts of those who hear of it, and even to myself it is so now; but when a man is in the field of slaughter he has none of those feelings. He is endowed with feelings suitable to the task he has in hand; he sees no horror, nor has he any time allowed for reflection.

Dear brother Mark, and myself lay within two hundred yards of each other that night and could not speak to one another. However, I learnt that he was safe, and sent him the pleasing news of my safety.

Day at last began to brighten the eastern skies, and no sooner could the two determined armies distinguish each other, than the roaring thunder of the guns resounded through the distant woods and plains. Every inch of ground was disputed with firmness on both sides, until 10 o'clock am when the French again retired into the forest of Ardinas [Ardennes]. Our noble duke saw the necessity of drawing the French army from this forest, which was a secure resource for them, when likely to be drove. He therefore

---

27. This letter is no longer extant.

ordered the British infantry to be drawn off, and the two brigades of heavy cavalry, together with a brigade of horse artillery and a troop of rocketeers to cover their retreat. They commenced their retreat by the Brussels road, and before the infantry were one mile, (which the enemy thought to be completely beaten) on the road, he sent out his cuirassiers (which are the choice troops of France, and clad in armour) to attack the British cavalry. The attack was furious on both sides, but the French were cut down wherever they came, and forced to retire with great loss. They advanced to attack the light cavalry several times, on the several hills we passed over, but would not face the heavy, any more that day. The British cavalry lost a number of men and horses on this occasion, chiefly by a brigade of French artillery which they brought to bear upon our lines. We retreated in this manner skirmishing together about 5 miles, and at last the duke gained the ground, for which he had been working the whole time. He formed his line with great skill and expedition, and placed his cannon ready for their approach; the rocketeers were placed on the road, and the cannon on a hill just over them. The moment the French army came within their reach, they opened a most dreadful fire of cannon and rockets upon them. The French was stagnated at our sudden stand, as they thought we were completely put to the rout, but the British boys gave it so hot that they were forced to retire out of the reach of our shot. Night again came on, and we lighted our fires on the ridge of the hill, and killed 2 or 3 bullocks for each regiment and set to work and roasted and boiled them and ate them, and drank our allowance of rum, as jovial together among the grass as if in the finest pavilion in Auld Edinburgh.[28] A stranger coming & seeing the army, could not have told that there had been any melancholy scene, on that day, or that they had any thought of seeing one.

We passed this night on this ground, which is called the plains of Waterloo; and on the morning of the 18th the French did not come up until 9 o'clock am.[29] This morning for the first time I saw my brother Mark, he was permitted by the colonel to come down the hill to our lines. He found me and we had just

---

28. This is strangely at odds with his journal regarding the ease of obtaining food and fruits to mention the heavy rain entirely.
29. His timings of the battle are consistently more than two hours out, the battle commencing around 11.30 am.

time to take a dram of each others' flask (as other warriors do) when the word was given to arms. We shaked hands and took a more than common farewell with each other, adding at the same time if we are both spared we must be sure to send word to each other as soon as possible after the battle, which we knew well was to be a serious one.

The brigade that our regiment belongs to was ordered to cover the highland brigade of infantry, and the French advanced, and attacked the right flank of the British line, about half past 9 o'clock, and about two hours after, both lines, extending about 6 miles in length were engaged, which filled the elements with smoke and fire and the noise of the guns could be compared to nothing but a continued roar of thunder. The scene I am not capable of describing, the good old Greys charged the enemy four times, and dashed through solid columns of their infantry (this was the first charge) but after they went through the infantry there was a line of those cavalry in armour, who they were obliged to engage at the rate of five men to one and a heavy fire kept up on them the whole time. They forced the French cavalry from the field and came back again upon the infantry; laid hundreds of the enemy lifeless wherever they went and brave General the Honourable Sir William Ponsonby being at our head the whole time, fought like a lion and when he was just in the act of crying out 'Well done Greys! This will be a glorious day' he received a musket ball through his heroic breast which laid him lifeless on the ground. Colonel Hamilton, our first colonel, was likewise killed on the same spot and 7 more of our officers.

Return of killed and wounded of the Royal Scots Greys, at the Battle of Waterloo on the ever memorable 18th day of June 1815.[30]

Killed Wounded											
Regiment	Officers	Sergeants	Corporals	Trumpeters	Privates	Horses	Officers	Sergeants	Corporals	Trumpeters	Privates	Horses
Scots Greys	8	4	7	1	95	183	7	7	9	1	74	67

30. These figures differ from those produced in *Cannon's Historical Record of the Scots Greys*.

I was one of the party who was sent next morning to bury the dead of our regiment as far as we was able to find them and to give a description of the field is far beyond my power. In the evening of the 18th I saw my dear brother walking to Brussels wounded; but I was happy when he informed me that he was not severely wounded, as it was only a flesh wound. I had the pleasure of hearing from him since and he informs me that he is recovering fast so that we have great reason to cry aloud to our heavenly father & return thanks for our preservation in the midst of so deplorable a massacre.

We advanced very quick after the French and we are now within 4 miles of Paris, to the right of it. It is garrisoned by British troops, and the king is again returned to his capital. Bonaparte has made his escape, supposed to be gone to Orleans, where a Prussian force is sent in search of him, and the fragments of his army. We expect as soon as he is *took* that the shattered remains of our brave Britons will return home, which I think cannot be long. I hope you will be good enough to write to me as soon as you receive this, and let me know how the world uses you all, as I am much delighted with reading the letters of my dear friends. We expect to go into quarters tomorrow, which will be the means of refreshing us, as we have not had a stitch of our clothes off since the 16th of June, only to change our shirts.

I heard yesterday by a letter from Dublin to one of my comrades, that my wife[31] has got another daughter since my departure.[32] God, I hope, will be with them. Adieu and may the God of Heaven bless you all. Your son William Clarke

This I have wrote, sitting by my good grey horse, at the root of a good old scotch fir tree in a wood near Paris.

---

31. This is one of the only references we have to his wife, who had clearly remained with her family in Dublin, probably because she was pregnant. Her name was most likely to be Mary.
32. Possibly Elizabeth Clarke, who was baptised on 22 June 1815 in Dublin, see the Foreword in this book for further details.

Chapter 22

The March to Paris

We now proceeded on our march and soon entered the village of Plancenoit,[1] the road still covered with the wreck of the French army, some dead men and horses lay on either hand and in the adjoining fields; the great road had been choked up with cannons, caissons and carriages of every description, which the enemy in their flight had left behind & which were now drawn to the sides of the way, for the purpose of making a passage for their pursuers. The few cottages which formed the village were stripped of every moveable article and such as were not carried away, lay broken in pieces in the houses or road. Two or three of the peasantry only were seen, and these sauntered in a state of stupor about the fronts of their pillaged houses. Some Prussian soldiers straggled about the village and along the road in the direction of Charleroi, whence their army had followed the enemy.

When we retreated through this place on the 17th, our rear was closely infested by Frenchmen, elated by the advantages they had gained; our brigade was ordered to front them and the covering artillery to open their fire, to check the progress of their advance. The rain fell in torrents, the lightning flashed through the murky elements and the thunder rolled with awful sublimity along the face of the heavens.

> Thus through the gloom pale lightnings flash
> Passed by with vivid glow.
> And roaring thunder around the clash
> Of striving arms below.

---

1.   He writes Plancenoit, but clearly means Genappe.

We passed this village and continued our route by the great road, which was a good pavement, passing through a fine open country; where scarcely any fences were seen to divide the farms or fields on either hand. The fine crops of corn &c although not totally destroyed, bore marks of the devastating torrents which had rushed over them. In some places it was levelled to the ground, save here and there a few straggling ears rearing their heads to show what the produce of these, now waste grounds, had once been.

Offal and fragments of bullocks, sheep, calves, pigs and poultry lay in great quantities on the ground where any part of the Prussian army had halted to refresh and in one field lay some skinned sheep which had been left uncut.

We took our way by a narrow lane to the right, which we followed a few miles & arrived at the environs of Nivelles. This town lies in a hollow and is so completely embosomed among clumps of trees and hedgerows, that it is not seen to the stranger till he is launched into its streets. However, perceiving ourselves at its entrance, we were withdrawn a short distance and dismounted at a hedgeback to rest till a party should enter quietly, to learn by whom it was occupied. In this situation we lay down by our horses nearly exhausted, to wait the return of the reconnoitring party; we were so much fatigued that in less than ten minutes we were all fast asleep. The calm shade of the darkening sky had lulled us into more peaceful slumbers than we had experienced for the three preceding nights and each, weary worn with fatigue, sunk with delight into this soft and unmolested remedy which had been denied for a time. However, the reconnoitring party returned, found every man and horse lying on the grass and with some difficulty made us understand that all was well in the town. We then with considerable exertion, conquered the slothful pressure with which nature had weighed us to the ground and entered Nivelles, but could collect no information respecting the situation of the British camp. However, we procured some refreshments for ourselves and horses and remained for the space of an hour wondering by what miracle the place had escaped the general pillage.

Previous to the commencement of hostilities, Nivelles had been headquarters for the Belgic troops and although both the British and French armies had touched upon it their passage was so rapid that it had sustained very little damage.

We having rested here about an hour again proceeded on our search for the regiment; we followed the road which led to Quatre Bras until we arrived at a small village named Houtain [le-Val]. Here, some of the British light cavalry were cantoned, but could give us no information respecting the two heavy brigades; our officer, consequently finding all his endeavours to join the regiment that night would be fruitless, and taking into consideration the great want of rest which we all laboured under, determined to consign a few hours to that purpose. We accordingly bivouacked in a clover field near the village till next morning, when I was again dispatched to Nivelles to make a more particular enquiry. I had just entered the town when I met some of the British horse artillery, who informed me that that the army was to advance the same morning, to the heights of Cateau [Cambresis], where (as report prevailed) the French army had made a stand. I returned with this news and we marched immediately, spent the day on the road and joined the regiment, in the evening, at the above-named place.

Our brigade had now collected the greater part of the men who had been employed on detached duties, in or after the recent battles and although much reduced in strength, their spirits were high and every man ready to meet the foe of his country. Their appearance was something singular, for many of them had lost in the battle their own helmets, caps &c and had substituted them by those of the enemy or other regiments. A robust dragoon, six feet high, was seen covered with the bonnet of a highlander divested of its plumage, where another of low stature strutted under the huge bearskin cap of a grenadier of the Imperial Guard and not a few, proud of the narrow escape they had made, displayed the holes in their own uniform head dress, through which some miscreant ball had passed without effecting its wicked mission.

We were however, mistaken as to the enemy waiting for us at the heights of Cateau and if such was their plan it was rendered abortive by their mortal enemies, the Prussians, who had harassed them on the night of the 18th to such a degree that they were driven from nine bivouacs where they had attempted to rest and not a moment allowed them to collect in any strength. They were discomfited and their courage lost; they were fatigued almost unto death and their pursuers full of vigour and elated by the scale of fortune thus turning in their favour, which neither left chance nor hope with the completely routed French army.

The country was still open and clothed bountifully with fine crops of grain; the marches of the cavalry indeed, did considerable damage to the farmers; they being generally through the corn fields to give the infantry the advantage of the roads.

General Order (Cavalry) 19 June 1815

The heavy brigades of cavalry will encamp at Bulleurs [Baulers]; Sir H. Vivian's and Sir Colquhoun Grant's Brigades of hussars to encamp at Houtain [le Val]; Sir J. O. Vandeleur's; Sir William Arentschildts & Sir Wiliam Dornberg's Brigades to encamp at Theunnis [Thines] and the Royal Horse Artillery not attached to brigades will encamp at Bulleurs.

General Order Belleurs [Baulers] 20 June 1815

The British cavalry will march immediately under the command of the senior officer in each camp to Arquesness [Arquennes] on the road leading from Nivelles to Rocules [Roeulx], where they will receive further orders. This order to be passed to the late Sir William Ponsonby's Brigade.

The cavalry marched to Arquesness [Arquennes] agreeable to the above order and received the following.

General Memorandum Arquesness [Arquennes] 20 June 1815

Major General Lord Edward Somerset will be pleased to move to Thieu with two brigades of heavy artillery. The headquarters of the cavalry and the reserve troops of horse artillery will also move to Thieu. The troops will canton if there be means of so doing in the place named and its adjacents, otherwise they must bivouac.

Signed Greenock Lieutenant Colonel & Acting Quarter Master General

The troops marched to Thieu, but could not be accommodated in cantonments and consequently compelled to bivouac until next morning when the following was received.

General Memorandum

Thieu 21 June 1815

The British cavalry will march immediately and assemble in rear of Mons, in Brigade columns of squadrons, right in front, where they will receive further orders; the artillery will also march with the cavalry.

Marched according to the above order, through a straggling village named Malplaquet, near which the cavalry were formed and dismounted on the roadside and the infantry continued their march past them to the front; the foot had no sooner come up and commenced to pass the cavalry than they were received by the latter with three hearty cheers, which was immediately answered by the former and the whole army continued their tremendous shouts of rejoicing, intermingled with beating of drums, while the pipers of the highland regiments

> Seren'd their pipes & gur'd them skirl!
> Till earth & atmosphere did dirl

At first we conjectured that the above movement had been made for the purpose of giving the horse and foot an opportunity of congratulating each other on their dear bought fame! But whether this was or was not the case, it is not in my power justly to say, for as soon as the whole of the infantry had passed, we were again mounted and marched back to the village which was nearly hid among hedges and trees and consequently an excellent place to bivouac.

The ground being pointed out to the regiment, our men bustled about in securing their horses to the trees and bushes, lighting their fires for cooking their rations &c &c while one of the sergeants who officiated as butcher, was also up to the elbows among some sheep which had been provided for the use of the regiment and everyone trying to out-vie another in making the necessary arrangements for a pleasant night in so comfortable a situation; when all in a moment, were suddenly alarmed by a brisk fire of musketry opening no great distance from us. All were for a moment, as if thunderstruck, the firing increased to a very heavy rattle which suddenly ceased and a yell followed which echoed through the surrounding woods and rang in every ear like the wild shout of an attacking enemy. The latter occurrence, immediately confirmed the doubt which had crept into every mind of some lurking division of the French army having stole upon us and the drums, trumpets and bugles proclaimed the fact by rousing the British troops to arms in the moment when anticipation had put them in the fairest track for a happy night.

Their peaceable preparations were immediately abandoned and every man flew to his horse; Mount! Mount! Was the cry and no time was lost in realising it; for a few minutes had only elapsed when the regiment was mounted, told off and ready for any service which might fall to their lot; the other two regiments which formed the brigade were also ready and the whole impatient to move, when a Staff officer who had been sent to reconnoitre galloped past us proclaiming a false alarm; and in a few minutes we were put in possession of the fact by being informed that what had created all the tumult was only a division of the Belgic troops who had imprudently adopted that method of rejoicing after the glorious victory gained over the enemy. However, the Belgic mode of rejoicing was no more allowed to disturb our social moments during the time the army continued together.

This eruption, although soon over, had done us a deal of mischief; for all our plans were deranged, and to be laid anew, and these not the worst! For while the hubbub continued, some of the Belgians, whose camp ground was separated only by some hedges from the little grove which we occupied, had watched the opportunity and made shift to deprive us of some pieces of the sheep which our butcher had cut up and left among the long grass. However, just as our men were again dismounted, one of these fellows was observed making another attack upon our field slaughterhouse and the officiating butcher being informed of it; ran after him with too much nimbleness of foot, to leave him any chance of ceasing the lash of his law. The Belgian seeing himself closely pursued, made the best of his way, no doubt; but having in his possession a good leg of mutton was a strong inducement for the butcher to crowd all sail, in which he was succeeding admirably, but still unlucky he could (in his course) fall in with no weapon to his mind, with which to execute justice upon the marauder; however as there was no time to lose and nothing else coming in his way, he (when scudding past the spot where the sheep had been killed) seized hold of a sheep's pluck[2] by the wind pipe and having come up with his object in the adjoining field, commenced battering it about his long thin jaws and continued the operation while a piece of his weapon stuck together, notwithstanding the poor Belgian having dropped his prize and bellowed for mercy with the voice of a Jupiter; he was sent into his own camp empty, besmeared with blood and dirt, while his punisher returned with his retaken prize.

We spent an unmolested night till early on the morning of the 22nd the following order was received.

---

2.   The sheep's innards.

General Memorandum
Camp Malplaquet 22 June 1815 half past one o'clock a.m.

The British cavalry, Colonel Estorff's Brigade, 2nd & 4th Divisions of British infantry, will march from Bavay this morning to Le Cateau. The several brigades of cavalry will therefore be assembled at Bavay from their respective bivouacs in the most convenient ground, in brigade columns of half squadrons, right in front, by five o'clock and will proceed at that hour in the following order to Le Cateau.

The heavy cavalry, hussars and light dragoons, with the two heavy brigades of artillery and two reserve troops, under the orders of Lord Edward Somerset to march to Aulnois [Suver?] after three o'clock.

The remaining artillery will march with the brigades to which they are attached.

Signed Greenock Lt Col
Acting Quarter Master General

The army marched agreeable to the forgoing order to Forest [en Cambresis]; nothing worthy of notice occurring on the march, unless being nearly smothered with dust be allowed to claim a place in our journal; for before we reached our nesting place, the clothes, accoutrements, arms and faces of the whole army were of one uniform colour.

We bivouacked at Forest and on the following day (the 23rd) received the following orders.

General Orders
Forest Camp 23 June 1815

No. 1 The Field Marshal takes this opportunity of returning to the army which he has the honour to command, his most sincere thanks for their gallant conduct in the glorious actions fought on the 16th, 17th and 18th days of this month and he will surely not fail to report his sense of their valour and determined courage, in the terms which it deserves to their sovereign.

No. 2 As the army is about to enter the French territory, the Field Marshal desires it may be understood by the troops of the several nations composing the army which he has the honour to command, that their sovereigns are in alliance with the King of France and the France therefore must be considered a friendly country. No article is to be taken from any individual without payment, by any officer or soldier of the British or allied troops. The commissaries of the army will supply the troops with all they may require in the usual manner and as requisitions are to be made direct on the country or its magistrates by any officer or soldier, the commissaries will receive directions, either from the Field Marshal or from the generals commanding the troops of the several nations (if these troops should not be supplied by the British commissaries) they will make such requisitions as may be necessary for their supply, for which they will give the usual vouchers and receipts and they will understand that they will be held responsible to issue and account for what they may thus receive from the country in France, in the same manner as they would if they purchased supplies for the troops in their own countries respectively.

No. 3 In order to preserve order and to provide for attendance in the hospitals at Brussels, the commander of the forces desires that one officer, one non-commissioned officer and three privates for one hundred men sent to Brussels wounded in the late actions of the 16th, 17th & 18th instants may be sent from the several regiments to the above-mentioned place tomorrow, who will place themselves under the orders of the commandant there.

No. 4 Regiments having in their possession horses belonging to other regiments, who had strayed in and after the recent battles, will immediately restore them.

This night (the 23rd) a heavy rain came on and continued all night, we were also under strict orders to be in readiness to turn out at a moment's warning, however the men crept under the hedges to which their horses were fastened and slept so sound, that when daylight appeared, many of them who were seated in the hollow and leaned to repose against the bank at the hedge bottom had dammed the current of the water, till it had found its way over their bodies, nor did some of them seem in the smallest degree disturbed by it till roused by their comrades. This place was no great distance from Cambrai and the battering train with a division of the army having been sent to reduce it; we were still kept in readiness to move. That garrison however, after being nearly two days bombarded, surrendered.

The rain continued all day on the 24th & the baggage, horses & belonging to the officers who were killed, were sold by public auction in the camp. Louis XVIII this day passed our camp on his way back to Paris.

On the 25th we marched to St Quentin; the fine country through which we passed was enchanting, the fields were refreshed by the late rain and the heavy corn waved to the very gentle breeze, the fruit trees reared their silvery heads round every cottage and ranked themselves along the waysides and the forests were folded in their verdant livery. We had not yet come upon the track of the flying French or pursuing Prussian armies, who had taken a route a little to our left.

Marched on the 26th to St Peige [Serain?] and encamped among a clump of trees in the middle of the village; some regiments took possession of the houses and occupied them all night.

Marched on the 27th to Goyncore [Jonqcourt], a village situated in a woody country some distance to the right of the great road leading to Paris. We bivouacked in a cherry orchard, where every tree was loaded with fruit and it may have been that the farmer had seen them as quickly divested of it before, but I should be inclined to doubt it; for in little more than half an hour there was scarcely as many left as would have suppered a blackbird.

There were no provisions to be purchased in the village, at least what it contained was soon swallowed up. However, two of my companions and myself having discovered a church and some farmhouses at a little distance, started off together to make such purchase as the place might afford. A few minutes' walk brought us to the spot, where in the first cottage we entered we purchased some bread and brandy; the next we came to was a small public house in which some of the peasantry sat drinking wine and having requested the host to bring each of us a bottle, which we intended to carry to the camp. A man who stood by and whose appearance bespoke something more than the humblest class, forbad the landlord to bring it & beckoned us to follow him; this we did without hesitation and were led into a handsome chateau and ushered into a spacious room, where an elderly woman immediately attended and after receiving our conductor's orders, spread the table with viands, which would not have disgraced him had his guests been of nobler descent. Our generous host accompanied us at the board and (in broken English) expressed his thankfulness that they were not visited by the Prussian instead of the English army, lavishing compliments on the latter as a brave and generous enemy, even when fortune crowned them with victory.

We enjoyed an excellent repast with plenty of excellent wine, but fearing our presence in the camp might be required, we dared not to make a long stay and our hospitable entertainer seeing us about to leave him, presented a quantity of fresh eggs and stowed in each of our haversacks a couple of pigeons and a bottle of wine. We indeed offered him money as payment, but he (as we expected) spurned the offer, inviting us to return and spend the evening with him, if we could with propriety do so; however, this we durst not promise, never being aware of what hour of the night the troops might move, we therefore took leave of our benefactor & returned to the cherry orchard loaded like bees and shared the fruits of our good fortune with our messmates who were busying themselves, frizzling some pieces of tainted beef, which had been issued to us at Le Forest, on a French cuirassier's steel jacket which was carried among our kitchen utensils to act the part of a frying pan and by adding our day's rations of brandy, made ourselves as happy as princes under the leafy boughs of the hedge till Morpheus used his influence in our behalf and folded us in his soothing mantle till four o'clock next morning, when we marched from our bivouacs and bore to the left till we again got upon the great road. We regained the road at Emans [Vermand] a considerable town, where the headquarters of the army had rested during the preceding night. Soon after we left this place we came upon the route of the French and Prussian armies. The change was obvious to all, the moment we entered upon the road, for the barley, rye and bean fields were beaten down on either hand, the trees stripped of their branches, particularly the cherry trees as this fruit was then in full perfection. Dead horses lay here and there, on the road and in the fields adjoining, where the bivouacs had in many places, also left their marks and could easily be pointed out by the corn being destroyed a considerable distance round the spot; the trampled ground covered with straw, branches of trees, feathers, paper, and the offal of other animals on which the men had feasted; it was frequently observed that dead sheep had been left lying on these camp grounds untouched. Most probably the neighbouring farmers had been plundered of them in greater numbers than the plunderers were able to make use of. We passed one camp ground this day, on which lay above twenty dead carcasses of the above kind.

There was not a farm house, cottage or any other kind of place of abode, on, or near the road, that had escaped destruction, their inhabitants were deserted, their doors and windows broken, their furniture within a heap of ruin scattered about the floor and wantonly broken to pieces. And in one word, the desolation which marked every human dwelling which lay in their way, were striking proofs that the greatest acts of cruelty against the French people could alone satisfy the horrid disposition which the Prussians had imbibed against them and consequently we frequently marched a distance of thirty or forty miles, without seeing a single smoking chimney.

We continued to advance by the great road till about one o'clock in the day, when we were again drawn into the fields and proceeding some miles to the right, entered a beautiful level plain, covered with clover and hay. On one side of this delightful green valley, a far expanse of level land appeared, and on the other a gentle acclivity presented its face, covered with farm houses, cottages &c enveloped in a wood of fruit trees.

This was such a situation for our bivouacs as we had never before experienced; it seemed as if nature had alone, meant it for that purpose and in her bounty we anticipated a night of more than common enjoyment! However, men are prone to err and dame fortune sometimes make them her laughing stock. For after we had taken our ground among the gardens and trees, lighted our fires and got our camp kettles set a boiling; having plenty of peas & vegetables of all kinds, at our will, as well as a good intention to dine on some good broth; orders was sounded and the cavalry ordered to march immediately. I must here leave to the judgement of the reader to consider how much we were disappointed, for my pen would fail in an attempt to describe the kind of look which wandered from every eye upon the cooks and batmen when they emptied the precious contents of their seething kettles among the long grass, that they might load them upon the animals for the march.

However, we were compelled to yield to the old lady's pleasure and accordingly were again in motion between four and five p.m. We were led forward inclining to the left through corn and hay fields until we regained the great road, by which we had not proceeded far before we arrived at a handsome little town names Pont St Maxence. This town was pleasantly situated on the banks of a river, but like all other places which lay in the route of the Prussian army, deserted by its inhabitants, the houses were all shut up (or had been so) but the greater part of the doors and windows now broken and according to appearance the place had undergone a complete pillage. A number of Prussian soldiers yet sauntered about the streets in a state of intoxication.

There were two good inns in the principal street to which some of their inhabitants had ventured to return on the approach of the British army and took advantage of the short sunshine, by selling liquers to both officers and men as they passed through and the headquarters of the army being established with them for the night, would give them a chance of making a pretty good harvest before the following morning.

Our brigade advanced to pass the river which might be about fifty yards in breadth and glided gently through the centre of the town; the passage was effected by a stone bridge (partly in ruins). It had been handsome, but having been blown up when the French were driven the same road the preceding year, was now made passable by planks and wooden supports in two arches. On the opposite height or fine rising ground which ran some miles above and below the town, covered with beautifying shrubs and trees, where we were told, that the French had posted themselves after destroying the bridge in 1814 and obstinately resisted their pursuers.

Our brigade passed the bridge by single files & at the end of the town, turned to the right & followed a narrow road which led along the bottom of the wooded hill, to a small village about five miles down the river. Here we rested all night, forming our bivouacs on the banks of the stream & at four o'clock next morning resumed our march.

On this day (the 29th) we marched to Chenvenis [Chennevières-lès-Louvres]; many dead horses seen on the road and in the fields, as well as the ground where several bivouacs had been formed on the line of our route. This village was small but situated in a fine country and surrounded with plentiful gardens; rows of cherry trees ranged themselves in every hedge, loaded with fruit.

The two heavy brigades of cavalry were encamped about this village; our regiment in a rye field and on the declivity of a gentle slope which lay directly opposite the sun at noon day. The weather was so extremely hot that we were compelled to carry green boughs from a wood at some distance to screen ourselves and horses from the powerful blaze that shot down upon the field in which we were bivouacked.

Soon after we encamped, a heavy cannonade was heard in our front; this continued till night, when we received orders to hold ourselves in readiness to turn out at any moment! This order kept us on the alert all night and our anxiety still more heightened by a rumour that we were to advance for the purpose of joining the Prussian army in the morning, who were skirmishing with the enemy before Paris. This report sounded well in every ear, for all were impatient to get forward;

however, morning brought no order to move, but that no man was (on any pretence) to leave his camp, also that 3 day's rations were to be drawn for the men; arms &c put in the best possible order &c &c. We accordingly continued in a state of anxiety the whole day and in the evening, men and horses well refreshed, we received the following order.

> Division Orders
> Camp near Chenvenis [Chennevières-lès-Louvres] 30 June 1815
>
> The troops to remain saddled all night and to be in readiness to advance tomorrow morning at daybreak. The baggage to be packed but not loaded on the animals. In the event of the troops moving in the night, they will assemble in their respective camp grounds ready to move as may be directed.

Remained saddled all night, agreeable to the above order. Heavy cannonading heard during the morning, but no orders to move, till one o'clock in the afternoon, when the army was put in motion and we marched (July 1st) to Chateau de Roissy [en-France] and encamped in the pleasure grounds and shrubberies of Marshal Ney's beautiful country seat at that place. A small village extended itself on each side of the road, near the chateau, which like all others on the road, was completely ransacked; it was truly a deserted village. No living creature was to be seen except a few crows who inhabited a clump of lofty trees in the neighbouring wood; the humblest cottage and the lordly hall were equally divested of the means of affording the slightest comfort. Their doors and windows stood open to whoever might choose to enter, but the cheerful swell of a human face welcomed none.

I accompanied two of my comrades into the village, after we had encamped; where we entered many of the houses, with no other intention but that of observing the destructive effects of war. We went into a fine large house, which had by its appearance, as one belonging to some person, of not the lowest capacity, attracted our notice. We visited several very fine rooms and found all the once spacious and costly furniture, broken to pieces and strewed about the floor; looking glasses, china, crystal ware &c in ruinous heaps in every corner and even the cupboards which these fancy wares had adorned were filled with their fragments and appeared as if the wanton deed had been completed by the stroke of a large stick or some other equitable weapon. In some rooms, picture or looking glass frames or part of them, still hung where they had adorned the walls, but the glasses broken and the paintings, (perhaps the once much admired work of some eminent master) lying in tatters and shreds about the rooms, with vast quantities of books, bed and window curtains, sheets and wearing apparel, torn in the same manner and thrown in promiscuous heaps of ruin.

We entered many other houses and found they had all (without exception) undergone the same kind of treatment.

The seat of Marshal Ney which was situated close to the village, was a large & ancient building surrounded by fine pleasure grounds and plantations. Some of the general officers took possession of the chateau, where they remained during the time we were in the place & the bivouacs of the troops were formed among the clumps of shrubs and trees around.

An invariable rule existed among the men on entering any new camp ground; viz, who to be first at such inhabited house or houses as lay in the neighbourhood, for the purpose of procuring provisions either by purchase or a more reasonable rate. Andrew J[ames][3] was an active fellow and generally led the van on these excursions; for he no sooner threw himself from his horse than he rushed off, leaving the care of the animal to his well-trained comrade and in this manner, bolting through hedges, over walls or any other obstacle that might lie in his direct course to the nearest hopeful chateau or cottage, he slacked not his buck-like pace till he had reached the spot! We were, this day, ordered to bivouac along the outside of a garden wall within which stood the grand chateau. This wall Andrew immediately sprung over and ran to the house, where after unsuccessfully rummaging some ill-furnished cupboards, he bounced into the kitchen and found a very genteel legged little French cook boiling a large metal pot of green peas by way of getting things in a forward state till other provisions should arrive for the dinner of the officers who had taken possession of the house.

Andrew, on entering the kitchen, knit his brows and flourished a look or two of an unpleasing kind over monsieur, but finding the house contained nothing else which would suit him, seized the pot and scampered off. The Frenchman dared not to complain while our hero was yet near him, but when he had gained a considerable distance,

---

3. Sergeant Andrew James of Captain Fenton's Troop. He was only 5ft 1in (1.55m) tall and came from Glasgow.

he mustered courage enough to enable him to call after. 'Mon Dieu! Cest le dinee pour le General Angloise.' However, Andrew could not understand French only when it served his own purpose and therefore took no other notice than that of increasing his pace to the point where he had entered the garden; but before he had reached it, the governor of the dripping pan had raised the cry of despair to such a height that the officers hurried to the rallying post and being informed of the depredation; ran after Andrew and gave him barely time to get the pot over the wall. However, Andrew was never taken at a nonplus, but always pregnant with invention. He clapped the pot down at the heels of the horses and seizing his comrade's dress jacket (which was something better than that of a private soldier), threw it over his prize and next moment applied himself vigorously to the grooming of his horse and was merrily singing 'Some one of a troop of dragoons was my daddy; nae wonder I'm fond o' a sodger laddie', when Lord G[reenock?] set his head over the wall and called out 'Stop that fellow with the pot.' Every eye was instantly turned in seeming surprise to the spot from whence the voice issued and then upon on another, Andrew seemed quite thunderstruck! Nor could a knowledge of the general's meaning be hammered into him by any means. However, a train of officers sprung over the wall, but finding themselves likely to be bilked, ordered a search to take place through the camp, which immediately commenced, but after rummaging every corner, hedge & bush as well as using fair and foul means to draw a discovery from some of the men who were near the spot where the pot scaled the wall. However, all their endeavours were to no purpose; they had seen anything but the pease-pot and consequently after a deal of fruitless labour the search was given up for a bad job. No one ever dreaming that a jacket of such a description could possibly have been used in such a stratagem.

The officers at last left our lines full of indignation and when the gloom of evening had summoned them to their tents or other covers and all declared in safety the contents of the pot was found very acceptable among a few of Andrew's most favoured friends.

On the following evening (the 2nd), I, with another comrade; strolled into a wood which was near our bivouac; a footpath which ran into the thickets seemed to invite us to explore a scene so full of beauty. The mantling foliage was gilded with the glorious rays of the declining sun and the birds warbled in endless variety throughout the echoing forest; we enjoyed the enchanting meld and unconsciously followed the pleasing path till we emerged at the other side of the wood; we issued near some cottages and entered one, the nearest to us, in which lay some men's garments clotted with blood, which gave reason to believe that some of its inhabitants had been murdered by the plunderers, who had evidently visited and spread distraction in these humble and lonely retirements. We proceeded from thence to a small farmhouse where an old man sat weeping on a stone at the door. He looked fearfully agitated as we approached him, however we beckoned him again, into a state of composure, assuring him that that we had no intention against his person or property, but of the latter the poor man was already deprived, for all was gone or destroyed; he arose from the weeping posture in which he sat and pointed to the door, as if inviting us to enter, which we did and were shocked at the destruction which filled the interior; all was desolation. Not an article of any description remained unbroken, and we turned from a scene of such cruelty, filled with a sensation of bitter disapproval of men who could be guilty of so much wantonness. The old man led us into the garden behind the house in which were still left some currants! Of these he invited us to partake, having nothing else to offer. He informed us that his family had fled to save their lives, he knew not where and night coming on we took leave of the lonely abode and its sorrow worn master, who again resumed his seat at the door.

We returned to the camp and as we remained some days in the place; many of our men went, not only to see the melancholy spectacle, but to carry provisions for the old man and to sooth his sufferings by their kind attentions.

This day, much cannonading was heard in the direction of Paris, from which we were situated only thirteen miles and the French army having taken possession of all the strongholds in its front, gave rise to much skirmishing with their outposts. Orders to hold ourselves in readiness to move at any hour.

3rd July No particulars.

4th July Some cannonading heard, but no particulars reached our camp till late in the afternoon, when we received the following orders.

General Orders
Headquarters Gonesse   4th July 1815

No. 1 The Field Marshal has great satisfaction in announcing to the troops under his command, that he has in concert with Field Marshal Prince Blucher, concluded a military convention with the commander in chief of the French army in Paris, by which the enemy are to evacuate St Denis, St Ouen, Clichy and Neuilly this day at noon; the height of Montmartre tomorrow at noon, and Paris next day.

No. 2 The Field Marshal congratulates the army upon this result of their glorious victory; he desires that they may employ the course of this day in cleaning the arms, clothes & appointments as it is his intention that they should pass him in review.

P Walters[4] Lieutenant Colonel
A A General

Address received by the cavalry on the same day, from the Earl of Uxbridge.

General Cavalry Orders   Brussels 25th June 1815

Lieutenant General the Earl of Uxbridge has the honour to announce to the cavalry and to the Royal Horse Artillery that he is about to proceed to England. He cannot leave them without feelings of regret at the separation, but he at the same time enjoys those of admiration and gratitude for their conduct whilst under his command.

The brilliant conduct of many of the brigades in the face of a cavalry so very greatly outnumbering them surpasses all praise that he'll attempt to offer.

He requests that the general officers and all other officers will accept his warmest thanks for the readiness and zeal with which they executed every duty, and that the non-commissioned officers and privates may feel assured that their general good conduct and their bravery in battle have made an indelible impression upon him.

Signed M Childers Major
Act A.A. General[5]

---

4.   As written in the journal, but should read J. Waters. Lieutenant Colonel John Waters, Assistant Adjutant General, had been one of the most famous of Wellington's 'Observing Officers' in the Peninsula.

5.   Major of Brigade to Vandeleur at Waterloo, Major Michael Childers 11th Light Dragoons. His letter to Siborne was published as Letter No. 55 in *Waterloo Letters*.

General Cavalry Orders   Camp Chateau de Croissy
4th July 1815

Officers commanding brigades of cavalry & troops of horse artillery are requested to send in immediately the names of such officers as they may wish to recommend for brevet promotion in consequence of the glorious actions of the 16th, 17th and 18th ultimo.

General Orders
Headquarters Gonesse (Received 4th)   2nd July 1815

The Field Marshal has great pleasure in publishing in general orders the following letters from the commander in chief, and the secretary of state expressing the approbation of his Royal Highness the Prince Regent, of the conduct of the army in the late actions with the enemy.

I have the honour to be &c Bathurst[6]
Horse Guards 25th June 1815

My Lord Duke,
I have the honour to acknowledge the receipt of your Grace's dispatch of the 19th instant conveying a report of the military operations up to that date, marked and distinguished, as these operations have been by the glorious and important victory gained over the French army on the 18th instant, I have infinite pleasure in communicating to your grace the high feeling of satisfaction and approbation with which the Prince Regent has viewed the conduct of the troops upon this memorable occasion.

No language can do justice to the sense which his Royal Highness entertains of that distinguished merit which has even surpassed all former instances of their characteristic bravery and discipline, allow me to desire, that your Grace will also accept yourself, and convey in my name to the officers, non-commissioned officers and troops under your command, the thanks of his Royal Highness, for the great and important services, which they have rendered their grateful country.

---

6.   Henry Bathurst, 3rd Earl Bathurst, Secretary of State for War and the Colonies.

From my partiality and well known opinion of the Prussian nation & their troops, your grace will readily believe, that I also concur in those expressions of admiration, and thanks which have emanated from the Prince Regent, for the important services rendered to the common cause by Prince Blucher, and the brave army under his command.

The triumph of success cannot lessen the regret which must be felt by all, for the loss of the many valuable lives which has unavoidably attended the accomplishment of this great achievement; and I particularly deplore the fall of Lt General Sir Thomas Picton,[7] and Major General Sir W Ponsonby.

> I am my Lord Duke
> Yours, sincerely
> Frederick
> Commander in Chief

War Department, London   24th June 1815

My Lord,

Your Grace will be pleased to convey to General His Royal Highness the Prince of Orange, the satisfaction the Prince Regent has expressed in observing, that in the actions of the 16th & 18th instant, His Royal Highness has given an early proof of those military talents, for which his ancestors have been so renowned, and that by freely shedding his blood in the defence of the Netherlands,[8] he has cemented an union of the people of the House of Orange which it is to be hoped will become thereby indissoluble.

The Prince Regent is fully sensible of the meritorious services performed by the Earl of Uxbridge who had the command of the cavalry in the Battle of the 18th and commands me to desire you will communicate to His Lordship his Royal Highness's most gracious acceptance of them.

The judicious and determined courage displayed by General Lord Hill, and by the other general officers in command of His

---

7. The fiery Welsh General Sir Thomas Picton was shot through the forehead when leading his troops forward during D'Erlon's attack.
8. The Prince was wounded at Waterloo. The Lion Mound was erected later reputedly on the spot where he was hit.

Majesty's forces upon these glorious occasions, have attained the high approbation of the Prince Regent has received the excellent and invincible valour manifested by all ranks and descriptions of the troops, serving under your Grace's command.

His Royal Highness commands me on no account to omit expressing his deep regret on receiving so long a list of officers and men, who have either fallen or been severely wounded in the actions of the 16th & 18th instant, and the Prince Regent particularly laments the loss of such highly distinguished officers, as Lieutenant General Sir Thomas Picton, and Major General Sir William Ponsonby.

It cannot be expected that such desperate conflicts should be encountered, and so transcendent a victory be obtained without considerable loss. The chance of war must at times expose armies under the ablest commanders to great casualties without any adequate advantage to be derived in the turn. But whoever contemplates the immediate effects, and the probable results of the battles of the 16th & 18th instants cannot but think, that although in the lists of killed & wounded several of His Majesty's most approved officers were unfortunately inscribed, many indeed well known to your grace, and whose names have become familiar to their country by their distinguished services in the peninsula, the loss however severe, and however to be lamented bears but a small proportion of the magnitude of the victory which has been achieved, and which have exalted the military glory of the country, has protected from invasion and spoil the territory of His Majesty's ally the King of the Netherlands, and has opened the finest prospect of placing on a lasting foundation the peace & liberty of Europe.

I have the honour to be &c Signed Bathurst

5th July No particulars.

General Order
Camp Chateau de Roissy   6 July 1815

The 1st & 2nd Brigades of cavalry will parade tomorrow morning at four o'clock in column of squadrons upon the ground of their respective camps right in front.

On the morning of the 7th we paraded agreeable to the above order and marched in the direction of Paris.

Soon after we left Roissy the country assumed the appearance of an immense vineyard; the plains with some gentle heights, were wholly clothed with the vine and many noble seats presented themselves to view. We left Paris about three miles to our left, passing the heights in its front, near where we crossed the river Seine by a pontoon bridge which had been thrown over for that purpose and continued our route down the banks of the river to a small town named Nanterre, about six miles below Paris.

On arrival at this place, we bivouacked on the outside of a high wall which enclosed the town, however the gates were ordered to remain open, that the troops might have access at pleasure & the camp being so close, many of the men entered in quest of provisions. However, whether it was an arrangement made on the approach of the British army or a previous precaution against losing their property, I cannot pretend to say, but true it was that the town contained but little comfort for a stranger. We could neither procure money and being of opinion that the inhabitants had concealed their provisions &c that we might be deprived of the use of them, we were sometime more anxious to discover where they were concealed.

Night came on and all was still; the weary gone to rest and others whose active minds had surmounted the fatigues of the day, sat gazing on the moon and musing on some favoured friend and spot in their native land, without taking any heed to the midnight prowlings of others who were determined (if possible) to find out the secret repositories of the unfavourable inhabitants who would not, by fair means, supply them with the necessary articles of food which the troops, at first, had no desire to obtain without payment.

It had been observed during the afternoon that many of the gardens (particularly those which could be seen from the streets) were newly turned up, which naturally created an idea that their stores were buried in the earth and when the silent hour of midnight arrived, many inroads were made as well as discoveries, by probing the ground with their swords.

A few of my most intimate comrades requested me to give them a hand with a prize they had discovered and after conveying a large cask of wine from one of these gardens to a snug corner in our bivouac, we made preparations for a convivial hour or two under the trees, behind the wall. Some of the party who were on this excursion belonged to the regiment which lay next to us in brigade[9] and by mustering a few

---

9. The Inniskillings.

more, we drained the wine cask before daylight, being aware it would not do to leave any traces by which we (as depredators) might have been detected. But how to dispose of the cask was still a matter which required some generalship and after several conjectures, a wag of our squad announced that he had [at] last hit the mark and discovered the very method to make all safe. He accordingly, with the assistance of two others, rolled the cask among the trees till it was completely clear of the camp ground occupied by the two regiments who had been partakers of the wine and having concealed it among some nettles in the lines of the other regiment which composed the brigade with us, returned undiscovered to the spot from whence they went.

The cry out [sic] which took place in the morning was not unexpected, we heard with some degree of confidence in our safety, the commanding officers of regiments called and the complaint which had been laid before the senior officer by the inhabitants, ordered immediately to be looked into. Lt. Colonel H[ankin][10] of our regiment was ordered to take two trusty non-commissioned officers with him and to begin at the one end of the lines and make a strict search to the other, for a wine cask, which had (with much other property) been pillaged from the inhabitants of the town during the night and would be a good landmark by which to find out the depredators.

The colonel accordingly called for two of the very individuals who had been principal actors in the wine affair and in whom he placed great confidence to accompany him; he made some short explanatory observations to his heroes and the work of justice began.

They searched the lines of our own & next regiment in the strictest manner, knowing there was no danger of making a discovery there and proceeded to the third,[11] among whose nettles they found the plundered barrel.

The work was at once at a close and it remained now only for the officer commanding that corps to find out his evil doers. Colonel H[ankin] protested that he was confident none of his men would have been guilty of such a breach of good order and the officers and men of the other corps seemed also to rejoice that they had no finger in the pie,

---

10. Major Thomas Pate Hankin was a lieutenant colonel in the army. He had not partaken in the charge at Waterloo, having been thrown by his horse, which had been startled by the explosion of a shell.
11. The 1st Royal Dragoons.

while the bustle of investigation went forward in every department of those in whose lines the cask was found.

Thus went on the investigation, a great part of the day; but as might have been expected, nothing could be brought home where no man was guilty! And after every possible experiment was tried that might lead to a discovery of the offenders, they were compelled to relinquish the task and monsieur, who made the complaint obliged to content himself under his loss and mortification of not being able to forward the punishment of any man for the sin of wine-bibing.

We remained in camp all this day (the 8th) & went into cantonments in the town on the following day.

Many noble seats of the ancient families of France were in this neighbourhood. St Cloud was situated one mile, at which beautiful place Lord Combermere,[12] the commander of the cavalry established his quarters.

> General Orders
> Headquarters Neuilly 7 July 1815
>
> No. 1 The commander of the forces has the greatest satisfaction of communicating to the troops, the thanks of the houses of Lords and Commons for their conduct in the battles fought on the 16th, 17th and 18th days of June last.
> Die Veneris 23 Juny 1815
> Resolved Nemine Dissentient [Without Dissent]
> By the Lords spiritual and temporal in parliament assembled, that the thanks of this house be given to General His Royal Highness, the Prince of Orange, Knight Grand Cross of the most Honourable Military Order of the Bath
> Lt General the Earl of Uxbridge, Knight Grand Cross of the most Honourable Military Order of the Bath
> Lt General Lord Hill, Knight Grand Cross of the most Honourable Military Order of the Bath
> Lt General Sir Henry Clinton, Knight Grand Cross of the most Honourable Military Order of the Bath
> Lt General Charles Baron Alten, Knight Grand Cross of the most Honourable Military Order of the Bath

---

12. General Sir Stapleton Cotton (1773–1865) became the 1st Viscount Combermere in 1814; he was given command of the British cavalry after Uxbridge was wounded and had to return to Britain to recuperate.

Major General Sir John Ormsby Vandeleur, Knight Commander of the most Honourable Military Order of the Bath
Major General George Cook, Knight Commander of the most Honourable Military Order of the Bath
Major General Sir James Kempt, Knight Commander of the most Honourable Military Order of the Bath
Major General Sir William Dornberg, Knight Commander of the most Honourable Military Order of the Bath
Major General Sir Edward Barnes, Knight Commander of the most Honourable Military Order of the Bath
Major General Sir John Byng, Knight Commander of the most Honourable Military Order of the Bath
Major General Sir Denis Pack, Knight Commander of the most Honourable Military Order of the Bath
Major General Lord Edward Somerset, Knight Commander of the most Honourable Military Order of the Bath
Major General Sir John Lambert, Knight Commander of the most Honourable Military Order of the Bath
Major General Sir Colquhoun Grant, Knight Commander of the most Honourable Military Order of the Bath
Major General Sir Peregrine Maitland, Knight Commander of the most Honourable Military Order of the Bath
Major General Sir Colin Halkett, Knight Commander of the most Honourable Military Order of the Bath
Major General Sir R. H. Vivian, Knight Commander of the most Honourable Military Order of the Bath
Major General Sir Frederick Adam, Knight Commander of the most Honourable Military Order of the Bath
And to the several officers under their commands for their indefatigable zeal and exertion upon the 18th of June when the French Army commanded by Bonaparte received a signal and complete defeat.
Die Lunae 26 Juny 1815
Ordered by the Lords Spiritual and Temporal in parliament assembled that His Grace the Duke of Wellington be requested to signify the said resolutions to them.
Signed George Ross, Clerk Parliament

Die Veneris 23 Juny 1815
Resolved Nemine Dissentient
By the Lords Spiritual and Temporal in parliament assembled, that this house doth acknowledge and highly approve, the

distinguished valour and discipline displayed by the non-commissioned officers and private soldiers of His Majesty's Forces serving under the command of Field Marshal the Duke of Wellington in the glorious victory obtained upon the 18 June 1815.

Ordered by the Lords Spiritual and Temporal in parliament assembled, that the same be signified to them by the commanding officers of their several regiments, who are desired to thank them for their gallant conduct and exemplary behaviour.

The thanks of the House of Commons were also received, being given to all the general officers, officers and men of the army for their distinguished valour & intrepidity in that hard fought battle.

On the 10th we received the following orders.

General Orders
Headquarters Paris 7 July 1815

No. 1 Major General Baron Muffling[13] of the Prussian service has been appointed Governor of Paris by the common accord of Field Marshal, the Duke of Wellington and Field Marshal Prince Blucher.

No. 2 The Allied Army under the command of the Field Marshal are to occupy the ports and barriers in six of the mairies on the right of the Seine; that is to say Numbers 1, 2, 3, 4, 5 and 6.

No. 3 Colonel Barnard of the 95th Regiment[14] is appointed to command in those mairies under the general direction of Major General Baron Muffling.

No particulars till [the] 13th, when the following Regimental Order was published.

General Orders
Headquarters Paris 11 July 1815
Lieutenant General Lord Combermere is to command the cavalry of this army; date of appointment 25 June last.

---

13. He was Prussian liaison officer to Wellington during the Waterloo campaign.
14. Colonel Sir Andrew Barnard had commanded 1st Battalion 95th Rifles at Waterloo.

Regimental Order
Nanterre, 13 July 1815
The troops will give in tomorrow morning, a Return of the officers and second chargers that were killed or taken by the enemy in the action of the 18th June last. Also a statement of the effects of the non-commissioned officers, trumpeters and privates who were killed on the 18th ultimo or have since died of their wounds.

General Cavalry Orders
Malmaision, 13 July 1815
Officers commanding brigades will be pleased to send in as soon as possible to the Acting Assistant Adjutant General, the names of the officers who commanded regiments & of those who succeeded to the command in the Battle of Waterloo.

The Emperor of Austria will receive the General officers of the Allied Army, officers commanding brigades and general staff tomorrow at twelve o'clock. The Field Marshal requests they will assemble at his quarters at half past eleven.

Malmaison 14th July 1815
General Cavalry Orders,
No. 1 Lieutenant General Lord Combermere feels very proud of the honour which his Grace the Duke of Wellington has conferred upon him, by appointing him to the command of the cavalry.

No. 2 The Lieutenant General has heard with the greatest satisfaction the great praise and admiration with which the British cavalry merited by their gallant conduct on the glorious 18th of June, under the late distinguished commander, the cause of whose temporary loss to the service he in common with the whole army most deeply regrets.

No. 3 Lord Combermere has to lament the loss of so many brave officers & soldiers who fell upon the 18th June, many of whom he had the honour to command, and to whose zeal & gallantry, he has upon so many occasions felt so much indebted.

No particulars until the 21st when the thanks of the Mayor and Corporation of the City of London were received; being given to the British troops as a mark of gratitude for their exemplary conduct in the recent battles in Flanders.

Headquarters, Paris 18th July 1815

General Orders,
A common council in the chamber of the Guild Hall of the city of London on Friday the 7th day of July 1815.

Resolved unanimously that the thanks of the court be given to General His Royal Highness the Prince of Orange, Knight Grand Cross of the Most Honourable Military Order of the Bath; Lieutenant General the Marquis of Anglesey K.G.C.B; Lord Hill K.G.C.B; Sir Henry Clinton K.G.C.B; Charles Baron Alten Knight Commander of the Most Honourable Order of the Bath; Major General Sir John Ormsby Vandeleur K.C.B, George Cook; Sir James Kempt K.C.B; Sir William Dornberg K.C.B; Sir Edward Barnes K.C.B; Sir John Byng K.C.B; Sir Dennis Pack K.C.B; Lord Edward Somerset K.C.B; Sir John Lambert K.C.B; Sir Colquhoun Grant K.C.B; Peregrine Maitland; Sir Colin Halkett K.C.B; Frederick Adam, Sir H Vivian K.C.B; and to the several officers under their command, for their indefatigable zeal & exertions upon the 18th June, when the French army commanded by Bonaparte in person received a signal and complete defeat, and that his Grace the Duke of Wellington be requested to signify the same to the officers above named.

Wood Thorpe[15]
W Drake Clark[16]
B[rigade] Major

A common council holden in the chamber of the Guildhall of the City of London, on Friday the 7th day of July 1815.

Resolved unanimously, that this court do most warmly admire and thank the non-commissioned officers and private soldiers of His Majesty's Forces, serving under the command of Field Marshal the Duke of Wellington for the distinguished valour and discipline displayed by them in the glorious battle on the 18th of June, and that his grace be requested to cause this

---

15. Woodthorpe, the extensive estate and mansion of Hugh Parker Esq. is pleasantly situated on the Intake road, 3 miles East of Sheffield. Taken from *White's Directory* 1833.
16. There is no such officer in the Army List for 1815. I suspect it should read Major Isaac Blake Clarke, Scots Greys.

note to be submitted to them by the commanding officers of the different corps.

Wood Thorpe
W Drake

About this time a regular mail was allowed to run to England and the army to correspond with their relatives, when many a budget of funny letters went off.

On the 22nd an order was issued by the commander of the forces, authorising officers commanding regiments to grant passes to a certain number of their men daily who might have a wish to see the City of Paris. This indulgence we frequently embraced and I myself spent several days, separately, in visiting its most remarkable ornaments. The road from Nanterre to the city was a capacious pavement with a double row of lofty beeches and elms on each side, and between the double rows of trees, a fine path for foot passengers over which the green boughs formed an agreeable arcade. The pavement had been torn up and entrenchments formed across at certain distances behind each other from Neuilly Bridge to the entrance of the Tuileries.

We entered the city by a large square or very open street, ornamented in several places with graceful marble statues; direct to the front was the gates which led through the gardens to the Palace of the Tuileries, this spacious street branching off to right and left.

Foot passengers only could be admitted by the way of the gardens and we consequently put our horses up at a hotel near the gates, after which entering and pondering among the beautiful walks, arbours, fountains and cascades, where the masculine statue of Hercules leaning on his ponderous club, peeped from the middle of an olive grove, with inquisitive eye to a more hidden recess among the combined foliage of the weeping willow and mantling myrtle, where stood a Venus de Medici[17] as a true representation of nature's work of perfection.

We passed through the archway which led to the inner court and spent about an hour in the splendid gallery of paintings. Afterwards proceeding through the court and triumphal arch surmounted by a beautiful golden car and four golden horses, into the city. Where we spent the day in visiting such places as we had been told were worthy

---

17. The Greek statue of Aphrodite had been taken from Florence and placed in the Louvre in 1803, but was returned to the Uffizi Gallery at Florence, where it can be seen today.

of attention and returned to our quarters in the evening, much satisfied with our day's pleasure. We repeated their visits to the city frequently during the time we remained at Nanterre.

Orders were received from the field marshal to get everything in the best possible condition, preparatory to a grand review of the whole army before the Emperor of Austria & arrangements for the formation of the lines as follows.

The cavalry and Royal Horse Artillery will form two lines and the different brigades will be posted as follows.

The first line on the centre of the paved road.
Lt Colonel Sir R Gardiner's[18]

Troop of Horse Artillery	- The right on the Place de Louis de XVI[19]
First Brigade Heavy Cavalry	- Left extending towards Saint Etoile de Champs Elysees.
Second Brigade Heavy Cavalry	- Directly on their left and in the same line
Major Bull's[20] Horse Artillery	- On the left of the 2nd Brigade and extending
Captain Morrison's Horse Artillery[21]	- across St Etoil des Champs Elysee in as
Captain Macdonald's Horse Artillery[22]	- close order as possible.
Captain Whinyate's Rocket Troop[23]	
Third Brigade Light Cavalry	- On the left of the guns of the centre and
Seventh Brigade Light Cavalry	- extending to the Barrier Saint Etoile

18. Lieutenant Colonel Sir Robert Gardiner.
19. Now La Place de la Concorde
20. Brevet Lieutenant Colonel Robert Bull had been wounded at Waterloo.
21. This troop was based at Vilvorde during the Waterloo campaign.
22. Captain Alexander Macdonald had taken command of Norman Ramsay's troop after his death at Waterloo.
23. Captain Edward Whinyate's Troop was equipped with both rockets and conventional guns.

Lieutenant W Smith's Brigade Artillery[24]

The second line in rear of the first and in the avenue, to be composed of the fourth, fifth and sixth brigades of light cavalry.

The officer commanding the fifth brigade will communicate immediately with the officer in charge of the pontoon bridges at Chateau and Argentieul and endeavour to get one of them re-established in time for the brigade to pass the river in the morning; should there however be the least doubt on the subject of either of these bridges not being possible, the 5th Brigade must move today by the bridge of St Germain and bivouac in the commune of Marley. At all events commanding officers of brigades must take the greatest care that everything shall be across the bridge of Neuilly before seven o'clock a.m.

The Royal Horse Artillery will be accompanied by all their ammunition waggons and spare carriages.

On the morning of the 24th we marched from Nanterre at five in the morning for the purpose of passing the bridge of Neuilly before the given hour, that the infantry brigades might not be restarted on their arrival at that place and the lines were formed agreeable to orders.

At nine o'clock the glittering cavalcade appeared on the right. The Emperor of Austria led the van along the front of the lines; the Duke of Wellington on his right and the Emperor of Russia on his left; followed by the King of Prussia, Prince Blucher, the Prince of Orange and a splendid and numerous retinue of officers of all the nations of Europe.

After these illustrious personages had viewed the lines by passing down the first and up the second; they stationed themselves at the gates of the Tuileries where the army marched past with music and saluted. The troops were highly complimented by the Emperor of Austria for their soldier-like appearance and steady discipline and returned to their quarters.

Nothing particular occurred till the 30th when the brigade marched by the pontoon bridge of Chateau to Pontoise, at which place the populace had assembled in vast multitudes to see the entry of the British troops. They were unlike the inhabitants of Nanterre, for as we remained all night in the place, we were treated with the greatest civility and kindness.

---

24. Lieutenant Colonel James Webber Smith's Troop.

31st. Marched to Magny [en-Vexin], where the other two regiments halted and that to which I belonged continued its march to St Clair [sur-Epte], a pretty village some miles on the Rouen road.

1st August. Marched to Ecouis.

2nd. The brigade marched to the city of Rouen. It was met about a mile from the town by the Duke de Caster and other men of distinction together with the magistrates of the city, who after the compliments had passed between them and the officers put themselves at the head of the troops and entered the town in procession. An immense concourse of people were assembled and accompanied the troops to a large cavalry barrack which the French troops had evacuated, for their reception the preceding day.

The men were now in high spirits with their good fortune being to occupy for a time, this fine town, which is large, pleasant in its situation and alive with gay and fashionable inhabitants. It is the capital of the province of Normandy and stands on a gentle eminence on the banks of the River Seine bounded on the north and east by inconsiderable hills and on the south and west by flat and fertile plains. The heights on the east command a fine prospect of the plains below and the windings of the river which glides gently through an agreeable landscape. Here are two churches of ancient and magnificent architecture and a very large hospital, said to be one of the finest in Europe.

The inhabitants of this ancient city tell us that it derived its name from a shepherd called Rouen who fed his flock on the banks of the Seine and built his hut on the eminence where the town now stands; his offspring multiplied and their habitations increased in number, thus laying the foundation of a town which now stands in rank among the foremost in France.

Near the middle of the city is an arched gateway which displays in its ceiling a figure of the shepherd Rouen, his dog by him, his crook in his hand and his flock grazing around. At a late period this was said to be the entrance gate from the north to the city, however it has now overshot its ancient boundary so far that the archway is near the middle of the town.

The place was much enlivened by the presence of our brigade, the inhabitants got very familiar with both officers and men. The officers formed a race course in the valley, by the riverside and opened a scene of amusement which was quite a novelty in that country and called together immense multitudes of spectators to witness a species of pastime which to all probability the greater part had never before seen.

We remained in Rouen till the 11th of October when we received a route to march for the purpose of making way for a Prussian corps which afterwards occupied our place. The inhabitants, especially those resident near the barracks seemed to lament our departure, not only on account of the slight acquaintance which had been formed between them and us, but on account of the Prussians coming to take our place, whom they utterly detested.

We marched off at seven o'clock in the morning of the 11th, accompanied (as on our arrival) by a great number of the citizens, who evinced their attachment by following & cheering us a considerable distance on the road.

We continued our march to Bolbec, where one regiment and the attached troop of horse artillery halted and took their quarters; the other regiment proceeded to Montivilliers and ours to Harfleur. Harfleur is a small but ancient town, it is situated on the banks of the river about four miles inland from Havre de Grace. It had in former ages been well fortified, but its now mouldering walls, which in distant wars had braved its besiegers, are hastening to decay. We arrived at our new quarters at nine o'clock at night, having marched during the day a distance of 54 miles, both men and horses considerably fatigued were desirous of getting under some friendly roof. However billets could not be arranged in any reasonable time and after standing about an hour in the streets, an order was proclaimed authorising the men to make their quarters good wherever they could obtain an entrance. This order gave great satisfaction and was no sooner given than put in force, the men taking possession of such houses as they anticipated (from outward appearance) might afford them a good supper and a well-supplied accommodation for their horses.

I with a comrade sergeant and our two men demanded at the house of a miller, where we were received and our horses put up without delay and after we had partaken of refreshments which were prepared for us, we desired we might go to rest and were conducted into a small apartment which contained a bed, boxed up like those used in many of the country houses in Scotland. Into this we crept, which with the aid of fatigue afforded us a sound repose till day break, when we were again aroused by the thundering of the mill which had been set a going and appeared to contain the little apartment in which we lay.

We now began to think the noisy quarters we had got into would not be very agreeable in case we had long to remain in the town and determined to sally out in search of a more peaceable habitation.

Therefore after we had breakfasted with the miller and his family, who showed every mark of kindness to us and seemed to exalt in our having chosen their house for our quarters, we walked through the town & at last fixed our affections on a handsome little house which presented itself in the middle of a tastefully laid out flower garden, some distance from the street which led past it. We rang a bell at the garden gate, which was shortly opened by a beautiful young lady whose manner at once awed us into a conduct of respectful civility. She did not (as might have been expected) appear in the smallest degree surprised on unlocking the door, but with a smile threw it open and desired us to enter. She led the way into the house and ushered us into a splendid apartment, where we were immediately visited by a respectable looking old gentleman accompanied by two other ladies, who all gave us a hearty welcome and an invitation to the adjoining room where they were just about to sit at dinner. We yielded to their entreaties and after dinner was over and the ladies had retired, our host informed us that he was a clergyman and a magistrate, begging that we would not persist in remaining in his house, he having no accommodation for us nor any inmate save himself and his three daughters, at the same time assuring us that he would furnish us with a billet on a house where, by his instructions, every attention should be paid to our comfort.

We immediately yielded to his wishes and after draining a few bottles of wine, receiving our billet as well as pressing invitations to visit them again, our host put a letter of introduction into my hand, which he desired me to deliver to the master of the house on whom we had received the billet and we took our leave impressed with feelings of the purest regard towards a family of such affability and becoming deportment.

Our next ramble was to find out our new quarters; our billet was on a Monsieur Jordan Chapelier;[25] to whose house we went and presented with our billet the letter of recommendation, which riveted the attention of the hatter and his wife so closely to our welfare that we were sometimes driven to peevishness by their importunate kindness. Mons. Jordan having his two marishals to attend to, for a time, laid aside the manufacturing of cocked hats and applied himself wholly to our services. He attended every day when the rations were issued, with a horse and cart, and demanded our allowance of bread, meat,

---

25. Hatter.

licquor, candles and wood, which he carefully carried home and betook himself to cooking, however, he was no loser, for our allowances united together was more than we were able to use and consequently a surplus of nearly one half was allowed to be his perquisite for his trouble. Some of the troops were quartered among the farmers round the country and as it very frequently occurred that a turkey or a goose, a couple of ducks or a brace of some kind of their kindred feathered tribe, found their way into our quarters in the night, Madam Jordan was always pleased to take them in of course, not dreaming but they were very honestly come by and in the evenings a few friends generally convened to extol our landlady's cooking and praise the assistant commissary's generosity (who often favoured us with his company) out of another gallon or two of brandy for our evening's entertainment. And thus our time passed in Harfleur till the 24th day of November when the route was again received and we marched to Fecamp, a considerable town 21 miles up the coast towards Dieppe. Fecamp was famed for harbouring English smugglers, its situation is in a valley, bound by mountains on all sides except that which looks to the sea.

Orders received on the 29th:

General Cavalry Orders
Headquarters, Paris, 27 November 1815

The 1st, 2nd & 6th Dragoons being three of those regiments which are to proceed to England, they will march agreeable to the following route.

Saturday 2nd December	Saint Valery [en-Caux]
Sunday 3rd December	Dieppe
Monday 4th December	Eu
Tuesday 5th December	Abbeville

Lieutenant General Lord Combermere will inspect the brigade at Abbeville

Marched agreeable to the above route to St Valery, a small fishing town on the coast and the following day to Dieppe where the following orders were received.

Dieppe 3rd December 1815

Orders by Major General Vandeleur

As agreeable to the route received from the Quarter Master General the 16th Light Dragoons will evacuate the Ville de Eu on the 5th instant. Only the 2nd Dragoons will halt tomorrow (the 4th) at Dieppe.

The 1st [Royal] Dragoons will halt tomorrow at Gueures St Dorne, Ouville [le Riviere] & Le Bourg Dun detaching 150 horses to Dieppe.

Lieutenant Colonel Clarke will be pleased to report this order, and the circumstance giving rise to it to Colonel Muter[26] and Lt Colonel Dorville.[27]

This order is not to interfere with the march of the Inniskilling Dragoons who will proceed according to route already received.

The Greys and Royals will march to Ville de Eu on the 5th & to Abbeville on the 6th.

William Armstrong[28]
ADC

Marched to Ville d'Eu agreeable to order on the 5th and received an order in the evening ordering a halt on the 6th at this place; which is a considerable town in point of size, but very irregular and possesses no ornament to recommend it to notice.

Marched to Abbeville on the 7th. This is a large and well-fortified garrison, strongly walled, with drawbridges at the entrances and the ramparts well furnished with heavy brass cannon.

On the 8th the brigade was inspected by Lord Combermere and a number of horses given up by the regiments destined for England to those who were to remain in the Army of Occupation in France.

This day was remarkable for the severity of the frost and excessive cold wind. It was allowed by all to be the most piercing day of cold they had ever experienced and many of both officers & men were quite speechless from the severity of the weather.

The following orders were received after the inspection.

---

26. Lieutenant Colonel Joseph Muter commanded the 6th (Inniskilling) Dragoons. Siborne published his letters as Nos. 43 and 44 in *Waterloo Letters*. He later took the surname Straton.
27. Lieutenant Colonel Philip Dorville commanded the 1st (Royal) Regiment of Dragoons after Waterloo. His letter to Siborne was published in the editor's *Letters From Waterloo* as letter No. 28.
28. Captain William Armstrong, 19th Light Dragoons, had served at Waterloo as aide de camp to Sir John Vandeleur.

Assistant Quarter Master Generals office, 332 Rue Saint Gilles
Headquarters of Cavalry, Abbeville 8 December 1815

Route for the march of the Royals, Greys and Inniskillings from
here to Boulogne.

9th December 1815	Greys	Rue & vicinity
	Royals	Nampont & vicinity
	Inniskillings	ditto
10th December	The 3 Regiments	Montreuil [sur Mer] & vicinity
11th December	The 3 Regiments	Samer & vicinity
12th December	The 3 Regiments	Boulogne & vicinity

The route for the Greys to Rue is by the great road to Calais
through the village Nouvion, and the route for the other two
regiments to Nampont, by the Montreuil road. The Greys will
march the 2nd day direct from Rue and rejoin the Montreuil
road at a village called Wailly [-Beaucamp].

At Montreuil the Inniskillings will be quartered in the town,
the Royals in the villages on the Boulogne side & the Greys in
those on the Abbeville side.

Marched to Rue on the 9th agreeable to order, which is a pretty village
situated some miles to the left of the great road. This day we passed over
the plains on which the Battle of Cressy[29] was fought. The village was
scarcely large enough to contain one troop, consequently the whole of
the regiment (except the commanding officer and staff) were scattered
among the farm houses &c round the country.

Marched to Montrieul [-sur-Mer] on the 10th, which is not only a
large town, but a handsome compact, clean and well-fortified garrison.
Its situation is naturally strong, being on the summit of a hill, from
whence a fine plain is overlooked which nearly surrounds it. Its walls
are strong and well supplied with heavy ordnance.

---

29. The Battle of Crécy was fought at Crécy-en-Ponthieu in 1346, which is not
on the road to Rue.

The frost this night was very intense, insomuch that the road the following morning was covered with a sheet of ice and compelled us to walk and lead our horses the greater part of the way to Samer. Samer is a small town situated on an eminence without anything else to recommend it to notice.

Marched on the 12th to St Leonard, a small village one mile from Boulogne. Remained on the 13th at St Leonard and marched on the 14th to Guines, a town of no great size, but pleasant in its situation about a league and a half from Calais. This day we passed Napoleon's Tower,[30] or Observatory, from which (it was said) some years before, he intended to see his flotilla cross the channel and land his troops in England.

Our march was very precarious owing to the severe frost, the roads and I may say the whole face of the country was covered with a sheet of ice. We were obliged to lead our horses nearly all the road and although many fell from being smoothly shoed, no particular accident occurred.

The troops reached Guines about 2 o'clock p.m. but the baggage was on the road till 12 at night.

The following orders were received here.

General Orders
Headquarters Paris 29th November 1815

No.1 The 1st Battalion 1st Guards are to be completed to twelve hundred rank & file by drafts from the 2nd Battalion.
No. 2 The 3rd Battalion of the Royals are to be completed to one thousand rank & file, by drafts from the 4th Battalion.
No. 3 The 1st Battalion 27th Regiment are to be completed to one thousand rank and file by drafts from the 3rd Battalion.
No. 4 The 1st Battalion 81st Regiment are to be completed to one thousand rank and file, by drafts from the 2nd Battalion.
Signed E. Barnes Adjutant General

General Order
Headquarters Paris 30th November 1815

---

30. Actually the Column of the Grand Army, which was erected to commemorate the successful invasion of England, which of course never took place. The first stone was laid in 1804 but work stopped in 1811 because of a lack of funds when the column stood about 20m high. It was completed in 1821 with a Fleur de Lys on the top, which was changed to a statue of Napoleon in 1841.

No. 1 The British troops which are to remain in France are to be formed as follows.

The 1st Dragoon Guards	
The 2nd Dragoon Guards	1st Brigade of Cavalry
The 3rd Dragoon Guards	
The 7th Hussars	
The 18th Hussars	2nd Brigade of Cavalry
The 12th Light Dragoons	
The 11th Light Dragoons	
The 13th Light Dragoons	3rd Brigade of Cavalry
The 15th Hussars	
The 3rd Battalion 1st Guards	
The 2nd Coldstreams	1st Brigade of Infantry
The 3rd Battalion Royals	
The 1st Battalion 57th	2nd Brigade of Infantry
The 2nd Battalion 95th	
The 1st Battalion 3rd	
The 1st Battalion 39th	3rd Brigade of Infantry
The 1st Battalion 91st	
The 1st Battalion 4th	
The 1st Battalion 52nd	4th Brigade of Infantry
The 1st Battalion 79th	
The 1st Battalion 5th	
The 1st Battalion 9th	5th Brigade of Infantry
The 1st Battalion 21st	
The 1st Battalion 6th	
The 29th Regiment	6th Brigade of Infantry
The 1st Battalion 71st	
The 1st Battalion 7th	
The 23rd Regiment	7th Brigade of Infantry
The 1st Battalion 41st	

The 1st Battalion 27th
The 1st Battalion 40th   8th Brigade of Infantry
The 1st Battalion 95th

The 1st Battalion 81st
The 1st Battalion 88th   9th Brigade of Infantry

Major General Lord Edward Somerset commands the 1st Brigade of Cavalry

Major General Sir H. Vivian commands the 2nd Brigade of Cavalry

Major General Sir C. Grant commands the 3rd Brigade of Cavalry

Major General Sir Peregrine Maitland commands the 1st Brigade of Infantry

Major General Sir Manly Power commands the 2nd Brigade of Infantry

Major General the honourable Sir Bart Robert O'Callaghan commands the 3rd Brigade of Infantry

Major General Sir Denis Pack commands the 4th Brigade of Infantry

Major General Sir S. Brisbane commands the 5th Brigade of Infantry

Major General Sir T. Bradford commands the 6th Brigade of Infantry

Major General Sir C. Kempt commands the 7th Brigade of Infantry

Major General Sir J. Lambert commands the 8th Brigade of Infantry

Major General Sir J. Keane commands the 9th Brigade of Infantry

The 1st Division of infantry is to be
Composed of the 1st, 7th & 8th Brigades
Lieutenant General the Honourable Sir L. Cole

The 2nd Division
the 3rd, 4th and 6th Brigades
Lieutenant General Sir H. Clinton

The 3rd Division
the 2nd, 5th and 9th Brigades
Lieutenant General the Honourable Sir C. Colville

267

Lieutenant General Lord Combermere will command the cavalry.
Lieutenant General Lord Hill will command the infantry.

The British troops going to England are to be brigaded as follows.

1st Life Guards	
2nd Life Guards	
Royal Horse Guards, Blue	Commanded by Colonel
3rd Dragoon Guards	Athorp
Royals	
Greys	Commanded by Colonel
Inniskillings	Muter
10th Hussars	
16th Light Dragoons	Commanded by Colonel
23rd Light Dragoons	Quinten
2nd Battalion 1st Guards	
2nd Battalion 3rd Guards	Commanded by Colonel
	Askew
36th Regiment	
38th Regiment	
73rd Regiment	Commanded by Colonel the
3rd Battalion 95th Regiment	Honourable Sir C. Greville
2nd Battalion 12th Regiment	
2nd Battalion 30th Regiment	Commanded by Colonel
	Stirke
33rd Regiment	
1st Battalion 41st Regiment	
1st Battalion 90th Regiment	Commanded by Lieutenant
	Colonel Evans
Detachment Royal Waggon Train	
3rd Battalion 14th Regiment	
2nd Battalion 35th Regiment	Commanded by Colonel
51st Regiment	Mitchell

54th Regiment	
2nd Battalion 59th Regiment	Commanded by Lieutenant
2nd Battalion 69th Regiment	Colonel Austin
4th Battalion Royals	
28th Regiment	
42nd Regiment	Commanded by Colonel Sir
92nd Regiment	C. Bilson
3rd Battalion 27th Foot	
32nd Regiment	Commanded by Colonel Sir
	J. Mclean
Detachment Staff Corps	
16th Regiment	
2nd Battalion 44th Regiment	Commanded by Colonel
1st Battalion 82nd Regiment	Tolley
58th Regiment	
2nd Battalion 68th Regiment	
64th Regiment	Commanded by Colonel
2nd Battalion 81st Regiment	Walker

The troops of the German Legion and the Hanoverian troops will march under the command of the officers commanding the several brigades of cavalry and infantry.

Upon breaking up of the army which the field marshal has had the honour to command, he begs leave again to return thanks to the general officers and the officers and troops of their uniform good conduct.

In the late memorable campaign they have given proofs to the world that they possess in an eminent degree all the good qualities of soldiers; and the field marshal is happy to be able to applaud their regular good conduct in their camps and cantonments not less than when engaged with the enemy in the field.

Whatever may be the future destination of those brave troops, of which the field marshal now takes his leave, he trusts that every individual will believe that he will ever feel the deepest interest in their honour and welfare and will always be happy to promote either.

Chapter 23

George IV's Visit to Scotland

Nothing worthy of notice, until 11 January 1816. This day an order was received for 20 men & horses to march for Calais for immediate embarkation. The above number of men and horses embarked accordingly and the transport sailed the same evening, but had not been long at sea when a violent storm arose and the sea ran so high that the greater part of the baggage, arms and appointments were swept overboard. However, with great difficulty, they got into port at Ramsgate at 4 o'clock on the morning of the 12th with eight of the horses dead in the hold and nearly all the others severely bruised and lamed by the vessel being tossed on the agitated sea during the night.

The whole of the regiment embarked on the 13th and 14th when the wind had moderated & landed safely either at Ramsgate or Dover (part of it having landed at each of these ports) and proceeded to Canterbury where the whole arrived on the 15th.[1]

Here we occupied the cavalry barracks and remained without any particular occurrence till about the middle of April when the commanding officer (Lieutenant Colonel Clarke) received a silver medal for every man who had served in the Battle of Waterloo. He ordered a parade & addressed the regiment as follows.

I have the pleasure this day to deliver these medals to the regiment, which is the most gratifying duty that has fallen to my lot, since I have had the honour of commanding one of the first (I was almost tempted to say the finest) regiment of cavalry in

1. On arrival at Canterbury, the regiment was immediately reduced to eight troops.

the British service, whose well known valour needs no comment from an humble individual like myself. Its fame is registered in the hearts of all men and its name will live revered and respected as long as history remains. May happiness be yours and may you all long live to enjoy these most honourable marks of your country's applause. May they stimulate those who wear them to further tell of bravery wherever their services may be required and may the bright example emulate the young recruit.

At this moment I feel but one regret, that it is not in my power to present every man in the regiment with a medal, but let those who are excluded from the honour, not feel the slightest uneasiness. I now allude to those who were serving at the depot. We all know that their hearts panted to share the glories of the day; but the various duties on which they were employed at home, were of the highest magnitude and it must also be recollected that many of them were actually engaged in providing comforts for their comrades on service.

It remains only for me to urge one request; that every man will most religiously treasure the medal given him by the Prince Regent, in the name and on the behalf of His Majesty as a testimony of his most gracious approbation of their well-earned fame. Let them guard the precious gift to the latest moment of their lives and when summoned from this to a better world, let them bequeath it to their children, who will proudly exclaim 'This was my father's who gained immortal honour at the victory of Waterloo; this was my father's who helped to hurl the tyrant Bonaparte from the throne of France to the rock of Saint Helena.

The regiment continued in Canterbury till the 20th July 1817, on which day two troops marched for Carlisle. On the 21st two [troops] for Newcastle upon Tyne and on the 22nd headquarters for Edinburgh.

Remained in the above stations until 4th June 1818, when orders were received to commence a march for Ireland. The two squadrons accordingly marched from Newcastle & Carlisle on their way to Portpatrick, concentrating at Dumfries, where they halted about a month and consequently were in this very loyal and spirited town on the anniversary of the Battle of Waterloo, which gave the inhabitants an opportunity of developing their warm wishes towards the regiment, which they did in the following manner.

As the 18th of June approached nearer, the inhabitants of Dumfries and its neighbourhood, made arrangements for showing some mark of respect for their national corps and came to a determination of inviting them to a dinner, which on the day alluded to, was sumptuously laid out in the town hall; the spacious room beautifully and tastefully decorated with oak and laurel boughs, garlands of flowers and wreaths of the mountain heath were also profusely intermixed.

The whole of the 4 troops sat down together and were attended by the clergy and most respectable inhabitants. The table was furnished in a most splendid style and after dinner the following address was delivered by the Reverend W. Wightman, minister of the parish of Kirkmahoe.[2]

Old Scotias sons whose swords like burnished mail
Flash'd terror on our foes, we bid your hail!
Warriors of Waterloo! Who nobly stood
Like walls of adamant in seas of blood.
Who checked the Tyrant's pride and crushed his power,
By a brave charge in one decisive hour,
We hear Napoleon praise the gallant Greys
We see his palled look, which fear betrays.
We hear your shout which rent the sulphury air
And struck his firmest troops with mute despair,
'Scotland for Ever!'[3] with electric roll,
Rings on our rear and ruffles up our soul;
As when through Soignes dark forest Zephyrs sweep,
Or curl the expanse of Caledonia's deep,
Our hearts are mov'd, our spirits wildly play,
In memory of that grand auspicious day,
When rose and thistle aye and shamrock join'd
To form the wreath which victory then entwin'd
When fames loud trumpet, hard through sea and land,
Proclaimed the honours of your noble band,
From your oun mountains, we fresh garlands bind.
Of blooming heath, fann'd by the northern wind,
The humble chaplets you will deign to wear.
And to your graves our warm affections bear,
Safe may you reach old Erin's fertile plains,
To guard her lovely nymphs and guileless swains,

---

2. The Parish of Kirkmahoe lies a few miles north of Dumfries, centred around Dalswinton.
3. A war-cry given by the regiment on advancing to a charge.

And happy may you be till lifes last flow,
May virtue in your dying bosom's glow.
When your cold dust is gather'd with the dead.
Soft be the turf that wraps the soldiers head,
When rests your spirits with the good and brave,
Sweet be the flowers that blooms upon your graves.

We remained in Dumfries till the 9th July, on which day we marched for Portpatrick on our way for Ireland. Routes were in readiness on arrival at Donaghadee, to conduct the regiment to Dundalk, Belturbet and Enniskillen, where it remained until the 15th June 1819 and marched on that day for Dublin.[4] Here we occupied Portobello Barracks[5] until the 21st July 1820, when an order was received to remove the regiment to the south. Headquarters accordingly marched to Cork, detaching two troops to Limerick, one to Fermoy and one to Bandon.

The troop to which I belonged was one of those appointed to occupy Limerick and on the day on which we were to arrive at our destination the squadron was met on the road by a sergeant and a private of the 79th Highlanders with an invitation for our officers of that regiment and a similar invitation from their sergeants to ours. These marks of friendship were (of course) accepted and at the appointed hour in the evening we repaired to a large room in the barracks into which a dinner was served, which would not have disgraced an equal number of nobler guests, the dishes were various, rich and numerous, but the sheep head's broth and highly seasoned haggis stood in popular favour above them a'. No sooner having made their appearance, than they called to memory that they had been favoured by our forefathers. The pipers immediately began their march round the table and blew their native pibroch till the trenchers [platters] seemed to dinnel [vibrate] in unison with the warlike mountain music. The pipes continued their wild cry till dinner was over, when the mountain dew began its march with mighty and enrapturing strides around the festive board, impregnating all hearts with hilarity, social friendship and national warmth, till the sun's streamers began to surmount the eastern horizon and will us again to our duty, but as the immortal Burns says of the moon waiting to will him and his two cronies hame; 'By my soul they waited a wee.' For the whole merry gang repaired to the barrack square and began to the more

---

4. He does not mention his wife and daughters at all.
5. Now known as Cathal Brugha Barracks.

273

agile exercise of running races, carrying each other on man-back &c, till the officers (who had spent a similar night) turned out and joined us! However, the overpowering influence of fatigue and drowsiness drove them individually to their beds, leaving myself and a sergeant J[ohn] C[ummings][6] of the highlanders, in possession of the field, from which we also retired and took post in a tavern near the barrack gate, where we drank better acquaintance to each other, till the sun had long sunk behind the hills in the west.

The two corps occupied the same barrack and between them, the first night begat a friendship which continued unbroken till we again received the route and left the highlanders where we found them.

We marched from Limerick on the 23rd of April 1821 and concentrated with the troops from Bandon and Fermoy at Clonmel, continued our march on the 2nd May for Waterford, where we were joined by the headquarters division from Cork and on the 3rd the whole regiment embarked and sailed for England.

A heavy gale of wind overtook us about the middle of the first night which dispersed our little fleet so that we saw no more of them till we entered the river below Bristol. We however, got into Bristol harbour without any accident on the 7th and disembarked the same day, where we remained in quarters till the 9th when we marched for Birmingham and on our arrival occupied the cavalry barracks at that place, detaching two troops to Coventry.

Nothing particular occurred until the first of July when the regiment received orders to proceed to London for the purpose of attending the coronation of King George the IV. The corps arrived at St Albans on the 6th and received orders to halt in that place, Hertford and Hatfield till further orders, but to be in readiness to move into the metropolis at any hour.

Remained in these quarters till the 16th and marched, agreeable to order received, into London and were quartered at Pentonville & Islington.

Regimental Orders
Pentonville, 18th July 1821

One field officer, one captain, one lieutenant, one cornet and fifty men mounted will parade in Review Order at ¼ past 12

---

6. Sergeant John Cummings had served at Waterloo in Captain Mylne's No. 3 Company.

o'clock this night & will be stationed at the Regent Park Barracks, sending out patrols agreeable to former orders.

One captain, two subalterns and fifty men mounted will parade in Review Order at ¼ past 12 o'clock this night and be stationed at Kings St Barracks, sending out patrols agreeable to former orders.

The above detachments are to arrive at their posts precisely at one o'clock a.m. 19th inst. and the remainder of the regiment to be saddled in readiness to turn out at a moment's notice. No officer or dragoon to quit his post on any pretence whatever.

Incessant patrols of the Life Guards, Blues, Greys, 4th Light Dragoons, 9th Lancers with several corps of yeomanry cavalry were kept in the streets and detachments stationed at many points to ensure an uninterrupted route of procession to Westminster Abbey and to preserve order and regularity and the ceremony was completed, the day passed away in the most tranquil manner and the troops retired to their quarters late in the night. Next day we received the following orders.

General Orders
Horse Guards 20th July 1821

The Commander in Chief has received the king's gracious command to express to the troops employed yesterday, in aid of the arrangements for the coronation, His Majesty's thanks for the orderly, soldier-like and exemplary conduct which they have evinced upon this occasion.

The commander in chief has received the King's further command, through the Secretary of State, to convey to the Light Horse Volunteers, the Honourable Artillery Company, the 1st and 2nd Bucks and Surrey and Berkshire Yeomanry Cavalry, His Majesty's thanks for their services upon the same occasion and his full sense and approbation of the loyalty and zeal which they have manifested in the offer of them.

By command of His Royal Highness, the Commander in Chief
Signed H. Torrance Adjutant General

Horse Guards 21st July 1821

Sir,
I have the honour to acquaint you that His Royal Highness the
Commander in Chief will review the
2nd (or R.N.B.) Dragoons
4th Light Dragoons
9th Lancers
At Wormwood Scrubs[7] at ten o'clock on the morning of Tuesday
next the 24th inst.
Signed H. Torrance Adjutant General

The review took place agreeable to the above order. The brigade under
the command of Lord Edward Somerset.

Previous to the hour appointed, a great concourse of people
assembled in the field; with a considerable number of carriages and
distinguished personages. Queen Caroline and suite was amongst the
first who appeared on the ground.

The Duke of York arrived at the appointed hour, attended by a
numerous retinue of distinguished officers and nobility, before whom
the brigade performed a number of movements and after the review,
the following order was issued.

Regimental Orders
Pentonville, 24th July 1821

By Lieutenant Colonel Clarke
The commanding officer is directed by Major General Lord
Edward Somerset to express His Royal Highness the Commander
in Chief's most gracious approbation of the appearance and
movements of the regiment this day; which the Major General
desires might be made known in Regimental Orders.

The headquarters division will parade in order of march
tomorrow morning at five o'clock.

Marched on the 25th and arrived again at Birmingham and Coventry
on the 31st.

Nothing particular occurred till 6th August when an order was
received for a reduction of two troops from the establishment of each
cavalry corps.[8]

---

7. Wormwood Scrubs is still a large area of open fields. From 1812 the War
   Office had rented 190 acres of this land for the exercise of cavalry horses.
8. The regiment was reduced to six troops.

The above reducement [*sic*] took place at the 24th of the same month and Lieutenant Colonel Clarke (an officer looked up to as a father to every man of the regiment) soon after retired[9] from the service. He issued the following farewell address in Regimental Orders previous to his departure.

> Lieutenant Colonel Clarke cannot retire without availing himself of this last opportunity of bidding his friends a kind farewell and of expressing his deep regret and unfeigned sorrow at resigning the command of the distinguished Greys; a regiment in which he has passed the best and happiest years of his life and in which he would joyfully have terminated his existence, had not the duties incumbent on him as a husband and a father compelled him to relinquish (for the sake of his family) what is, has been and ever will be most truly dear to him.
>
> Although removed from the regiment, Lieutenant Colonel Clarke's attachment to it can never cease but with his life and the honour, welfare and happiness of every individual in it, will be ever uppermost in his heart.
>
> Men are so prone to error, it would be presumption in Lieutenant Colonel Clarke to expect, or even to flatter himself, that he alone should have been so fortunate an individual, during his long period of service, as to have steered wholly clear of it. He however hopes that when at any time he has mistaken his duty, or so far forgotten himself as to cause any individual a moment's pain, that it may not in every instance be attributed to personal animosity (which he disclaims) but to an ardent zeal for the credit of a regiment he most dearly loves. He therefore, hopes that his faults will be buried in oblivion and his few merits remembered by those who have still the honour of belonging to a corps excelled by none and equalled by few.
>
> Lieutenant Colonel Clarke once more takes a painful but sincere farewell of the regiment & he prays God to take it under his special protection and providence and to power down his blessings upon it abundantly, for ever and ever. God bless you all.

No particular occurrence from this period till after His Majesty's return from his visit to Ireland,[10] when a rumour arose that he intended to

---

9. He retired in October 1821.
10. George IV made an eighteen-day visit to Ireland in August 1821. It was a triumph.

honour Scotland also with a similar visit. However, although the report continued to be the discourse of the day for some months, it appeared to be a matter of uncertainty and many doubts were afloat until they were removed by a letter which the Lord Provost of Edinburgh had received from Lord Viscount Melville, Lord Privy Seal for Scotland, intimating that His Majesty had positively resolved to visit that city during the summer and might be expected to reach Edinburgh about the 10th of August [1822].

Our regiment immediately received orders to march from their station, at Birmingham and Coventry; for Scotland. We marched accordingly by the way of Manchester. Here the regiment was inspected in conjunction with the 7th Dragoon Guards by Lord Edward Somerset and continued its march to Glasgow and Hamilton.

A similar letter to that received by the Lord Provost, was received by the Deputy Keeper of the Palace of Holyrood,[11] in order that the

---

11. **William's Note** – The more ancient parts of this venerable edifice, consisting of the north west towers, were built by James V about the year 1528, as a royal residence; though for ages before, the Scottish King's seem to have occasionally resided there.

During the minority of Queen Mary, the Palace of Holyrood House was burnt along with the city, by the English forces under the Earl of Hertford, Soon after this period, however, it was repaired and enlarged far beyond its present size, said to have extended more towards the south and to have consisted of no less than five courts.

Great part of the Palace of Holyrood House was burnt by the soldiers of Cromwell. At the restoration, however, it was again repaired and altered into its present form by King Charles 2nd.

Of this palace, which is now almost the only entire regal residence which remains in Scotland, the Duke of Hamilton is heritable keeper and although he and many others of the Scottish nobility have lodgings within it, yet a great part of the building remains uninhabited and was hastening to decay till in 1793 apartments were fitted up for the residence of the Comte d'Artois, brother to the King of France with the Dukes d'Angouleme and Berri and others of the French exiled nobility. Adjoining are the remains of the Abbey of Holyrood House, in its time the most richly endowed in Scotland. It was founded by David 1st, who for his liberality to the church was canonized as a saint.

After the Reformation the building was converted into a parish church and on the accession of James VII it was converted into a Royal Chapel. A throne & stalls for the Knights of the Thistle, were also erected.

necessary preparations might be made for His Majesty's reception. It was also announced that His Majesty was to reside at Dalkeith House, the seat of the Duke of Buccleugh, but to hold his court at his own Palace of Holyrood House; therefore the attention of the public authorities directed to its repair and improvement.

It being understood that His Majesty would proceed to the castle in state, there to receive the Royal Diadem of Scotland; the magistrates determined upon the removal of every obstruction or deformity along the route of the procession. The weigh house[12] at the head of the west bow, which had stood upwards of five hundred years was accordingly removed and an uninterrupted view opened from the Castle Hill of that noble street, which has, even in the 16th Century, extorted the admiration of travellers and which Smollett[13] pronounced to be one of the noblest in Europe. The castle also underwent a thorough inspection and repair. The exact distance from which to Holyrood House is one mile and twenty-five yards.

Various improvements were also made in the high church of St Giles'[14] and a seat erected in this venerable fabric of the most becoming magnificence for the sovereign.

It being the intention of the magistrates to invite His Majesty to a banquet, the Parliament House[15] was fitted out for that purpose. The Great Hall in which the Scottish parliament used to assemble was agreed upon and a more proper place than this noble hall could not have been selected. The height of which in its walls is 60 feet, its length 142 feet and its breadth 49. Its grand Norman roof which is of carved oak is much admired.

At the Revolution it suffered grievous dilapidations at the hands of the populace. In 1758 an architect having agreed for a large sum of money to repair its roof, covered it with flag stones, the weight of which was so disproportioned to the strength of its walls, that in 1768 the roof fell in and the rubbish was afterwards sold and a house in Baxter's Close was built with the figured stones!!

12. Weigh houses were set up in cities during the Middle Ages to ensure the correct dues were paid in taxes on the weight of goods transported etc.

13. The poet Tobias Smollett.

14. St Giles Cathedral which stands on the Royal Mile.

15. Parliament Hall had been built in 1639. It was used as a court building after the Act of Union.

In order to support the dignity of the city, a carriage and six was prepared for the Lord Provost, having the arms of the city on the panels and livery of the city colour. Dresses such as worn by the beefeaters (properly the Yeomen of the Guard) were also prepared for 30 men, who were appointed to the service of the Lord High Constable and the Knight Marshal.

Our regiment being ordered to furnish all escorts and guards of honour over his majesty during his stay, were ordered to Edinburgh where it arrived on the 22nd and took post at Dalkeith, being the place appointed for the royal residence, detaching one squadron to Piershill Barracks.

A proclamation was issued by the magistrates intimating to the inhabitants that on the evening after his majesty's arrival there would be a bonfire on the summit of Arthur's seat, an immense hill which overlooks the Palace of Holyrood. It rises 656 feet from its base and above 800 from the level of the sea. Also a display of fireworks at the west end of George Street and recommending a general illumination.

The materials for the above named bonfire were transported by horses to the top of the mountain, to which, in all probability no horse had ever before ascended. These animals presented an amusing spectacle to persons at a distance, dragging their slow lengths towards the summit.

Sir Walter Scott was delegated by the ladies resident in Edinburgh as the bard of chivalry and romance, to greet the approach of their sovereign to the Scottish shore and to do homage in their names, by laying a Saint Andrew's cross, the ancient emblem of Scotland at the feet of His Majesty. It consisted of a rich cross of pearls raised on blue velvet and enclosed within a belt of gold on which was embroidered with pearls. The Gaelic motto of 'Riogh ah bhain gu brath' (Hail to the King of Scotland). The belt is attached by a brilliant diamond buckle and from its extremity is suspended a magnificent pearl, the produce of Scotland and probably the finest ever found in this country. The whole is surmounted by the Imperial crown, girt round with brilliants and richly decorated with rubies, emeralds and the topaz, alternating with pearls in the manner of the ancient Scottish crown, which was so long forgotten, but auspiciously brought to light a little before this period.

No improvement which could add to the appearance of the noble city of Edinburgh was omitted; scaffolds were erected for the convenience of the spectators, in all the open parts along the route where the procession was to pass on the day of their monarch's landing and great improvements were also made on the theatre for his reception, in case he should visit it.

It was agreed upon that the guard of the king's person in the palace, should be entrusted to the ancient and honourable company of archers, who were to discharge that duty the same as the gentlemen pensioners of England.

This society had diminished very much till within these few years, when it was revived by the attention of the late Mr St Clair of Roslin.[16] It consisted of about 300 members among whom are the most distinguished of the Scottish nobility, their uniform is elegant, viz, a Robin Hood tartan jacket, tartan trews, Highland hose, flat blue bonnet, the ruff, Robin Hood belt, a white satin bow case worn as a scarf. They are commanded by the Earl of Hopetoun. The society is very ancient, it appears that a prize silver arrow given by the town of Musselborough has been shot for by it as early as the year 1603.

They prepared two barbed arrows of exquisite workmanship on this occasion, which were to be presented to His Majesty on his arrival. The shafts were of snakewood and the barbs of silver, with the following inscription on each.

> To His Majesty King George IV
> Reddendo of Royal Company of Archers,
> Holyrood House, August 1822.

The Celtic Society also formed four companies in complete Highland costume and were appointed the guard of the Lord High Constable and Knight Marshal also over the regalia of Scotland.

This society was instituted in 1820 to promote the general use of the ancient highland dress, it was established at Edinburgh and even at the period consisted of many of the nobles and gentlemen of Scotland.

So active was the feeling of loyalty which now pervaded all ranks and so ardent the desire to see the king, that legions from all quarters of the kingdom to the metropolis. The universal stir which prevailed was well described by the following quotation from a Glasgow paper.

> Glasgow, as far as we can learn, will be almost deserted on this occasion, every vehicle of conveyance is fully employed and

---

16. Mr William Sinclair was also the first Grand Master of the Scottish lodge of Free Masons.

engaged for coming days. Extra boats on the canal are insufficient for the number of passengers. Where the moving mass from all corners of the land are to stow themselves in Edinburgh, we know not, but understand that many are provided with, or providing themselves with tents, by which it appears they mean to encamp and bivouac in the fields. A great number of gentlemen from Ireland, are passing through Glasgow, for Edinburgh, to attend there during the joyous occasion.

While preparations were thus going on and the city thronging to excess with all descriptions of people gazing upon each other, an amusing spectacle presented itself at the west end of the town, in the approach of a body of highlanders, the tennantry of the Earl of Breadalbane, which this worthy and spirited nobleman had equipped in the complete highland costume; they marched in to the old favourite tune 'The Campbells are Coming' and proceeded with their mountain music to the Palace of Holyrood House where they were received by the Countess of Breadalbane.

Twelve pieces of cannon were placed on the summit of the Calton Hill and tents pitched for the artillerymen and six guns were also mounted on the top of that part of Salisbury Crags which immediately overlooks the palace where additional tents were lined along the crest of the abrupt precipice and formed a beautifully romantic encampment.

A great number of tents were also pitched on the Castle Hill which produced a very grand effect and in fact the city altogether would have presented (to one who was unacquainted with the real cause) rather the appearance of a place occupied by a victorious army, than one about to welcome its sovereign.

Dalkeith House was fitted up in the most magnificent and costly manner and every improvement made upon the own; even the cottages on the road leading from Edinburgh to that place, which was selected for the Royal residence, were neatly whitewashed. The road repaired and hedges and trees pruned into a state of uniformity, that no object might prove offensive to the eye of the beloved monarch of the land.

A beautiful triumphal arch composed of various flowers, was thrown over the principle entrance from the north, to the town of Dalkeith, surmounted by a tastefully interwoven Imperial crown with an inscription in large characters 'A thousand welcomes to the King of Scotland.'

The inns, as the joyous day drew nearer, crowded to excess as many of the company who had tried in vain to thrust their heads into some place of cover in Edinburgh had repaired to Dalkeith in hopes of being more successful & at last, lodgings, even there, could not be procured but at an exorbitant price. The Butcher's Market was fitted up with racks and mangers and served as stabling for two troops of our horses.

The period was fast approaching when His Majesty's arrival was expected and the immense throng became hourly more animated. The streets of Edinburgh thronged to a degree almost inconceivable and the beauty of the scene greatly heightened by the fine appearance of the Highlanders (who were now arrived in great numbers) all plaided and plumed in their tartan array, each distinguished by some badge belonging to their different clans. The Highland chieftains in particular were conspicuous objects amongst the moving multitude and the public exulted in perceiving these gallant gentlemen parading freely in the full and imposing costume of their forefathers.

The minds of the public which now began to load with anxiety were somewhat relieved by the removal of the regalia from the Castle to the Palace of Holyrood, this took place on the 12th of August. The regalia consisted of the crown sceptre and sword of state, which is (by one of the articles of the Treaty of Union) to be forever kept as they were then in Scotland.

Accordingly, soon after nine in the morning the Duke of Hamilton, the Knight Marshal, the Lord Provost and Sir Walter Scott, with the Celtic Society and Clan MacGregor, also the Edinburgh troop of Mid-Lothian Yeomanry Cavalry.

Sir Walter Scott
Lord Rolla
The Honourable General Leslie Cumming &
McLeod of McLeod in full highland garb

The whole proceeded to the castle gates; the herald sounding a trumpet. The gates being shut, the Officer of the Guard within challenged 'Who's there' and was answered by the Herald 'The King's Knight Marshal comes to receive the regalia which are deposited within your castle and he demands admission in the name of the king.' The officer (from within) answered, 'Throw open the gates and make way for the King's Knight Marshal.'

The gates were then thrown open, the Knight Marshal and other official personages entered the castle, where they remained a short time and returned surrounded with beautiful banners of white and blue silk, exhibiting the St Andrew's Cross, with the crown and other regalia on a crimson velvet cushion which was supported to the carriage of the Knight Marshal and the procession moved along followed by a band of Highland pipers playing select ancient Scottish airs.

The arrangement of the procession follows:

Mid Lothian Yeomanry Cavalry Flanking	Guard of Celts		Mid Lothian Yeomanry Cavalry Flanking	Guard of Celts
		Advanced Guard of Yeomanry Cavalry		
		Trumpeter		
		Guard of Celts, General Graham Stirling		
		Coach and four, Duke of Hamilton Hereditary		
		Keeper of the Palace of Holyrood House.		
		Chariot and four, two Marshal's Esquires.		
		Coach and four, two Marshal's Esquires.		
		Coach, Sir Walter Scott.		
		Coach and six, Sir Alexander Keith		
		Knight Marshal & Captain Ferguson.		
		Deputy Keeper		
		With the Regalia of Scotland.		
		Guard of Celts, Colonel David Mellart		
		Clan McGregor, Sir Evan McGregor Bart.		
		Squadron of Yeomanry Cavalry.		

The regalia being thus deposited in the Palace under the charge of the Knight Marshal, a Guard of Celts, consisting of twelve, were mounted over it, until it was again conveyed to the castle.

As this procession moved along the street an immense crowd of spectators forced themselves upon one of the scaffolds which was in an unfinished state and although warned of the danger, so strong was the desire to see the moving spectacle that persuasion had no effect till the platform gave way and came down with a dreadful crash. The consequence was as might have been expected, a great number of the unfortunate people who had thus, imprudently mounted it, severely hurt and bruised and many were carried to the infirmary with broken limbs.

Preparations for the reception of His Majesty in the Scottish metropolis being now in a forward state, it may be gratifying to take a view of the monarch's embarkation and departure from his English subjects.

Greenwich (being the place chosen by His Majesty for his embarkation) was not in the memory of any of the present generation, known to be so much crowded, not even at the melancholy and memorable spectacle of Lord Nelson lying in state, was there witnessed such an influx of strangers. The demands for accommodation in the taverns were beyond the possibility of gratification and this congregated multitude also kept in suspense from the 8th to the 10th, which day was at last finally settled upon for the day of embarkation. Accordingly, the Royal squadron assembled with the Lord Mayor and city barges, in state to accompany the royal traveller down the river.

As the hour of three p.m. approached the public expectation was at the highest possible pitch, the vessels were crowded to excess, the shrouds and yards manned, so that the river at this time presented a spectacle of the most impressive nature. A few minutes past three a general 'Huzza' announced the approach of His Majesty. He arrived at the Royal Hospital in a plain carriage & four bay horses, escorted by a party of the 15th Hussars. He embarked amid the acclamations of tens of thousands, about half past three o'clock and at 20 minutes before four, the *Royal George* was in rapid motion off the East India docks. A fine breeze sprung up and filled the sails of the *Royal George*[17] while she stood before it down the river amid the air rending shouts of an immense multitude who were congregated on either shore.

About half past 7 the Royal squadron reached Gravesend on its way to the Nore, where the Lord Mayor took his leave of the *Royal George*, His Majesty intimating his sense of his lordships loyal and respectful attention, by repeatedly bowing and kissing his hand till the city barges commenced their return to the metropolis.

The Royal squadron proceeded on its voyage visited by immense collections of boats from every town they passed on the shore, filled with loyal subjects anxious to manifest their respect and gain a glimpse of their sovereign, during which visits His Majesty frequently appeared upon deck and acknowledged their greetings by taking his hat off and bowing on all sides.

It appeared that even the muses were roused from a state of inactivity on this great occasion, for several pieces connected with it appeared about this time. The following came to view in the shape of a congratulatory address to His Most Gracious Majesty.

---

17. The Royal Yacht *Royal George* was built in 1817 and used until 1842.

Dread sovereign! I've been spa bund lang [at a watering place],
Or I'd hae todl'd doon to meet ye,
For which I send a humble song,
For my ain country men to greet ye.
My muse oft fancies wi' great glee
When auld kirk bells are set a ringing
And Royal Geordies face they see,
How they'll 'God Save the King' be singing!

Congratulatory Address

Hail! Royal Liege! To Scotia's shores.
Hail to famed Lothians bonny city.
Where ilka Scottish heart implores
Your presence wi' a welcome ditty
Blest be the day that brings ye here
Whaur nane gainsays my glade opinions
O'millions; wha' wi' joyful cheer,
Hail you to Scotia's auld dominions!
Dear Geordie! Welcome to the North!
Thrice welcome to our cocky leeky
Thrice welcome to the banks o'Forth
An thine ain palace in auld reeky
Ye'r welcome to a cog o'brose
A dainty, nane but coofs disparage.
Ye'r welcome to our barley bree
Or weil pang'd bicker ful o'parritge.
The English roose their roast and fry'd
Nae doubt, its dainty to the moo.
But sheep-head keal! Come Lad! And try't
Frae scaup divested o'the woo.
And gif ye dinna say yersell!
That broth; frae head o'troop or eue!
Bangs a'their English muslin keal,
I'se eat the horns that on it grew.
They crack o'puddings too! Sae mare
Row'd up sae nice, in cloots and baggies
But, see's tow! Can they e'er compare;
Wi' chappit dainties o'our haggis.
Wow! We'll be glade to see ye here
Twill gar us a' look unco frisky,

Twill gar us pledge for ane sae dear
Fue, monie a quaigh! O'Highland whisky
Ilk freeborn las wi lightsome glee
Will snod her hair wi cocker only
And kilt her coats aboon her kull
To strew your path wi flowers sae bonie
Dear Geordie! Bless yer sonsey face.
We a'are fidgin fain to meet ye
For deil a norlan's i'this place
But has an open heart to greet ye
Ilk lass, Frae John o'Groats, to Tweed
Ilk Leezie, Maggie, Kate and Janet
Are a'maist daft to see ye cleed
Yersell in plaid and plumed bonnet,
There's ne'er a lad among them a'
Frae Lewis Isle doon to Dumbarton
Wha'll look mair comely sire or bra
Array'd in Philabeg and tartan
The lasses lang had fashous fears
In southern dudds ye'd mak ye'r show
But glad ye'r like ye'r ain forbears.
Shantreus, ye ken! They'r fondest o.'
Faith, but ye'r belt will look fae weil
Ye'r dirk and broad sword, made a-far-a
Whaur skilful Andrew forg'd the steel
To mak ye'r Royal keen Ferrara;

The Procession

When ye gae up the Castle Hill
Nae doubt ye'll mak a grand procession
For then stands forth ilk sturdy chield
The cleverest lads o'ilk profession.
Our rich regalia for our king
Shall frae its coffers be forthcoming
And bells, many loud acclaims well ring
Many skirling bag-pipes, fifes and drumming
Frae ilka toon on hill or glen
O'Caledonia's ancient nation
Ilk Royal burgh will feel fue' fain
To send their king a deputation
And could the lame, the halt, the blind

Poor, rich or muddling, hobble hither
Lord man! Ye'd find them o'ae mind
To come and greet ye o'the gather
Our provost and our baillies a'
(and nane ye'l find mair staunch or loyal
For joy to think, they fairly crow.
O'entertaining one sae Royal
Convenor, deakens, city trades
Will a be crying 'God be thanket'
When they unfurl the banner ca'd
'The Palestine perubian blanket.'[18]
Our advocates and great law lords
Our clerks and writers o' the signets
Will gee ye welcome, whilst the fair
Will deck their brows in comely cignets.
Ilk student, ilk colegiat spark
Will their obesience humbly tender,
And ministers, o'holey kirk
Will hail wi' joy, the faith's defender.

The Royal Guard

Then for your guard. O'archers braw
Wi merry pibrochs Geordie greeting;
Say Royal Sir gif e'er ye saw
Clansmen sae tight at ony meeting?
And then for sodgers! Sic as thae
Na either monarch e'er cou'd boast of.
For you! Ouer a'the world they's gae
And frae the bravest bear the roast off,
Ye'll see around ye! Veterans bauld
On who's achievements aft we've reckoned

---

18. **Note by William** – The blue blanket is the standard of the incorporated trades of Edinburgh and is kept by the convenor 'At whose appearances therewith' observes Maitland 'tis said that not only the artificers of Edinburgh are obliged to repair to it, but all the artificers or craftsmen in Scotland are bound to follow it and fight under the convenor of Edinburgh as aforesaid' and according to an old tradition, this standard was used in the Holy wars, by a body of crusading citizens of Edinburgh and was the first mounted on the walls of Jerusalem, when that city was stormed by the Christian army under the famous Richard.

But ne'er yet could the tale be tauld
Their banner wore disnonours speck on't.
Here on our Greys but turn ye'r see
Wha mony a bluidy muir hae pranced on
They've muckle pride ye'r guard to be
For lang sin-syne! Ye'r faes they've done'd on.
Wi'Malborough aft they stood the field
And Charlie, Prince Loraine! In Flanders
Wha gav'd the bands of Gallia yield
In thousands to his hardy hunders.
Prince Ferdinand o'Brunswick too
Hae often led them victorys winding
Where flow'd around the crimson dew
And dy'd the fields! 'La feldt 'aud Minden'
Their king at home they'll guard wi' care
And think them happy when beside him,
And gif he takes the caller air
They'll watch and see nae skaith betide him.

On the morning of the 14th the Royal Squadron entered the Firth of Forth and received royal salutes from the batteries of Dunbar and the Bass and were received in like manner by the ships of war in Leith roads. The *Royal George* cast anchor off Leith and the guns of Edinburgh Castle, Calton Hill, Salisbury Crags and Leith Fort opened like thunder.

The troops, clans, trades &c &c were posted in readiness to receive His Majesty on shore, but the weather proving very unpropitious, the landing was postponed and the troops returned to their quarters with orders to assemble at ten o'clock the following morning in the same order.

The following new words to an auld spring are by Sir Walter Scott Bart.

The news has floun frae mooth to mooth,
The north for once has bang'd the south;
The diel a Scotsman's die o drouth,
Care now the kings come!
Care now the kings come!
Care now the kings come!
Thou shalt dance and I will sing,
Care since the kings come!

Auld England held him lang and fast;
And Eren had a joyful cast,
But Scotlands turn has come at last;
Care now the kings come!

Auld Reeky in her rockclay grey,
Thought never to hae seen the day;
A weary time he's been away;
Care now the kings come!

She's skirling frae the Castle hill;
The carlin's voice has grown sae shrill;
Ye'll hear her at the Camson Mill;
Care now the Kings come!

'Up bairns' she cries 'beath great & sma,'
And busk ye for the wapon shaw;
Stand by me and we'll bang them a';
Care now the kings come!

Come frae Newbattles antient spires;
Bauld Lothian with your knight and squires;
And match the mettle o' your sires;
Care now the kings come!

Y'ere welcome hame my Montague!
Bring in your hand the young Buccleugh,
I'm missing some that I may rue,
Care now the kings come!

Come Haddington the kind and gay!
You've grac'd my causeway monie a day!
I'll weep the cause if thow should stay;
Care now the kings come!

Come premier Duke and carry down
Frae yonder craig his ancient crown
Its had a lang sleep and a swoon
Care now the kings come!

Come Athol frae the hill and wood,
Bring down your clansmen like a cloud

Come Morton show the Douglas bluid
Care now the kings come!

Come Tweesdale true as sword to sheath
Come Hoptoun fear'd on fields of death
Come Clark and gie your bugle breath,
Care now the kings come!

Come Wemyss who modest merit aids,
Come Rosebery, frae Dalmeny shades
Breadalbane bring your better plaids,
Care now the kings come!

Come stately Niddery, auld and true
Girt wi' the sword that Minden knew
We hae ouer few sic lairds as you,
Care now the kings come!

King Arthur's groun a common crier
He's heard in Fife and far Kintyre,
Fie lads, behold my crest o'fire
Care now the kings come!

Saint Abb roar'd out 'I see him pass'
Between Tantalan and the Bass
Calton glour'd wi keeking glass
Care now the kings come!

The Carlin stopp'd & sure I am,
For every glee had ta'en a dram,
But Oman help'd her to a dram,
Care now the kings come!

She toom'd her quaigh o'mountain dew
It rais'd her heart the higher too
Because it came frae Waterloo
Care now the kings come!

Again I heard her summonds swell
Wi' sic a dirdum and a yell
It droun'd St Gilles's saving bell,
Care now the kings come!

My trusty provost tried and tight
Stand forward for the guid toon's right
There's waur then you been made a knight
Care now the kings come!

My reverend clergy see ye say,
The best o' thanksgivings ye hae,
And warstle for a sunny day
Care now the kings come!

My doctors look that you agree;
Cure a' the toon without a fee,
My lawyers dinna pike a plea
Care now the kings come!

Come forth each sturdy burghers bairn,
That dunts on wood, or clanks on airn,
That fires the o'en or winds the pirn
Care now the kings come!

Come forward wi' the blanket blue
Your sires were loyal men and true
That Scotlands foemen oft might rue
Care now the kings come!

Scots dinna loup and rin and rave,
We're steady folks and something grave,
We'll keep the causeway firm and brave,
Care now the kings come!

Sir Thomas thunder frae your rock
Till Pentland dinnels wi' the shock,
I'll hae a braw new snood o'smoak
Care now the kings come!

Melville bring oot your bands sae blue
O'Lothian lads beath stout and true
Wi' Elcho, Hope and Cockburn too,
Care now the kings come!

And you wha on yon bluidy braes
Compell'd the vanquished foemans praise

Rank out, rank out, my gallant Greys
Care now the kings come!

Cock o'the north, my Huntly braw
Whaur are ye, wi your forty twa
Ah! Waes my heart that ye'r awa
Care now the kings come!

But yonder comes my canty Celts
We dirk and pistole at their belts,
Thank God we've still some plaids and kilts
Care now the kings come!

Come cock ye'r cap each archer spark,
For ye'r to guard him light and dark,
Faith lads, I trow ye've hit the mark
Care now the kings come!

Young Errol take the sword o'state.
The sceptre paviemorarchate,
Knight marshals see ye clear the gate,
Care now the kings come!

Kind Cummer Leith ye've been miset,
But dinna be upo' the fret
Ye's hae the handsell o' him yet,
Care now the kings come!

My daughters come wi' een sae blue
Your garlands weave, your wild flowers strew
He ne'er saw fairer flowrs than yow
Care now the kings come!

What shall we do for the propine
We us'd to offer something fine
But diel a grot's I'pouch o'mine.
Care now the kings come!

Diel care for that, I'se never start
We'll welcome him wi highland heart
What'er we hae he's get a part
Care now the kings come!

I'll shew him mason work this day
None o'the bricks o' bable clay
But louers will stand till time's away
Care now the king's come!

And here's Sir John, a'projects rife,
Will win the thanks o' an auld wife
And brings her health and length o'life
Care now the kings come!

The morning of the 15th proved extremely fine and the troops, clans, trades &c &c took their posts soon after nine o'clock and the immense multitude which had collected from all parts of the kingdom were seen thronging from every direction towards the point of landing or the route by which His Majesty's procession was to proceed.

Our regiment marched from Dalkeith and were posted at the landing place on Leith Pier, detaching a small squadron with the King's standard, which was posted at the barrier or city gate for the purpose of saluting as His Majesty entered the city of Edinburgh.

All being thus in readiness and every mind loaded with anxiety, for the arrival of the hour at which His Majesty intended to land till within a few minutes of 12 o'clock, when a gun from the *Royal George* announced that the king had entered his barge. A simultaneous shout from the tens of thousands assembled on the shore followed, the effect of which was indescribably striking. The guns on the Castle of Edinburgh, Leith Fort, the ships in the roads, Calton Hill and Salisbury Crags opened their royal salutes at the same moment, and for a time it appeared like a determined contest for the mastery between the roaring of the cannon and the unremitting shouts of the populace, while the joyful tumult was rendered still more impressively grand by the stillness that prevailed in the background.

> His Majesty was accompanied in his barge by the
> Marquess Conyngham
> Lord Graves
> Sir Charles Paget – Commodore
> Mr Russel – Flag Lieutenant
> Mr Tucker – Midshipman

And rowed by sixteen sailors in blue frocks and black velvet caps, Sir Charles Paget at the helm.

The Royal Barge was proceeded by that of the admiral on the station and followed by the barges of all the captains of the king's ships in the roads, arranged by seniority and these again followed by an immense number of private boats gaily trimmed to take a place in the grand aquatic procession.

As the royal barge came within hail of the pier, the royal standard was hoisted on the lighthouse and the multitude who had unconsciously dropped into silence, again sent forth a tremendous cheer. The barge passed the pier head, where a band of mountain bagpipers were posted & struck up their wild music amid the enthusiastic and rapturous shouts which now continued without intermission.

His Majesty stood in the barge; his countenance glowed with pleasure, he pulled off his hat and bowed incessantly to the spectators.

The ships in the harbour were clothed with flags and their shrouds and yards crowded to excess with the sailors, as the royal barge approached the landing place. His Majesty appeared most sensibly to feel the affectionate greetings of his subjects & on coming alongside the platform he again took off his hat and bowed repeatedly on all sides. His Majesty was dressed in an admiral's uniform with a thistle and a sprig of heath in his hat; wearing the St Andrews cross, presented to him by Sir Walter Scott in the name of the ladies of Edinburgh on his breast. He landed at twenty minutes past twelve o'clock and was received at the top of the steps leading from the platform, (which he ascended with great alacrity) by the port admiral.

- ➤ The Magistrates of Leith
- ➤ The Lord Provost
- ➤ The Lord Justice Clerk
- ➤ The Lord Chief Baron
- ➤ The Lord Clerk Register
- ➤ The Lord Advocate
- ➤ Sir Thomas Bradford – Commander of the Forces
- ➤ Sir Walter Scott
- ➤ The Marquess of Lothian – Lord Lieutenant of the County
- ➤ The Marquess of Winchester – Groom of the Stole
- ➤ Lord Charles Bentwick – Treasurer of the Household
- ➤ Two naval officers and other persons of distinction.

The guns again opened, which with the shouts of the people and warlike notes of trumpets and other martial instruments, now announced the landing of King George IV on Scottish ground.

His Majesty having received the congratulations and homage of the assembled noblemen & gentlemen, which he most graciously acknowledged and having heartily shaked hands with several personages about him, he proceeded with a firm and dignified step, attended by the Port Admiral and senior resident Magistrate of Leith. Flowers were strewed before him to the royal carriage, which he entered accompanied by the Duke of Dorset [Master of the Horse] and the Marquess of Winchester [Groom of the Stole].

It would be utterly impossible to describe the enthusiastic acclamations which burst from all ranks at this moment.

After His Majesty was seated a few minutes in his carriage, which was an open landau drawn by eight beautiful bay horses, with coachman and postilians in state livery, the procession moved slowly towards Edinburgh in the following order.

> ➤ Three trumpeters of Mid Lothian yeomanry cavalry in front
> ➤ A squadron Mid Lothian yeomanry cavalry
> ➤ Two highland pipers
> ➤ Captain Campbell and tail of Breadalbane
> ➤ A squadron of Scots Greys
> ➤ Two highland pipers
> ➤ Colonel Stewart of Garth and Celtic Club
> ➤ Sir Euan McGregor mounted on horseback & tail of McGregor
> ➤ Two equerries on horseback
> ➤ Sir Alexander Keith, Knight Marshal on a black horse
> ➤ Pages and grooms
> ➤ Sherriff mounted
> ➤ Sherriffs Officers
> ➤ Deputy Lieutenants in green coats mounted
> ➤ Two pipers
> ➤ General Graham Stirling and tail
> ➤ Barons of Exchequer
> ➤ Lord Clerk Register
> ➤ Lords of Justicary and Session in carriages
> ➤ Marquess of Lothian, Lord Lieutenant mounted
> ➤ Two heralds mounted
> ➤ Glengary mounted and grooms
> ➤ Young Glengary and two supporters; tail
> ➤ Four herald trumpeters
> ➤ White Rod, mounted and equerries

- ➤ Lord Lyon Defuite, mounted and grooms
- ➤ Earl of Errol, Lord High Constable mounted
- ➤ Two heralds mounted
- ➤ A squadron of Scots Greys
- ➤ Royal carriage and six containing
    - – The Marquess of Graham, Vice Chamberlain
    - – Lord George Berrisford, Comptroller of the Household
    - – Lord C. Bentwick, Treasurer of the Household
    - – Sir R. H. Vivian, Equerry to the king
- ➤ Ten royal footmen, two and two
- ➤ **The King**
- ➤ Attended by the Duke of Dorset, Master of the Horse and
- ➤ The Marquess of Winchester, Groom of the State
- ➤ Sir Thomas Bradford and Staff
- ➤ A squadron of Scots Greys
- ➤ Three clans and Highlanders and banners
- ➤ Two squadrons Mid Lothian yeomanry cavalry
- ➤ Grenadiers of the 77th Regiment
- ➤ Two squadrons of the third Dragoon Guards.

And in the rear of the procession were observed, in their carriages, a great number of nobility &c who were present to welcome His Majesty, among whom were.

- ➤ The Duke of Hamilton
- ➤ The Duke of Argyle
- ➤ The Duke of Athol
- ➤ The Duke of Montrose
- ➤ The Duke of Roxburgh
- ➤ The Duke of Buccleugh
- ➤ The Marquess of Queensberry
- ➤ The Marquess of Tweedale
- ➤ The Earl of Caithness
- ➤ The Earl of Lauderdale
- ➤ The Earl of Breadalbane
- ➤ The Earl of Elgin
- ➤ The Earl of Moray
- ➤ The Earl of Home
- ➤ The Earl of Hopetoun
- ➤ The Earl of Morton
- ➤ The Earl of Eglenton

- ➤ The Earl of Cassilis
- ➤ The Earl of Amboyne
- ➤ The Earl of Kellie
- ➤ The Earl of Northesk
- ➤ The Earl of Balcaris
- ➤ The Earl of Aberdeen
- ➤ The Earl of Roseberry
- ➤ The Earl of Glasgow
- ➤ The Earl of Wemyss
- ➤ The Earl of Leven
- ➤ The Earl of Wilton
- ➤ The Earl of Fife
- ➤ Viscount Arbuthnott
- ➤ Viscount Dunblain
- ➤ Viscount Maitland
- ➤ Viscount Montague
- ➤ Baron Forbes
- ➤ Baron Aylmore
- ➤ Baron Gray
- ➤ Baron Cathcart
- ➤ Baron Saltoun
- ➤ Baron St Clair
- ➤ Baron Blantyre
- ➤ Baron Reay
- ➤ Baron Elibank
- ➤ Baron Belhaven
- ➤ Lord Binning
- ➤ Lord Strathaven
- ➤ Lord Glenorchy
- ➤ Lord Robert Kerr
- ➤ Lord Frederick Leveson Gower
- ➤ Lord Elcho
- ➤ Lord Kilburn
- ➤ Lord J. Scott

The Lord Provost, magistrates and town council of Edinburgh had taken their station at the city gate, over which floated a variety of flags and when the procession was yet at a considerable distance, the Depute Lyon, King at Arms and the Usher of the White Rod, preceded by two heralds, sounding their trumpets, galloped up to the gate (which was locked) and the Usher of the White Rod knocked three times and was challenged by the city officer (from within) to whom it was communicated that His Majesty desired to visit his ancient city of Edinburgh. The Chamberlain answered, that the gates would be opened to his majesty and the Depute Lyon, King at Arms and the Usher of the White rod, with the Heralds returned with the answer. The gates were immediately thrown open and the procession passed through till His Majesty's carriage was within the barrier, which then drew up and the Lord Provost who held the cushion on which the keys of the city were placed addressed the sovereign as follows.

'May it please your Majesty, we your Majesty's most faithful and dutiful subjects, the Lord Provost, magistrates and town council of Edinburgh, animated with the warmest feelings of attachment to your Majesty's sacred person and government, have embraced the earliest moment of approaching your royal person for the purpose of congratulating your majesty on your safe arrival in your ancient hereditary kingdom of Scotland and of offering for your most gracious acceptance, the keys of your majesty's good town of Edinburgh.'

'This dutiful ceremony sire; does not as in former times represent the direct command of gates and fortifications, these having long since been rendered unnecessary by the internal peace and happiness which Edinburgh has enjoyed under the mild and paternal government of your majesty and your majesty's father of happy memory. This ceremony now implies that we place, with loyal devotion, at the disposal of your majesty, the hearts and persons of our fellow citizens and bid your majesty a heartfelt welcome to this metropolis, so long the residence of your majesty's ancestors.'

His Majesty replaced the keys upon the cushion and replied. 'My Lord Provost, I return you these keys being perfectly convinced that they cannot be placed in better hands than in those of the Lord Provost and magistrates of my good City of Edinburgh.'

During this ceremony a profound silence reigned among the multitude, which (on the Royal carriage again moving) burst into a tremendous shout of approbation and thus the monarch cheerfully received into the city.

The procession advanced slowly along the walk, Picardy Place, York Place, North & South St Andrews Street, Princes Street, Waterloo Place, Calton south side, where thousands upon thousands were clustered round Nelson's pillar and rent the air with joyful acclamations.

His Majesty appeared struck with astonishment at the grandeur displayed throughout the whole route of the procession, but here he again took off his hat, waved it several times to the multitude and exclaimed 'How superb!' The procession descended the Abby Hill and proceeded to the front door of the Palace of Holyrood, where (as His Majesty entered) a deafening shout broke forth from the congregated mass; the guns on Salisbury Crags, which immediately overlooked the palace, as well as those of the castle fired another royal salute; the numerous bands of music played 'God Save the King' & were joined by the voices of the multitude in the same strain till His Majesty was quite out of their sight.

The conduct of the people throughout, was admirable, their steadiness and the absence of all tendency to disturbance or riot was truly praiseworthy. The remark of a certain nobleman say that 'there was not one whose behaviour would have been offensive in a private drawing room; and but few comparatively whose appearance might not have entitled them to admission into one'.

That the manner of his reception was as grateful to our king as it was solemn and impressive, is put beyond all doubt by a remark which he was pleased to make to the gallant Lord Lynedoch after he arrived at the palace. His Majesty observed that 'he had often heard that the Scots were a proud nation; and the surely had reason to be so, for they appeared to be a nation of gentlemen, and he himself was proud of them.' We may also add that one of the king's household, an English nobleman, when His Majesty landed, exclaimed 'Surely never before did a monarch meet such a reception!'

His Majesty remained some time in the palace, where the regalia was presented to him, with some addresses from the Lord Provost and magistrates.

A squadron of Greys was dispatched to Dalkeith to receive His Majesty on his arrival there, and another posted at the Palace of Holyrood to escort him thither; under which he took his departure at half past three o'clock and arrived at Dalkeith House in 22 minutes.

On the 16th His Majesty remained at Dalkeith House and frequently expressed himself much delighted with his residence.[19]

---

19. **Note by William** - Dalkeith House is about six miles from Edinburgh, in the immediate vicinity of the town of Dalkeith, on the site of an ancient castle, once the property of the Douglas family; which (when occupied by the Regent Morton, during the minority of James VI) was called the Lion's Den. The park

His Majesty also expressed his satisfaction of the reception he had met with on landing and repeatedly spoke of the very orderly appearance of the people. He received visits during the day from many of the nobility, among whom were

> The Duke of Buccleugh
> The Marquess of Lothian
> The Earl of Fife
> The Earl of Lauderdale
> Lord Montague
> Lord Melville
> Lord Ravensworth
> Lord John Scott &c &c

This evening the citizens of Edinburgh, the inhabitants of the towns of Dalkeith, Mussleborough and all the surrounding villages, did honour to His Majesty's landing by a most brilliant illumination; all ranks vied with each other in giving effect and splendour to the scene and inscriptions, ornaments, devices and emblems were displayed in endless and dazzling variety. The streets were crowded to excess and blazed in more than noontide splendour. When the whole was viewed from the Calton Hill, the mind was lost in wonder; Waterloo Place, Princes Street, the North Loch and the gigantic outline of the castle were rendered perfectly visible by the numberless lamps which ornamented the windows and houses; and the torches which blazed on the battlements of the ancient fortress, cast a lurid glare on the shelves of the precipice on which it reposes. Picardy Place & George Street with its two noble squares were incredibly splendid; but nothing could exceed the grand and romantic effect of the high street with its lofty sides shining with innumerable lights reflected from heights apparently inaccessible.

A large crown was erected on the top of the gas work chimney which was brilliantly lighted every night during His Majesty's stay and

---

is much admired for its extent and beautiful scenery, the two crystaline rivers of north and south Esk, after meandering through the most romantic course, enter the park, the one in front, the other in rear of the house and continue their rugged way through a dell, exhibiting profusion of the beauties of nature and art, and uniting a little below the house, they role their combined streams through the remainder of the grounds.

the lofty summit of Arthur's Seat shone radiantly on the surrounding country.

Great quantities of rockets were discharged from all quarters and about ten o'clock salvoes of cannon were fired from the castle, Calton Hill, Salisbury Crags, Leith Batteries and the ships in the roads; with feu de joie from the infantry in the castle. The whole combined gave to the scene a sublimity which is beyond the power of description.

On the 17th His Majesty held his first levee at Holyrood House and the concourse was so great and so splendid as to surprise all who beheld it. The halls of Holyrood once more exhibited a scene the most gay and most exhilarating to the mind of the patriot and the presence of the sovereign recalled its former consequence; the composition and appearance of the company which now thronged its courts, forced upon the mind of the spectator the salutary changes which time had introduced since it ceased to be the seat of a monarchy. Beneath its gloomy arcades where ambitious partisans used to hatch their ruthless schemes; where fiery chieftains, whose greatness consisted of a power to oppress and to set the laws at defiance, bearded each other in fierce altercation. Here now appeared in peaceful mien, their more fortunate representatives, all who were respectable by birth and station, cordially united in the performance of a common duty, that of rendering homage to a constitutional king. A king who was bound by the same laws, which it was his office to administer; whom craft or violence could not render the instrument of injustice; whose greatness was identified with the liberty and happiness of his people; who might exalt, but of his own will, could not degrade or injure the meanest of his subjects.

About ten in the morning, the carriages began to draw up and continued to arrive without intermission till three.

His Majesty arrived from Dalkeith escorted by a squadron of the Greys, at a ¼ before two o'clock. He appeared in the complete highland costume of the Royal Stewart Tartan, which displayed his graceful figure to great advantage.

A guard of honour, consisting of a squadron of Greys and detachments of the 13th and 77th Regiments of Foot, was posted in front of the palace. A squadron of Greys was also posted at His Majesty's private entrance, while detachments of the Royal Archers and Celtic Society formed the guard within. And in the entre room were the following noblemen &c

> The Duke of Hamilton, Keeper of the Palace
> The Duke of Argyle, Great Master of the Household
> The Earl of Errol, Lord High Constable
> The Marquess of Lothian
> The Honourable W. Dundas, Lord Clerk Register
> The Lord President
> The Lord Advocate
> The Lord Justice Clerk
> Sir I. Berrisford, Admiral of the Station
> Sir J. Bradford, Commander of the Forces
> The Lord Chief Baron
> The Lord Chief Commissioner
> The Earl of Kinroule, Lord Lyon
> Sir Patrick Walker, Usher of the White Rod

About the throne were

> The Duke of Montrose
> The Marquess of Coynyngham
> Lord Melville
> Sir George Berrisford
> Lord Graves
> Lord Charles Bentwick
> Sir Edward Nagle
> Mr Peel
> Mr Butler &c &c

About 2,000 persons were presented to His Majesty; the chieftains of clans and many other noblemen and gentlemen were dressed in complete highland costume, among whom were observed.

> The Duke of Hamilton
> The Duke of Argyle
> The Earl of Breadalbane
> Lord Guydir
> Lord Glenorchy
> Sir H. Curtis &c &c &c

The levee closed and His Majesty took his departure about four o'clock, under his usual escort, accompanied by the Duke of Dorset and the Marquess of Coynyngham.

The 18th was passed by His Majesty in privacy, while thanks were offered up in all the churches for his safe arrival &c.

On the 19th His Majesty held a court and closet audience at Holyrood Palace; he drove into the courtyard about two o'clock, attended by the Duke of Dorset and Lord Graves. He was dressed in a Field Marshal's uniform, received several addresses &c and departed under the same escort for Dalkeith.

On the 20th His Majesty held a drawing room at Holyrood Palace, which was attended by about 500 ladies of the most distinguished rank in Scotland. The appearance of the palace at two o'clock was most splendid. His Majesty arrived from Dalkeith soon after two, escorted as usual, when the presentations took place & were finished about ½ past three. He was dressed in a Field Marshal's uniform and set out for Dalkeith at ¼ before four.

On the 21st His Majesty entertained a select party at dinner and expressed much satisfaction with the performance of Gow's[20] celebrated band after dinner.

On the 22nd His Majesty's grand procession from the Palace of Holyrood to the castle, took place, to witness which, early in the morning, Immense crowds of people flocked from the surrounding country, which so accumulated the mass already sojourning in Edinburgh that every spot, from the palace to the castle gates, where a foot could stand, and every window & balcony from whence a sight could be caught, was crowded to excess, many hours before the given period. The view of the High Street towards midday was animated beyond conception. The windows and balconies were covered with green, crimson & scarlet cloths, the public bodies, incorporations and trades took the ground assigned them & lined the street from the abbey to the castle. They were dressed (with very few exceptions comparatively) in blue coats with yellow buttons on which the word 'Welcome' was inscribed, white waistcoats and white trousers, a white rod in the hand and a thistle or a sprig of heath[er] in the hat with a St Andrew's Cross on the breast.

The 3rd Dragoon Guards, 7th Dragoon Guards and Midlothian Yeomanry cavalry were also lined in extended files along both sides of the street.

The open space in front of the palace now presented a most lively scene. The Scots Greys formed a square in the front court, where detachments of the 13th Regiment of Infantry were also on duty; the Royal Archers marched into the quadrangle of the palace to the

---

20. The renowned Bandmaster Nathaniel Gow.

sound of the bugle, the gathering of the clans followed and presented a spectacle of astonishing grandeur. But when the noble and official persons who had places assigned them in the procession appeared and mingled in the throng; their plumes nodding in the air and their gorgeous trains sweeping the ground, When 'Steed nigh'd to Steed', when the fairest dames of the land pressed to the palace windows to overlook the glittering scene. All that was attractive & captivating of chivalry, seemed to have been revived in more than its pristine magnificence, without any of its barbarous accompaniments. At two o'clock His Majesty arrived from Dalkeith, escorted by his usual guard of Greys and about ¼ past two the procession moved from the palace in the following order.

- ➢ Trumpeters Midlothian Yeomanry Cavalry
- ➢ Squadron Midlothian Yeomanry Cavalry six abreast
- ➢ Division of Marshal's Guard (Breadalbanes & McGregors) 12 abreast
- ➢ Band of Music
- ➢ Squadron of Scots Greys six abreast
- ➢ Two State Trumpeters
- ➢ Marchmont Herald
- ➢ (I. Small Esquire)
- ➢ Marshal Trumpeters
- ➢ Marshal Guard of Highland Gentlemen, twelve abreast
- ➢ A Marshal Yeoman
- ➢ Three Marshal Yeomen abreast
- ➢ Six Marshal Esquires, three abreast mounted and attended by
- ➢ Four Marshal Yeomen
- ➢ Henchman – Knight Marshal – Henchman
- ➢ Marshal Yeoman – Sir Alexander Keith – Marshal Yeoman
- ➢ Division of Lord High Constables Highland Guard
- ➢ Two Pursuivants in their tabards
- ➢ Four State Trumpeters
- ➢ Islay Herald
- ➢ (John Cook Esq.) supported by two pursuivants in their tabards
- ➢ Assistant – Usher of the White Rod Sir Patrick Walker – Assistant
- ➢ Lord Lyon, King at Arms, Lord Kinnoul, attended by two grooms
- ➢ Constables guard of partisans
- ➢ Six Constables Yeoman, three abreast
- ➢ Six Constables esquire three abreast

- ➤ Three macers, the exchequer mace in the centre
- ➤ Six grooms, 3 abreast attendants on the sword of state
- ➤ Two Esquires
- ➤ Sword of State Carried by the Earl of Morton
- ➤ Two Macers
- ➤ Four pages abreast, attendants on the sceptre
- ➤ Four Esquires abreast
- ➤ The Sceptre carried by the Honourable John M. Stewart
- ➤ Two Macers
- ➤ Six Grooms three abreast attendants on the Crown
- ➤ Two Esquires
- ➤ The Crown carried by the Duke of Hamilton, his horse led by 2 Equerries
- ➤ A Royal Carriage drawn by six bays,
- ➤ Containing the Duke of Argyle, The Marquess of Coynyngham, Lord F. Coynyngham & Sir H. Vivian
- ➤ Squadron of Scots Greys six abreast
- ➤ Flanking Guard His Majesty accompanied by the Flanking Guard
- ➤ Of Archers Duke of Dorset & Lord Glenlyon of Archers in a carriage drawn by six horses
- ➤ The Earl of Errol as Lord High Constable of Scotland
- ➤ Dressed in his robes of office and Earls Coronet on his head, rode on the right of the carriage by the express appointment of His Majesty
- ➤ Squadron of Scots Greys six abreast
- ➤ Constables Guard of Highland Gentlemen twelve abreast
- ➤ Detachment of Scots Greys six abreast
- ➤ Division of Constables Guard of Highlanders (Drummonds & Sutherlands) twelve abreast
- ➤ Squadron of Mid Lothian Yeomanry Cavalry

The procession was most impressively splendid, the variety of different costumes was admirably calculated for effect, the intermixture of the clans with their tartan habiliments and of the troops formed a happy relief to the official splendour which marked other parts of the pageant.

His Majesty was dressed in a Field Marshal's uniform and appeared in excellent spirits. All eyes seemed to be riveted on the regalia, as it was carried triumphantly along by the ancient nobles of the land, whose ancestors had often fought and bled for that independence of which they were the sacred and venerable symbols. Every heart seemed to fill with patriotic emotions at the sight of the same diadem that had invested the brows of the Royal Bruce, of his warlike descendants and of the lovely and unfortunate Mary. Their feelings were often expressed in boisterous shouts and loud cheerings, which was still increased as His Majesty advanced.

When the royal carriage reached the Netherbow,[21] six beautiful girls, dressed in white, with blue satin sashes across their shoulders, from which descended the St Andrew's Cross and their heads adorned with wreaths, proceeded before and strewed the way with flowers, and on arriving near the castle gate, a herald announced to the governor, the approach of His Majesty; and when the royal carriage reached the barrier gate, His Majesty got out on a platform covered with crimson cloth, where the keys of the castle were tendered to him by Lt General Sir Alexander Hope accompanied by Major General Sir Thomas Bradford.

After this ceremony His Majesty returned the keys and walked to the inner gate where he got into another carriage and the procession moved through the windings of the castle, to the Half Moon Battery, where His Majesty ascended a platform covered with scarlet cloth and presented himself to the full view of his admiring subjects. At this moment a Royal Salute was fired from the batterys and the bands played 'God Save the King.'

His Majesty remained a considerable time on the platform cheered by the considerable multitude who occupied the Castle Hill, whose royal greetings he most graciously acknowledged by taking off his hat and returning three hearty cheers to the people. He expressed his admiration on viewing the surrounding scenery. The broken outline of crags, cliffs & stupendous buildings peering above the fog which had settled in the hollows, forced upon the eye of the spectator, a scene the most singular & romantic.

His Majesty re-entered his carriage and the procession returned by the earthen mound, Princes Street, Regent Bridge and the road over the Calton Hill, which was literally hid by the thousands who had

---

21. The Netherbow port was one of the original gates of walled Edinburgh. It stood between High Street and Canongate and formed the 'End of the World' for many poor residents, as if they passed out of this gate, they had to pay a toll to re-enter, hence the name is retained in a local public house. The gate was demolished in 1764 but the site is still marked in the pavement by brass plaques.

assembled on it. This mass cheered their sovereign in one united body as he passed and the procession again reached the palace at four o'clock.

This day, after His Majesty's return to the palace, he conferred the honour of knighthood on Lt. Colonel Thomas Pate Hankin of the Greys and at a few minutes past four he proceeded under his usual escort to Dalkeith.

On the 23rd a Grand Review of cavalry took place on Portobello Sands, consisting of the following corps:

> ➤ Commanded by Major General Sir Thomas Bradford

> ➤ Royal Horse Artillery
> ➤ 3rd Dragoon Guards
> ➤ Royal Scots Greys
> ➤ Glasgow Troop of Yeomanry Cavalry
> ➤ Peebleshire Corps of Yeomanry Cavalry
> ➤ Selkirkshire Corps of Yeomanry Cavalry
> ➤ Fifeshire Troop of Lancers
> ➤ Fifeshire Corps of Yeomanry Cavalry
> ➤ Berwickshire Corps of Yeomanry Cavalry
> ➤ East Lothian Corps of Yeomanry Cavalry
> ➤ Midlothian Corps of Yeomanry Cavalry
> ➤ West Lothian Corps of Yeomanry Cavalry
> ➤ Roxburghshire Corps of Yeomanry Cavalry
> ➤ The ground kept by the 7th Dragoon Guards.

At half past one o'clock His Majesty arrived on the ground under escort of a detachment of Greys. His approach was hailed by loud & continued cheers from the vast multitude assembled on the sands and a royal salute from a battery on the pier.

His Majesty got out of his carriage and mounted a fine grey horse which he had purchased from Cornet and Riding Master Edlmann[22] of the Scots Greys, with such a degree of freedom and activity that the congregated spectators sunk into a state of wonder-bound stillness, which continued for a few seconds and was expressed by a tremendous and simultaneous shout as he galloped towards the right of the line, followed by a numerous retinue.

---

22. Cornet James Caspar Edlmann, who had joined the regiment on 14 December 1815.

His Majesty proceeded along the front of the line and after again returning between the ranks to the right; he galloped at a sharp pace to the front of the centre and posted himself close to the multitude, from whom another burst of approbation issued, which made sea and atmosphere echt [join].

Here the line marched past His Majesty in a column of half squadrons right in front with music &c &c. The Greys (who stood highest in popular favour) was led by their colonel, General Sir James Stuart Denham Bart. And on their band striking up the ancient national air 'Garb of Old Gaul.' The multitude testified their regard by loud and universal cheers.

After the cavalry had thus passed His Majesty, the clans followed in order as underneath with their leaders in the full ancient costume of the land.

	Led By	No.
Celtic Society	Duke of Argyle	100
Breadalbane men	Earl of Breadalbane	50
Strathfellan	Stuart of Ardvorlich	100
Clan Gregor	Sir Euan McGregor	50
Glengary's	MacDonal of Glengarry	12
Marchioness of Stafford's	Dunrobin men	50
Lord F. Leveson-Gower		
Clan Drummond	Lord Gwydir	30

Sir Walter Scott acted as Adjutant General to the mountaineers.

His Majesty expressed himself much satisfied with the appearance of the troops and seemed much delighted with the garb of the clans. However it may be that His Majesty's partiality to the tartan did not originate here, for he had uniformly expressed his approbation of the dress to MacDonald of Clanranald, who had for years before, been in the habit of appearing at court in it. And on one occasion when Clanranald appeared in the full costume befitting the chief of the MacDonalds and the representative of the Lords and Kings of the Isles (and was introduced as such) His Majesty received him most graciously and presented to him a magnificent sword, which the City of Glasgow had presented to Prince Charles. His Majesty's words to Clanranald on that occasion were 'I will always be happy to see you in that dress. This sword belonged to the unfortunate chevalier and I now give it to you, as the person best entitled to wear it.'

After the Review, His Majesty proceeded to Dalkeith and from thence (in the evening) to a ball given by the peers of Scotland. The preparations for his reception were splendid in the extreme, he was received by all the Scottish nobility (with very few exceptions). The gentlemen mostly in the mountain garb and the ladies in rich white with abundant plumes of snow-white ostrich feathers whose constant motion like foaming waves, gave to the scene a most magnificent appearance.

His Majesty after some time, expressed his entire approbation of the richness and beauty which was displayed in the preparations for his reception and took his departure under his usual escort for Dalkeith.

On the 24th the regalia of Scotland were carried from Holyrood Palace and re-deposited in the Crown Room in the castle. The procession moved as follows:

Flanking Scots Greys and Celts	Sir Euan McGregor mounted Banner and a Piper Major H. McGregor and division of Clan McGregor Sir A. Keith Knight Marshall (Attended by his esquires) In his carriage with the regalia. Major D. McGregor Of the Clan McGregor	Flanking Scots Greys and Celts

The procession moved to the castle gate and obtained admission in the usual manner. The crown was then carried by the Knight Marshal, the sceptre by the Honourable M. Stewart and the Sword of State by Captain Ferguson, Keeper of the Regalia.

This evening a splendid banquet was given to His Majesty, by the Lord Provost, Magistrates and Town Council of the City of Edinburgh in the Parliament House, where His Majesty attended at half past six in the evening.

Dinner being over, a silver basin containing rose water, was brought to His Majesty by Mr Howison Crawford younger of Braehead and

Crawford-Land, who in right of his mother as proprietrix of Braehead in Midlothian, claims his privilege. This service being the ancient tenure by which the estate of Braehead is held, and originated in the following interesting story, viz.

One of the Kings of Scotland, James II or III, travelling incognito in the neighbourhood of Cramond Bridge, was attacked by a gang of gypsies, who were then very numerous in Scotland. The King long bravely defended himself, but was at last, by manly assailants brought to the ground and at the critical moment a husbandman of the name of Howison who was threshing in a barn hard by, hearing the noise, came out and seeing one man attacked by so many, sided with the weaker party and dealt such blows with his flail among the gypsies as speedily put them to flight. The stranger being rescued from his perilous situation, was conducted by the honest rustic to his humble abode, where his guest requested a basin of water and a towel to remove the blood; which was done and the farmer placed before him such refreshment as his habitation afforded and suspecting from something he had observed in His Majesty's dress that he was some person of distinction; desired in token of respect, that he would sit at the head of the table. This the King at first resisted, but was so stoutly pressed by the farmer, that he was obliged to comply & before departure, the stranger after many thanks, invited his deliverer to visit him in Edinburgh and directed him to enquire at the castle for 'Ane Jamie Stewart', who would gratify the curiosity he had expressed of seeing that fortress. 'Wow man' said the farmer 'but I would like to see the castle', perhaps considering this a remuneration sufficient for flailing the gypsies &c.

The farmer however, at no distant day availed himself of the invitation; he presented himself at the castle gate and to his great astonishment was ushered into an assembly of courtiers, among whom, much to his relief, he speedily recognised his auld friend Jamie Stewart, who informed him that the king was present and that he would know him by being the only person in the room who was covered. 'Then' said the confounded farmer, 'It maun be either you or me' having in his bewilderment neglected to doff his own blue bonnet.

After having diverted himself with the farmer's simplicity, the now disclosed monarch again expressed his gratitude and desired him to name a boon, such as he could bestow for his deliverance, when the honest deliverer modestly replied that the summit of his earthly wishes was to become proprietor of the land he cultivated as bondsman. This was instantly complied with and a crown charter of the lands of Braehead (which then were Crown lands) forthwith prepared. The redendo of the charter is the service of holding a basin of water and a napkin, when required to do so, for the King to wash his hands in commemoration of the office performed by the farmer after rescuing his sovereign from the gypsies.

Mr Howison Crawford was attended in performing this ceremony to King George the IV, by Masters Charles and Walter Scott, the one a son, the other a nephew of Sir Walter Scott Bart., as pages attired in splendid dresses of scarlet and white satin, the one holding a silver ewer and the other a salver with a damask napkin of Scottish manufacture. In offering the basin, Mr Howison Crawford knelt down and His Majesty performed his part of the ceremony with his usual affability and grace.

After dinner, the Lord Provost arose and proposed the health of His Majesty, 'Who' (said he) 'has this day honoured us with his presence, thereby conferring a signal mark of favour upon this good town of Edinburgh, which will never, never, be obliterated from the memory of the present generation.'

A previous arrangement having been made to announce to the city the moment of drinking His Majesty's health, which was done by two rockets from the Parliament House and instantly proclaimed by a discharge of artillery from the castle, Calton Hill, Salisbury Crags, Leith Battery and the ships in the roads.

'God Save the King' by a vocal band

His Majesty then said 'In rising to return thanks for the expressions of attachment now made to me, after what I experienced on my arrival, what I have since seen and what I now see before me, words would fail me were I to attempt to describe to you my feelings in this situation, I must appeal to your own. I assure you I consider this one of the proudest days of my life, and you may judge with what truth, with what sincerity and with what delight I drink all your good healths.'

By the Lord Provost 'The Duke of York and the Army.'

By the Lord Provost 'The Duke of Clarence and the Army.'

His Majesty then addressed the Lord Provost as follows: 'My Lord, you may have heard that it is my intention to make you a baronet.'

His Lordship replied that he had heard that such was His Majesty's gracious intention.'

'Have you any objection to it?' enquired His Majesty;

His Lordship observed that he could not fail to consider it a very high honour.

'Then' said His Majesty 'Call a bumper.'

A toast was announced, His Majesty arose and said, 'Gentlemen, I am sure you will cordially agree with me in drinking the health of the Lord Provost of Edinburgh, Sir William Arbuthnot Baronet, and the Corporation of the City of Edinburgh.'

Loud cheering followed and the band struck up.

The Garb of Old Gaul & Highland Laddie

His Majesty retired about nine o'clock and Sir William Arbuthnot on his return from attending him to his carriage was congratulated by the company.

A mans a man for a'that

Sir William took his seat at the head of the table and again gave the health of the King.

God Save the King & Highland Laddie

By the Duke of Hamilton, 'The Lord Provost'

By the Lord Provost 'The auspicious days of the 14th, 15th & 24th of August, the first being that on which the King cast anchor in Leith Roads, the 2nd his public entry into the city and the last, that on which he had honoured the Corporation with his presence. The British constitution and may that constitution, in church and state, which is the envy of the world, be transmitted unimpaired to the latest prosperity.'

Kind Robin Loe's me

By the Lord Provost 'Health of Mr Peel'

By the Lord Provost 'Health of Viscount Melville'

By Viscount Melville 'The Duke of Hamilton and Peerage of Scotland'

By the Lord Provost 'The Earl of Errol'

By Lord Strathmore 'Lady Arbuthnot and the flowers of Edinburgh'

Here's a Health to all good Lasses

By the Duke of Argyle 'The Church of Scotland'

By the Lord Provost 'The distinguished strangers of England, who have this day honoured us with their presence' (loud cheering)

By the Earl of Errol 'Sir Walter Scott and thanks to him for the which he had in bringing us together'

By Lord Strathmore 'The King's young landlord; the Duke of Buccleugh'

By the Lord Provost 'The Duke of Montrose'

By the Lord Provost 'The Duke of Wellington' (loud applause)

See the Conquering Hero Comes

By Lord Lauderdale 'The rectors of the universities of Scotland and may they long maintain the honour they have acquired.'

By the Lord Provost 'The brave companions in arms of the Duke of Wellington, the Earl of Hopetoun, Lord Lynedoch, Lord Beresford & Sir David Baird'

By Sir Walter Scott 'Both sides of St George's Channel'

By the Lord Provost 'The memory of Lord Nelson who seemed only to live till his glorious mission was accomplished and expired in the act of giving the exterminating blow to the naval power of the combined enemies of Britain'

By the Lord Provost ' The chieftains and the clans who have come forward on the present occasion, to grace His Majesty's court, particularly the Marchioness of Stafford, Lord Gwydir, Earl of Breadalbane, Sir E. McGregor & Glengarry'

By Sir E. McGregor 'The chief of chiefs, the King'

By the Duke of Athol 'May the radiant son of royalty, see what the sons of Scotland are made of' (loud applause)

By the Earl of Kinnoul 'The Duke of Argyle and the Highland Society of Scotland'

By Sir M. Shaw Stewart 'The King as Baron of Renfrew'

By the Earl of Elgin 'The health of the Duke of Athol and particularly alluding to the national monument of Scotland, in which His Majesty evinced so great an interest'

His Grace said he was a Scotsman born and bred, he loved his country most sincerely and he wished that every action of his life might be such as to do good to his country and meet the approbation of his countrymen. He had taken an interest in the national monument to be erected in the memory of those brave men who had fought the battles of our king and conquered all the enemies of our country. He hoped he had been somewhat instrumental in bringing this great work to a conclusion; the foundation stone of which was to be laid on the next Tuesday and from the situation in life in which providence had placed him, much was expected from him, and as he had said before, his best endeavours should ever be exerted for the good of his country, in doing so, he only did what he trusted every Scotsman would do – his duty! There was not an individual in Scotland who would sacrifice more for the improvement of his native land; and he would at all times, stand forth a decided supporter of the King and of those measures which tended to the good of Caledonia.

By Lord Ashburton 'The National monument that will last, when a monument of stone and mortar has passed away. The author of

Waverley, whoever he may be and his works'

By Glengarry 'The memory of Henry Lord Melville'

By the Duke of Athol 'The memory of his associate Mr Pitt, we shall never see his like again'

By the Lord Provost 'Sir J. P. Beresford and the Northern Squadron'

By the Honourable Captain Napier 'The Baronet of Renfrew, Sir M Shaw Stewart & the Yeomanry of Scotland'

By Sir M Shaw Stewart 'The Yeomanry of Scotland'

Bold Dragoon

By Sir W. Maxwell 'The Lord Provost and the rest of the company, not yeomen'

A song by W. McGrath, 'Scots who hae we Wallace bled'

By the Earl of Elgin 'The convenor and trades of the City of Edinburgh'

By Glengary 'The health of His Majesty as the King of the Isles' (first in Gaelic and then in English)

By the Lord Provost 'The City of London & Sir William Curtis'

By the Lord Provost 'The City of Dublin'

By the Lord Provost 'The City of Glasgow & prosperity to its trade and manufactures'

By the Lord Provost 'The rose, the thistle & shamrock'

By the Lord Provost 'King George the IV'

The company broke up about ten o'clock and the Lord Provost gave orders that the wine remaining after the banquet should be distributed to the Royal Infirmary and the Destitute Sick Society and the broken meal to the poor and prisoners in the jail.

On the 25th His Majesty attended divine service in the High Church of St Giles, where a great number of the nobility also attended.

The King arrived at the palace at about 11 o'clock attended by the Duke of Dorset and Lord Glenlyon with his usual escort of Greys, where a vast multitude were assembled, and many of whom not a little amused by a worthy couple, who had come frae the country to hae a glour among the leave at the great man. The auld care, a guid natured looking chield, wi' a rauchin row'd aboot his shouthers and a rent in his neive, his teeth weil smesr'd wi tobacco juice and his bonnet set a wee thought ajee to let fock ken that domestic thraldom, had nae yet putten oot a'the spunk o'his youth. This original showed a hantle o'indifference aboot the matter; but his spouse, a wee wiffie wi' sma' grey ferrety een keeking oot frae among rigid muscles that betokened absolute rule and was dressed in a chintz goon o' the largest pattern wi' a galash on her head, was on the qui vive, wi' curiosity. As the royal carriage drove up, her guid man exclaimed 'Noo Jennet noo! Dinna gang hame flyting on me as ye hae done this sax bygone days because ye haena seen him. There woman! He's coming noo, be sure an tak a guid look o'him, noo, noo, noo!'

However, Jennet who thought she could never see too much of His Majesty, first cast her wee een upon the carriage, then upon the coachman, footmen and guard, whose finery altogether quite dazzled her busy sight and before she could rally all her faculties of memory, reflection &c the King was within the porch of the palace. Poor Jennet discovering her fatal error too late ejaculated 'The Lord preserve us, I've tint him again' and the two withdrew from the crowd, Jennet flying most unmercifully and John countermarching his guid and ruminating, no doubt, on another day's sojourning in the metropolis.

His Majesty set off in a few minutes for church and was extremely gratified with the stillness and appearance of the streets which were very imposing and characteristic of a Scottish Sabbath; as he passed along the people reverently took off their hats, but not a voice was raised to hail his appearance. There did not reign in the most sequestered glen in Scotland a more profound stillness then was now observed in the streets of Edinburgh! Nor is this to be wondered at, the spectacle of a monarch proceeding to humble himself before the King of kings, could scarcely fail with a national people, to act as an example.

When the royal carriage was near the cross, a few boys took off their hats as if about to cheer, but some old men dissuasively held up their hands and the most prompt obedience was yielded to the signal. This circumstance was particularly noticed by the King and we have reason to believe that no part of the behaviour of his Scottish subjects was more admired by him, than their conduct on this solemn occasion. His Majesty was dressed in a Field Marshal's uniform and wore a ribband of the Order of the Thistle on his breast. The officiating clergyman was Doctor Lamont, who delivered an excellent discourse on the 3rd & 4th verses of the 3rd Chapter of the Epistle of St Paul to the Colossians.

'For ye are dead and your life is his with Christ in God, when Christ, who is our life, shall appear, then shall ye also appear with him in Glory.'

In the prayer which followed the discourse, he made use of the following words.

May thy choicest blessings descend upon the head of our

sovereign King George. Grant him, O God, a long, a happy and a prosperous reign; may he be adorned with every Christian virtue, may he be happy in this life and happy in the life to come. May the paternal regard he has shown in visiting this part of his dominions, which has diffused joy throughout the land, have a lasting influence on the hearts and conduct of his people.

As His Majesty returned from the church, the people observed the same reverential silence, which they had done in the fore part of the day, of which His Majesty repeatedly expressed his admiration.

On the 26th His Majesty paid a private visit to the Palace of Holyrood, for the purpose of inspecting its apartments. He arrived about two o'clock and being received by the Duke of Hamilton (Keeper of the Palace) proceeded to Queen Mary's apartments. Previous to His Majesty leaving London he gave orders that these apartments should be preserved sacred from any alteration; and when shown the bed and blankets in which the ill-fated Mary slept, he caught one of the blankets in his hand and remarked; how wonderful it was that they had been kept in a state of preservation so long. His Majesty remained about an hour in the palace and returned privately to Dalkeith.

This evening a Grand Ball was given to His Majesty in the Assembly rooms, by the Caledonian Hunt, of which institution he had previously condescended to become a patron. The front of the Assembly rooms was elegantly illuminated and His Majesty arrived at half past nine o'clock attended by the Duke of Dorset, Lord Graves and an escort of Greys. He was received by a great number of the peerage and many of the principle landholders of Scotland, with officers of every rank belonging to the Army and Navy. Dancing began soon after his arrival and His Majesty seemed quite delighted with the Scots reels and Strathspeys. He wore his uniform as Colonel of the Guards and a St Andrew's Cross on his hat.

None contributed more to the hilarity of the company than himself for he was in excellent spirits and his whole deportment was most affable, gracious and condescending.

His Majesty left the Assembly at 11 o'clock and set off for Dalkeith, attended and escorted as he came; when country dances commenced and were kept up by some of the company till seven in the morning.

On the 27th the foundation stone of the great national monument, to be erected on the Calton Hill to the memory of the warriors of Scotland and which His Majesty was graciously pleased to patronise, took place.

This noble edifice was to be erected on the model of the celebrated

Parthenon of Athens and consecrated to the duty in testimony of the nation's gratitude for the signal success of the British arms during the late war and in commemoration of the valour of our countrymen engaged in the eventful contest. This ceremony was performed with all the honours of masonry; the procession was guarded by the Greys and 3rd Dragoon Guards and moved from the Parliament Square, by High Street, North Bridge to the Calton Hill, where the multitude of spectators was prodigious, every spot that afforded a resting place for a foot was occupied and the rugged fronts of the precipice under Nelson's pillar, which had for ages past, braved the western storms, only seen! The procession passed by the south side of the hill and when it arrived at the place where the stone was to be laid (which is on the summit of the mount) the Royal commissioners with the Magistrates &c ascended a platform which was erected on the opposite side, with the lodges &c arranged round the platforms and site; the accompanying band playing 'God Save the King.'

The stone measured 7 feet 8 inches square and 15 inches thick, about six ton weight. The Duke of Hamilton, after several speeches and ceremonies from other noblemen, addressed the bretheren and said, that having received His Majesty's commands, it was now their duty to proceed with the work. The band then played 'Hail Masonry' after which the Reverend Doctor Lee offered up an excellent prayer on the occasion and the Grand Master directed the Grand Treasurer and Secretary to place in the cavities of the stone bottles hermetically sealed, containing the coins, Newspapers &c of that present day and the inscription plates; the inscription on one of which was as follows.

> To
> The glory of God
> In
> Honour of the King
> For
> The good of the people
> This monument, the tribute of a grateful country
> To
> Her gallant and illustrious sons
> As
> A memorial of the past & incentive
> To the future heroism of the men of
> Scotland

Was founded on the 27th day of August in the year of our
Lord 1822, and in the third year of the glorious reign of
King George IV
Under his immediate auspices and in commemoration
Of His most gracious and welcome visit to his antient
Capital and the palace of His Royal ancestors
John Duke of Athol
James Duke of Montrose
Archibald John Earl of Rosebery
John Earl of Hopetoun
Thomas Lord Lyndoch

Officiating as commissioners in name and behalf of and by
special
Appointment of His August Majesty, the patron of the undertaking.
The celebrated Parthenon of Athens being the model of the
edifice.

Other plates containing the names of the Magistrates of Edinburgh,
office bearers of the Grand Lodge &c were deposited, with the bottles,
in their proper situations and the stone laid, the band playing 'Grand
Light will shine.' The Grand Master &c &c then descended to the
stone and the senior Grand Warden applied the square. The junior the
plumb line. The substitute Grand Master, the levee. The Grand Master
gave the stone three knocks with a mallet and craved the following
benediction on the work: 'May the Almighty Architect of the universe,
look down with benignity upon our present undertaking and crown
this splendid edifice with every success and may it be considered for
time immemorial a model of taste and genius and serve to transmit
with honour to posterity, the names of the artists engaged in it.' This
was followed by three cheers and the Grand Master then received a
cornucopia containing corn and two cups containing wine and oil and
having poured them upon the stone said:

Praise be to the Lord, immortal & eternal who formed the
heavens, laid the foundation of the earth and extended the waters
beyond it; who supports the pillars of nations and maintains
in order and harmony surrounding worlds, we implore thy aid
and may the continued blessings of an all bounteous providence
be the lot of these our native shores; and may the Almighty ruler

of events, deign to direct the hand of our gracious sovereign, so that he may pour down blessings upon his people; and may his people living under sage laws, in a free government ever feel grateful for the blessings they enjoy.

Loud cheering!

At this moment a signal gun was fired from the Calton Hill, which was immediately followed by a salute from the guns of the castle, Salisbury Crags, Leith Fort and the ships of war. His Grace the Duke of Hamilton afterwards made a handsome address to the people and so the ceremony of laying the foundation of the Grand National Monument ended.

This day His Majesty honoured Lord Viscount Melville by visiting his noble mansion, Melville Castle, to which place a guard of honour was marched to receive His Majesty on his arrival and a party to preserve order in the walks and pleasure grounds. And the Midlothian corps of Yeomanry Cavalry was drawn up on the lawn near the castle, for the purpose of saluting as His Majesty passed.

His Majesty arrived at half past two under an escort of Greys and was received by Viscount Melville in the uniform of the yeomanry cavalry (he being their colonel), he remained at the castle about ¾ of an hour and returned under the same escort for Dalkeith.

This day also; a chair of curious workmanship was presented to His Majesty through the medium of the Right Honourable the Lord Justice Clerk, by Mr Auld of Ayr. It was of exquisite workmanship in the Gothic state and made from the rafters of Alloa kirk, containing on the one side of the back a polished brass plate on which was inscribed at full length the well-known tale of 'Tam o'Shanter.'

And on the other side a painting representing 'Heroic Tam' mounted on his grey mare Meg and dashing onward amid the appalling horrors of the midnight storm.

> Whyles hauding fast his guid blue bonnet
> Whyles crooning ouer some ald Scots sonnet
> Whyles glouring round wi prudent cares
> Lest bogles catch him unawars

His Majesty most graciously received the gift and in respect to the genius of the great national bard, gave orders that particular care should be taken of it.

The same evening His Majesty visited the theatre, where he was received by all ranks with the utmost demonstrations of joy and respect, 'Rob Roy' was performed by particular desire of His Majesty with which he was much delighted.

On the 28th His Majesty visited New Battle Abbey, the seat of the Marquess of Lothian, where he remained about an hour and returned to Dalkeith House.

No particulars until the morning of the 20th when His Majesty took his departure from Dalkeith House and proceeded under an escort of the Greys to Hopetoun House, about ten miles up the banks of the Forth, where he remained some [time] and embarked at Port Edgar near the Queens Ferry and bid adieu to the Scottish shores.

Our regiment was now sent to its station for the winter, the headquarters occupied Piers Barracks, detaching a squadron to Perth on the smuggling duty, this squadron furnished parties at Crieff, Auchterarder, Forfar &c. The troop to which I belonged remained at Edinburgh till about the 15th of December when it went to Perth with another troop and relieved the squadron stationed there. Here the smuggling was carried on to an extraordinary pitch, which compelled us to be very often out during the night, ranging the mountains after the whisky mongers. In this way we continued until the end of April and marched by Dunblane,[23] Stirling, Kilsyth & to Glasgow Barracks, which we occupied about 3 weeks and marched for Edinburgh where we joined the headquarters and about the 13th of July 1823 again marched for Carlisle and occupied quarters there till beginning of 1824 when we were again moved to Newcastle upon Tyne where the headquarters had been stationed during the time we had occupied Carlisle. We remained in Newcastle till the 7th June [1824] and marched for Manchester Barracks, where we remained till 10th May 1825.

The regiment was then ordered to London to attend a grand review and were quartered in Hammersmith from 14th June until the 1st of July when the review took place on Hounslow Heath and we again commenced our march on Norwich. Here we bid farewell to the good old regiment.

'And now gentlemen having got to the end of my ragged tale; I beg leave to drink a good health to our brethren in arms, whom we have left behind!' And so saying the veteran grappled the tankard and took a heart pull to his country and his King. Then flourishing the

---

23. Just north of Bridge of Allan.

tankard round his head, gave three hearty huzzas for little Britain and sunk to repose on the bench where he sat, perhaps enjoying more real contentment than falls to the lot of many of the rich & the great on beds of doune [down].

*****

William left the regiment at Norwich, and he presumably returned to Scotland. 'We' may well mean his family, but again nothing is known. Mark left the regiment a month or so later and it is nice to think that they may well have met up again in Scotland. Unfortunately all attempts to find William's grave have failed to date.

It is hoped that the publication of William's story may well uncover his final resting place.

Appendix 1

Scandal Hushed

William Clarke was clearly proud to have served with such a distinguished regiment and his account appears to be an honest and frank account of the service he saw. His description of Waterloo and particularly of its aftermath is superb and full of detail; but there appears to be one matter on which he remains silent, just like the rest of his colleagues. Not everybody's actions under fire are the same, but given the great celebrations after the great victory of Waterloo, no regiment wanted its reputation tarnished by any whiff of scandal of any description and it would seem that the Scots Greys, among many others, were guilty of such a cover-up. As William had produced his 'journal' with the undoubted intention of seeing it published, it is therefore not surprising that he chose to draw a veil over this embarrassment.

Recently, a journal of an officer in the cavalry at Waterloo[1] has been published for the first time in English, which makes an accusation against two officers, who were guilty of cowardice at Waterloo, one in his own regiment and the other in the Scots Greys!

The Hussar officer, Lieutenant George Woodberry of the 18th Hussars records in his private journal on 20 June 1815 that

> Lieutenant G … who had been 'absent assumed killed', his horse being killed under him: during the battle of the 18th, returned today. He mounted another and left for Brussels. Colonel Grant is so angry regarding the case that he has removed him from his

---

1. *The Journal of Lieutenant George Woodberry 18th Hussars*, was bizarrely originally published in French in 1896, but has never been published in English until 2017.

command of his troop and he has put McDuffie in his place. If we can admit, like Hudibras,[2] that:

He who fights and runs away
May live to fight another day,

We do not think so in the 18th Hussars. He also wants the officers to meet and consider whether to request G… to leave the regiment immediately. General Vivian said that if Lieutenant G. . . does not leave the corps of hussars, he will have him court martialled.

A little investigation reveals that the officer referred to is Lieutenant John Rolfe Gordon, who was 'persuaded' to resign from the army by early 1816, to avoid the ignominy of a court martial.

On the following day, he then records the rumours of the army, including 'On the 18th a captain of the Scots Greys by the name of [Blank] fled the field of battle and took most of his troop with him.' On a short inspection of the list of officers serving with the Scots Greys at Waterloo, it becomes patently clear that he is referring to Captain Edward Payne who also quit the army within months of the battle: is this why?

Stuart Mellor[3] has analysed the Returns and found that the average mortality rate (at or post the battle) of the six troops was a staggering 21.2 per cent of all ranks; the highest being Vernor's at 29.7 per cent and Payne's the lowest at 8.2 per cent, a clear 5 per cent less than the next lowest, Cheyney's at 13.3 per cent. The wounded are much more difficult to identify easily or separate from those who were simply sick or those with light wounds, which were not recorded. However, it would appear that Payne's troop suffered sixteen wounded out of sixty-four officers and men, a casualty rate of 24 per cent (excluding all those who were killed or died of their wounds); whereas Cheyney's Troop (the next lowest mortality rate) suffered twenty-seven wounded out of sixty-four officers and men, a casualty rate of 42 per cent. Therefore Payne's troop clearly suffered substantially less injuries and deaths combined, than any other troop, by a significant margin.

---

2. *Hudibras* is a sort of imitation of *Don Quixote* by Samuel Butler who was born in 1612 in Strensham (Worcester) and died in 1680.
3. S. Mellor, *Grey's Ghosts, Men of the Scots Greys at Waterloo 1815*, London, 2012, p. 29.

But, this alone is not enough to condemn anyone, the losses often being affected by numerous external factors including their position, the forces opposed to them and a healthy dose of luck.

There are also however, testimonies that help explain Captain Payne's actions during and immediately after the great charge. An unknown sergeant of his troop states[4] that 'Captain Payne was not hurt, he helped the lieutenant colonel out of the field when he was wounded and slept in Brussels two or three days, he sent for me, told me if he lived to get to England he would do something handsome for me that will do me good in my old days. He is a gentleman of his word and has got plenty . . .'

It is unclear whether the Lieutenant Colonel he escorted from the field was Clarke or Hankin (both being of this rank in the army, although both majors in the regiment). Paymaster William Crawford records that 'I remember Lieutenant Colonel Hankin's going to the rear in consequence of his horse having fallen with him; but this took place *some time before we charged.*'[5] [Author's emphasis] and this is backed up by Lieutenant Charles Wyndham who records that .' . . we were in a hollow and had suffered from the guns in question before we charged, and it was at this period (not in the charge . . .) that Sir T. Hankin fell off his horse. I saw him on this side of the hedge taken to the rear . . .'[6] So if Payne had helped Hankin from the field then he never took part in the charge at all.

If, however, it was Clarke that he helped, it is stated that he was wounded soon after they had crossed the ridge, when they were attacking a second column/square and Captain Cheney then took command of the regiment. This occurred somewhere on the allied side of the shallow valley and would be before the regiment rode on up to the line of the French cannon on the intermediate ridge where they became virtually surrounded by the French lancers and suffered so badly.

If as I suspect, Captain Payne and part of his squadron pulled up here to aid Lt Colonel Clarke, then this would explain the disparity in the numbers of casualties suffered by this troop.

The fact that Payne then retired to Brussels with Clarke and stayed there for three nights, whilst the regiment was left desperately short of

---

4.   *Waterloo Archive* I, p. 32.
5.   *The Waterloo Letters*, p. 82.
6.   *The Waterloo Letters*, p. 78.

officers whilst he was absent and uninjured, would certainly not have gone down well with his fellow officers.

It is also intriguing to note, that a high proportion of the vacancies in the other troops for sergeants was made up from NCOs from Payne's Troop. I do not like conspiracy theories, but was their silence rewarded?

Payne received a Waterloo Medal, which was posted on to his family home at Broadwater Farm, near Worthing as he had already left the regiment before it was issued in 1816. However, Payne did not receive any Waterloo Prize Money when it was issued the following year.

There is clear evidence that Payne's troop suffered very much lower numbers of casualties than the other troops, this linked with Payne's rapid departure from the army would seem to confirm that he, just like Lieutenant Gordon of the 18th Hussars had been 'persuaded' to leave the army rather than face the embarrassment of a court martial.

The regiment then 'closed ranks' and it would seem that the incident was never mentioned again.

Bibliography

Anon., *Army Lists*, various.

Anon, *The Waterloo Medal Roll*, Dallington, 1992.

Beamish, N.L., *History of the King's German Legion* 2 vols, London, 1832–7.

Canon, R., *Historical Record of the Royal Regiment of Scots Dragoons, now the Second or Royal North British Dragoons, Commonly called the Scots Greys*, London, 1840.

Dalton, C., *The Waterloo Roll Call*, London, 1904.

Eaton, C., *The Battle of Waterloo, Ligny & Quatre Bras By a Near Observer* 2 vols, London, 1817.

Glover, G. (ed.), *Letters from The Battle of Waterloo*, London, 2004.

Glover, G. (ed.), *The Waterloo Archive* Vols 1–6, Barnsley, 2010–15.

Glover, G. (ed.), *With Wellington's Hussars in the Peninsular and at Waterloo. The Journals of Lieutenant George Woodberry 18th Hussars 1813-1815*, Barnsley, 2017.

Groves, J.P., *History of the 2nd Dragoons – The Scots Greys 'Second to None' 1678-1893*, London, 1893.

Gurwood, J., *Duke of Wellington's Dispatches 1799-1815*, London, 1832.

Mellor, S., *Grey's Ghosts: Men of the Scots Greys at Waterloo*, London, 2012.

Philippart, J., *The Royal Military Calendar* Vols 1–5, London, 1820.

Siborne, H.T. (ed.), *The Waterloo Letters*, London, 1891.

Index

329